The Grea

The rugby league career o

By Robert Gate

The Brian Bevan statue
(St James' Church in background)

LONDON LEAGUE PUBLICATIONS Ltd.

For our Katharine

The Great Bev
The rugby league career of Brian Bevan

Cover photos: Front: Warrington versus Carcassonne October 1950. Back: top: Bevan in action; bottom: Wembley 1954 Challenge Cup final.

First published in Great Britain
in August 2002 by:

London League Publications Ltd,
P.O. Box 10441, London E14 0SB

ISBN:

1-903659-06-X

Cover design by:

Stephen McCarthy Graphic Design
46, Clarence Road, London N15 5BB

Layout and design:

Peter Lush

Printed and bound by:

Bath Press Limited
Lower Bristol Road, Bath BA2 3BL

Introduction: Family memories

Jeanette Lane, née Bevan

It is particularly poignant and relevant that I sit, on this the 11th anniversary of Dad's passing, to write a fitting tribute to a much loved and sadly missed father. I wish to add that my mother would have loved to have written a contribution but has sadly had a stroke and so this is also on her behalf. She is delighted to know a book about Dad's genius on the football field is at last in print.

Some folk are born with silver spoons in their mouths. Dad was born with a rugby ball tucked well under his arm. I understand Dad was a breech birth - he was probably side-stepping his way into the world!

There are millions of memories, obviously too many to mention. However, some stand more prominent in our minds than others. Dad was methodical, meticulous and a perfectionist - just as he was with his rugby.

There were certain rituals, for example, prior to matches. Mum used to drop Dad off along Wilderspool Causeway, about one mile short of the ground. It had to be at the same spot each time. He liked to walk - always briskly - no matter what the occasion to the ground to warm up a little.

Then there were the socks. He always wore the same pair, if he'd had a great game, which invariably he had, for the following game.

Even now we can smell the wintergreen ointment Dad used for his knees, and see the cod liver oil and malt he took on a spoon nightly. He was a great believer in the good old-fashioned remedies and pick-me-ups and regularly took a beaten egg in warm milk with sugar at night.

As children, we lived in a shop in Grappenhall. We both recall the Wembley Cup taking pride of place in the shop window following Warrington's success. It was at the same shop premises I recall so often hearing the jingle-jangle of old irons tied to Dad's ankles and feet, as he was doing sit-ups - by the thousand! Free weights and empirical research into sports science and performance were unheard of. That is what makes his achievements so unbelievable. For example, whilst on holiday at Butlins as young children, with the late John Bebe (ex-Wigan RL) and his wife, life-long great friends, I believe Dad ran the 100 yards sprint in just over nine seconds. That indeed was a world record. Unfortunately, because it was an unofficial race-meet, it could not be recorded as such.

Our father was a great all-round sportsman and watched sport on the TV by the hour. He loved cricket, football, athletics, boxing, swimming, etc, and, of course, no one dare even ask if he'd like a cuppa when his beloved rugby was on! He played cricket, swam and participated in athletics to a very high level at school, and all his school reports state what a gifted sportsman he was. It was not just sport. Dad was an accomplished pianist and banjo player and loved music. He had a fine singing voice, which I only discovered in a Baptist church near Latchford once, when I heard him singing hymns.

His fads food-wise caused the family great amusement. He loved cornflakes and toast in a morning and liked to be first to the kitchen. Peanut butter on bread was another favourite, as was lashings of gravy on his food. He never needed to watch his weight and had a really sweet tooth, apple pie and iced buns being his favourite.

The Bevan family - a photo published in 1962

Dad was incredibly proud of his native Australia and regretted never donning the green and gold, due to rules of abode, even though he won many caps for Other Nationalities.

Much has been written in Australia about Dad and his career, and Owen, Dad's brother, even now sends regular clips. It bothered Dad that Owen did not have fair praise and acclaim while here in the UK. He apparently was a superb goal-kicker but inevitably followed in Dad's shadow, and returned to Sydney eventually, being somewhat homesick.

Dad's job at Portland Naval Base gave him immense pleasure and he was delighted with his promotion and 'lot' in the south of England. However, once retired, my parents moved back to the north of England to be closer to family. Dad had played a few seasons with Blackpool Borough and liked to be close to the coast. They settled on the South Shore between St. Anne's-on-Sea and Blackpool.

It is with phenomenal pride, yet great sadness, that we observe his statue as we pass by Wilderspool. Warringtonians were indeed incredible in their tributes at the time of his passing. it is a great pity my father did not live to see the statue, the Brian Bevan roundabout and stand, and the Warrington Rugby League Football Club were rightly criticised by the public for the fact that nothing had been done to honour him prior to that. It was indeed disgraceful.

Even now, as I pass Wilderspool, I half expect to hear chants of "give it to Bev" echoing from the ground. I have vivid memories of the stand erupting and everyone jumping to their feet when Dad got the ball. He never failed to come up with the goods. Time and again I remember hat-tricks, interceptions, seven-tries-a-match and sprints and side-steps the length of the field. I can see Dad now waving furiously for the ball as he flew down the wing in his number 2 strip.

Not because he is our father, but because it is fact, there has never been a winger before or since him able to hold a candle to his skills and genius. I believe it was Harry Bath who sent a tribute to his funeral stating that much had been written about Martin Offiah, and yet why? He was not fit to lace up Dad's boots. What a tribute indeed.

As a father, Dad was so proud of our sporting, ballroom dancing and academic achievements. I was a great enthusiast on the athletic field, my sister a super swimmer and trampolinist, and we both won a great many trophies for ballroom dancing. Many a time we were introduced to the floor as Brian Bevan's daughters - we did not need other names.

Dad did not even want sons, apparently, which may seem surprising. He always wanted two daughters, of whom he was very proud.

He was a shy, fiercely private man, totally modest about his sporting prowess. He would blush as folk recounted this and that try on one of the many grounds he played at, and he was always polite and courteous to his fans, no matter how long they detained him. He was always the last autograph-signer to leave the ground, usually being mobbed as he signed.

Wonderful tributes have been accorded my father, verbally and written. The word "freak" is a word my father hated and we, his family, repudiate. It is not true, kind or appropriate. A genius, yes, freak, no.

It is true, Dad's world record will probably never be broken. That indeed is an amazing achievement. Yet he never mentioned it, never bragged, never blew his own trumpet about anything. There are so many world class sportsmen who let you know one way or another that they are great. My father never did. His game was evidence.

It is now nearly 40 years since Dad retired and still folk talk about his unpredictable, brilliant play, saying repetitively, "There'll never be another Bev".

It is an incredible honour to see the Brian Bevan stand, roundabout and statue and to see your mementoes in the Rugby League Hall of Fame. Thank you, Dad, for all the memories both on and off the field. You are sorely missed and may this book be a fitting tribute to your great career.

Jennifer Aldis, née Bevan.
Having lived on Merseyside for over 30 years, I am now an avid soccer fan but I have always felt immense pride whenever rugby league and inevitably "Bev" is mentioned.

My first real memories of Dad's rugby days were when he used to go to training every Tuesday and Thursday nights. Saturdays in our house were always a bit fraught, especially before a really big match, as Dad still got quite nervous.

My earliest memories of spectating at Wilderspool aren't actually the matches. They are of sitting in the tea-room with the players' wives and children and of watching the players and directors congregate after a match.

When we eventually made our way outside, there were always what seemed like thousands of fans clamouring for Dad's autograph. He never refused a single one of them. Outside the tea-room was a sea of primrose and blue scarves, everyone shouting for "Bev".

I think I only ever truly appreciated how famous he was when the BBC sent television cameras to our house to do a spot on Dad on *Look North*.

As we got older Mum often drove Dad to his away matches and, of course, we went along too. It was a wonderful feeling sitting in the stands hearing people cheering for your father. At school everyone used to ask me whether I was really related to the Brian Bevan.

The trips home from matches could be either great fun - Dad loved a good laugh and had an infectious, hearty laugh - or, in fact, rather sombre, always depending on the result of a match or how well Dad had played. There were not many sombre occasions! Dad's concept of not having too good a game was what others would consider an outstanding performance, one which no doubt was the talking point of both home and opposition crowds on their homeward journey.

Like all good things, it one day had to come to an end. I remember that day as though it were yesterday. Warrington was the busiest I'd ever seen it. There were hundreds and hundreds of people walking from town towards Wilderspool, all in primrose and blue. Inside the stadium it was the same - rattles, flags, scarves, whistles, cheers and chants. The vast majority were turning out to see Bev's last game with Wires.

When the teams came out Dad had been made captain for the day and proudly led out the Wires. The cheers and shouting of Dad's name were deafening.

Warrington won. Dad scored. The crowd erupted. At the end of the game, on the final whistle, the pitch was invaded and dad was carried shoulder high to the tunnel. He was then escorted up to the stand, where Mum, my sister and I were sitting. By this time, just about every fan was on the field cheering and shouting, "We want Bev, we want Bev". Once he appeared the crowd went wild, then fell silent after shouting for a speech.

My father was moved beyond words and was never one to show emotion in public, or indeed to sing his own praises. The crowd knew it was a mutual respect and that my father was indebted for all the support over the years.

It was a perfect day and a very touching finale to his final match at Wilderspool.

Mike Lane, Brian Bevan's son-in-law

Meeting Brian Bevan for the first time was quite an ordeal. I had never met anyone famous before and as a new boyfriend of his younger daughter I felt that I would be under real scrutiny.

At the time the family were living on Portland Naval Base, as Brian had retired from rugby league and was a military policeman on the base. When I arrived and eventually gained entry to the base Brian was on duty at the gate on Incline Road. Jeanette took me up there to meet her father. I was rather nervous at the idea of meeting a living legend but I need not have been because I think that Brian was equally ill at ease. I learned early on that Brian was not the easiest person to have a conversation with until you got to know him. This was not a personal thing, but rather a very reserved and modest nature. I wanted to know all about his career but he seemed almost embarrassed to talk about it. For someone who had achieved so much in a sport I could not believe the level of modesty he displayed.

However, he was a sport fanatic - any sport, it did not seem to matter, he would watch them all with absolute concentration. He admired the skill of all sports people and had great analytical insight into the tactics of so many sports. I always felt that it was the greatest pity that he was never involved with rugby league after his playing career ended. Had he been a more forceful and outgoing person, he would have made a great coach, manager or commentator. He loved the game, it had been such a huge part of his life, he had been so successful and he missed it dearly. He never voiced this opinion but you could see it in his eyes whenever he watched the game. He didn't have to say anything.

While I knew him he was a pipe smoker and I used to wonder if he was playing out some game tactic in the ashtray, as he arranged the spent matches in lines with such precision.

I was never fortunate enough to see him play when he was at his peak, only having had the opportunity to see him a few times in testimonial games long after his retirement from the game. Even then I was amazed by the reaction of the crowd when he got the ball - a cocktail of excitement, exhilaration and expectation.

I will never forget the sentiments of Colin Welland at Wilderspool Stadium during the memorial service which followed Brian's sad demise. He stated that, in all the sports he had watched, he had never seen any player create such excitement when he had the ball.

He really was a true legend. So few have ever reached the heights he did. He leaves a history in the way that so few can. I am so happy to see this book in print so long after his playing career ended. That in itself is a tribute to the genius of the man.

Owen Bevan

When Brian was about 10 years old, our parents thought he may have some future in rugby league, be it as a coach, commentator, even, perhaps, a player. He entertained himself by playing a game on a small table covered with a blanket with marbles of two sets of colours. I think it was about seven-a-side and each marble had the name of a prominent player of that era. He gave a running commentary as he moved the players about with some dexterity. Perhaps that dexterity translated into some of the freakish ability he displayed later in his life. One day I touched one of the marbles during the game. It was as if a spectator had run on the field! He sent me to the sin bin with a clip over the ears.

Brian was a lover of brass band music and spent hours listening to his records and "conducting" the band. When he had to mow the lawn for our parents he paid me threepence to do the job while he listened to the music at high volume. It was some combination - a noisy old lawnmower and the Royal Coldstream Guards Band!

Like every other family member, I am immensely proud of Brian's phenomenal achievements and even more proud to have been his brother.

About the author

Robert Gate is a pioneering and prolific rugby league historian. A life-long Halifax supporter, and former archivist at the Rugby Football League, he lives with his wife Myfanwy in Ripponden in West Yorkshire. He has written for a number of rugby league publications, and has written the following books:

Gone North: Welshmen In Rugby League (vol 1) [RE Gate], 1986
The Struggle For The Ashes [RE Gate], 1986
Champions [RE Gate], 1987
Gone North: Welshmen In Rugby League (vol 2) [RE Gate], 1988
The Rugby League Quiz Book [Mainstream], 1988
Rugby League: An Illustrated History [Weidenfeld], 1989
The Hall Of Fame Brochure [Rugby Football League]. 1989
An Illustrated History Of Saints v Wigan Derby Matches [Smiths Books (Wigan)] 1990
The Guinness Rugby League Fact Book [Guinness]. 1991
They Played For Wigan [Mike RL Publications], 1992, with Michael Latham
There Were A Lot More Than That: Odsal 1954 [RE Gate], 1994
When Push Comes To Shove (vol 2), [Yorkshire Art Circus]. 1995, co-editor with Ian Clayton and Ian Daley
The Official Rugby League Centenary Magazine [Grandstand Publications], 1995, with David Howes
The Struggle For The Ashes II [RE Gate]. 1996
Bradford, Northern and Bulls [Tempus], 2000

Preface

I am acutely aware that this book probably fails to do complete justice to Brian Bevan, nor is it intended to be a biography of the great man. It is hoped that it will, however, serve as an accurate and definitive account of his phenomenal playing career with Eastern Suburbs, Warrington, Blackpool Borough and the renowned Other Nationalities international team.

It is now 60 years since Bevan made his first grade debut for Eastern Suburbs, 57 years since he first donned the primrose and blue of Warrington and 38 years since he last played in a first-class fixture for Blackpool. The fact that no one has deemed the most prolific try-scorer in the game's history worthy of recording in book form is an indictment of rugby league's lack of respect for its heritage and for its greatest practitioners. This is a theme I have often repeated in my own writings on the sport down the years. Unfortunately, as the instigators of Super League repeatedly told the world, history does not pay the bills. As far as I am aware, no one ever thought it did, but we forget it at our peril. Certainly such rare and sublime talents as Brian Bevan's deserve to be better cherished by the game in which they were fashioned.

As a subject, Brian Bevan probably gave me as many problems as he gave his bewildered opponents on the field of play. Collating the facts and figures of his monumental career was the easy part. Trying to fathom the inner man was more problematic. The fact that he was such an intensely private person was obviously a hindrance to research. It would have been much easier if he had been a gregarious, outgoing, more stereotypical sportsman as there would have been more extra-curricular tales to tell. But he was not, and the fact that he was so self-effacing and retiring actually made him a more sympathetic and interesting subject for me.

My personal experience of Brian Bevan was minimal. I know that as a child I saw him play for the first time in 1958, when Warrington beat my team Halifax 17-12 in a second round Challenge Cup-tie at Thrum Hall. I cannot remember anything about the game except the profound disappointment of defeat. It had been the first big cup-tie I had attended. The records tell me that Bev scored one of the Wire tries. I saw him again in September 1960 on a dull Monday evening at Thrum Hall. This time 'Fax won 8-4 in a dire game, which still remains in my mind 42 years on. In 1961 I was present at the Warrington-Leeds Championship final at Odsal, when a different balding genius in the shape of Lewis Jones took all my attention and Bev did not get a look in as Wire were hammered.

My fourth and final view of 'The Great Bev' on the pitch was, however, unforgettable. I was fortunate enough to be at Thrum Hall for the Halifax International Sevens Tournament on 30 May, 1964. It was Bev's last official appearance in rugby league. He had announced his retirement a couple of months earlier and it was his last hurrah. It was a glorious, sunny Saturday afternoon, but there were only 4,114 of us there, including my German pen-friend, Wolfgang Goos, from Heidelberg. Wolfgang could not understand what all the fuss was about but, then again, he was completely mystified about rugby league and its hold on me and my schoolmates.

We kept taking him along to the games and he still did not seem to be succumbing to the disease. Bev's last game was also Wolfgang's. A few weeks later he went back to Germany and I have never seen him since. It's a pity really, as he had a fantastically good camera, which I had made him point and click at Bev as he ran towards us on a lap of honour. The crowd had seen him score two astonishing tries playing for an Other Nationalities VII. The scores had rolled back the years for the old-timers and had given us gob-smacked youngsters an idea of just how sensational this old bloke in the green jersey must have been before he had started drawing his pension. I remember it was all very emotional, and I have been upset ever since because Wolfgang never did send me that historic photograph of Bev on his last lap.

The next time I came across Brian Bevan was 23 years later. I was then the researcher for the Rugby Football League's Hall of Fame and Bev was one of the nine original inductees. In the course of my duties I visited him several times at his home in Blackpool during 1987 and 1988. Naturally, I had heard all the tales about both his tries and his taciturnity. The tries I could deal with, but I was a bit worried about the taciturnity. I need not have been. After the initial formalities we got on splendidly. He was courteous, open and informative. There were cups of tea and biscuits every time I visited and Bev was genuinely gratified that he had been recognised for the highest honour the game could bestow on an individual. The last time I met him was at the Hall of Fame induction on 24 October 1988, when I got him to sign my menu card along with the three other living legends, who were being admitted to the Hall of Fame - Gus Risman, Billy Boston and Alex Murphy. It was a truly joyous occasion.

My visits to see Bev usually consisted of several hours of chat, which means by all other accounts that I did very well. It was apparent that Bev would have dearly liked to have told his story in print and had produced a small manuscript himself with which he had got nowhere, as far as publishing was concerned. Less than three years after his elevation to the Hall of Fame Brian died. I hope that this testament to his life and times in rugby league would have met with his approval.

Robert Gate
Ripponden, May 2002

Notes on the text

The statistics presented in this book are based on the game's official records, as laid down by the Rugby League Record Keepers Club. As such they do conflict with the records, or lack of them, of contemporary journalists. For many years appearances and scorers from the annual Wardonia Cup matches between Warrington and Wigan, plus other friendly fixtures, were included in records, but have subsequently been deemed unacceptable. Some confusion also surrounded the eligibility of some of Bevan's representative appearances. Consequently, many of Bevan's landmark records were erroneously highlighted by the press, usually too late. The scoring of his 500th, 600th and 700th tries are good examples of such confusion. In such cases, I have recorded both the contemporary and amended versions.

During Brian Bevan's time with Warrington, his club played in four annual competitions: the Rugby League Challenge Cup, the Northern Rugby League Championship, the Lancashire Challenge Cup and the Lancashire League Championship. There were no separate fixtures for the Lancashire League Championship - this was based on the Northern Rugby League fixtures. They also played for and won a one-off floodlit competition in 1955-56 - the ITV Trophy. In his two seasons with Blackpool Borough, the Western Division Championship replaced the Lancashire League Championship, and the league was split into two divisions, Borough playing in Division 2.

Attendance figures for club fixtures are shown in the end columns. All, except those for the 1946-47 season, have been taken from the official attendance books at the Rugby Football League. The 1946-47 figures were mostly drawn from *Rugby League Review*. For a handful of games no attendance figures have been found, including, frustratingly, that for his English first-class debut against Oldham on 17 November, 1945. Home fixtures are shown in **bold**.

Abbreviations in the statistics sections at the end of each chapter are as follows:

Ch Cup	Rugby League Challenge Cup	LC	Lancashire Cup
CH	Championship	WD	Western Division
T	Tries scored by Bevan	G	Goals kicked by Bevan
dnp	(Bevan) Did not play		

Acknowledgements

The author is indebted to many people for help in the compiling of *The Great Bev*. Four individuals have been of inestimable assistance. Without their contributions the book would have been much more difficult to assemble and unquestionably a much poorer creation.

Mike Rowan substantially altered the original form of the book by providing a vast store of material, both printed and illustrative, which allowed me to create a much fuller narrative account of Bev's playing career at Wilderspool. Mike's own written account of Bev's career and many informative and entertaining conversations with him only served to reinforce my admiration for his knowledge and insight.

Anthony Quinn provided invaluable assistance by furnishing descriptions of the vast majority of Bev's tries, gleaned from innumerable visits to Warrington library to scour the microfilms of the *Warrington Guardian* and the *Warrington Examiner* - a monumental example of interest, diligence and persistence, especially as Anthony is a Widnesian. Anthony also played his part in persuading me to entitle the book *The Great Bev*.

Ernie Day, the Warrington RLFC historian, has been a friend for many years and has done me, and many others, countless favours in terms of research and information. Ernie has read the manuscript and ensured that I have not made errors of fact relating to local events, places and people in Warrington. He has been the source of many of the statistics in the book.

David Middleton, the great man of Australian rugby league history and statistics, did me an enormous service in providing Brian Bevan's career record with Eastern Suburbs. He also supplied more than the bare bones of the stats, however, for he was kind enough to add contemporary observations and material, which otherwise would not have seen the light of day.

I am also indebted to the following for supplying information, illustrations, reminiscences and written contributions:
Jeanette Lane, Jennifer Aldis, Mike Lane, Owen Bevan, Peter Atkinson, Philip Ball, Wally Barnes, Bob Batten, Owen Bevan, John Blacklock, John Buckle, William Burgess, Bernard Cain, Terry Clawson, Arthur Clues, Tony Collins, Gerry Collingwood, M. Darbyshire, Alan Davies, Harvey Davis, Geoff Dawber, Glen 'Bumper' Dwyer, Harry Edgar, Reuben Edge, Harold Farrimond, Phil Fearnley, Brian Flaherty, Raymond Fletcher, Jim Forster, Bob Fox. Eric Frodsham, Eddie Fuller, Charles Gate, Keith Gilbert. Alec Givvons, Jim Graves, David Gronow, Ray Hewson, Joseph Higham, Reg Hughes, Colin Hutton, Curtis Johnstone, Stan Kielty, Eric Lafferty, Michael Latham, *League Express*, Alan Leigh, Stan Lewandowski, George Lunn, Bill Lythgoe, Bert Maguire, Kevin Maguire, Bernard Mahoney, Alan Marchant, Tom Mitchell, George Morrison. John Mounfield, Johnny Noon, Brian Nordgren, Keith Nutter, Clarrie Owen, David Parr, Mike Parsons, Colin Perkin, Albert Pimblett, Anthony Quinn, Emlyn Richards, Peter Robinson, *Rugby Leaguer*, Bob Ryan, Alex Service, Roger Shackleton, Bob Shuttleworth, Henry Skrzypecki, Gary Slater, Brian Smith, Eddie "Aber" Smith, Geoff Smith, Peter Smith Sen., Roy Smith, Stuart Smith, Michael Turner, Tom Wadsworth, Brian Walker, Joe Warham, *Warrington Guardian*, Andrew Wheelwright, Denis Whittle, T. Williams, Fred Worrall, Joseph A. Wright.

Thanks also go to Michael O'Hare, Dave Farrar, and David Ballheimer for their help in producing the book...
...and finally, boundless thanks to Peter Lush, of London League Publications, for ensuring that this project has finally come to fruition. He has soldiered on gallantly in the face of my eccentricities and occasional bouts of cantankerousness. Fancy a Londoner producing a rugby league book by a Yorkshireman about an Australian. Who would ever have thought it?

Robert Gate

Contents

The unveiling of the Brian Bevan statue

Top: Jennifer Aldis, Doreen Bevan and Jeanette Lane with
former Warrington players at the unveiling of the statue
Middle: The plaque on the statue
Bottom: Colin Welland with Doreen Bevan

1. Strange bedfellows

"Great", "legend", "genius" are all words which are routinely spouted or written to describe sportsmen, who in truth are nothing of the sort. Brian Bevan, who died in 1991, had probably never heard the word hyperbole. It was not of his time. These days sport, and particularly rugby league, Super League-style at least, is all about hype. It is the best, the most, the greatest and because they keep saying so, it must be true.

The hype merchants would have found Brian Bevan a nightmare. They would have been redundant. There was absolutely no need for hype with Bevan. No amount of hype could persuade those who saw him that even the most extreme superlative was excessive in his case. He was genuinely great, he was truly a legend, undoubtedly he was blessed with genius.

He was also mysterious, enigmatic, reclusive - a sporting conundrum. He did not act or look like a stereotypical rugby league player, particularly an Australian rugby league player. He was not big, he was not brash, he was not bronzed, he did not seek the spotlight. He wove dream patterns on the field and when the games were over he merged into the scenery. Fame was his constant companion but anonymity was his best friend. Fame and anonymity do not mix well. They are strange bedfellows.

Many of the things Brian Bevan did on the pitch were hardly believable. He found space where none existed. He went through gaps which were mere slivers of light. He outran athletes and sprinters who were supposedly faster than he. He made monkeys out of outstanding players. He appeared to move backwards as fast as some players moved forwards and sometimes he went in two directions at once, although everyone knows that is impossible. When he had the ball in his hands the crowds were in a constant state of excitement. He was bewildering, he was lightning, he was elasticity, he was rolling athleticism, he was here, he was there, he was gone. He was also at times comical, almost Chaplinesque in that his movements could be as dementedly jerky as in an Edwardian film. One man I interviewed remembered Bevan running round in ever-decreasing circles until he eventually ran out of options and subsided unmolested to the ground. It was hilarious, he said - should have been a penalty for a voluntary tackle.

Opponents, however, found nothing hilarious about Bevan's antics. There was not much anyone could do about him though. Yes, he was only human but often he defied the laws of physics. Opponents swore they had him but somehow he had dematerialised, escaped from their grasp like an eel coated in soap. There was no explanation. It was just Bevan. Teams could not really legislate for him. Individuals like Dai Bevan, one of the best defensive wingers of the era, could contain him in some games, but man-on-man marking was generally hopeless. He would humiliate his adversary at some point and three more points would be added to the score-board. The great Cumbrian administrator Tom Mitchell said that there was no point in his Workington Town team devising plans to stop him - just deal with the other 12, hope for the best but don't be surprised when he performed a miracle. Tom was so keen to capture Bevan for Workington in the late 1940s that he made an illegal approach to him, although he did not know it was illegal at the time. It was one of Mitchell's great regrets that Brian remained at Warrington rather than enjoying life on the West Cumberland coast.

Brian Smith, a winger of considerable class with York and Bradford Northern and a 1958 Australasian tour trialist, said Bevan was one of the easiest of wingers to play against. Once the game had kicked off he would hardly see Brian again, let alone touch him. Bevan would just run off in another direction, the one no one expected. Alan Davies, one of the very best centres Great Britain ever produced, recalled many games for Oldham against Warrington. Bevan was notorious for claiming shoals of interception tries against the men from Watersheddings, so many that Davies and his colleagues had a brotherhood of half-backs and centres, who could all claim to have been "done" by the king of the interception. One particular game a centre, who had not had the experience of giving away an interception try to Bev, but lived in dread of doing so, had reached half-time with his record intact. He was so nervous, however, that even the encouragement of his colleagues could not allay his fears and, sure enough, Brian did him twice in the second half. He had joined the brotherhood.

One of the most striking features of discussions with rugby league fans about Brian Bevan is the almost tangible awe in which they hold him. To a man or woman, they are grateful that they were privileged to witness his performances. Many express a real sorrow that they are simply incapable of describing the things he did. They talk of the apparent impossibility of some of his tries. They saw them with their own eyes, yet they can still hardly believe what they saw. Physically Bevan appeared to be able to perform almost outside the laws of science. The most astounding aspect of all this is that Bevan did not perform these near-miracles just occasionally. He did it over and over again for most of his 19 year career in England. Another thread of regret for many is the lack of filmed evidence of this great man's deeds. They fear that in years to come those who never saw him will simply not believe how extraordinary he was.

Fortunately, for most of his career Brian Bevan's performances were recorded by Cyril Briggs in the *Warrington Guardian*. Briggs wrote under the nom de plume of 'Jack Steel' and was, like many of his contemporaries, a writer with well developed descriptive and narrative powers. 'Criticus' of the rival local paper, the *Warrington Examiner* also bequeathed us a fine collection of descriptions of Bev's impossible tries. Their reports, so unlike the modern variety which rely largely and lazily on parroting the thoughts and clichés of the club coaches, are scattered throughout the book and give us the possibility of glimpsing at least a trace of Bevan's overwhelming brilliance.

It is not really possible to distil just what made Brian Bevan so deadly dangerous as a rugby league wingman. Genius is always difficult to define. Certainly Bevan could not define it himself. Of course, he was gifted. He was naturally quick on his feet. He could have been an international sprinter, as his track times indicated. He had a body wobble which totally debilitated opponents, appearing sometimes to have swivel hips. He did everything at speed. Many wingers have excellent side-steps but can only perform them off one leg. Bevan could side-step equally well off both feet, a rare asset. More devastatingly, he could side-step and hardly lose any pace in doing so. His deadliest weapon, however, was probably instant acceleration. It carried him out of harm's way and left tacklers nonplussed. Alarmingly for defenders, he could summon up extra speed at will during his straight dashes or labyrinthine meanderings over the length of the field.

Apart from purely physical skills of speed and elusiveness, Bevan had the priceless gift of anticipation. He knew when and how to intercept an opponent's pass, he had an uncanny awareness of how a ball would bounce when he pursued colleagues' kicks and he intuitively turned up in places where orthodox wingers would never stray. He did not wait for the ball to come to him, believing a good wingman went looking for action.

His handling was outstanding, having the knack of being able to catch the most awkward of transfers. Disturbingly for his opponents, his eyes and deadpan, phlegmatic demeanour never betrayed his intentions.

If he had a fault, it was in tackling. He was not in the business of tackling, however. He could tackle if it was necessary but he preferred to leave such basic tasks to the inside backs. Who cared whether he could tackle, anyway?

Brian Bevan's job, like all other wingers, was to score tries. It would be interesting to know what Bev would think of the role of wingers in the modern game. No doubt he would be appalled. Even in the early 1960s, when he was still featuring as a newspaper columnist, he was bemoaning the trend for forwards to take more of the limelight. He argued that back play was becoming more stereotyped, wingers were getting fewer running chances and backline moves were being devalued. What would he have made of wingers who took the ball up from acting half-back to relieve forwards? He would certainly have been amused by modern articles on leading wingers in which their contribution to a game is dissected in the minutest details - how many times they carried the ball, how many tackles they made, how many knock-ons they committed, how many litres of water they drank in the first 10 minutes, how many off-sides they managed without being penalised. In short, just about every useless statistic imaginable. The only thing missing from the list is how many tries they scored. He would be just as mystified to know why arguably the best rugby league wingers (Robinson, Sullivan, Rogers and Sailor) now ply their trade in rugby union.

In Bevan's days rugby league was a game of specialisms. Players had specific duties to perform and were usually instantly recognisable by their height, weight and body shape. Wingers were expected to score tries, from any point on the field. They were usually excellent sprinters. Some were light and elusive, others heavier and more direct. Their common currency was tries and if they failed too often to provide them, they were dropped. The 1940s, '50s and early '60s were a golden age for try-scoring wingers. The daddy of them all was Brian Bevan.

However, it was not entirely natural instinct and God-given genius which kept Bevan at the top of his trade for so long. He worked at it. As the modern axiom goes, the more he practised the better he seemed to get. There is no question that Brian was a perfectionist. He would leave nothing to chance in preparing for games. He was an assiduous trainer, who would put in extra work at the end of club training sessions and in his own time. He was obsessed with maintaining his speed and loved to use spikes in sprinting. He was a fervent believer too in stamina training, undertaking longer road runs and enjoying the benefits of shadow boxing and tennis to sharpen his reflexes. His obsession with fitness and attention to detail undoubtedly gave him an edge but also prevented him from understanding those who were less dedicated. Players like Albert Pimblett at Warrington and Alec Givvons at Blackpool were the types he appreciated most - men prepared to put in the extra work after regular training and who would practice combinations and join in sprinting sessions with him.

The work ethic was paramount for Brian and that extended into protecting the vulnerable parts of his body. He often said that legs were a footballer's main attributes. They had to be looked after. Toes, ankles and knees were potential sources of injury. Consequently, he made sure they were taped, bandaged or padded. So too were his shins, elbows, shoulders and any other body parts he felt were suspect at any particular time. At home his wife Doreen tended devotedly to any cuts, wounds or bruises he sustained. Attention to detail was all-important.

Mentally too Brian prepared thoroughly for games. Once a game was over he was thinking about the next one. In 1962, he told Derek Marshall of the *Daily Mail*: "I think and plan in private as well as at practice. By Saturday morning I am so tense that my wife and two daughters discreetly steer clear of me". He often admitted that he had a type of tunnel vision, that he switched off from outside distractions in order to psyche himself up for games. His concentration was total. In that respect he would be in tune with today's sports psychology. Bevan had a passionate love of rugby league and an insatiable appetite for scoring tries. He displayed the dedication necessary to maintain his hunger for almost two decades.

Psychologically, he needed routines. His drive for perfectionism dictated his pre-match schedules and there are many tales of his reliance on Warrington's groundsman Jackie Hamblett, who was, next to his father, perhaps the biggest influence on him. Jack Hamblett was part of the furniture at Wilderspool, having been on the groundstaff from the age of fifteen. By the time Brian Bevan arrived in Warrington Jack had already put in 25 years as kit-man and general factotum. He was to remain a fixture for another 35 years or more. Ernie Day, the Warrington club's historian, wrote the following: "How Bevan came to be affectionately known as 'Old Knobbly Knees' is worth relating. In his early days at Warrington Bev used to suffer from grazed knees and after a game he would turn up at the ground on the Monday morning seeking treatment. The only person there who could give any kind of medication was Jackie Hamblett, the Wilderspool jack-of-all-trades. At that time Jack was the official kit man with responsibilities for seeing that the kit was washed and aired, the boots cleaned and repaired and generally doing the kind of jobs nobody else would do. Unofficially though Jack was the friend and confidant of all the players. So, when Bev came along asking for treatment, Jack in his usual caring way would clean the grazed knees with peroxide and put dressings on. The treatment went on throughout the week and was successful enough for Brian to be fit to play the next game. After the match, with new tissue scraped away, the ritual cleaning and dressing began all over again.

After a week or two like this, Jack suggested that perhaps prevention was better than cure, and found Brian an old pair of knee pads that had been discarded. Bev agreed to wear them and as they were already second hand and a

Bev in tackling mode

little slack, by stuffing cotton wool in, the problem was solved and the legend started.

The relationship between the two was quite unique in that while Bev found it very difficult to form a relationship with his team-mates, and conversely, they with him because by nature he was a shy, reserved and very private person, Jack was the friend of almost everyone, who came to know him, and his magic worked with Brian. Probably, he was the only member of staff at Wilderspool who was able to get close to Bev, whom Jackie in his last years reverently called 'The Old Man'.

On and off the field Bevan was perhaps a little finicky. Sometimes during a match, when he felt he was not getting his expected quota of passes, he would trot to the touchline, complaining to the bench that the cord in his shorts was not right or his strapping was uncomfortable. Jack would sit him down and, fussing over him like a mother hen, see to his problems and pat him on the head. Reassured, Bev would return to the fray and, like as not, immediately latch on to the ball and score one of his specials. As he walked back to the applause, he would nod to the bench and to Jack in particular.

There was one story Jack loved to tell. During a game in which Bev had had a very lean first half, he came off at half-time complaining bitterly to Jack that he had been given the wrong boot. Now, Jack had never been known to lay out the wrong boots but, knowing the ways of his hero, he immediately took the offending boot into his kit room, wiped it over with a little dubbing and returned to the players dressing room and apologised profusely for making such an unforgivable mistake. Bev thanked him and trotted out with the same boot he had been sure was the wrong one."

Ironically, Jack Hamblett died, aged 86, in February 1991, just a few months before Brian passed away.

Brian Bevan presented a strange figure on the field. Even as a young man of 21 he had lost most of his hair and looked older than his years. As he grew older, balder and more toothless, people assumed his age to be increasingly greater than it was. Exacerbating the effect was his apparent frailty, all that padding and bandaging appearing to be the means of holding him together. Contrary to appearances and popular belief, however, there was nothing frail about Brian Bevan. In his long career he remained largely immune to injury, especially serious injury. No one plays over 600 games of professional rugby league without a considerable degree of toughness. Brian may not have given off the aura of a 'tough guy' rugby league player, but there was nothing wrong with his physique. Tom Mitchell recalled that he had breast bones like armour plate and others noted he had a back like a professional boxer. At around 5ft 10in and 11st 8lbs, he was not the biggest of wingers, but he was by no means the smallest. It is a truism that appearances can be deceptive. In Bev's case they certainly were, for his performances were those of a sublimely talented athlete.

If Brian Bevan was a mystery to opponents, he was no less mysterious off the field. Reticent, home-loving and a dab hand on the piano, he was not the stuff of which tabloid editors dreamed. Tales of his taciturnity abounded. It was said that when he worked for Siddall's Printers he used to put on his apron and work silently for hours. Then at dinner-time he would send out for ten cigarettes and two packets of sandwiches. On rare occasions, however, it was said that he would talk non-stop for ages. Frank Keating was one of those who tried and failed to get much out of Brian. In November 2000, he wrote in *The Guardian*: "Even in my sheltered 1950s west country boyhood, news seeped down of this phenomenon who could jink like a crazed pinball and run like a barmy hare and who weekly for winter after winter thrillingly injected with adrenaline the north's sporting culture and self-esteem... I interviewed him once, in the week of the 1975 Challenge Cup final - a reprise of his own first Wembley final for Warrington in 1950 against Widnes... I cannot remember a more unrewarding interview. Some questions brought only a 'No' or 'If you say so' in reply, but mostly it was 'I can't remember' and a dismissive suck of gaunt cheeks as if both question and questioner were a total irrelevance."

Many fans remember Bev habitually standing in his austerity gabardine waiting for the team bus with a brown paper parcel under his arm. The parcel contained his pads and strapping. Not exactly a glamorous image but what would he be worth to Nike or Adidas today? He was so reclusive in retirement that when he was elected to the rugby league *Hall of Fame* in 1988 most people thought he was dead, even though by that time he had returned from Dorset to live in Blackpool and, as far as scientists are aware, the Fylde coast is not on the dark side of the moon. Just as he had been able to ghost silently through the midfield mayhem, he was able to slide into private obscurity.

2. Something in Brian's genes

In Russia in January 1924, the Soviets mourned the death of Lenin while in Great Britain Ramsay MacDonald became the country's first Labour Prime Minister. In June, the first wireless link was established between Britain and Australia. That same month, on the 24th, a son was born to Veda and Eric Bevan in Waverley, a district in the Eastern Suburbs of Sydney. He was christened Brian Eyrl Bevan and was destined to make an unsurpassable reputation as the greatest try-scorer in the history of rugby league.

Eric Bevan, a linotype operator with the *Sydney Sun*, had been a rugby league player himself, a useful three-quarter or full-back, who had played in lower grade matches for Newtown - the famous old Bluebags - and for Eastern Suburbs. Two of Brian's uncles, Roy and Lance, had also been on the books at Newtown. There was, therefore, possibly something in Brian's genes predisposing him to genius as a rugby league player. Certainly he grew up with his brother Owen and sister Gwenda in an environment which positively encouraged any child with sporting ambitions. Bondi beach was, almost literally, his backyard. He would later recall: "In the warm summer months, like thousands of other Australians, I kept myself fit by regular surfing with the local club. It was great fun and later on I think it helped me to stand up to the rigours of professional sport. For swimming, to my mind, is one of the greatest muscle-builders of all. I know it helped to give me strong shoulders and legs, those two essential attributes of a rugby player."

Brian was educated at Bondi Primary and Randwick Intermediate High schools, where sport figured prominently in his universe. Swimming and sprinting were his initial favourites. It was clear that the young Bevan had spring in his heels.

He was a schoolboy sprint star from an early age and, by the time he was 12, he was champion sprinter of New South Wales for his age group. Cricket and tennis also competed for his attention. At one point he thought it was a toss-up as to whether rugby or cricket would eventually claim him. Captaining the school XI, he later cherished the memory of once scoring 127 not out.

Inevitably, however, he was drawn more and more to rugby. In 1937 and 1938 he was selected as stand-off for New South Wales in interstate fixtures against Queensland. This was, however, rugby union. It was a case of playing union for his school on Saturdays and league in impromptu pick-up games at Bondi and Tamarama beaches at any time he could. Brian did not really relish playing stand-off, admitting that he found the experience "too fierce" It was, perhaps, a blessing in disguise when he suffered a badly broken elbow at the age of 15. He and his father decided that playing at centre or wing would be a less hazardous option

From the age of about nine, Brian had become increasingly absorbed by rugby league. His father, naturally enough, encouraged his growing passion for the game by taking him to big matches every Saturday at the Sydney Cricket Ground. It was at the SCG that Brian's imagination was fired in 1932 when he attended a test match in which the great Welsh full-back and goal-kicker Jim Sullivan led a magnificent Great Britain team to Ashes victory over Australia. In 1936 he was again among the Sydney crowds enthralled by the visit of Jim Brough's victorious Lions.

It was on his numerous visits to the SCG that Brian indulged in a pursuit to which he ascribed much of the credit for developing his elusive qualities on the playing field. In 1962 he recalled: "Every Saturday I went to Sydney Cricket Ground to watch the match of the day. Vic Hey, Bill Shankland and other stars of the period were great heroes to me. My father had me practising sidesteps as I passed telegraph poles, and I remember that after Cricket Ground matches I would go out of the Paddington side exit and sidestep my way past white poles all the way up the slope leading from the ground to Moore Park Road... My father always said the ability to elude a rival was the biggest asset in football and he taught me when I was a schoolboy how to sidestep. He showed me where my feet should go in executing a sidestep by placing pieces of wood in position in our backyard. And he taught me to sidestep off either foot, for he knew that many players could step off one foot but not many off both. I think my sidestep has always been equally strong off either foot."

By the time Brian finished his education his focus on rugby league was razor-sharp. He wanted to play for Australia and the signs were that he had what it took - natural athleticism, blistering pace, the gift of elusiveness, abundant enthusiasm and a quiet but steely resolve to succeed in his chosen field.

Above: A boy and his ball - the young Bev. Right: In the Navy - Bev at 17

3. To war and back

On leaving school at the age of 15 Brian took up an apprenticeship as a compositor or typesetter in the printing trade, thereby following in his father's footsteps. It may have been the fact that English was his favourite subject at school that prompted him into this line of work, but later life would show undoubtedly that he did not regard a life in compositing as a vocation. Sport and, inevitably, the ever-widening and increasingly horrific Second World War would occupy his mind and time as he approached his late teens.

In the meantime his youthful energies were directed into furthering his career as a rugby league player. He took to playing in the local Eastern Suburbs competition with the Graham 'C' Grade Club and was invited eventually to play for Eastern Suburbs at the start of the 1941 season. His debut in Reserve Grade on 19 April 1941, was inauspicious as Easts went down 5-16 to Souths at the Sydney Sports Ground. Brian was still two months short of his 17th birthday and wisely he was played on the wing by an Eastern Suburbs management which clearly recognised that here was a star in the making. The following week he stepped out for the first time as a Grade player on the Sydney Cricket Ground, helping his team draw 7-7 with Norths.

Frustratingly, there is very little written material on Brian Bevan's early career in Sydney football. Certainly in interviews Brian himself skips over the period in a sentence or two whenever asked about it. It must have been fascinating to watch his development in this period as he began to change from boy to man. Understandably, perhaps, given that he was playing against older, stronger opponents, he appears to have started somewhat slowly to make a mark. His first four games on the wing failed to yield a solitary try and then on 17 May, in a 13-5 win over Canterbury at the SCG, he broke his duck, playing at centre. *Rugby League News* gave him his first real write-up on 24 May 1941, saying: "Brian Bevan, since being moved into the centre, is showing the form he displayed in the trial games in scoring his try last Saturday. This is his first year in Grade football, having played in the Graham 'C' Grade Club in our Junior Competition last year. He learnt his football at the Bondi School, and captained the NSW Schoolboys against Queensland."

Even then it was not all plaudits. A dedicated Easts supporter, F. W. Boyd noted that against Souths on 21 June "Bevan dropped all his passes". A week later - three days after Brian's 17th birthday - playing at five-eighth (stand-off) against Wests at Pratten Park, Boyd pointed out that "Bevan spoilt a lot of Walsh's openings". Easts drew that encounter 10-10 and the following week, after a run of nine games in Reserve Grade, Brian was relegated to Third Grade for a fixture against Norths at Trumper Park. He scored a try in a 12-0 victory and Boyd tersely noted: "Bevan much improved".

Mr Boyd was much happier by 26 July when Easts hammered Newtown 21-5 at the SCG. This time he wrote: "Bevan moved to inside centre after ten minutes. Rafferty and Bevan brilliant. Bevan got ball behind own line, sidestepped to 25, passed to Rafferty, to O'Donnell, to Sinclair, to Rafferty, to McCallum, to Rafferty, to Sinclair, who stumbled and bumped his head on goal post and lost ball." On 9 August Brian had a busy afternoon. Playing for the Third Grade against Canterbury at Belmore "Bevan was the best back on side", according to Boyd. At the conclusion of the game Brian was sent out again in the Reserves fixture with Boyd able to report that "Bevan sidestepped through the whole side for his try".

By the time the play-offs took place, Brian was really taking the eye with some wonderful wing play. In the Third Grade semi-final against Souths at the SCG on 23 August, Bevan won the match with a sensational try. According to Boyd: "Bevan received in his own 25, raced out to the wing, sidestepped the winger, ran down the wing, veered back infield, sidestepped the full-back and scored between the posts."

Rugby League News, the Premiership's official weekly programme wrote: "Brian Bevan's try last Saturday against South Sydney was a gem and fully deserved the applause of the crowd... There is no doubting this player's ability, and with a few minor faults to rectify, he is sure to reach the top."

The Third Grade final at the same venue a week later pitted Easts against Wests. The only score of the game was an interception try by Brian. Wests would not be the last team to perish from this trademark type of score. Probably no player in history - certainly no winger - ever mastered the devastating art of interception more completely than this incipient maestro. Coincidentally this Third Grade Final was a curtain-raiser to one of Australian rugby league's most momentous occasions. Easts had qualified for the First Grade Final against St. George and a massive attendance of 39,957, a fair number of whom would have witnessed Brian's killer try against the Magpies, packed the SCG, the biggest crowd at a club fixture since 1921. Easts' legends Dave Brown and Sid Pearce played their last games for the club that afternoon but it was St George who ran out winners by 31-14 to claim their first ever Premiership.

The 1941 season may have ended for the Easts First Graders on that traumatic afternoon of 30 August, but for Brian Bevan it had another week to run. On 6 September, his debut season ended in joy as he helped Easts to win the Third Grade Grand Final with a 14-4 defeat of Balmain at the SCG.

After an uncertain beginning Brian Bevan had clearly begun to make a favourable impression on Easts officials and on the club's supporters. They knew that they had snared a good one. With a little more experience he would surely make the grade. Sure enough, Brian's next appearance for Easts was in First Grade. He made his senior debut on 2 May 1942. By coincidence, it was a mirror image of his Reserve Grade debut a little over a year earlier. It was at the Sydney Sports Ground, against Souths and once again Easts lost (14-18) and Brian failed to score. The only Premiership rugby league Brian would play for Easts in 1942 was in First Grade where he made seven appearances. Amazingly he did not score a solitary try, but did kick a goal in a 22-15 beating of Souths at the Sports Ground on 20 June.

Addicted to rugby league though he was, Brian had embarked on more serious matters. After completing his apprenticeship, he had volunteered for the Royal Australian Navy. Matters in the South Pacific had become extremely grave. In December, 1941 the Japanese had attacked Pearl Harbour. Soon Hong Kong, the Philippines, the South Pacific Islands, Malaya and Burma were overrun and

A young Brian Bevan in his
Eastern Suburbs blazer

Australia was threatened. In the circumstances Brian Bevan decided to do his duty, although he was still not yet 18.

As the Allies stemmed the Japanese advances in the Battles of the Coral Sea and Midway in May and June of 1942, Brian juggled his time between naval training at Flinders Training Depot, near Melbourne, and a little rugby league in Sydney whenever possible. Indeed he was so anxious to play that on 18 July 1942 *Rugby League News* reported: "Brian Bevan, who came from Melbourne to play against North Sydney expects to obtain leave next weekend to play against the leaders, Canterbury-Bankstown. There is no doubting Brian's keenness to travel 1000 miles for a game of football." In the event Brian did not make it back for the Canterbury fixture, but he did manage to figure in the business end of Easts' season, assisting them in their 20-14 victory over Balmain in the First Grade semi-final, but suffered disappointment as they went down 5-18 to St. George in the final on 5 September. It would be the nearest he would come to winning a Premiership. In fact he would not play again for Easts for almost two years.

Rugby union was played in the services and Brian Bevan played a few games for his depot at Flinders as a centre-threequarter. After three months training there, his naval service took him to Townsville in North Queensland where he joined his first ship, *HMAS Katoomba*, a corvette. *HMAS Katoomba* was constantly on patrol from Townsville and another northern base at Cairns, transporting troops or engaged in anti-submarine operations. There was certainly little time to contemplate the joys of playing rugby.

Brian Bevan's war service was not uneventful and on at least one occasion it was damned nearly fatal. In a series of articles entitled *The Brian Bevan Story* in the (British) *Daily Mail* in April, 1962, Derek Marshall ghost-wrote the following: "Eight - or was it nine - Japanese Zeros screamed out of a dusky Pacific sky and nearly ended my football career before it had really begun. It was in November 1942 and *HMAS Katoomba* was pitching placidly in the seas just north of New Guinea. I was off watch at the time and enjoying the moments of precious relaxation after the heat and fumes of the engine room. I had found a comparatively comfortable spot in the stern of the corvette when the dive-bombing attack began. Within seconds I found myself hanging on for dear life as the bombs began to fall. One of them landed in the sea only ten yards from where

I was standing, and the whole ship heaved with the explosion. Miraculously we suffered only slight damage, but that was altogether too close an escape for a man who was already beginning to dream of rugby fame." After such a harrowing experience, the perils of the rugby league field - the odd stiff-arm or wayward boot - would probably hold few terrors for the young sailor, if and when he could ever get a game.

Eventually the Navy decided to post Brian to a depot ship at Cairns where he remained for several months. During that time he was able to renew his acquaintance with rugby league. In 1961 George Crawford, a distinguished writer for the (Australian) *Daily Telegraph*, recalled his own times in the forces and his first encounter with Brian Bevan: "Back in the war years I was a soldier posted for a time on Trinity Beach, a few miles north of Cairns in Far North Queensland. Quite a deal of rugby league was played in the Services around the Cairns district in those days. The Navy had a particularly good side organised mainly from *HMAS Platypus*. My mind goes back to the last round of a competition in which the undefeated Navy team was drawn to meet an undefeated Cairns side. The men from the *Platypus* knew a bright young footballer was on the *HMAS Lithgow* some five miles off shore. Signals flashed and on the day of the match a small boat was sent out to pick up this youngster. The way back to shore was not easy and just as the Navy team, with 12 men, strolled out on to the field after having dawdled as long as possible a Navy truck dashed up to the field.

The lad from *HMAS Lithgow* jumped out of the back of the truck, tearing the seat out of his oversize khaki shorts in doing so. Not concerned about the badly tattered shorts, he dashed straight on to the field. In the first 10 minutes of the match the youngster, swerving and side-stepping in brilliant fashion, scored two tries. It was Brian Bevan."

Another often told tale of this period has Bevan again turning up late for a match, borrowing a strange assortment of kit, which provoked a good deal of mirth amongst the spectators, who were then stupefied by his virtuoso performance in bagging six tries. After a few months in Cairns, Brian was returned to more dangerous duties on another corvette before finally returning to Sydney in 1944. There he was stationed at the Balmoral Naval Depot which allowed him the opportunity of turning out again for Eastern Suburbs. His return at the tail end of the season saw him make three appearances in the centre, two of which were in Reserve Grade and the last in the Third Grade semi-final on 26 August when his two tries helped his team to a 20-5 victory over Balmain.

The 1945 rugby league season began with Brian restored to the wing and scoring both of Easts' tries in a 10-5 win against Newtown in Third Grade. He was then promoted to the Reserves for whom he played a further four games in April and May. By now the war had turned decisively in favour of the Allies, Germany had surrendered on 7 May and the Japanese were being rolled back to their own shores. Brian must have thought that life was about to settle down for him, but he could not have been more mistaken. One of the casualties in the Philippines had been *HMAS Australia*, the Royal Australian Navy' s flagship. She had been sent to Sydney for repairs and the day after her arrival Brian had been drafted to her. Almost immediately he learned that he was to accompany the ship to England where she would be refitted.

4. To Warrington and back

Whether Brian Bevan had ever harboured serious thoughts about playing rugby league in England before the news of his imminent voyage to the dockyards of Plymouth is not known. What is clear, however, is that the prospect of visiting England suddenly galvanised his ambition to really make a name for himself in the hardest of all rugby league arenas - the north of England. During this period, and for a long time past and for years to come, rugby league at the top level was much more competitive in England than in Australia. Australia's brave, but fruitless, attempts to wrest the Ashes for the last quarter of a century were eloquent testimony to that truth. The Sydney (New South Wales) Premiership, after all, consisted of a mere eight clubs who, by definition, could not all be winners. If rugby league in England could be defined by the cynics as parochial, then the game in Sydney must have been positively claustrophobic.

Whatever his previous priorities, hopes and ambitions, Brian now focussed his mind on the possibility of a career in the English game. It was a measure of his self-confidence that he could even contemplate such an enterprise. Certainly he must have felt in his bones and soul that he had what it took to succeed, even if his career so far had, in real terms, hardly begun.

It took *HMAS Australia* almost two months to travel from Sydney to Plymouth. Brian doubtless enjoyed the journey via Panama and New York and in all the whole tour of duty took up the best part of a year. The world had changed by the time Brian and his crew-mates had settled down to face an English winter. Hiroshima and Nagasaki had been obliterated in August, Japan had capitulated and the Second World War had finally ended. In Britain a Labour landslide had swept Winston Churchill from office and 43,000 dockers were on strike as *HMAS Australia* hove into British waters.

Back in Australia, Brian's Eastern Suburbs playing colleagues had won the Premiership on 1 September after beating Balmain 22-18 in a spellbinding Grand Final. Perhaps the possibility that, as champion club, Easts may not have any real need of his services on his return, whenever that might be, gave him added incentive to make good in England.

There was an opportunity to play some rugby on the south coast as a ship's rugby union team was quickly formed and met various teams in the local area. While Brian enjoyed such outings, he was bursting to travel north to try his luck in the professional game. His father had already warned his friend and former Australian Star Bill Shankland, now living in England, to expect a call from Brian and Bill had agreed to help fix up his old colleague's son with a trial if he could. Bill had become the professional at Temple Newsam golf club in Leeds. As soon as Brian was given some leave he shot up north to stay with Bill and more or less placed himself in his hands.

The oft recited tale that Leeds took one look at Brian and turned him away without a trial, and that he was similarly treated by Hunslet is pure invention. The truth is that Shankland only got as far as telephoning Leeds to enquire whether they would trial Bevan. Most clubs were in some turmoil recovering from the war and Leeds were particularly afflicted. It appears that they simply did not have the

13

time nor inclination to pursue the matter. Brian never even saw Headingley. Nor did he get any nearer to seeing Hunslet's Parkside home. Shankland's third gambit was to contact his old club Warrington, who had the sense to agree to have a look at the young Australian. It was Jack Knowles, acting secretary-manager of the club, who arranged with Shankland to run the rule over Brian. If ever a man hit the bull's-eye, Jack Knowles did when he agreed to Shankland's telephone request on Thursday, 8 November 1945. It is tempting to wonder if Bill Shankland had any other line of enquiry in mind had Warrington followed Leeds's and Hunslet's example.

Wilderspool debut

It must have been with a mixture of trepidation and excitement that Brian Bevan boarded the train from Leeds to Warrington early on the morning of Saturday, 10 November 1945, the good wishes of Bill Shankland echoing in his ears. Later that afternoon, Brian Bevan made his debut in English rugby league in a low-key reserve team match at Wilderspool. Warrington 'A' versus Widnes 'A' in the Lancashire Combination was decidedly not the big league, but, as a landmark in the history of the sport it certainly holds some significance. Brian had not played a competitive game of rugby league for almost six months. The last time had been back on 19 May, when he won the match with two tries for Easts' Reserve Grade who beat Norths 13-8 at Sydney Cricket Ground. From the SCG in May to Wilderspool in November must have seemed like entering another universe to the aspiring Aussie, and he could have been forgiven any apprehension he might have felt in view of his English experiences to date. It was definitely make or break time.

More than half a century later, it is surprising how many people claim to have been present at Brian Bevan's British baptism. Well, wishful thinking is no crime. Two who were present, however, were Jackie Parr and Edie Spilling, one on the pitch and one on the terraces. Mike Rowan, local boxing coach and Warrington supporter, has recorded their recollections of the occasion. Edie recalled that "when he came out we all laughed. I mean everybody laughed because we couldn't believe it when we saw him. He looked so thin with his shorts right down to his knees. His hair was almost gone too. But boy, oh boy, when he ran! Well, we just gasped - I suppose that's the word for it. I don't suppose we considered what he could do but when he took off - well, I mean, that's it. He just seemed to take off. He was exciting. You were hoping he would get the ball."

Jackie Parr played at Warrington for a good few years, and he was in the team for Bevan's debut against Widnes 'A'. He remembers: "Bevan hadn't a chance in the first half so when the players took a rest at the interval, I was approached to see if I could work out something. During the second half I was able to open them up and I gave him the ball. You should have seen him go. He didn't half pick 'em up. He flew and left the lot of us behind."

The *Warrington Examiner*'s match report was headlined: "Shankland's Protégé Scores Dazzling Try At Wilderspool."

Warrington 'A' won 23-8 and the match report glowed with praise for the debutant: "Appearing on the right wing was a youthful member of the Australian

14

Navy, who while on leave came along on the recommendation of Bill Shankland ... and he proceeded to give one of the most promising displays on the part of a newcomer ever seen at Warrington capping it with a grand try from halfway for which the crowd gave him an ovation which must have made him blush! Accepting a pass from his centre he sped down the wing with head up and shoulders back and at a speed which amazed the onlookers. At various intervals were no fewer than four opponents and it seemed they were all in a position successfully to challenge him. But sweeping past them in a straight dash he simply left them standing and went on to score in the corner without a finger having been laid on him. This was the last of a number of fine things he did. He frequently came inside and cut down the middle in a manner most disconcerting to the opposition and, what is more, he used a deceptive sidestep."

The *Warrington Guardian* match report recorded Bevan's debut a little less comprehensively but their reporter was equally impressed: "The player on the right wing astonished all with his fine turn of speed and will be an acquisition. We were pleased to see the crowd recognised his abilities when a minute before time he scored a try in brilliant fashion."

Brian had done enough to whet the appetite of Warrington. Although he had to return to his ship after the game, the club acted quickly to secure further leave for him to play in the first team against Oldham at Wilderspool the following week.

More than half a century later Bert Maguire recalled that day. His father, Tom, ran a garage and taxi service in Bridge Street. "I remember my father returning from Wilderspool after watching the 'A' Team match and talking about how the stand members were all on their feet every time Bevan got the ball. A week later I got a message to meet a certain train at Bank Quay Station and that Brian Bevan would be on it. I was to take him to a certain director's house. I think it was Jack Knowles's. I soon spotted Brian as he had his service bag. I remember we talked about service life. I had been on an Australian destroyer, *HMAS Stuart*, when it sailed into Tobruk when it was under siege. If only the Warrington directors had known just what a star they were getting, they would have had a red carpet all the way from the station to Wilderspool."

The game, played on 17 November 1945, was an open one, but two resolute defences kept the scoring down to only three tries, two of which fell to Warrington who ran out winners by 12-3. Bevan uncharacteristically failed to trouble the scoreboard operators but he certainly made his mark.

FOR YOUR INFORMATION.

The young man who played such a good game on the wing for our "A" team last Saturday was an Australian who is serving in the Australian Navy and is at present stationed in this country. Our old captain and friend, Bill Shankland, recommended to the boy that he should come and have a game with Warrington. Thanks Bill for giving our supporters an opportunity of seeing this boy. As a matter of fact he is the A. N. Other who is on the team sheet for to-day's game and if he can get leave from his ship he will play for our team against Oldham this afternoon.

From the Warrington versus Oldham programme

The *Oldham Evening Chronicle* reporter noted that: "Warrington had an Australian Naval man on the right wing and it was his fine side-stepping which led to the home team's first try." In truth, however, he was more interested in Oldham's own newcomer, John King, a trialist full-back who was said to have fielded and kicked well.

The *Warrington Examiner's* correspondent, 'Criticus', understandably more concerned with the Wire's new man, was bowled over by Bevan's showing. He wrote: "Chief interest from a Warrington point of view was the appearance of Bevan, the young Australian winger, who had done so well with the 'A' Team the previous week. The crowd rose to him in the second half when from a standing start he flashed past three opponents with as neat a sidestep as one could wish to see and, dashing into the middle of the field, started the movement which resulted in L. Jones scoring after the ball had passed through several pairs of hands. Everything he did went to confirm the impression I gained when I first saw him that he has real football skill. He combines pace with the ability to beat a man and he has the gift of being able to cut inside and do the unexpected, which is so disconcerting to a defender."

The teams on this historic occasion were:

Warrington: Belshaw; Bevan, Les Jones (try), Higginbottom (3 goals), Ratcliffe; Helme (try), Fairclough; H. Jones, Cotton, Miller, Bennett, Gregory, Taylor.

Oldham: King; Lees (try), Gummer, Mitchell, Large; Kenny, Smith; Ogden, W. Flanagan, Rostron, Griffiths, Moore, Pugh.

George Phillips, the famous Widnes official, was the referee.

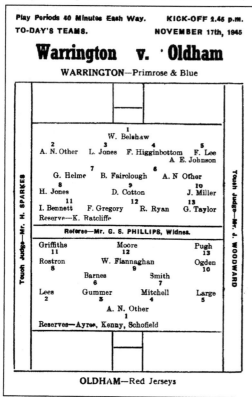

Warrington lost no time in signing their trialist winger. Immediately after the match, Brian agreed to a three-year contract with the club. The contract would run from the time he returned to England on completion of his demobilisation. The fact that they were prepared to wait almost a year before seeing him again indicates that the Wire directorate recognised a good thing when they saw it. Bevan's signing-on fee was £300 and many people have, in hindsight, remarked upon how cheaply Warrington got their man. Of course, Brian repaid that outlay many times over, but when it is remembered that he had only played a handful of first-team matches in Australia, Warrington were taking a risk

16

which could have backfired. In the immediate post-war years £300 was not a figure to be sneezed at, especially by an unknown 21 year-old. Such a figure represented more than a year's wages for a working class man and, given any sort of success, he could expect to earn as much again in match fees per season, in addition to which he would be found a full-time job.

Farewell to Oz

Brian returned with *HMAS Australia* to Sydney, arriving home in January 1946. He was demobbed and resumed work in the printing trade until July. By coincidence, that English summer saw the Great Britain touring team in Australia, although they were still called England by all and sundry in both hemispheres. The presence of Gus Risman's 'Indomitables' must have added piquancy to Brian's anticipation of what would soon be happening to him. Within a few months he would be playing against most of those Lions. Risman's men went through the Ashes series undefeated and lost only five times in a 27-match itinerary. They played four times in Sydney, twice in tests and twice against New South Wales, and it is almost certain that Bevan would have been present at some, if not all, of those occasions, studying those great men and weighing up his own prospects. Certainly none of those games on the SCG clashed with his own infrequent appearances in grade football that campaign. He would undoubtedly have seen newsreel footage of the tour games at the cinema and listened avidly to the wireless coverage. Doubtless he took particular notice of the tourists' wingers, Arthur Bassett, Jim Lewthwaite, Eric Batten and Albert Johnson, especially the latter, who was the sole Warrington representative among the Lions.

Brian's last season with Easts comprised only four games - three in the reserves and a solitary first team appearance against Balmain at Leichhardt Oval on 13 July 1946. Easts lost 8-11 to the Tigers and Brian failed to score. Significantly, that Eastern Suburbs team contained three other men who were to follow Bevan to England - Lionel Cooper, Johnny Hunter and George Watt. Hooker Watt and winger Cooper had played in all three tests against the Lions, while Hunter would surely have given even Clive Churchill a stern challenge for the Australian test full-back jersey, had he remained in Sydney.

Brian Bevan made his final appearance for Easts in a reserve game, however, on 27 July. He made a winning exit and scored a try in a 12-5 victory over St. George at the Sydney Sports Ground. Ironically Sydney's last glimpse for fifteen years of one of its greatest sporting sons was as a centre, a position he would never fill again. A week later, on 3 August, *Rugby League News* reported that: "Brian Bevan expects to leave for Warrington, England, this week. All members and supporters join in wishing this popular player *bon voyage* and the best of luck in his venture."

By the time that sentiment had been published, Brian Bevan had taken leave of his family and was sailing to England and sporting immortality.

Brian Bevan's playing record for Easts

Date	Grade	Opponents	Venue	Result	Bevan	Position	
1941							
19 Apr	Reserve	Souths	Sydney SG	5-16		Wing	
26 Apr	Reserve	Wests	Sydney CG	7-7		Wing	
3 May	Reserve	Norths	North Sydney	0-10		Wing	
10 May	Reserve	Balmain	Sydney SG	·5-0		Wing	
17 May	Reserve	Canterbury	Sydney CG	13-5	T	Centre	
24 May	Reserve	Newtown	Henson Park	8-4		Centre	
31 May	Reserve	St George	Sydney SG	2-9		Centre	
21 June	Reserve	Souths	Sydney SG	5-7		Centre	
28 June	Reserve	Wests	Pratten Park	10-10		5/8	
6 July	Third	Norths	Trumper Park	12-0	T	Wing	
12 July	Third	Balmain	Sydney SG	9-8	T	Centre	
26 July	Third	Newtown	Sydney CG	21-5		Centre	
2 Aug	Third	St George	Hurstville Oval	13-3	T	Wing	
9 Aug	Third	Canterbury	Belmore SG	11-12		Wing	
9 Aug	Reserve	Canterbury	Belmore SG	10-15	T	Wing	
23 Aug	Third	Souths	Sydney CG	15-10	T	Wing	Semi-final
30 Aug	Third	Wests	Sydney CG	3-0	T	Wing	Final
6 Sep	Third	Balmain	Sydney CG	14-4		Wing	Grand Final
1942							
2 May	First	Souths	Sydney SG	14-18		Wing	
6 Jun	First	Wests	St. Luke's Park	7-16		Centre	
13 Jun	First	St. George	Sydney SG	9-17		Wing	
20 Jun	First	Souths	Sydney SG	22-15	G	Wing	
11 Jul	First	Norths	Sydney CG	12-9		Wing	
29 Aug	First	Balmain	Sydney CG	20-14		Wing	Semi-final
5 Sep	First	St George	Sydney CG	5-18		Wing	Final

(Bevan also played in a City Cup Reserve Grade match v Wests at Sydney Sports Ground on 15.8.42. The result is not known. Bevan played at centre. This was not a Premiership game)

Date	Grade	Opponents	Venue	Result	Bevan	Position	
1944							
5 Aug	Reserve	Souths	Sydney CG	6-20		Centre	
12 Aug	Reserve	Balmain	Sydney CG	5-13		Centre	
26 Aug	Third	Balmain	Sydney CG	20-5	2T	Centre	Semi-final
1945							
21 Apr	Third	Newtown	Sydney CG	10-5	2T	Wing	
28 Apr	Reserve	Canterbury	Sydney SG	7-12		Wing	
5 May	Reserve	Souths	Sydney SG	10-12		Wing	
12 May	Reserve	Balmain	Leichhardt Oval	12-8	T	Wing	
19 May	Reserve	Norths	Sydney SG	13-8	2T	Wing	
1946							
29 Jun	Reserve	Wests	Pratten Park	0-11		Wing	
6 Jul	Reserve	Norths	North Sydney	14-14		Wing	
13 Jul	First	Balmain	Leichhardt Oval	11-8		Wing	
27 Jul	Reserve	St George	Sydney SG	12-5	T	Centre	

Summary

First Grade (1942, 1946):	Played 8	Goals 1	Points 2
Reserve Grade (1941, 1944-46)	Played 19	Tries 6	Points 18
Third Grade (1941, 1944-45)	Played 10	Tries 9	Points 27
Premiership matches (All grades)	Played 37	Tries 15 Goals 1	Points 47

5. 1946-47 'Get the ball to Bevan'

Brian Bevan disembarked at Tilbury Docks on Wednesday, 4 September, 1946, some five or so weeks after leaving Sydney. He was met by Fred Davies and Arthur Catterall, two directors of the Warrington club. Even in those days local newspapers liked to be one up on their rivals and the *Warrington Guardian* scooped the *Warrington Examiner* by persuading Bevan to send its readers an exclusive message from Tilbury, which read: "My best wishes to all Warrington supporters. I am fit and well and eager for my first match."

Following an overnight stay in London, the trio decamped for the north of England by train. After a journey of more than four hours they were greeted at Bank Quay Station by more members of the Warrington management, including the team manager, Chris Brockbank, and directors J. W. Gibbs, J. Craik and R. Appleton. The *Warrington Guardian* rugby league reporter Cyril Briggs, using his *nom de plume* of Jack Steel, was quick to ensure that his paper had Brian photographed outside their offices in Sankey Street and noted that: "Bevan certainly looked fit enough when I met him at Bank Quay. He said he had been training hard on the boat and had included boxing in his routine. Bevan stands 5' 10" and weighs 11 st 9 lbs."

The *Warrington Guardian* stole another significant march on its local rival by employing Brian in its printing department, while Jack Knowles provided him with accommodation at his own home in Flers Avenue. Materially, therefore, Brian Bevan's needs were more than adequately satisfied. He had a contract, a job and a roof over his head. He was, however, a 22-year-old bachelor, separated from his family by 12,000 miles. He was shy, friendless and stranded in an alien culture - a recipe which could have spelled disaster. There were distractions, however. Brian was a proficient pianist and the club encouraged him to entertain at old peoples' homes and hospitals. Pubs and clubs too welcomed him, rugby fans being able to rub shoulders with the man who was destined to bring them such joy in the coming years.

The term culture shock had probably not been coined in 1946, but there is every likelihood that Brian experienced it. Warrington and Sydney were 12,000 miles apart, but it may have seemed nearer a million miles. He had left behind home and hearth, family and friends, sea and sand and a benign climate which positively encouraged outdoor activity. In exchange he was now domiciled in Warrington, an industrial town in Lancashire, bounded on the south by the less than exotic Manchester Ship Canal and some 16 or so miles to the east of Liverpool. Its population of around 80,000 was engaged in a variety of trades ranging from the manufacture of iron, steel and wire products to leather and cotton goods, chemicals and soap and from engineering to brewing.

Britain and her allies may have won the Second World War but there had been a huge price to pay. Apart from the obvious evidence of Luftwaffe bombing and the presence in the country of thousands of German and Italian prisoners of war, the United Kingdom had been seriously impoverished, a quarter of the national wealth had been lost and the empire was firmly on the road to extinction. Economic and financial stringency was the order of the day. Brian had arrived just in time for the age of austerity, when everything from petrol to sweets was rationed. In retrospect, Bondi beach and the possibility of a peace-time career with Eastern Suburbs may have crossed his mind as a preferable option.

The boss - Chris Brockbank

It is well known and documented that Brian Bevan was not the most gregarious of men. He was, as they sometimes say, backward at coming forward. He has variously been described as introverted, shy, introspective, uncommunicative, reclusive, off-hand, a loner. From the beginning, tales of his taciturnity abounded. Exaggerated or not, they merely added to his mystique. A case in point was his relationship with Chris Brockbank, secretary-manager at Wilderspool from Brian's arrival until 1951.

Chris Brockbank knew all about wing play. He had been a star wingman for Swinton when they became the last team to win all four cups in 1927-28, and had been capped by England against Wales in 1927 and twice by Lancashire. In 1928, he had come close to Lions tour selection having been a try-scorer in the first tour trial at Headingley. He had certainly tried hard enough. The conditions that day had been so atrocious and the ground so stamina-sapping that he was carried from the field exhausted in the final minutes, while several other players were also noticeably physically distressed. Brockbank had also played for Salford and Bradford Northern, had coached Huddersfield to great success, including Wembley appearances in 1933 as winners, and 1935 as runners-up, and was so highly regarded that he was poached by soccer club Bradford Park Avenue in 1935. By the 1936-37 season, however, he had been lured back to rugby league as manager of Warrington. There is no question that Chris Brockbank was a skilful man-manager and a deep thinker about the game. He refused, for example, to allow any dressing-room criticism of players after games, believing that things were more profitably discussed later in the week when minds were clearer.

Apart from having been a wingman himself, Brockbank had something else in common with Bevan. Both served in their countries' navies during the war. Indeed, Brockbank was still in the Royal Navy when Brian had made his first trip to England. He was then serving as a sports and welfare officer based in the Glasgow area and travelled down to matches at weekends when his duties allowed. He had been present at Brian's 'A' team debut and was duly impressed. However, he later intimated that initially he felt Brian would simply not settle to England and English conditions - not, of course, through any lack of talent, but because temperamentally he was too retiring, almost anti-social.

Brian and Brockbank may have had some things in common, but Brockbank experienced severe difficulty in communicating with his Australian protégé. Many stories have been told of Brian's frequent visits to the manager's office, during which Brian would sit for up to a couple of hours while barely saying a word. Brockbank was undoubtedly mystified by the young player's behaviour, the like of which he had not previously encountered among footballers. In an autobiographical series of articles for the *Sporting Chronicle & Athletic News* in 1950, Brockbank recalled another Australian - the prodigious Dave Brown, like Bevan a former Eastern Suburbs player and also prematurely bald, but, unlike

Bevan, already a world star when he signed for Warrington for the 1936-37 season. Brown did well enough by any normal standards in three seasons at Wilderspool but not quite as well as his towering reputation promised.

Brockbank wrote that Dave Brown "often came into my office to talk football, and it was always a pleasure to see him for he had a charming personality."

On arrival in England, Brown, naturally, had more maturity and, in footballing terms, vastly more experience than Brian. He had been Australia's youngest test captain, had toured Europe with the 1933-34 Kangaroos and skippered Easts to two Premierships. Australian rugby league had already deified him before he arrived for his stint with Warrington. It would doubtless have been easier for him to strike up a rapport with Brockbank and other notables than for the nervous Brian Bevan. Crucially too, Brown had brought his wife over with him, having been married only six weeks prior to arriving in England.

Chris Brockbank may have had little insight into Brian off the field, but he quickly came to recognise his special talents on it. In that same series of articles in 1950, he wrote: "I will go so far as to say that our game can have seen no better wing threequarter than Brian Bevan. He is the best player in that position I have seen. What is it that has made him the most talked of player in the game? He has been endowed with terrific speed and, added to this, I believe him to be the most unorthodox winger who has played during my connection with the game. He attempts things - and gets away with them - that star wingers I have admired in the past would never have attempted, nor even thought of."

Whatever problems his reclusiveness may or may not have presented to his employers, there were no such problems as far as the Warrington supporters were concerned. From the off they simply adored him. Thoughts of hardship and austerity, memories of war-time terror and horror were banished as Bevan cast his spells for 80 minutes each Saturday.

Warrington was certainly hard-core rugby league territory. The club had a long and illustrious history and was a founder member of the Northern Union back in 1895. In the decade leading up to the Second World War Warrington had been a constant threat to the other leading clubs in the league, but somehow never quite broke into the elite ranks. They had lost at Wembley in 1933 and 1936, and had failed in Championship Finals in 1935 and 1937. The biggest prizes always just eluded them, although they had lifted the Lancashire Cup in 1932 and 1937 and the Lancashire League Championship in 1937-38. In the 1930s their Wilderspool ground housed many big games - Lancashire Cup Finals, the 1934 Championship Final when more than 31,000 were packed in, county and representative fixtures. Support was so solid that Wilderspool came to be known as the venue which would fetch a good crowd when the authorities needed a sure thing.

The potential for success was certainly present in Warrington, but the Second World War put everything on hold. Warrington had continued to operate until December 1940, when all rugby activity ceased because the ground was requisitioned for storage purposes by the United States Air Force establishment based at Burtonwood. The club went into hibernation for almost five years.

When normal service resumed for the 1945-46 season Warrington performed reasonably well in finishing 10th in the Northern Rugby League Championship.

They had a smattering of pre-war warriors in the team, especially in the pack, with old familiar names such as 'Cod' Miller, Dave Cotton, Ivor Bennett and Bill Chapman. Mel de Lloyd, Les Jones and the great Billy Belshaw were among the pre-war backs who returned to action. Most, however, would soon be retired or gone to fresh pastures. Some excellent younger players were coming through the ranks, notably Gerry Helme, destined to be one of the game's finest and most controversial scrum-halves, and future test forwards in Jim Featherstone and Bob Ryan, as well as a couple of England wingers in Ossie Peake and Albert Johnson. The basis of a good team was in place, but that first post-war season proved that more pieces were needed to complete the jigsaw. The Wire's experience in the crucible of the Challenge Cup in 1946 emphasised that, as Warrington struggled desperately to overcome Cumbrian amateurs Kells by a paltry 3-0 away in the first leg of the first round, although a 27-0 win at home in the second leg followed. The ignominy of a 8-2 loss at perennial strugglers Bramley in the second round must have focussed a lot of minds at Wilderspool.

Tries and Goals

So it was to a team of as yet unfulfilled promise that Brian Bevan was introduced in September of 1946. The Warrington directorate had the good sense to delay Brian's return to match action for 10 days, allowing him to acclimatise to his new surroundings. On Saturday 7 September, he went to watch his new colleagues take on Salford before a crowd of 13,000 in the first leg of a first round Lancashire Cup tie at The Willows. The game ended in a 10-3 defeat. The second leg was staged at Wilderspool the following Saturday and Bevan replaced Glyn Williams on the Wire right wing, Williams moving into the centre. Brian was faced by Salford's Syd Williams, a dual Welsh international and a searching test for any novice to take. The Wire's team was: L. Jones; Bevan, Williams, Dixon, Helme; De Lloyd, Davies; Norris, Cotton, H. Jones, Featherstone, Rothwell, Chapman.

Bevan had a decent game. It was not his fault that Warrington could only manage a 10-5 victory over a team which played a man short for most of the match. The tie was thus lost 13-15 on aggregate and Warrington got a flogging from the local press.

However, Bevan was singled out for praise, the *Warrington Guardian* noting that he "showed amazing speed when chasing two high cross-kicks from Featherstone and in the 15th minute neatly side-stepped two opponents to dive over for Warrington's first try." One down. Only 795 to go!

Brian also landed a goal and, for a time, it seemed as if his prowess in this department might outweigh his try-scoring as he kicked goals in his first twelve games in 1946. By the season's close he had booted 34 and finished as the club's top goal-kicker. He would, however, never kick another goal in his entire professional career.

Brian's next game was also to end in defeat for Warrington, who went down 2-16 at Oldham on 21 September 1946. Bev landed a 35-yard penalty to score his side's only points. The local paper criticised his kicking action: "The lift and carry was there but the direction was faulty." His tackling technique was also dissected as suspect and too high. Tackling and goal-kicking were not, thankfully, to be the measure by which he would ultimately be judged. The *Oldham Evening Chronicle*'s reporter was much kinder, commenting that the "star of the visitors' team was elusive Australian winger, Bevan, signed on three weeks ago following his release from the Australian Navy. A useful place-kicker and showing a certain individuality, he is obviously a capture."

Warrington's fortunes soon perked up, however. Eight consecutive victories from the close of September onwards and only three more defeats before the turn of 1947 saw them firmly established in the top four alongside Widnes, Wigan and Bradford Northern. Brian Bevan was a match-winner in several of those games, and he was fast becoming the idol of Wilderspool. The first of 101 hat-tricks came his way in a 19-10 home victory over St Helens on 5 October when he also popped over a couple of goals. Not for the last time, opponents would try to dull his attacking edge illegally, and on this occasion Saints' hooker Ike Fishwick got his marching orders and a three-match suspension for having a go at the pesky Australian wing. Ike would later become a colleague of his victim at Wilderspool and be grateful that he did him no lasting harm.

'Criticus' wrote in the *Examiner*: "It's a long time since we saw such an exhibition of speed and determined running. The crowd gave him a tremendous ovation. When he scored two of his three tries opponents were that close that it seemed impossible to clear them but his amazing acceleration was such they looked as if they were static. Twice he went over and didn't realise they were that well beaten he could have gone behind the posts."

Jack Steel, in the *Guardian*, was mightily impressed but somewhat fearful that Bevan's talents might be bludgeoned out of him. He wrote that "a dangerous complex is fast becoming apparent in the Warrington team... get the ball to Bevan and he will do the rest. Speed, grit, determination, all these the Australian possesses and at the moment they are bringing tries. But a potentially great player must not be 'burned out' before he has had a chance to show his true worth."

In hindsight, there was little danger of Bevan burning himself out and the crowds certainly thought that he should be given the ball at every opportunity. They loved every moment he was in possession. He won matches and that was what counted. On 19 October his try from Gerry Helme's cross-kick gave Warrington a 7-5 win at Workington, on 9 November his penalty goal stunned a 22,000 crowd at Central Park as Wigan were downed 4-3 and the following week in a local derby against Leigh at Wilderspool, the Wire found themselves trailing 3-5 with eight minutes left. Again it was left to Bevan who collected de Lloyd's cross-kick to score the winning try, which, just for good measure, he converted from three yards from the touchline. Even then he was not finished, for he added another try at the flag before the final whistle, but this time proved his mortality by hitting the crossbar with the conversion.

The frozen North

One thing Brian had not experienced was a winter in the north of England. It must have come as a rude shock to his system. Christmas took care of itself - professional rugby league players' concentration in those days focussed more on football than festivities. Bev spent Christmas Day afternoon at Naughton Park, Widnes, where Warrington went down 3-7 to their local rivals. Boxing Day was better as he scooted over for a hat-trick against Liverpool Stanley at Wilderspool and two days later on the same ground he bagged a spectacular try as Castleford were pipped 10-9.

The winter of 1947 unleashed all its fury in February. Brian Bevan had apparently never seen snow. He had certainly never experienced such numbing cold. The country endured widespread blizzards. It was one of the snowiest winters ever recorded, and plummeting temperatures ensured that no substantial thaw would move the snow for weeks. To add to the misery of an arctic climate, a Britain bedevilled by shortages, power cuts, travel difficulties, rationing and growing problems of industrial absenteeism and under-production was also requested by the Home Secretary to desist from playing midweek sporting fixtures. It must all have seemed a long way from sunny Sydney.

On 1 February, only three fixtures survived the weather, one of which was Warrington's home game against Wigan which drew a crowd of 27,500 hardy souls. Bevan scored the only Wire try as Wigan won 11-3. The game was notable because half-back Jackie Fleming made his debut for the Wire against his former club. It was also the first time that Bev came into direct opposition with Brian Nordgren. Nordgren, a New Zealander, who was studying to become a barrister, was to have many an epic confrontation with Brian over the next seven years. Tall and athletic, he was a lethal finisher and his record of 312 tries in 294 games for Wigan was testimony to an exceptional talent. Bev found out all about his power when Nordgren brushed him aside in scoring a try of his own.

The following week, conditions were so bad that the entire first round of the Challenge Cup was postponed. Warrington instead managed to stage a league fixture against Rochdale Hornets. The club had taken the extraordinary measure of covering the Wilderspool pitch with 180 tons of sand. It did not do the grass much good, but remarkably Warrington did not lose a solitary game to the weather that season, an amazing justification of their actions as chaos ruled everywhere else, particularly across the Pennines in Yorkshire. So severe was the disruption of fixtures that the season did not end until 21 June, five weeks behind schedule.

As other clubs failed to fulfil fixtures, Warrington played nine consecutive home matches between 1 February and 4 April. Brian Bevan scored 18 tries and 16 goals in the first eight of those games. It did not seem to matter to him that he was playing on a surface resembling the beach at Blackpool on a bad day. In the first round Challenge Cup tie against Brookland Rovers, played over two legs, he plundered six tries and nine goals. A much sterner test was anticipated for the second round tie against St Helens. By this time, however, Bev was in overdrive. On 22 March, a crowd of 23,500 saw Saints squashed 24-2, with Bevan streaking over for three tries, as well as kicking three goals. They were the last goals he would land in his career. Of more relevance to the ecstatic Wire fans was the fact that their new hero broke the club record of 34 tries in a season which had been established in 1938-39 by Welsh winger Islwyn Davies. At this point he had amassed 36 tries in 29 matches.

The following week, 18,000 turned up at Wilderspool for the third round, Castleford being the opposition and putting up stern resistance before succumbing 5-0, with no prizes for guessing who scored the Wire try.

The Warrington supporters could hardly believe their luck. The team was ensconced in the top four, had qualified for the semi-final of the Challenge Cup and had unearthed a winger who seemed to produce tries out of nothing with a frequency which alarmed all who played against him. By this time, too, Bevan had shot to the top of that season's league try-scoring lists, edging ahead of the Wigan trio of Ernie Ashcroft, Gordon Ratcliffe and Brian Nordgren and Barrow's flying winger Roy Francis. They were not to catch him.

Warrington had to negotiate four games before they were to meet Ernest Ward's formidable Bradford Northern in the Challenge Cup semi-final at Station Road, Swinton. Their form dipped somewhat as they lost narrowly at home to Widnes and disappointingly at Batley. Sandwiched between those defeats were victories at St Helens and Halifax, Bevan scoring crucial tries in both. Yet, paradoxically, it was an incident in which he failed to score which was burned forever on the memories of those privileged to see it. The *Warrington Examiner* reported of the game at Thrum Hall on 7 April: "The feature of the match was a sensational run by Bevan. He has given us some thrills since joining Warrington but I have never seen an effort quite like this. When he fielded the ball at half-way and close to the touch-line there seemed not the slightest danger to Halifax. But he suddenly started an electrifying cross-field dash, the unexpected nature of which had opponents as well as spectators amazed. Weaving in and out, feigning to pass three or four times using a peculiar half-turning motion to escape the clutches of would-be challengers and all the time maintaining a thrilling pace, he must have beaten seven or eight opponents in this sensational run but as he dived to complete the effort the ball shot from his grasp and he was denied tangible reward for what everybody agreed was the finest effort they had ever seen. The crowd rose to him and the cheers continued all the time Bevan came back to his place on the wing. He had some consolation later when he nipped in to intercept an opponent's pass and raced from well beyond half-way to score near the posts."

It is doubtful if any other player in the game's history has so often earned such idolisation from crowds at opponents' grounds. Even the most partisan of supporters were moved to rapturous applause whenever Bevan's genius was given full rein. The years that followed were littered with such references. The fact that

A FEW OF THE LEAGUE'S WINGMEN   **By Jim Forster**

25

reporters chose so frequently to record these spontaneous accolades was a measure of the impact and spectacle Bevan could bring to the most mundane of matches.

The biggest game of Brian's life thus far saw more than 33,000 fans squeezing into Station Road on 19 April for the semi-final clash with Bradford. His hopes were dashed, however, as Bradford won more easily than the 11-7 scoreline suggested. Still, there was the Championship to play for. The Wire were still looking to clinch a place in the top four and right down to the final fixture, at Rochdale, on 2 June, it seemed that they would win a place in the semis. They only needed to draw to pip Leeds for fourth place and Hornets were next to bottom of the league. Nobody bothered to show Rochdale the script, however, and it was the Hornets' right winger, Harry Nicholson, noteworthy for being a canal shipwright in Wigan but certainly not one of the great figures of rugby league history, who stole the limelight with two tries which brought his side an improbable 8-7 victory and condemned the Wire to fifth place in the table. So near and yet so far... perhaps next season?

Season 1946–47

Warrington finished 5th in the League: P36, W26, L10; For 432, Against 236
Bevan scored 48 tries and 34 goals for Warrington

Date	Opponent	Score	Bevan	Crowd	
31 Aug	**Hunslet**	27–5	dnp		
7 Sep	Salford	3–10	dnp	13,000	LC1
14 Sep	**Salford**	10–5	1T, 1G	15,000	LC1
21 Sep	Oldham	2–16	1G	10,000	
28 Sep	**Workington T**	13–7	2G		
5 Oct	**St Helens**	19–10	3T, 2G	8,000	
12 Oct	Belle Vue R	15–4	1T, 1G		
19 Oct	Workington T	7–5	1T, 1G	11,000	
26 Oct	**Barrow**	12–6	3G	10,000	
2 Nov	**Batley**	15–2	1T, 2G	9,000	
9 Nov	Wigan	4–3	1G	22,000	
16 Nov	**Leigh**	11–5	2T, 1G	15,500	
23 Nov	Wakefield T	11–17	2G	5,000	
30 Nov	**Salford**	14–7	1T, 1G	7,000	
7 Dec	Salford	2–0		6,000	
14 Dec	Barrow	4–5		7,625	
25 Dec	Widnes	3–7		14,500	
26 Dec	**Liverpool St**	25–6	3T	12,000	
28 Dec	Hunslet	11–0	1T	8,000	
1 Jan	**Castleford**	10–9	1T	13,000	
4 Jan	**Belle Vue R**	5–2		10,000	
11 Jan	Swinton	13–5	1T	8,000	
18 Jan	**Halifax**	25–5	3T	13,000	
25 Jan	Castleford	0–12		8,000	
1 Feb	**Wigan**	3–11	1T	27,500	
8 Feb	**Rochdale H**	21–0	2T	6,000	
15 Feb	**Brookland R**	46–3	3T, 5G	10,500	Ch Cup 1
1 Mar	Brookland R	32–3	3T, 4G	8,000	Ch Cup 1 (at Wilderspool)
8 Mar	**Liverpool St***	29–0	4T	8,500	
15 Mar	**Oldham**	23–3	1T, 4G	13,000	
22 Mar	**St Helens**	24–2	3T, 3G	23,500	Ch Cup 2
29 Mar	**Castleford**	5–0	1T	18,000	Ch Cup 3
4 Apr	**Widnes**	2–4		27,000	
5 Apr	St Helens	10–6	1T	15,000	
7 Apr	Halifax	12–2	1T	8,000	
12 Apr	Batley	7–13		7,000	
19 Apr	Bradford N	7–11		33,474	Ch Cup SF (at Swinton)
26 Apr	Leigh	4–5		13,000	
10 May	**Featherstone R**	15–7	1T	8,000	
17 May	**Wakefield T**	19–16	3T	12,000	
21 May	Liverpool St	16–11	1T	5,000	
24 May	**Swinton**	22–7	1T	7,000	
31 May	Featherstone R	23–5	3T	3,000	
2 Jun	Rochdale H	7–8		5,000	

* The fixture against Liverpool Stanley on 8 March should have been played at Liverpool but because of ground conditions Liverpool agreed to play at Wilderspool. The Rugby Football League declared the match void and ordered the game to be replayed at Liverpool on 21 May.

Warrington 1946-7
Standing (left to right): J. Fleming, B. Day, H. Jones, B. Ryan, D. Cotton,
J. Featherstone, J. O'Toole
Sitting: B. Bevan, I. Davies, C. Brockbank, L. Jones (captain), J. S. Tilling,
M. De Lloyd, F. Higginbottom, A. E. Johnson
(Photo taken in March or April 1947)

Two great Wire wings - Albert Johnson
and Brian Bevan, circa 1947

6. 1947-48 'At the 37th attempt: Champions'

Brian Bevan's first season of English rugby league had been a personal triumph. He had topped the League's try-scoring list with 48 tries, 14 ahead of Wigan's splendid centre Ernie Ashcroft and Bradford Northern's Welsh winger Emlyn Walters. His try tally was the highest recorded since 1935-36, when fellow Australians Eric Harris of Leeds and Huddersfield's Ray Markham had scored 63 and 53 tries respectively. His achievement was unique in that no other Warrington player had previously topped the try-scoring charts. He had smashed the Warrington club record and had even been the club's leading goal-kicker with a total of 34. It beggared belief then how the trade paper *Rugby League Review*'s panel of experts could fail to include him in their five 'stars of the season' or even their five 'discoveries of the season'. The "stars" were Willie Davies and Ernest Ward of Bradford, Wigan's Jack Blan, Workington Town's Billy Ivison and Dewsbury's Jimmy Ledgard. At least Bev had not been excluded from the "discoveries" list on the grounds of xenophobia, for none of the five were English. Bert Cook of Leeds and Wigan's Cec Mountford were New Zealanders, Hagan Evans of Bradford Northern and Oldham's Selwyn Evans were Welsh and Huddersfield's Johnny Hunter was an Australian and former team-mate of Bevan at Easts.

Just how lucky Warrington's fans were to have Bevan in their midst was brought home to them when the Rugby Football League imposed a five-year ban on signing Australian rugby league players on 7 August 1947. On 15 December, the ban on signing New Zealanders was extended until 15 December 1949. These measures were taken to safeguard the game down under, because there was a real danger of undermining the test strength of the Kangaroos and Kiwis. Since the war ended Australia had already lost more than enough test or potential test players to predatory English clubs.

Staggeringly, the best of the lot, Brian Bevan, had probably cost the least and he had come begging for a trial. What a bargain he was at £300. In December 1947 *Rugby League Parade*, a short lived magazine edited by Stanley Chadwick, produced a list of Australians who had recently been signed by English clubs. Huddersfield had splashed out £1,000 for Lionel Cooper, £1,300 for Pat Devery, both of whom were test stars, and £750 for the unheralded full-back Johnny Hunter. Hull had forked out £1,250 for Bruce Ryan, a fine winger from Newtown but certainly not four times as good as Bev. They had also contracted scrum-half Duncan Jackson for £1,000 and test hooker George Watt for £650. Forwards, of course, were cheaper than backs in those days. Harry Bath had moved from Balmain to Barrow for £800 and Leeds had a real snip in Arthur Clues for £750, especially in comparison to their expenditure of £1,000 each to Queensland backs Len Kenny and Ted Verrenkamp. Reportedly Don Graham cost Hunslet £1,000, Denis Boocker cost Wakefield Trinity £850 and even Bramley were able to lay out £500 for Wollongong centre Bob Bartlett.

With an influx of New Zealanders to add to the Australians, and the return of most of the men who had been caught up in the services, the standard of play in the 1947-48 season was expected to hit new heights. Warrington's performances in the 1946-47 season had kindled high hopes of future success, but the Challenge Cup semi-final defeat and the disastrous loss at Rochdale had indicated to the club management that substantial team strengthening was required if a genuine challenge for honours was to be sustained.

Fortunately Warrington were in a good position financially and under Chairman Joseph (J. S.) Tilling the board of directors was prepared to provide the required monies to fund an ambitious recruitment campaign. The 1946-47 accounts had revealed a club record profit of £2,850. The profit for 1947-48 would fall to around £1,500, but that was after almost £2,000 had been invested in restoring the Wilderspool pitch to a semblance of normality and the expenditure of a massive £7,000 on new players. Tilling, president of the club for the previous 10 years, had a sound management team in place with Chris Brockbank as secretary-manager, Bob Anderton as the club's representative to the Rugby League Council and a newly appointed coach in Emlyn Jenkins, the former Salford, Wales and Great Britain stand-off and one of the brainiest players of the pre-war period. Jenkins had the support of excellent training staff in Fred Ryder and Fred Worrall.

Team building

The season did not begin at all well. Bevan bagged a brace of tries in the Wardonia Cup charity match at Wigan, but Warrington were beaten 28-15 and, in the first league game of the campaign, Oldham beat them 14-3 at Watersheddings. Bevan missed his first game for almost a year, but was back for a two-legged first round Lancashire Cup-tie at Wigan on 30 August. Another defeat ensued, but Warrington put in a fine performance. The first fruits of the recruitment campaign were on show in the rather large shapes of props Bill Derbyshire and Bill 'Spiv' Riley, both signed from Liverpool Stanley for a combined fee of £1,800.

The second leg drew a club record crowd of 30,150 to Wilderspool, but again Wigan were just too good, winning 15-10, and Warrington went out of the Lancashire Cup 31-23 on aggregate. They had begun with four straight defeats, hardly championship form. There was a silver lining, however, to this particular cloud. Three of those reverses had been to Wigan, who were undoubtedly the best team of the immediate post-war era. They all been tough games. Warrington fans, officials and players knew that there would be few more daunting encounters as the season unfolded. They were strangely optimistic. Their optimism was increased when they witnessed that second-leg Lancashire Cup-tie and they realised what a capture they had made in debutant loose-forward, Harold Palin.

Palin, Warrington-born and a former pupil at Evelyn Street School, had started his professional career as a full-back with the Wire in 1936. He had, however, moved to Swinton within a few months and spent a decade at Station Road before returning to Wilderspool. Swinton had turned him into a second-rower good enough to win a couple of Lancashire caps, but by 1947 they clearly thought he was past his prime. He was already 31 when he returned to Warrington. Chris Brockbank was obviously more astute than the Swinton management for Palin -

'Moggy' to all and sundry - proved a catalyst in transforming the Wire into real contenders. A magnificent tackler, a wily tactician and a brilliant goal-kicker - a skill Swinton had failed to utilise - Palin was handed the loose-forward's jersey and was soon promoted to the Warrington captaincy. He was a revelation in all areas.

Brian Bevan certainly admired Harold Palin as a player and leader, but he must have wondered what the management had in mind when they signed Bill Gore, a Welsh rugby union international hooker from Newbridge, just before the season proper began. Gore, at almost 28 a very late conversion to league, was supposedly destined to take Dave Cotton's place. Cotton, one of the best hookers to have laced on boots, deferred his retirement, however, and at the age of 36 decided to play on, so Gore was limited to a solitary appearance in the first team that season. With Derbyshire and Riley already pushing 30, Palin 31 and Cotton 36, the pack looked seriously geriatric. The regular second-rowers, Jimmy Featherstone and Bob Ryan, both 24-year-olds, restored the balance somewhat. The distinguished rugby league writer Tom Longworth quickly realised that this pack, despite its preponderance of ageing members, was mobile and skilful. By November 1947, he wrote that Warrington's forwards were the best in the league in loose play, even if Wigan's was a better scrummaging machine.

Warrington's opening home league fixture against Rochdale Hornets on 6 September brought a 23-2 victory. Bevan scored two tries, the first his 50th for the club. More importantly, it marked the start of an eight-match winning run which catapulted the team to the top of the league. Bevan scored 15 tries in this spell, which shot him to the top of the try-scoring lists. The home fixture with Belle Vue Rangers on 27 September saw Bill Gore make his debut, but more momentously it was also the debut of Albert Pimblett, signed from Halifax two days earlier for £1,500. Pimblett partnered Bevan for the first time that afternoon to begin a fruitful, if relatively short, association. Many believed Pimblett was the best centre to have served Bevan. He was big, strong, fast and was prepared to take the knocks to protect his winger.

Pimblett and Bevan were paired together on the Wire right wing 86 times over the next three years. Having Albert inside him was just Bev's cup of tea. Brian was a perfectionist, he understood the value of rigorous training and that hard work brought rewards. He appreciated the fact that Albert was happy to spend hours with him after official training had ended, practising the various elements of centre-wing play and sprinting. Albert rated very highly in Brian's pantheon of centre-threequarters.

Warrington's most significant victory in that eight-match winning streak and the one that fired their self-belief came on 11 October. Inevitably it was against Wigan who went down by the amazing score of 17-0 before an ecstatic Wilderspool crowd of more than 26,000. If they could do that to Wigan, every other team had better watch out. Bevan scored a try but it was Moggy Palin who put on a virtuoso performance grabbing two tries, three goals and a drop goal to bag the remaining 14 points. The following week 22,000 turned up at Wilderspool to see Leeds thrashed, Bevan and Albert Johnson both running in for three tries while another debutant centre, former Belle Vue Ranger, Stan Powell booted over three goals.

At the beginning of November Warrington and Brian set off for pastures new. They travelled to the South of France and took on Perpignan on 1 November and the French Cup-holders Carcassonne the following day. The French teams were despatched 30-5 and 26-6 with Bevan scoring a try in the first match and two in the second. Although the wins were comprehensive Brian later remarked how impressed he had been with the determination of the French teams to persist with an open game and to try to be inventive throughout. He admired their style.

The trip to France helped build up further an already excellent team spirit and extended the winning run to 10 games. However, it must have had a seriously tiring effect on men who, like everyone else, worked for a living from Monday to Friday. Tiredness and the absence of Albert Johnson and Harold Palin, who were on test match duty against the Kiwis, certainly contributed to their 17-2 defeat at Workington on their return to league action. Yet, by the following week the return to a normal routine had them well prepared for a momentous occasion for Brian and the club.

The fourth New Zealand touring team arrived in Warrington at 2.15pm, four hours after leaving their Ilkley headquarters. It had snowed in Yorkshire and this was the coldest day the Kiwis had yet encountered on tour. This was a fine touring team which had just levelled the test series with victory at Swinton, having lost the first test at Headingley, both extremely tight matches. Among their other scalps had been current champions Wigan, Challenge Cup-holders Bradford Northern, Leeds and Wales. The New Zealanders paid Warrington the compliment of fielding 12 test men in their side while the Wire were at full strength, apart from skipper Harold Palin. For Brian Bevan there must have been a feeling of keen anticipation as he faced the prospect of facing a touring XIII for the first time.

More than 20,000 turned up to run the rule over the Kiwis, despite the inclement weather. The pitch was a disgrace, treacherous after some heavy showers earlier in the day. The game was, however, brilliantly contested. Dave Cotton monopolised the scrums, but the New Zealanders' defence was almost impregnable. It faltered only once. Needless to say, Brian was involved. In his tour book, *The Kiwis 1947-1948*, E. M. Gibson wrote: "Bevan, brilliant ex-Sydney wing, switched to unorthodox which harassed the defence. Strained dangerously, this snapped when Bevan cut through with Pimblett to a point near the line. Derbyshire won a play-the-ball and whipped to Featherstone, who charged in for a try which Powell converted." It was the only score of the first half and in the end it was a second half penalty goal by Powell which decided the match as Warrington won a famous victory 7-5.

On 22 November, Wigan brought the Wire back down to earth when they scraped a 6-3 victory before 30,000 at Central Park, their fourth win in five games against Warrington so far that season. Two weeks later, Bradford Northern triumphed 12-0 over a weakened Wire at Odsal. At that point, however, Warrington embarked on a sequence of games which broke all kinds of records. Between 13 December 1947 and 6 April 1948 they played 20 league games, winning all but one - a 5-5 draw at Headingley on 31 January. By the turn of 1948, it was clear that Warrington would push Wigan all the way for the coveted top spot. Bevan was also having a personal battle for top spot in the try-scoring stakes and he too was running second to a Wiganer. Bev had piled up 25 tries by 1 January, but lion-hearted Gordon Ratcliffe had scored 27 for Wigan and, for good measure, another two for Lancashire and one for England.

Thwarted by Wigan

Warrington's great run began on 13 December with a 45-13 home rout of Salford, a game notable for the debut of the former Barrow captain Bryn Knowelden. Knowelden, a polished footballer and a 1946 British Lion, had cost £1,400, according to the newspapers. He was the last piece in the jigsaw that completed Warrington's back division, which at its strongest now read: Les 'Cowboy' Jones, Brian Bevan, Albert Pimblett, Bryn Knowelden, Albert Johnson, Jackie Fleming and Gerry Helme. Within a year all of those players, except Bevan, had been capped as internationals and there were two more internationals in Ossie Peake and Stan Powell, who figured more often in the Warrington 'A' team. Bryn Knowelden certainly got off on the right foot against Salford as he ran in a hat-trick.

Harvey Davis remembers
They say that Brian Bevan's length of the field try at Wigan in the Wardonia Cup of 1948 was his greatest. Earlier that year I saw a similar effort by Bevan against Leeds at Headingley. It was a very important league fixture that ended up 5-5.

On this occasion Bevan received the ball inside his own 25 on the South Stand side and he finished up on the try-line at the St. Michael's Lane end, not far from the corner where the players came out. I forget now exactly what happened as he got to the line but I know he did not score. He was brought down right on the line and somehow lost the ball when everyone thought he had scored the match-winning try.

I particularly remember the occasion as there was a transport strike on in Leeds and everyone - 29,000 of us - had to walk to the ground.

At that time it was rare for a wingman to leave his touchline side. However, with Bevan one never knew where he was going to finish up. He just spotted gaps and raced through them, using all his natural talents, either to create the gaps himself or to get into those that appeared. Only those who saw Brian in action in his prime can imagine how exciting he was to watch. He had everything - blistering pace, side step either way at top speed, acceleration, swerve, controlled kicking abilities. You name it; he had it, the lot.

By the time the cup-ties came round at the beginning of February, 10 straight league victories had been recorded followed by the drawn game before 30,000 fans at Leeds. Warrington received a tough-looking first round draw - over two legs - against Workington Town. Fortunately, the first leg was at home and a 10-0 win gave the Wire a good platform for the return in Cumberland on 14 February. There was very little between the teams and only one try was recorded, but what a thrill it gave the Wire supporters in a Borough Park record crowd of 19,478. Inevitably it was Brian Bevan who broke the deadlock. The *Examiner* report ran: "Workington were making one last all-out effort and when an attack developed

33

just inside the Warrington '25' a try for the Cumbrians looked probable. As the pass reached Risman, who had come up to make the man over, he failed to hold the ball which fell to his left. Very quickly he bent and flipped it to his wingman but Bevan nipped in, stole the ball practically from Large's chest and was away in a flash. Carr pursued him for a few strides in desperation but Bevan sailed away with head thrown back and, as the Warrington enthusiasts roared themselves hoarse, was soon out on his own to cross the line near the corner and then go within a few yards of the posts for a magnificent try after a thrilling run of more than eighty yards. His colleagues hugged him, patted his face and shook his hand while cheer after cheer rolled out."

Wally Barnes remembers

I am now in my 70s and I have always loved Rugby League. I do a lot of work for charity in and around Warrington. Brian Bevan was a good friend and was guest of honour at many of my charity shows. I remember him as a wonderful man, very quiet, and he had a lovely family.

I remember the first time I ever saw him play was when I was home from Palestine on leave from the army. The try I remember most clearly by Brian was scored up at Workington in a first round cup-tie. We had won the first leg 10-0 at Wilderspool and a huge following went up from Warrington for the second leg. Anyway, as was quite common in those days, there was a bit of betting going off. This time it was about one of my in-laws, Harold Palin. Harold, by the way, was a great worker for charity. He was the best loose-forward and captain Wire have ever had in my view. Harold was our goal-kicker and the Warrington folk were betting that he would score more points himself than Workington.

Anyhow, there was a lot of money put on this bet - about £15, which was a lot in those days and a Workington chap held the money. Harold kicked a goal and that was the only score until very near the end when Workington Town were really hammering the Warrington line. If Town had scored, the Warrington folk would be out of pocket. It was then that Bevan shot into a ruck of players and came out the other side with the ball, having made one of those famous interceptions of his. He went the length of the field to score with no one getting anywhere near him. When the excitement had died down, we looked around for the man holding the betting money only to discover that he had buggered off with it! Joe Palin, Harold's brother, went looking for him but could not find him. Good job really as I think he might have killed him!

Lots of people say Brian was no good in defence but I recall that he was very good at ankle-tapping opponents. I do remember an occasion against Leeds when Bob McMaster, a massive Australian forward, got the ball twenty yards out with only Brian to beat. I felt really sorry for Brian. McMaster looked at Bev and you could see that he thought he was going to trample him into the ground. Just as the two met I closed my eyes, not daring to watch. There was a mighty cheer and when I opened them Bev had somehow managed to bring the giant Aussie down. So he could obviously tackle sometimes.

Warrington won the tie 7-0 (17-0 on aggregate). A home tie against neighbouring Leigh was their reward in the second round. Leigh proved difficult opponents as

27,514 shoehorned themselves into Wilderspool. Tries by Bevan and Bill Riley and a goal from Palin saw them off 8-2, however. The following week, 6 March, another 21,000 turned up to see St Helens defeated 21-3 in a league game with Bevan, the game's star, claiming his fourth hat-trick of the season.

Warrington had now gone 16 games without defeat. They were ready for anything, or so everyone thought. But were they ready for Wigan in the third round of the Challenge Cup? The game, at Wilderspool on 13 March, was declared all-ticket and the 29,300 who got in had their money's worth. Bevan put his team into the lead with a try after 12 minutes, but Wigan struck back to lead 8-5 before Jackie Fleming, the man-of-the-match, brought the house down to score a try which restored Warrington's lead at 10-8. With five minutes to go it looked as if the Wire would extend their run to 17 undefeated games. Brian and his team-mates may well have had visions of Wembley, but they were cruelly dashed when Wigan full-back Martin Ryan engineered a match-winning try for right winger Brian Nordgren. Ted Ward's touchline conversion gave Wigan a 13-10 victory. They would go on to win the Cup, beating Bradford Northern at Wembley.

Despite this reverse, Warrington had plenty to play for. They had 10 more league games left, but on form were almost certain to finish in the top four. They may even have entertained thoughts of pipping Wigan, with extra cup commitments and the pressure of aiming to win all four cups, for top spot.

Four days after the Wigan defeat, Warrington had a run-of-the-mill fixture with Featherstone Rovers at Wilderspool. Spice was added, however, because Harry Bath, just signed after an unhappy time with Barrow, made his debut in Warrington's second-row. Bath, a compatriot of Bevan, made a satisfactory start, scored two tries and landed the first of 812 goals he would pile up for the club over the next nine years. Albert Johnson too, with four tries, enjoyed himself on the left wing. Despite awful conditions, lashing rain and a waterlogged pitch Warrington ran in 11 tries to win 43-2. One man who was not amused was Brian Bevan. It seemed he was destined to be thwarted of a touchdown whatever he did, and as the ball began to be continually moved towards the left wing, he protested very publicly by sitting down on the puddle-strewn pitch looking as miserable as the weather. Even more provocatively, as Ernie Day, the Warrington historian, recalls: "As the crowd were acclaiming yet another try for Warrington, Bevan returned to the corner flag on his own try-line, leaned on the flag and gestured to the crowd in a manner that was obviously belligerent and angry. The crowd's reaction to this was understandable and they began to jeer and laugh at his antics. Bevan then stepped over the mark when he turned his back to the terraces and half dropped his shorts. Such behaviour now could bring a charge of disrepute, but fortunately for him the animosity that could have been levelled against him was dissolved in a flash, when, straight from the kick-off, he beat three or four defenders in a 40-yard run that only ended with him tackled a yard from the Featherstone line. He had managed to redress his misdemeanour with his own brand of brilliance - but only just." Bevan may not have been amused but many of the crowd probably were.

That game against Featherstone was the first of seven more consecutive league victories. Brian failed to score in the next couple of games at Salford and Widnes, but then proceeded to run riot with 11 tries in the space of a week, all in the familiar surroundings of Wilderspool. First to suffer were Bradford Northern, who were due to play in the Challenge Cup semi-final a week later. Bevan claimed a hat-trick as they were despatched 21-5 on Easter Saturday, 27 March. Two days later, Leigh were the visitors. The Wire won 28-8. The *Examiner* reported: "A magnificent scoring feat by Bevan dwarfed everything else ... Seven of Warrington's eight tries were claimed by the flying wingman. When the final whistle sounded, excited enthusiasts surrounded him patting his back and shaking his hand until he was rescued by police."

No Warrington player had ever scored as many tries in a match, not even the fabulous winger of Edwardian times, Jack Fish. The record had, in fact, been held by Tommy 'Tubby' Thompson, a left-winger, who had claimed six tries in a 38-12 triumph over Bradford Northern at Wilderspool on 6 April 1933. Even Bevan was never able to beat his own newly created record, although he would equal it just over five years later. His seventh try equalled his own club record of 48 tries in a season. Amazingly, Leigh's left-winger, Harry Dagnan, scored both of his side's tries and, with Pimblett bagging the only other Wire try, all 10 touchdowns emanated from the same flank.

Workington Town were Warrington's next victims, losing 15-8. The Wire were not particularly convincing, but a local paper reported: "Bevan was the only back who looked like making progress and he once again provided thrills with his scintillating running. What a roar when he reached a bouncing ball over the head of Large, his opposing number, took it on his fingers after a juggling act and raced forty yards for a try at the corner." His 49th try of the season broke his own Warrington club record.

Onto the Championship

On 10 April Warrington finally lost a league match. An unfancied Castleford brought their four-month 20-match undefeated run in the league to an end with a 12-2 win at Wheldon Road. Bev had a bit of a stinker opposite the Welsh pairing of Len Skidmore and Reg Lloyd. In the end, Bev was so frustrated that he hurled the ball into the crowd in another show of petulance.

Peter Atkinson remembers
I have been a Castleford supporter for 50-odd years, through thick and thin and I have only ever seen one man tackle Brian Bevan out of a game. Bevan was unbelievable - I think they once measured his side step some way or another and it was about six feet. He would run right across the field and back again to find an opening. Anyway, once Warrington came to Castleford on the back of a fantastic 20-odd games winning run, which was some sort of record at the time. Bevan was up against a Welsh winger called Len Skidmore. Len only had a short career with Cas and had to retire through ill health. Anyway, on this particular occasion Bevan couldn't find a way past Len at all and Cas won 12-2 and ended Warrington's unbeaten record. What I remember most clearly was Bevan's actions at the end of the game. He ran a considerable distance to shake Skidmore's hand and you could tell that he was genuinely congratulating Len on

his performance, even though it must have been really disappointing for Warrington. It really showed how gentlemanly Bevan could be.

However, Warrington's subsequent victory at Halifax in the penultimate League game of the season set up a fascinating climax. The Wire's last game was against Oldham at Wilderspool on 17 April. That afternoon Wigan were hosts to Belle Vue Rangers. Both Warrington and Wigan were expected to win comfortably, but a slip by either would hand the Lancashire League Championship to the other. After 25 games Warrington had gained 44 points to Wigan's 43. Victory would give the title to Warrington for the first time since 1937-38, the last time that they had won a major honour. Moreover, a Wire victory would deny Wigan the opportunity to create history by becoming the fourth team in history to win all four major trophies in a season.

Almost 18,000 were at Wilderspool to see what turned out to be both a formality, as Warrington coasted to a 45-3 victory and a triumph, as they took a trophy for the first time in a decade. Bevan, who had failed to score in the last three games, took it out on the Roughyeds. His third try gave him his century in the primrose and blue jersey, and he went on to take his tally to 102 with his fifth. In future years Oldham were to be a team who seemed incapable of stopping Brian from scoring. The *Examiner* reporter was so astounded by Bev's performance that he merely remarked: "Personally I do not know which try to admire the most" - a sentiment that would be repeated by many a scribe.

Although Warrington had snatched the Lancashire League title from Wigan, they had finished in second place to Joe Egan's men in the League Championship. That set up a possible seventh clash of the season between the two if both came through their semi-finals on 24 April. Wigan expected to qualify even though their opponents Bradford Northern were to play them again the following week at Wembley and, if they did reach the Championship Final, they also knew they seemed to have a hoodoo on Warrington. But there was a major surprise. Northern shocked a 38,000 Central Park crowd by winning 15-3 to claim a place in the Maine Road final.

For their part Warrington did all that was expected of them. Their opponents in the semi were third-placed Huddersfield, arguably the best footballing team of the period, if not quite as ruthless or successful as Wigan. Apart from the intrinsic importance of the match, Brian Bevan faced a special challenge. On Huddersfield's left wing was Lionel Cooper, Bevan's former team-mate at Easts and a member of Australia's 1946 test team. Over the next seven years the clashes between Cooper and Bevan were to be highlights of their own personal seasons and those of countless thousands of fans. In this first confrontation Bevan definitely came out on top. Albert Pimblett played one of his greatest games. His combination with Bevan was irresistible, both men touching down twice in a 17-5 victory. The high point of the game, however, was an unlikely score by hooker Dave Cotton, his first try for more than two years. It was Brian who gifted the old warhorse his moment of glory, *Yorkshire Sports* reporting that "Five minutes after the resumption, Bevan, receiving the ball near the touchline, ran through almost the whole of the Huddersfield team before passing to Cotton, who scored unopposed."

Warrington had never won the Rugby League Championship. They had reached the final in 1926, 1935 and 1937 only to lose to Wigan, Swinton and Salford respectively. Incidentally, Dave Cotton had scored another of his rare tries in the 1937 final. Maine Road, Manchester was the venue for the 1948 Championship Final. For the first time the Wire were to meet Yorkshire opposition in the final, perhaps an omen of better fortune? Again Brian Bevan had special reason to be on tenterhooks. This time he was up against the Welshman Alan Edwards. Although a veteran, Edwards was still quick and quirky enough to give any opponent severe problems. Brian no doubt recalled Edwards's great performances in Sydney on the 1936 Lions tour and he would later admit that Edwards was the best British winger he encountered. Edwards had been Bradford's try-scorer the previous week at Wembley, when Wigan had exacted swift retribution on Northern for beating them in the Championship semi.

A massive crowd of 69,143, containing at least 15,000 Warringtonians, assembled in the hope of seeing a classic. The game never quite reached that status, but Tom Longworth summed it up pretty well in saying: "At the 37th attempt, Warrington have secured the title of Rugby League champions. They are worthy of it... Bradford Northern, jaded and stale, were overplayed and beaten by three goals and three tries to a goal and a try. In a contest 100 per cent better than the spectacle presented at Wembley, it was clear from the outset that Warrington were supremely fresh. They delivered their attacks with a crispness which Bradford lacked."

Warrington were never behind, Palin kicking them into the lead with an early penalty after which Bevan streaked over untouched from an overlap for a try. The score remained 5-0 at half-time but was doubled to 10-0 when Stan Powell scored on the other flank and Palin landed the conversion from the touchline. Bradford briefly threatened when their centre Des Case, playing his last official game for the club, scored a try around the hour mark. Ernest Ward's conversion struck the post and rebounded into the playing area. To the amazement of almost everyone in the ground, Albert Dobson, the referee, who had been behind the posts, awarded the goal. He later explained that the ball had passed inside and over the bar before being blown back by the wind, a contingency allowed for by Law 34.

The Wire weathered this minor storm, however, and Pimblett, in some of the best form of his career, scored a gem of a try dummying inside to Bevan and then flying down the wing to ground the ball near the flag. Palin landed a magnificent penalty from half-way to complete the scoring at 15-5 and, after over half a century, Warrington were finally crowned champions, receiving the trophy from the Earl of Derby. 'D'Artagnan', in *Rugby League Review*, chose Brian Bevan as the outstanding figure in the match, just shading Bradford skipper Ernie Ward. He wrote: "This flying Australian, when in possession of the ball, is one of the most electrifying sights in the game. His will-o'-the-wisp side-stepping, allied to a fine turn of speed, leaves the opposition grasping thin air." Thousands thronged the streets to greet their victorious heroes on their return from Manchester to Warrington. The team was received at the town hall by the Mayor, W. L. Challinor, himself a Wire supporter and a Warrington director. All was well with the world and Brian Bevan would soon become used to, if not entirely comfortable with, civic receptions in his adopted home town.

Warrington RLFC 1947-48

Back row: W. Riley, I. Davies, D. Cotton, H. Bath, W. Derbyshire, R. Ryan, O. Peake;
Centre row: A. J. Pimblett, B. Knowleden, S. Powell, H. Palin (captain), L. Jones, A.
E. Johnson, B. Bevan; Front row: J. Fleming, G. J. Helme.
The trophies are the Rugby League Championship and the Lancashire League

14 March 1948, Challenge Cup
third round.
Brian Nordgren cannot prevent
Bev from scoring.
His effort was not enough,
however, to stop Wigan
from winning 13-10 before a new
Wilderspool
ground record of 29,300. Billy
Blan looks on.

12 April, 1948.
Bev is sent flying by Halifax's Stan
Kielty (7) and Arthur Daniels (2)
with second-rower Harry Greenwood
racing to cover.
Wire won 9-3.

Season 1947–48

Warrington finished 2nd in the League: P36, W30, D1, L5; For 688, Against 232
Bevan scored 57 tries for Warrington

Date	Opponent	Score	Bevan	Crowd	
23 Aug	Oldham	3–14	dnp	13,000	
30 Aug	Wigan	13–16	1T	25,000	LC 1
3 Sep	**Wigan**	10–15		25,000	LC 1
6 Sep	**Rochdale H**	23–2	2T	6,000	
13 Sep	Liverpool St	19–6	2T	3,000	
20 Sep	Featherstone R	43–7	3T	3,200	
27 Sep	**Belle Vue R**	21–16	1T	8,000	
4 Oct	Barrow	18–10	2T	7,589	
11 Oct	**Wigan**	17–0	1T	26,014	
18 Oct	**Leeds**	38–13	3T	22,000	
25 Oct	Belle Vue R	28–8	1T	15,000	
8 Nov	Workington T	2–17		12,800	
15 Nov	**New Zealand**	7–5		20,682	
22 Nov	Wigan	3–6	1T	30,000	
29 Nov	**Liverpool St**	30–3	1T	7,000	
6 Dec	Bradford N	0–12		6,000	
13 Dec	**Salford**	45–13	1T	8,000	
20 Dec	**Barrow**	37–7	3T	6,000	
25 Dec	**Widnes**	15–4	1T	20,000	
26 Dec	Leigh	29–0	2T	16,500	
27 Dec	Swinton	6–5	dnp	12,000	
1 Jan	**Dewsbury**	19–6	1T	10,270	
3 Jan	Rochdale H	9–0	2T	4,500	
10 Jan	St Helens	8–2	1T	20,000	
17 Jan	**Castleford**	9–2	1T	6,000	
24 Jan	**Swinton**	17–7		8,000	
31 Jan	Leeds	5–5		30,000	
7 Feb	**Workington T**	10–0		19,460	Ch Cup 1
14 Feb	Workington T	7–0	1T	19,478	Ch Cup 1
21 Feb	**Halifax**	28–6	2T	6,000	
28 Feb	**Leigh**	8–2	1T	27,514	Ch Cup 2
6 Mar	**St Helens**	21–3	3T	21,000	
13 Mar	**Wigan**	10–13	1T	29,300*	Ch Cup 3
17 Mar	**Featherstone R**	43–2		10,921	
20 Mar	Salford	13–5		18,000	
26 Mar	Widnes	5–4		20,286	
27 Mar	**Bradford N**	21–5	3T	19,597	
29 Mar	**Leigh**	28–8	7T	18,794	
3 Apr	**Workington T**	15–8	1T	14,000	
6 Apr	Dewsbury	14–8		7,000	
10 Apr	Castleford	2–12		7,000	
12 Apr	Halifax	9–3		11,000	
17 Apr	**Oldham**	45–3	5T	17,922	
24 Apr	**Huddersfield**	17–5	2T	25,070	CH Semi
8 May	Bradford N	15–5	1T	69,143	CH Final (at Maine Rd)

* Ground record

7. 1948-49 'Yon man should carry a 15 pound penalty'

Brian Bevan felt that the 1947-48 Warrington side was the best in which he ever played. In reminiscing he said: "I was privileged to play with lots of good sides but the 1947-48 team had something special. Collectively and individually, both on and off the field, they were the best set of lads you could hope to meet." The sports editor of the *Warrington Examiner*, Percy J. Kay, agreed. While admitting that Bevan was the outstanding individual figure in the team and that the half-back pairing of Helme and Fleming had been inspirational, he wrote that: "It was not in individuals or even in one section of the team that lay the secret of success. It was all-round team work on and off the field, physical fitness and a deeply instilled understanding one with the other."

The 1947-48 campaign had certainly been a joy for Brian Bevan. Once again he had topped the try-scoring lists in extending his own club record to 57 tries. Gordon Ratcliffe (49) and Lionel Cooper (37) had been his nearest rivals. This time too, the *Rugby League Review* had had the sense to include him in their five stars of the season, alongside Alan Edwards, Joe Egan, Gus Risman and his colleague Harold Palin. He was now in the company of the blessed. Harry Bath was named as one of the discoveries of the season, Palin the best captain and Albert Pimblett the most improved player, along with Bradford loose-forward Ken Traill. Warrington were rated the outstanding team, which would not have gone down too well in Wigan. All in all, a good season's work.

No less was expected for 1948-49. The close season had brought two more fine players to Wilderspool. On 11 July, Roy Francis had been signed from Barrow for £800. A centre or wing of the most entertaining and unorthodox style, he had played for Wales at rugby league and, despite his Welshness, for England at rugby union in services internationals - men did what they were told to do in the army. In the 1947 series against New Zealand, he had become the first black player to represent Great Britain when he scored two tries from the right wing in the third test at Odsal. Albert Johnson was on the left wing that afternoon. To many it had been scandalous that he had not been selected as a 1946 Lion, but Australia's colour bar, excluding non-white players, was then in operation. Then on 20 July, Warrington handed over another £750 to St Helens for full-back Eric Frodsham. Eric was one for the future, however, and it would be two years before he took over the Wire's number one jersey.

Warrington's season began at Wigan on 14 August with the annual Wardonia Cup fixture. Nominally these encounters were 'friendlies'. However, absolutely no Warrington-Wigan clash in those days could be termed a friendly, any more than a Hunslet-Leeds, Halifax-Huddersfield or Oldham-Rochdale Hornets pre-season meeting could. A crowd of 31,960 definitely thought it was a serious matter. The gash in Dave Cotton's head, and the ankle injury which was to keep Bob Ryan out until the following March, were adequate testimony to the seriousness with which the whole thing was invested. When all was said and done, Warrington and Wigan were currently the sport's two top teams. Pride and the prospect of gaining a psychological edge for the coming season were enough of an incentive to win, even if the game was for charity.

The match ended in an 18-8 victory for Warrington, a real tonic for the Wire supporters and a good omen for the months to follow. Bev scored two of the four tries for the winners, his first arguably the most sensational of all the tries he ever concocted, so sensational that it features elsewhere in this book.

The league season began well with an 18-2 victory in Noah's Ark weather at Halifax. Brian had a mixed afternoon, however. He scored Wire's last try but was subject to close attention from the Halifax defence, receiving a cut eye and a badly bruised face. When he attempted to get some of his own back, as it were, the Thrum Hall crowd gave him a dose of what Jack Steel referred to as "Bevan-baiting". It was all part of the fun, no doubt. Bev did not think it funny though when his injuries kept him out of a 40-8 romp at Liverpool Stanley, particularly because his deputy Ossie Peake grabbed three tries.

He was back two days later, however, picking up a try in a 19-7 win at Bradford to begin a sequence of scoring in a dozen consecutive games, all of which ended in Warrington victories. His try tally in this spell was 23. The most important league fixture in this period was the home game against Huddersfield on 25 September. A record crowd for a league game at Wilderspool - 29,450 - gathered in the expectation of a classic. They did not get one - Huddersfield had half a dozen absentees and their captain Lionel Cooper was crippled for most of the game - but they did see Wire victorious by 25-2. Among the crowd was the RFL's President, Lord Derby.

On the following Tuesday, Warrington met Oldham in the semi-final of the Lancashire Cup, having previously disposed of Barrow and Leigh. Close on 20,000 piled into Wilderspool expecting to see a rip-roaring cup-tie. Again they were disappointed for Warrington did as they liked in an astonishing 55-0 rout of the Roughyeds. Brian was simply mesmerising and finished with five tries, while Albert Johnson on the other wing grabbed four in his first game of the season. Four days later, the two teams met again at Watersheddings in a league match. Despite the embarrassment of the Lancashire Cup debacle, almost 17,000 fans turned out. The result was not quite as bad for Oldham. This time they lost only 37-0, but Bevan again tormented them with another five tries. He had now scored 15 tries in his last three games against them. 'Criticus' reported that the Oldham fans were so impressed and exasperated that he heard one declare: "Yon man should carry a 15 pound penalty".

Bevan was on fire in this period. Mike Rowan has this to say: "The overriding impression he left week-by-week ranged from thrills to bewilderment. His style, if it could be regarded as ostentatious, belied his personality. How could such an unimposing figure do those things? Seeing is believing, they say, but how do you believe what you have seen if you cannot comprehend just what has been done? Many years later I was asked to do a painting of the great man. In studying various photographs and pictures one thought struck me that was alien to everything that I employed as a boxing coach. Balance is so important to control a situation yet the images captured by the camera belied my tenets. His legs ate up the ground while his upper body was markedly jerky in movement. He appeared to be off balance yet he flew past men without appearing to lose any speed. His

25, September 1948. Bev meets the Earl of Derby, President of the RFL prior to Wire's 25-2 home victory over Huddersfield. There was a record crowd of 29,450 .

head was back. His head was past his knees. His head went from side to side. A sprint coach preaches, like a boxing man, 'eyes on the target'. Brian Bevan contradicted this. As he flew over the ground the brain and instincts functioned most sharply. It was as if he just reacted instinctively, on impulse, if you like. Bevan did not depict the image one might associate with a great player but the outcome was just the same. Usually it was a great score.

He was a complete one-off. If genius is interpreted as highly original then Brian Bevan was a genius... His upper body movement was baffling and he feinted opponents into error. All the time he was in control of his blistering pace and while opponents went one way he was usually going the other way. He could stop dead. As Cec Mountford said, 'He did things so sharply he was gone before you realised it'. Cec himself was regarded as a special player and on many an occasion he was in close proximity to witness the elusiveness of Bevan - 'He appeared to step in and out of tackles without breaking stride and just change direction. Nobody else could do that. He was something else, for whatever he did it was done at top pace'."

Bevan's scoring run ended with a couple against Whitehaven and a hat-trick against Halifax two days later, both easy wins at Wilderspool. In the latter game Harry Bath also scored three tries. It was a game notable for the debut of Halifax's Jack Wilkinson, one of the toughest forwards ever to have played the game, and the first appearance of a new referee, Matt Coates, who, according to the *Halifax Courier & Guardian*'s reporter Frank Williams: "was a star in the game". Williams also wrote: "The second half showed Bevan and Bath as the shining lights. The former is the fastest and most deceptive three-quarter I have seen for a long time." Frank Williams knew what he was talking about. He had been an international wingman himself, having taken part in the 1914 'Rorke's Drift' test in Sydney. Brian then went four games without scoring, an unprecedented occurrence in his English career. The sequence included his 100th appearance for the club, a 15-6 home win over Rochdale on 23 October. Bev's try drought did not stop Warrington winning all four matches, however. Among those victories the most notable was on 30 October, when the touring Australians attracted almost 27,000 to Wilderspool. Dave Cotton's 35-14 superiority over

Kevin Schubert in the scrums went a long way towards securing Warrington's 16-7 triumph. Tries from Gerry Helme and Jimmy Featherstone and five Harold Palin goals accounted for their points. Brian's direct opponent Johnny Graves scored all the Australians' points. It must certainly have crossed Bev's mind that, had he remained in Sydney, he could have been on this Kangaroo tour. It must also have provoked thoughts of what might have been whenever Gerry Helme, Albert Pimblett and Jimmy Featherstone, on Ashes duty, were missing from the Wire line-up.

The following week, 6 November, Helme and Pimblett were missing when they helped Britain to a 16-7 Ashes-clinching victory at Swinton. Warrington journeyed north to Barrow and scraped a 6-5 victory against doughty opponents, thanks to a drop goal from Les Jones. Bev did not touch the ball in the first half and hardly at all in the second. Still, a win was a win and Warrington had now won all 17 games played so far. In fact their winning run stretched back over 21 games, when the previous season was included.

Lancashire Cup Finalists

Next up were Wigan in the Lancashire Cup Final at Swinton on 13 November. It was crunch time again. Warrington, undefeated, conquerors of the Australians, top of the League and reigning champions went into the game as favourites. Wigan too had beaten the Australians, but a fortnight earlier had surprisingly gone down 14-7 to Belle Vue Rangers and had been well beaten at Fartown early in the season. Warrington certainly had the wherewithal to beat Wigan but chickens, as they say, should never be counted before they are hatched and Wigan - Mountford, Ashcroft, Ryan, Egan, Gee, etc - were no chickens. They wanted to remain top of the pecking order.

Everyone wanted to see this final. Despite a murky, rain-sodden afternoon and a muddy pitch, a record crowd for a Lancashire Cup Final turned up at Station Road - 39,015. That was almost 3,000 more than had been at the same venue the previous week for the second Great Britain versus Australia test. Under the circumstances they were treated to a rousing game. Warrington did not receive the rub of the green - crucial decisions went against them - but Wigan were at their best. Gordon Ratcliffe and Ted Ward scored first-half tries to which Ward added three goals with only a Palin penalty in reply. Just before the interval, Albert Johnson brought the Wire back to a 12-5 deficit with a try at the corner. Brian Bevan caused plenty of problems for Wigan on the few occasions he had the ball and bagged a try when he finished off a passage of play following a troublesome up-and-under from Moggy Palin. That try and another Ted Ward penalty goal were the only second half scores. Wigan won 14-8 and proved once more that no matter how many consecutive games the Wire won, their Central Park foes were still their nemesis.

The Lancashire Cup Final proved to be the last appearance for both Dave Cotton and Ossie Peake in primrose and blue. Cotton finally retired on doctor's orders and Peake soon transferred to Widnes. The directorate acted quickly to replace Cotton by securing Ike Fishwick from St Helens for £2,500, big money for a hooker but cheap at the price as Ike was to give excellent service and would win five Lancashire caps as a Wire.

Despite the setback in the Lancashire Cup, Warrington bounced back to win their next nine league matches. Gone briefly, however, was the dazzling, open play which had pulverised opponents in the first third of the season. As the weather conditions worsened, Warrington depended increasingly on dreadnought defence to wrest victories. The most important game in this spell was the return fixture at Huddersfield. The Earl of Derby had so enjoyed the Wilderspool encounter that he insisted on being at Fartown on 11 December. The game was a spellbinder and for most of the encounter it seemed as if Warrington were about to lose their unbeaten league record. Bevan, from two yards for a change, and Johnson had scored tries against one by Lionel Cooper and three goals from Pat Devery, leaving Warrington 6-9 down. It was Roy Francis who rescued the game. Vincent Firth in *Rugby League Review* described the try: "Two minutes later [after Bevan's try] came the supreme thrill of the match. Francis, who had been a little uneasy in the first half but who had atoned wonderfully by his brilliance in the second, scored a try that will never be forgotten by those who saw it. From a point near the half-way line he made a dash up the centre of the field, fanned out to the wing, passed the dummy in a manner which deceived players and spectators alike and ran over to touch down near the posts. A spontaneous burst of cheering arose from the crowd naturally consisting mostly of Huddersfield supporters. The further round of applause which accompanied Francis back to his own half demonstrated how much his prodigious effort was appreciated by true followers of the code." Harold Palin, who had missed several shots, landed the conversion and Warrington escaped with an 11-9 success.

Marching orders

Warrington next met arch rivals Widnes at Naughton Park on Christmas Day. They won well enough 14-2, but Brian Bevan was given a torrid afternoon by the Chemics' defenders. At one point, while playing the ball after a vigorous challenge, he gestured toward a Widnes player and was penalised by the referee, Frank Smith from Barrow. In the very last minute Stan Jolley, the Widnes left-winger, shot away down the flank and was laid low when Bev's right arm shot out and caught him under the chin. Pandemonium!

Jack Steel wrote in the *Guardian*: "As the Widnes players surrounded their dazed comrade, Bevan walked back to his place amid a terrific din... Then Bevan was called up by the referee and sent from the field. Warrington players and supporters were stunned. It was the last thing they expected to happen, and yet the drama was not finished by any means.

A spectator on the popular side jumped the rails, waded through the piled-up straw and ran straight up to Bevan. At first I thought he was about to pat Bevan on the back, but evidently he had different ideas because he appeared to argue with the player. A policeman, though hindered by his greatcoat, ran towards the couple now in the centre of the field, and persuaded the intruder to walk towards the barriers.

Policeman No 2, anticipating further interruptions, escorted Bevan to the tunnel, where he received thunderous applause from a sympathetic Warrington contingent."

Merry Christmas, Brian. Roy Francis certainly enjoyed it, as he again stole Brian's thunder with a fine hat-trick. Bevan was never sent off again, although his patience must have been severely tried in the remaining 512 games of his career at Warrington.

Over 56,000 saw Warrington complete a four-day holiday treble with a 13-0 home win against Leigh and a 14-0 success at Leeds. The latter fixture saw the debut of former Maesteg second-rower Bill Hopper in the Wire pack. The Welshman's career at Wilderspool was to last barely a year before he was transferred to Leeds. Brian failed to score in any of those festive fixtures, but on New Year's Day he was back on the scoresheet at Whitehaven as Warrington's game-breaker. New Year's Eve had been spent en route in Keswick and Warrington were no doubt expecting an easy win over a side which had been butchered 61-0 at St Helens in their last match. It did not turn out as they anticipated. Horrendous conditions prevailed at the Recreation Ground. The pitch was ankle-deep in mud and it was mind-numbingly cold. Whitehaven defended like demons, but eventually succumbed 3-2 to a piece of Bevan magic. The *Examiner* match report from their 'Whitehaven Representative' described his effort thus: "His try was magnificent and it made the crowd rub their eyes in wonderment. Seizing on a loose ball at half-way, Bevan swerved and danced his way through a packed defence like a ballet master, before scoring."

The Whitehaven game marked Stan Powell's last appearance for Warrington before he was transferred to Castleford. It was also Bev's last game for a couple of weeks because he was suspended for two matches following the episode at Widnes. At that point in the season he had rattled up 32 tries for Warrington although his rate had slowed down since the middle of October. Even so, he was trailing his great rival Lionel Cooper, who had crossed the line 42 times for Huddersfield.

The games Brian missed were both against Workington Town. The first at Wilderspool was won 29-7, but the return at Borough Park on 15 January 1949 marked the end of Warrington's fabulous unbeaten league record. They had won all 22 of that season's league fixtures and the last three of the previous season. The game at Workington represented their chance to equal Huddersfield's record 26-match winning run in league fixtures established between March 1912 and January 1913. Gus Risman's men had other ideas, however, quickly establishing a 6-0 lead with three drop goals before Warrington levelled with tries from Johnson and Francis. A draw seemed likely until Town second-rower Jimmy Wareing won the match with a try at the corner with 15 minutes left, Risman converting.

The following week presented Warrington with another huge challenge. Wigan were the visitors to Wilderspool and a ground record crowd of 34,304 rolled up with the gates closed 25 minutes before kick-off. Bev was back and no doubt aching for a victory over Jim Sullivan's wondermen. It was a truly pulsating game. G. A. Brooking, a writer with more than 60 years' experience of watching rugby, remarked that he could not recall a game with more thrills and excitement. Again the luck seemed to run against Bev's team. Bill Derbyshire broke his collarbone around the hour mark, just after Les Jones had dropped a marvellous goal to put Warrington 4-3 ahead. The game finally swung Wigan's way 15 minutes from time when Ernie Ashcroft scored after grand work by Gordon Ratcliffe and Frank Barton. Ted Ward's conversion made the final score 8-4 to the cherry and whites. It had been Warrington's first defeat at Wilderspool since Widnes had won there on 4 April 1947.

There was no shame in losing to Wigan but the following Saturday, 29 January, people were wondering whether the Wire bubble had burst as they went down 11-6 at Belle Vue Rangers. True enough, they lacked Pimblett, Helme and Featherstone away on test duty at Odsal, but few pundits anticipated defeat. This was the first time that Brian Bevan came up against Dai Bevan, who had taken over from Stan McCormick on Rangers' left wing after the latter had been sold to St Helens for a world record transfer fee of £4,000 10 days earlier. Dai was one of the few men who could be relied on to keep Brian in check as the passing years were to prove. Cope, the Belle Vue left-winger, stole everyone's limelight, however, by scoring all three of his side's tries.

Settling down

Fortunately, the gloom of suspension and defeats was lightened by events in Brian's private life. He had become engaged to a girl from Grappenhall, Doreen Allison, who worked in a local bank and there was more exciting news when Warrington announced on 4 January that they had signed Brian's younger brother Owen. Owen, an accountant, had been playing for Eastern Suburbs Rugby Union Club for several years. He was more versatile than Brian, being able to play full-back, wing, centre and in the back-row of the pack. He was a blue-eyed six-footer, who weighed around 12 stones. From the reports in the local papers anyone would have thought that Warrington had signed a film star. Owen arrived at Heathrow airport on 1 February to be met by Brian, Chris Brockbank and the club chairman Mr. P. F. Ward. Another group of directors greeted him at Bank Quay station, along with hordes of supporters. A report headlined "Tall, Tanned, Terrific" ran: "If his play is as good as his looks, the eagerly awaited Owen Bevan... may bring about the impossible and displace brother Brian as the idol of the Warrington crowd... if he can win over that section of the Wilderspool fans which looks upon Brian in much the same way as Bobbysoxers regard Frank Sinatra, Owen will fill the bill to a T."

Apparently the brothers' father and other folk back home regarded Owen as a more likely candidate for greatness as a rugby player than Brian. Warrington must have been impressed with the reports given to them by such experts as Dave Brown for the reported fee was £2,000, £1,700 more than Brian had received. Brian later wrote that "Owen was a natural player and a left-hander, and during his high school days was no mean cricketer. Although perhaps lacking a little weight, he nevertheless possessed plenty of speed, a neat side-step and a clever dummy. The problem was finding his correct position on the field. I somehow think it was loose-forward".

Warrington decided to play Owen at centre alongside Brian in the home game against Liverpool Stanley on 15 February. Stanley were bottom of the league and despite three consecutive defeats Warrington could afford to experiment. If Owen had not believed how good Brian was before the game, he did after it. A crowd of 15,000 assembled, a remarkable figure in the circumstances, many doubtless curious about Bevan Mark 2. Brian stole the show and was at his coruscating best, running in three tries in a 29-3 victory. 'Criticus' declared that his "attacking play was as near perfection as possible". He was sure that no description of his second try could really do it justice - "his colleagues mobbed him, opponents shook his hand and the crowd just went frantic".

'Homer Genn' was prepared to proffer a description. He was in no doubt that it was even better than the wondrous effort in the Wardonia Cup back in August. He wrote: "Against Stanley he received an unexpected pass, almost on his own line, which necessitated his turning round and gathering a dancing impish ball, and then viewing his possible objective, which lay some 100 yards away. Facing him was the whole Stanley team who, in addition to eleven of his colleagues - 24 players in all - were scattered here, there and everywhere. To get through such congestion looked utterly impossible, and let it be remembered that despite their short-comings, Stanley have a reputation for being gallant, enthusiastic and determined defenders. Bevan sized up the situation in a flash (his quick thinking is one of his greatest assets). He sprinted forward at full speed in a straight line, until he had the whole opposition moving wingwards, and then he switched inside and set a diagonal course. It was from this point that the movement became majestic and delightfully rhythmic in its execution, and, viewed from the vicinity of the press box, was indeed a poetic joy. Here we saw the long, raking strides suddenly shortened as he accelerated, his body swaying and swerving as he evaded would-be tacklers (I saw at least six such attempts) and his almost invisible side-step as he flashed through each opening as it presented itself. It was fitting that a final desperate effort by the last defender should fail, as with energy exhausted, Bevan reached his objective, prompting a prolonged burst of cheering, which did us all good, no-one being more obviously delighted than his brother Owen."

The Challenge Cup presented Warrington with an easy tie against Hull KR in the first round. Bev scored four tries over the two legs and bagged an almost inevitable hat-trick against Oldham in the following league match. Warrington were back in winning mode and Brian had reverted to type with 10 tries in four games. Another supposedly easy tie in the cup at Belle Vue Rangers followed. The Zoological Gardens looked more like Arctic tundra on the afternoon of 5 March, however. Warrington got the shock of their lives. They had not come to play blizzard-type football. They persisted in trying to pass the ball. Rangers played perfect rugby in the snowy conditions, taking no risks but accepting whatever chances fell their way. Even so Warrington should have had the tie wrapped up by half-time. Ike Fishwick had opened the scoring with a try but despite total superiority Warrington only led 3-2 at the interval. Rangers turned the screw in the second half to win a deserved 8-3 victory. Bev uncharacteristically blew a couple of chances he would normally have translated into tries and the Wire's Wembley dreams evaporated once again, along with the icy air.

It was back to league fare and Warrington had all to play for. They were still top of the table and in a three-cornered fight with Wigan and Barrow for the Lancashire League title. Five games on the trot were won, including a vital 19-10 home victory over Barrow. Belle Vue Rangers were finally overcome when Bev scored a hat-trick in a 32-0 win at Wilderspool on 30 March, a game which saw Harold Palin land seven goals, the last of which created a new club record of 126 goals in a season. Palin took the record from Cumberland full-back Billy Holding who had landed 125 back in 1932-33. By the season's close Harold extended the record to 146 goals. In the next match at Salford on 2 April, Brian ran in his eighth and last hat-trick of the season, his third try being his 50th of the campaign. He had now overtaken Lionel Cooper in the scoring lists, the Fartowner scoring his own 50th a week later.

On 9 April Warrington travelled to Central Park for a crucial engagement with Wigan. A win for Warrington would probably have clinched top spot for them and Wigan had to win to retain hopes of displacing the Wire. A crowd of 42,500 saw an early try by Jack Fleming give Warrington an ideal start and 10 minutes into the second half the scores were still level at 7-7. Warrington then fell apart and Wigan ran riot scoring 19 further points to win 26-7. This Wigan jinx must have been giving Brian and his team-mates an inferiority complex. In 10 league and cup games against them Brian had only twice been on the winning side.

The humiliation at Central Park did not deter almost 29,000 from turning up at Wilderspool on Good Friday for a hard-earned 21-14 success against Widnes. There was a promising debut for stand-off Ron Ryder, son of the club trainer Fred Ryder. On Easter Monday Bev scored two tries in a 25-12 home victory over cup finalists Bradford Northern, the second from 75 yards bringing the house down. The next day another key fixture loomed at Leigh. The fate of the Lancashire League Championship rested on Wire's result and that of Wigan who were playing at Salford. A draw by Warrington would give them the title but a loss accompanied by a Wigan victory would hand the honour to Jim Sullivan's charges. Warrington looked to have done enough at 2-2 with eight minutes to go when Welsh centre Norman Harris put the cat among the pigeons by scoring a try to give Leigh a 5-2 victory. Relief and joy followed despair, however, when the news came through from the Willows that a late penalty by another Welshman, Salford's ex-Harlequins rugby union stand-off, Jack Davies had snatched a 9-9 draw from Wigan. The end result was that Warrington had retained their Lancashire League title and Bev had another medal to add to his growing collection.

Two days after the Leigh saga Brian had an even more important match, for on 20 April he was married to his sweetheart Doreen at St. Wilfred's Church in Grappenhall. Owen Bevan had arrived in England in good time to be his brother's best man. The happy couple spent their honeymoon in North Wales. Among their wedding presents were a wireless set from the club and an eiderdown and blankets from the players.

Married man or not, the season was still not over. Warrington finished the league programme in style walloping Hull 36-7 to finish five points clear of Wigan at the top of the table. Bev scored two tries, one a gift from debutant centre

Austin Heathwood, who presented the ball to his winger when actually over the line.

That week Brian received his first call-up to representative rugby when he and Harry Bath were selected in an Empire squad to play games in Bordeaux and Albi at the end of May. Unfortunately he was unable to make the trip to France but his career in representative football was soon to take off.

On 30 April the semi-finals of the Rugby League Championship took place and lightning did strike twice in the same place - Central Park. Wigan went down again to Yorkshire opposition on their own ground, this time their conquerors being Huddersfield. A ground record 43,700 saw Huddersfield win 14-5 and emulate Bradford Northern's feat of the previous year. Meanwhile at Wilderspool before a more moderate crowd of 18,309, Warrington accounted for third-placed Barrow by 23-8. It was not a vintage performance by any means, but it was good enough to carry them through to another Championship Final on 14 May and a chance to retain their champions title. Brian played his part with a couple of tries.

No stopping Huddersfield

The omens looked good for Warrington. Wigan, thankfully, had been taken out of the equation, the Wire had completed the league double over Huddersfield already and no Yorkshire side had beaten Palin's men all season in 12 attempts. Enthusiasm for the game was astronomically high. The previous week's Challenge Cup Final had drawn a world record crowd of 95,050 to Wembley for the Bradford Northern versus Halifax match. The Championship Final drew 75,194 to Maine Road, the largest attendance for a rugby league match anywhere in the world apart from Wembley.

Warrington were confident and Brian Bevan's own confidence must have received a subconscious boost when the appointed referee Frank Smith failed to arrive from Barrow. Apparently Mr Smith had never received confirmation of his appointment. Smith, it will be recalled, was the man who sent Brian off at Widnes. Matt Coates, a 29-year-old Pudsey touch-judge and the reserve referee, was given the whistle while a familiar figure to Warringtonians came out of the crowd to take Coates's touchline role. This was Warrington's own Paul Cowell, a renowned referee of the 1930s and 1940s, who had officiated in three Championship finals and five Challenge Cup finals.

W. E. Riley, in *The Sporting Chronicle & Athletic News*, wrote of the game: "It provided a classic encounter between two teams bent on playing attacking football and ended in such an exciting tempo that rugby enthusiasts and the non-initiated alike were sent away with nerves tingling and appetites satiated with a feast of good football." Harry Sunderland agreed, saying: "The match was the classic we hoped for. Thousands went away with the firm idea that it is the Championship final and not the Challenge Cup final that should be put on show at Wembley for Southerners."

Unfortunately for Warrington, they met Huddersfield on a day when only their very best would have done and they did not quite produce it. Huddersfield were better than the 13-12 score-line in their favour indicated. They were ahead from the 13th minute when Irish prop Jack Daly scored under the posts for Pat Devery to convert. After 35 minutes they went into an 8 point lead when Lionel Cooper claimed an astonishing try created by magical play from Devery and Billy Banks. Bevan launched himself at Cooper in a last desperate effort to prevent the try but was stopped dead by a powerful hand-off as Cooper crossed at the corner for his 60th try of the season. On 53 minutes it became 13-0 when Devery converted his own touchdown after a comedy of errors by the Warrington defence.

It was not until the 63rd minute that Warrington got on the score-board when Palin piloted a penalty goal. The final 10 minutes, however, seethed with tension as Warrington almost ripped victory from defeat. Seven minutes from time Roy Francis crossed. Although held in a two-man tackle, fortune smiled on the Wire at last for he clearly lost the ball, yet unsighted Matt Coates allowed the try. Harry Bath, Palin having been taken off injured, converted from wide out and at 13-7 hope sprang eternal. Four minutes later the Wire fans were beside themselves when Billy Jackson grabbed a brilliant try after superb play from Helme and Francis. Bath's touchline conversion brought the score to a nerve-jangling 13-12. If the game had lasted five minutes longer onlookers were convinced that Warrington would have stolen the spoils. It would, though, have been an injustice to a fine Fartown team.

Brian Bevan could have altered the course of events, but fate was not on his side. In the very first minute he stole between full-back Johnny Hunter and Cooper as Hunter tried to get his winger away. Bev got a hand to the ball and it looked momentarily as if he was going to pull off one of his trademark interception tries. Alas, with Bev facing an open field, the ball went to ground. Later, he ran almost the length of the field only to see Francis drop his pass in a scoring position. Finally, Warringtonians were incensed when Bevan chased a short kick by Albert Pimblett, ran out of play to get round Cooper, gathered the ball and flew unopposed toward the Huddersfield goal-line, only to be brought back unrewarded when Paul Cowell's flag was seen to be raised. The touch-judge had decided that Bev was in touch when he collected the bouncing ball, a ruling which did not go down well with the townsmen he met over the next few days.

Warrington's season had promised much more than the team finally delivered. Even so, most other clubs' supporters would have been pleased enough with appearances in the County Cup and Championship finals, the retention of the Lancashire League title and a position at the top of the table. There is a very fine line between success and failure sometimes. For most Wire fans and players, the team had just fallen on the wrong side of the line. The civic reception and high tea at the town hall were less joyful than in 1948, but there was always next season.

Brian's season had not quite finished. Despite missing the trip to France and the games on 26 and 29 May, he did play for a joint Warrington-Wigan XIII which defeated Trevor Foster's XIII 37-13 in an exhibition match in Llanelli on 28 May. His spectacular running thrilled a crowd of more than 11,000 and brought him two tries. Modern day Super Leaguers can note that 50 years ago the concept of taking games "on the road" was alive and kicking. In the 13 days between 16 and 29 May 1949, apart from the Llanelli game, the following rugby league games were staged: Bradford Northern, Wigan and Leigh met Roanne; Huddersfield and St Helens met each other at Pontardulais, Bridgend and Abertillery; and Empire XIIIs were in action in Bordeaux and Albi.

Season 1948-49

Warrington finished top of the League: P36, W31, L5; For 728, Against 247
Bevan scored 56 tries for Warrington

Date	Opponent	Score	Bevan	Crowd	
21 Aug	Halifax	18-2	1T	6,000	
26 Aug	Liverpool St	40-8	dnp	5,135	
28 Aug	Bradford N	19-7	1T	23,000	
4 Sep	**Barrow**	30-8	2T	20,000	LC 1
8 Sep	Barrow	7-4	1T	8,289	LC 1
11 Sep	Rochdale H	17-7	1T	8,270	
16 Sep	Leigh	15-10	1T	24,285	LC 2
18 Sep	**Leeds**	39-17	1T	21,032	
25 Sep	**Huddersfield**	25-2	1T	29,450*	
28 Sep	**Oldham**	55-0	5T	19,500	LC Semi-final
2 Oct	Oldham	37-0	5T	16,759	
9 Oct	**Whitehaven**	48-15	2T	17,670	
11 Oct	**Halifax**	36-4	3T	13,481	
16 Oct	St Helens	12-4		29,774	
23 Oct	**Rochdale H**	15-6		18,562	
30 Oct	**Australians**	16-7		26,879	
6 Nov	Barrow	6-5		11,903	
13 Nov	Wigan	8-14	1T	39,015	LC Final (at Swinton)
20 Nov	**Salford**	15-12	2T	16,680	
27 Nov	Swinton	21-7	1T	10,400	
4 Dec	**St Helens**	15-5	2T	24,075	
11 Dec	Huddersfield	11-9	1T	25,232	
25 Dec	Widnes	14-2		16,317	
27 Dec	**Leigh**	13-0		24,784	
28 Dec	Leeds	14-0		31,880	
1 Jan	Whitehaven	3-2	1T	8,376	
8 Jan	**Workington T**	29-7	dnp	16,246	
15 Jan	Workington T	6-11	dnp	15,000	
22 Jan	**Wigan**	4-8		34,304*	
29 Jan	Belle Vue R	6-11		7,000	
5 Feb	**Liverpool St**	29-3	3T	15,800	
12 Feb	**Hull KR**	17-7	1T	17,000	Ch Cup 1
19 Feb	Hull KR	28-5	3T	16,000	Ch Cup 1
26 Feb	**Oldham**	34-12	3T	15,575	
5 Mar	Belle Vue R	3-8		14,000	Ch Cup 2
12 Mar	Hull	24-2	1T	15,000	
19 Mar	**Swinton**	18-3		17,770	
26 Mar	**Barrow**	19-10	1T	18,454	
30 Mar	**Belle Vue R**	32-0	3T	14,000	
2 Apr	Salford	18-2	3T	12,000	
9 Apr	Wigan	7-26		42,500	
15 Apr	**Widnes**	21-14		28,989	
16 Apr	**Bradford N**	25-12	2T	18,357	
18 Apr	Leigh	2-5		19,000	
23 Apr	**Hull**	36-7	2T	16,916	
30 Apr	**Barrow**	23-8	2T	18,309	CH Semi
14 May	Huddersfield	12-13		75,194	CH Final (Maine Road)

* Ground record

8. 1949-50 'Guts, glamour and gumption'

The season of 1948-49 had marked the high tide of rugby league as a spectator sport. Rugby league, along with other major sports, enjoyed a phenomenal surge of interest following the dark days of the Second World War. A record 6,867,189 paying customers passed through the turnstiles, including 4,749,223 at league games. The following season the aggregate at all matches had dipped slightly to 6,811,796 but an all-time record 4,982,160 paid to watch the league programme. By the time Brian Bevan finished playing professionally in 1964, the league aggregate had more than halved to only 1,972,901. As the 20th century ended, the total for league fixtures (Super League and the rest) hovered at around 1.2 to 1.3 million.

Warrington certainly provided their share of spectators in this halcyon period. In 1948-49, for example, Wilderspool never drew a crowd of less than the 13,481 which attended the game against Halifax, which was played on a Monday evening in October. There were crowds in excess of 20,000 on eight occasions and the average league crowd of 20,199 was bettered only by Wigan's 22,535 (*Rugby League Review* figures, June 1949). Nine clubs drew average crowds in excess of 10,000 while Barrow, Halifax, Hull, Hunslet, Oldham and Widnes all exceeded 9,000. Only seven of the competition's clubs experienced falls in attendance. The game was a compelling spectacle and Brian Bevan was arguably its biggest individual crowd-puller.

One thing that would have disappointed Brian was the fact that he lost his position at the top of the try-scorers to Lionel Cooper. A third consecutive top try-scorer title was snatched from him when Lionel came with a late flurry of scoring to finish with 60 tries to Brian's 56. Gordon Ratcliffe of Wigan had finished third with 36. By the time the 1949-50 season dawned Brian was raring to go and fit as a fiddle. He had proved he was as fast as ever in a sprint at Warrington Rugby Union Club's ground in August. His opponent was St Helens winger Stan McCormick, currently the world's costliest player. Astonished spectators saw Bev finish five yards ahead of Stan over the 100 yards which was covered in 9.6 seconds. This was almost world-class sprinting and was all the more remarkable for being performed on a bumpy rugby football field.

While hopes were high for Warrington, now to be captained by Harry Bath, there were to be a number of surprises and setbacks during the season for both the club and for Bevan. There was something of a seismic shift in the league table as Halifax shot up from 25th in 1948-49 to fourth in 1949-50 and other big movers were Swinton (ninth to third), Leigh (18th to sixth), Dewsbury (20th to ninth), Leeds (14th to eighth) and Castleford (19th to 12th). There were also a couple of massive fallers in Bradford Northern (10th to 21st) and Warrington who collapsed from top to 11th.

One thing that was as sure as death and taxes, however, was the pre-eminence of Wigan in this period. They proved it immediately the season opened when they completely outclassed the Wire in winning the Wardonia Cup on 13 August. The Central Parkers won 28-11 at Wilderspool before 23,300 mostly bemused Warringtonians. The press absolved only Bevan and Fishwick. Bev scored two tries and held the formidable Brian Nordgren in check, but could do nothing about the other Wigan winger Gordon Ratcliffe who ran in a hat-trick.

It was not a good start. The first league fixture, however, was more encouraging as Bev bagged another brace in a 39-10 rout of Hull at Wilderspool, Palin booting nine goals. Optimism faded four days later when Barrow blotted out the Wire attack to win 7-0 at Craven Park. Progress was made in the Lancashire Cup with a couple of good victories over a Salford team which would ultimately just be pipped for a place in the top four at season's end. A daunting trip to Fartown followed on 3 September. Huddersfield had won their first four games and were ready to prove to a crowd of 26,700 that their Championship triumph over Warrington at Maine Road had been no fluke.

'D'Artagnan', in *Rugby League Review*, was bewitched by the game. He wrote: "Once again Huddersfield and Warrington have shown how it should be done. This was rugby in *excelsis* with attack predominating." Each side scored five tries and the lead changed hands five times. Bev was in sublime form, scorching in for the first and the 10th try and fitting in another to register a hat-trick. Opposite him, Lionel Cooper ran over for two himself, his second as spectacular as Bevan's own second. This was one of their most fascinating duels - Bev all speed, instinct and eccentricity, Lionel direct, potent, full of menace. In the end Lionel was happier for Huddersfield won 25-17, as Jeff Bawden landed five goals to Harold Palin's one.

After a midweek 30-7 romp against Bradford Northern, Warrington went down to a third successive away defeat when Workington Town beat them 17-7. Things were clearly not right, but there were mitigating circumstances. Les Jones was missing from the full-back position - he did not play until February - and Albert Johnson and Roy Francis also missed the first five games. Johnson was drafted to full-back when he did reappear and proved a surprisingly good stand-in for Jones. As worrying as anything, however, was the loss of form exhibited by Pimblett and Helme, who had been regarded as prime candidates for the 1950 Lions tour.

Capped by the Other Nationalities

The cracks were papered over with comfortable 40-point victories over Belle Vue in the second round of the Lancashire Cup and at Liverpool in the league. Then on Monday, 19 September came a red letter day in Brian's career. He won his first international cap when he played for Other Nationalities against England at Workington. The RFL had decided to organise a full-blown European International Championship involving England, Wales, France and Other Nationalities. The short tour to France by the Empire squad in May had been a precursor to the formation of the Other Nationalities international team. The tournament was immensely successful but was discarded in 1956 in favour of more regular World Cups and test matches against the French. Other mitigating factors for its dissolution were the declining numbers of Welsh imports and the complete drying up of Antipodean stars due to the international transfer bans.

3 September, 1949. Warrington lost 17-25 to Huddersfield at Fartown but Bev still scored a hat-trick. He is pictured touching down ahead of Jeff Bawden, a prolific points-scorer from Cumberland.

However, while the Other Nationalities did exist as an international force, players considered it a signal honour to represent them, especially as many of them had contracts which precluded them from ever having a realistic chance of winning test recognition for Australia or New Zealand if their long term interests - financial or otherwise - were best served in England. Wearing the famous green jersey of the Other Nationalities was a real mark of excellence, for there was a plethora of world-class men vying for the privilege, scrum-half probably being the solitary position where a genuine top-ranker was lacking during the period. For the wings Other Nationalities had a superabundance of talent but always chose the twin godheads of Bevan and Cooper, unless injuries kept them out. The other contenders included brilliant players in Wigan's Brian Nordgren, Huddersfield's Empire Games sprinter Peter Henderson and big Jack McLean (Bradford Northern), all New Zealanders, the latter pair being former All Blacks. Australians Bruce Ryan (Hull and Leeds) and Bob Bartlett (Bramley and Leeds) and Scots such as the prolific Drew Turnbull (Leeds) and George Wilson (Workington) simply added to the competition.

In that inaugural international fixture Brian took his place in the following team: Wilson (Huddersfield); Bevan (Warrington), Paskins (Workington), Bartlett (Leeds), Cooper (Huddersfield); Devery (Huddersfield) captain, Jackson (Hull); McMaster (Leeds), Kearney (Leeds), Pansegrouw (Halifax), Bath (Warrington), Mudge (Workington), Valentine (Huddersfield). The England team read: Ledgard (Leigh); Lawrenson (Workington), Kerwick (Leigh), Ashcroft (Wigan), Clark (Dewsbury); Horne (Barrow), Bradshaw (Wigan); Naughton (Widnes), Egan (Wigan) captain, Hayton (Workington), Featherstone (Warrington), Armitt (Swinton), Ivison (Workington).

Over 17,000 crammed into Borough Park on a lovely Cumbrian evening, many of them miners coming off shifts which had begun at 1.00am. England were tremendously disappointing and Other Nationalities won far more convincingly than the scoreline of 13-7 suggested. The *Workington Star* reporter wrote: "Other Nationalities had two extremely fast and dangerous wingers in Bevan and Cooper. England's wingers never got the same chances of showing their paces, though Lawrenson shone both in attack and defence, and two tackles on Bevan which saved certain tries were highlights, as he had to race from the opposite wing." Bevan scored the try which gave the Others an 8-0 lead at half-time. England fought back to trail 7-10, but then came the try of the match, the game-breaker, when Bevan finished off excellent work from Cooper, Jackson, Bartlett and

Paskins. Bev would go on to score 26 tries in 16 internationals, a phenomenal strike rate for that level of competition.

A couple of days later Bevan was back in Cumberland with Warrington, who went down yet again, 9-2 to a gutsy, fired-up Whitehaven. The Wire had been lucky to get off so lightly by all accounts. Bevan had been partnered for the first time by Ron Ryder at the Recreation Ground, but had hardly seen any ball as the 'Haven tacklers swarmed all over the pair. The two had better fortune in a 50-13 thumping of Batley on 24 September when Bevan claimed three tries. Even so, both Jack Steel and 'Criticus' suspected that he was below his best and was carrying a leg injury sustained at Whitehaven.

On Monday, 3 October Warrington faced their most important engagement so far that season, a trip to resurgent Leigh in the semi-final of the Lancashire Cup. A crowd of 22,000 was witness to as grim and tense a cup-tie as could be imagined. Warrington, with Pimblett incapacitated for half the game, had nonetheless held Leigh to 7-7 as the closing minutes approached. A penalty from 30 yards out to Warrington looked as if it would be the match-winner, but Harold Palin's kick skimmed just outside a post and Leigh came roaring back. They won the game when Harris, Kerwick and Cec Ryan - brother of Warrington's Bob - sent right-winger Jack Wood slicing through a wrong-footed defence for the winning score.

To rub salt into Warrington's wounds, news came through of Wigan's 30-17 victory over Workington Town in the other semi-final. There was a silver lining for Warrington, however, in that Wilderspool was chosen to host the final on 29 October, despite Wigan's preference for the game to be staged at Swinton. The game was made all-ticket and all 35,000 were sold, yielding ground-record receipts of £4,751, although only 33,701 actually attended. Unsurprisingly Wigan won the trophy for the fourth year running. Two days after the defeat at Leigh, Wilderspool housed the Roses Match, drawing a crowd of 15,000 who saw Lancashire victorious over Yorkshire by 22-13.

A brief flurry of success came Warrington's way with a rare away victory at Hull and a splendid 30-9 flogging of Huddersfield before almost 25,000 at Wilderspool on 15 October. The following week was a case of riches to rags again, as the team went down once more at Belle Vue Rangers with the enigmatic Roy Francis playing his last game for the club. Francis, who went on to become a master player-coach at Hull, was filling in for Bevan who was on international duty again for Other Nationalities. After a very dry and hot summer and autumn it came as something of a shock when torrential rain reduced the crowd for the game against Wales at Abertillery to a mere 2,000 for 10 times that figure had been expected. It was fortunate for the Others that their wings were so potent as tries from Bev, after seven minutes, and Cooper won the match 6-5. Conditions were so awful that many of the players begged Warrington referee Charlie Appleton to abandon the game with 20 minutes to go. By the time 80 minutes had elapsed the players were on the point of exhaustion, according to Harry Sunderland in *The Daily Mail*.

On Bonfire Night, a Johnson try and a Palin goal gave Warrington a hard-earned 5-4 victory at Swinton, who were pushing for a top-four spot. It had been an uncompromising encounter and Brian had suffered an incapacitating leg injury. Ironically, six days later, an article appeared in *Rugby League Review* written by Tom Reynolds extolling the virtues of the training and fitness regime at Wilderspool. Amazingly for the time, Warrington had the following staff: Chris Brockbank (secretary-manager), Fred Ryder (trainer and coach), Tom Lomax (physical training instructor), Griff Jenkins (sprint specialist), Fred Worrall (masseur and trainer), Fred Higginbottom and Jack Goodall (general assistants) and Tommy Flynn (ground worker). There was a fantastic amount of expertise available in these men. "Each to his needs" was the collective credo, although Karl Marx was probably not on the staff. "When a player is thoroughly wound up," wrote Reynolds, "the (training) process is eased off accordingly. At the moment Brian Bevan, for instance, needs next to no training, and is treated accordingly."

Being the perfectionist he was, Bevan unquestionably relished this professional environment. However, his leg injury, his first real injury problem since coming to England, kept him out of action for six weeks. In that period Warrington lost at home to St Helens, away at Oldham and were losing 2-0 at Bradford before the game was fogged off. A home victory over Belle Vue provided the only league points in this depressing period, although Harry Bath had little reason to smile because he had his jaw broken in a clash with former Wire, Bryn Day. Brian was unlucky in again missing a trip to France as Warrington recuperated with a couple of wins, on 10 and 11 December, over a South of France XIII (6-3) at Toulouse and Albi (16-8).

On that trip to France, Ally Naughton had made his debut for Warrington, having transferred from Widnes for a world-record fee of £4,600 on 30 November. Ally, a bone-jarring tackler and a good footballer, was to play at left centre for the remainder of the season but, in the years ahead, would strike up a successful partnership with Bevan when he moved to right centre.

Bevan returned to duty on 17 December and scored a try in a 17-0 home win over Whitehaven. He claimed another in a close victory over Widnes on Christmas Eve to take his season's tally to 20, but he was slipping behind Brian Nordgren (30) and Lionel Cooper (24) in the individual try-scoring stakes, injuries and Warrington's abysmal form proving considerable handicaps. A lacklustre Boxing Day defeat at Leigh saw Jackie Fleming and 'Spiv' Riley play their last games in Warrington's colours as the old order gradually continued to change. Both were transfer-listed, Fleming mainly because he refused to play anywhere but stand-off and eventually moved to Widnes at a reported fee of £2,500. Bryn Knowelden took over at number six for the rest of the season.

On 27 December Warrington entertained Cardiff in a friendly. Rugby league was having one of its periodic flirtations with Wales. Cardiff were part of a new Welsh League and would enter the Northern Rugby League itself in 1951. At this juncture, they were happy to play friendlies with the first-class clubs. Warrington won 35-10 with Bevan piling up five tries, one an 80-yarder. Cliff Rosser, playing opposite him, had the satisfaction of scoring both Cardiff tries. A crowd of 12,603 paid £870, half going to Cardiff after tax, and then contributed to a collection for the Welsh club. Apparently this was the first time Cardiff showed a profit on any game. Four days later Bev confirmed his return to form and fitness with another hat-trick against Wakefield Trinity.

The team's erratic form continued through January 1950, with home successes against Rochdale Hornets and Barrow and away defeats at Batley and Wigan, the latter played before a crowd of 35,000. Nordgren gave a master class on Wigan's right wing to touch down three times.

It was now Challenge Cup time. Warrington were down in 12th position in the league with no chance of retaining their title. They were certainly not the side they had been a year earlier. Hopes were not high, although they rose when the first round draw pitted them against lowly Hull KR on 4 February. Les Jones made his reappearance in this game allowing Albert Johnson to return to the left wing, a position which had been a real problem all season with eight men tried there.

Back to form

Astonishingly, the team suddenly turned everything around. Confidence returned and the result was a loss of only four of their remaining 18 fixtures.

The first leg of the first round of the Challenge Cup took Warrington to Craven Park where Bevan scored half the team's four tries in a 12-2 win. Wire won the second leg twice as decisively, 24-4. All of a sudden, interest in the club rocketed with each of the next five games, four of them at Wilderspool, attracting 20,000 plus crowds. The only defeat in this spell came at St Helens on 4 March. The week before, Warrington had overcome Swinton 17-2 in a potentially difficult second-round tie. Added import was given to this result because Leeds disposed of Wigan 7-2 and opened up a whole new set of possibilities for the rest of the surviving clubs.

The third round draw was kind to Warrington again. A home tie with mid-table Hunslet on 11 March was much easier than top-four club Swinton in the previous round - on paper, at least. Brian Bevan had been having a lean time with only three tries in his last seven games, although his new centre Ron Ryder had done well enough with five. Hunslet were not fooled, though. They switched their captain, Welsh international Les Williams, from centre to wing to counter the brilliant Australian. On 2 March, Williams had been selected as a winger for the forthcoming Australasian tour along with two Warrington forwards, Jim Featherstone and Bob Ryan, the latter a real surprise selection.

Warrington were never behind, although Hunslet held them to 4-8 at the break. In the final 20 minutes the game was sewn up. Up to that point Williams had repeatedly checked Brian, despite some lovely play from the Wire right wingman. Williams was helpless though when Bevan raced through for two tries in that final quarter. 'Criticus' wrote: "He simply flew along the touchline, and the second time finished with a determined headlong dive, which three opponents together tried in vain to check. If he saw one route to the line closing Bevan tried another in his own inimitable way and altogether he gave the defence a most uncomfortable time." The final result of 21-7 was a little harsh on Hunslet, but Warrington fans were beginning to believe something special might be in the offing.

They were certainly delirious the following Saturday when almost 25,000 poured into Wilderspool for a league clash with Wigan, who would go on to win

11 February, 1950. Bev leaves Hull KR full-back Lewis in his wake after chasing a kick-through to touch down, only for his score to be disallowed. Many of Bev's tries came from his own and colleagues' kicks.

three of that season's major trophies. For a change Warrington ended up beating their great rivals. It was a close run affair - 12-9 - tries from Johnson and Knowelden and three goals from Bath doing the trick. Jack Steel wrote in *The Guardian*: "Warrington won because they had equally as much guts, glamour and gumption as their opponents. Sooner or later the bogy had to be chased out of the stadium and the victory could not have been achieved at a more appropriate moment."

Steel was dead right but the following week there was anti-climax when Wire were turned over 23-11 at Salford, a game which marked Albert Pimblett's last appearance for the primrose and blue. It was not ideal preparation for Warrington's next encounter - Leeds in the semi-final of the Challenge Cup at Odsal on April Fools' Day. Leeds had been installed as favourites to win the competition after their ejection of Wigan. The press believed that Leeds might be too powerful for the Wire in the forwards and too clever and quick at half-back, although they were less impressed with the Loiners' three-quarters than with Warrington's. Former Wire, Bill Hopper, was at prop for Leeds instead of suspended Australian Bob McMaster.

A record Odsal crowd of 69,898 expected a titanic struggle, but were let down. Many were still queuing to get in when the old warhorse Bill Derbyshire scored the opening try after sloppy Leeds play. Warrington never looked back and were superior at all points. By half-time they led 14-0 with further tries from Johnson, Bath and Helme and ran out winners by 16-4, with Leeds very flattered by the score. Warrington were back at Wembley for the first time since 1936 but had not lifted the Challenge Cup since 1907, when Jackie Fish had scored 11 points in their 17-3 defeat of Oldham at Broughton.

Their opponents proved to be near neighbours Widnes, who ended Bradford Northern's hopes of a fourth consecutive Wembley final with an 8-0 victory in the other semi-final at Central Park. As luck would have it, the two finalists were due to clash six days later in the Good Friday, 7 April, fixture at Naughton Park. Nearly 23,000 attended, looking for signs and portents of what might occur at Wembley a month hence. Warrington heartened their fans by winning 17-8, with second-rower Gerry Lowe making a sound debut and Ally Naughton excelling against his former team. There were few thrills, however, although Bev did bring the house down with one of his specials.

The next day, Easter Saturday, at Wilderspool he scored again against Workington Town, but it was Albert Johnson's try which finally killed off the Cumbrians 14-13. On Easter Monday, Leigh came to Warrington and beat the home men 10-7, their third victory over the Wire that season. Bev failed to score in any of the games against Leigh, Jack Wood being his opposite winger on every occasion. Two more home games followed, making four within seven days. It was therefore small wonder that the crowds for the games against Oldham (7,991) and Liverpool Stanley (11,147) fell markedly, for with the expense of a trip to London for the Cup Final many fans had to adjust their budgets.

There was a scare for Warrington in their 26-12 win over Oldham when Brian was forced off the field with a damaged shoulder. He consequently missed games against Liverpool, Bradford and Wakefield. In 1949-50 Bev had missed seven games through injury, more than he had missed in the three previous seasons put together. It was a worry to him, making him more keen to find ways of avoiding mishap, a trait that would last throughout his career.

He was back, much to everyone's relief, for the final league game of the season on 26 April, 10 days before Wembley. Warrington made hard work of beating lowly Rochdale 11-5 at the Athletic Grounds. It was a poor do all round with only 2,016 people in the crowd. 'Criticus' remarked that "Bevan handled badly", but he was among the try-scorers, claiming his 30th of the season for the Wire.

Wembley winners

There may have been only 2,000 at Rochdale, but there was definitely Wembley fever in south-west Lancashire. All 95,000 tickets for the Challenge Cup final had been sold, although the official attendance was later returned as 94,249, the largest crowd either team had ever entertained.

Amazingly, Warrington and Widnes had never before met at any stage of the Challenge Cup. Warrington had reached the final on eight occasions but had only won the trophy in 1905 and 1907. Widnes had also won it twice but had only reached the final three times. All Widnes' finals had been at Wembley, whereas the Wire had played there only twice and on both occasions they had suffered defeat. History did not matter, however. The pundits strongly favoured a Warrington victory. They might have fallen from grace in terms of their league position, but they were a team full of genuine class. Ten of the Wembley side were past, present or future internationals, whereas only ex-Wire stand-off Jack Fleming could say the same for Widnes. Both teams had, however, lost two forwards through selection for the Australasian tour, Warrington lacking Featherstone and Ryan while Widnes were shorn of Dan Naughton, Ally's brother, and Fred Higgins. Higgins' absence enabled another Naughton brother, Johnny, to claim a place in the Chemics' second-row.

Widnes had finished 16th in the league, five places below Warrington. Their strong point was undeniably their defence. They had conceded only 316 points in 36 games - leaders Wigan conceded 320. In five cup-ties they had let in only one try in scoring 74 points to 13. Warrington had been equally miserly in defence, their points ratio standing at 90-19, with only Hunslet managing to claim a try against them. The big questions were (a) could Widnes actually score enough points to win if their defence held and (b) how could they stop the more talented Warrington backs? The answers turned out to be (a) no and (b) with extreme difficulty.

The teams lined up as follows:

Warrington: Jones, Bevan, Ryder, A. Naughton, Johnson, Knowelden, Helme, Derbyshire, Fishwick, Fisher, Bath (captain), Lowe, Palin

Widnes: Bradley, Parkes, Hutton, Sale (captain), Malone, Fleming, Anderson, Rowbottom, Band, Wilcox, Leigh, J. Naughton, Reynolds

John North, of *The Daily Dispatch*, summed it up pretty accurately: "Almost the whole rugby league world owes an apology to Widnes. We thought they would keep the ball close and stage a dull, uninteresting final. Instead, they played open football when they could, and earned the praise of the southern critics. Widnes had every excuse for closing up the game. They started the second half in an impossible position... with little prospect of overhauling opponents who played the best football I have seen at the stadium in five post-war finals. Instead they continued to throw the ball about in lively style, which helped us to overlook the one-sidedness of a game that produced the highest margin since the final was taken to London."

Warrington were never in danger with the game largely following the pattern of their earlier victories over Hunslet and Leeds. Harold Palin gave them the lead with a left-footed drop goal after 16 minutes and doubled the advantage with a difficult penalty goal a few minutes later. After 22 minutes, Gerry Lowe, in his first cup-tie of any description, drove to the line, and quickly played the ball to Palin who delivered a pass to the onrushing Harry Bath. Bath shattered the defence to score a try which Palin converted from an oblique angle and Wire were nine points clear. Bath had a storming game despite carrying an injured shoulder which had needed a pain-killing injection 20 minutes before kick-off.

Seven minutes before the break Ronnie Ryder went over near the corner flag, after lovely passing from a scrum. Palin missed the conversion but landed another fine penalty in the 38th minute. At 14-0 at half-time there was no way back for the gallant but over-powered Chemics. However, despite the obvious difference in speed and class they did restrict Warrington to only five second half points. Palin landed his fifth goal in the 58th minute from a penalty after Anderson was caught off-side. The scoring ended at 19-0 after 67 minutes when Gerry Helme, a clear winner of the Lance Todd Trophy, stole around the scrum and gave a delicious reverse pass to Bryn Knowelden who caught the Widnes defence in a tangle to touch down. Harold Palin needed to land the conversion to finish as the season's top goal-kicker - he was level with Wigan's Ken Gee on 133 goals - but the ball struck a post and bounced out. Palin's 10 points had, however, ensured that he finished as the league's leading points-scorer with 290 to Gee's 281.

Brian Bevan did not score a try on his Wembley debut, a surprising feature in view of the openness of the play. He did nonetheless provide plenty of thrills. John Ridgway, in *The Yorkshire Post*, wrote: "A southern rugby union follower I spoke to afterwards was impressed with the final... In particular he liked the Warrington wingers - Brian Bevan and Albert Johnson - both masters of the sidestep and body swerve. Bevan succeeded with many runs which looked impossible when he set off." John North was also full of praise, saying: "The wingers took the eye, especially the spectacular Bevan, slowing a little nowadays, but still able to provide thrills, with his brushes along the touch-line and sudden swerves into the centre to throw the defence off their guard. Johnson did not get as much of the ball on the left flank but his attacking play was dazzling at times."

Brian may have taken exception to the remark about "slowing a little" - injuries had taken their toll, but he would soon recover. He was, however, thrilled to bits about his winners' medal, presented by Clement Attlee, the Prime Minister, not to mention the £40 match fee, his biggest pay-packet yet. He would later recall: "Memories of that first Wembley appearance will never fade - the build-up to the game, the atmosphere, apprehensive thoughts as to how I would shape up ... my first glimpse of the magnificent Wembley dressing-rooms, spotlessly clean and tiled all over, the nervous long walk up the tunnel onto the playing area, the feel of the lush, green, carpet-like turf, which can sap the energy from any player. After playing in a game at Wembley Stadium one is left with the impression that one has run literally a thousand miles... My only disappointment was to be recalled for a forward pass after crossing the Widnes line."

On Monday, 8 May Brian and his team-mates arrived back in Warrington with the Cup. If they thought the celebrations for the 1948 Championship-winning side were special, they were nothing compared to the reception this time. All the town and surrounding districts seemed to have turned out to welcome them. The local papers reported that there were eight miles of cheering fans as the trophy was paraded through the main thoroughfares, the town hall was bedecked with primrose and blue floral decorations and the mayor, Councillor W. Higham, was as excited as the most delirious fan. The players were repeatedly brought to the balcony, speeches were made and, after high tea, the Challenge Cup was filled with six bottles of 1943 champagne. It is not recorded if any was kept for Gerry Lowe who had to miss the reception in order to sit a chemistry degree examination.

The Challenge Cup had finally returned to Wilderspool after a 43-year absence. Brian Bevan had now won all the domestic honours the game had to offer with the exception of a Lancashire Cup-winners medal. He had won his spurs as an international, and he had scored more tries than any other player in post-war rugby league. He was still only 25. How much more could he achieve? At that moment he had other things on his mind. Two days after the civic reception he and Doreen were off to Australia for his first home visit for four years. They were due back on 11 August.

Wilderspool, 11 March, 1950, Challenge Cup third round. Hunslet centre Sinclair wonders what the hell happened as Bev beats him all ends up.
Unfortunately, the master has stepped on the touch-line.

Wembley 1950: Bev slices between two Widnes defenders

Bev joins Harry Bath and Warrington Mayor, Councillor W. Higham, in celebrating Wire's 1950 Challenge Cup final victory over Widnes, one of the many civic receptions Bev would attend as a Warrington hero.

Season 1949–50

Warrington finished 11th in the League: P36, W22, L14; For 579, Against 367
Bevan scored 30 tries for Warrington, plus 3 for representative teams

Date	Opponent	Score	Bevan	Crowd	
20 Aug	**Hull**	39–10	2T	15,636	
24 Aug	Barrow	0– 7		13,130	
27 Aug	Salford	22–9	1T	17,000	LC 1
31 Aug	**Salford**	17–2		15,000	LC 1
3 Sep	Huddersfield	17–25	3T	26,700	
7 Sep	**Bradford N**	30–7	1T	18,141	
10 Sep	Workington T	7–17		14,753	
14 Sep	**Belle Vue R**	45–7	2T	16,070	LC 2
17 Sep	Liverpool St	40–7	1T	1,850	
21 Sep	Whitehaven	2–9		8,766	
24 Sep	**Batley**	50–13	3T	13,987	
1 Oct	**Swinton**	20–12	1T	18,159	
3 Oct	Leigh	7–10		22,000	LC Semi
8 Oct	Hull	18–5		14,964	
15 Oct	**Huddersfield**	30–9	1T	24,688	
22 Oct	Belle Vue R	5–14	dnp	6,000	
5 Nov	Swinton	5–4		11,000	
12 Nov	**St Helens**	3–7	dnp	19,636	
19 Nov	Bradford N	0–2	dnp	10,052	(abandoned)
26 Nov	**Belle Vue R**	16–5	dnp	9,660	
3 Dec	Oldham	3–10	dnp	9,436	
17 Dec	**Whitehaven**	17–0	1T	9,550	
24 Dec	**Widnes**	12–7	1T	19,001	
26 Dec	Leigh	3–7		14,382	
31 Dec	**Wakefield T**	23–5	3T	15,267	
7 Jan	Batley	9–10		7,000	
14 Jan	**Rochdale H**	39–8	1T	13,234	
21 Jan	Wigan	11–21		35,000	
28 Jan	**Barrow**	13–12		14,004	
4 Feb	Hull KR	12–2	2T	9,280	Ch Cup 1
11 Feb	**Hull KR**	24–4		14,444	Ch Cup 1
18 Feb	**Salford**	11–7	1T	20,127	
25 Feb	**Swinton**	17–2		20,652	Ch Cup 2
4 Mar	St Helens	3–12		22,152	
11 Mar	**Hunslet**	21–7	2T	21,583	Ch Cup 3
18 Mar	**Wigan**	12–9		24,921	
25 Mar	Salford	11–23	1T	12,498	
1 Apr	Leeds	16–4		69,898	Cup Semi (at Odsal)
7 Apr	Widnes	17–8	1T	22,729	
8 Apr	**Workington T**	14–13	1T	15,540	
10 Apr	**Leigh**	7–10		15,630	
11 Apr	**Oldham**	26–12		7,991	
15 Apr	**Liverpool St**	16–5	dnp	11,147	
17 Apr	Bradford N	23–5	dnp	5,154	
24 Apr	Wakefield T	16–27	dnp	5,464	
26 Apr	Rochdale H	11–5	1T	2,016	
6 May	Widnes	19–0		94,249	Ch Cup Final (Wembley)

Representative Matches:

Date	For	Opponent	Score	Bevan	Venue
19 Sep	Other Nats	England	13–7	2T	Workington
22 Oct	Other Nats	Wales	6–5	1T	Abertillery

9. 1950-51 'The work of a genius'

Despite the delightful intoxication of winning at Wembley, both Brian Bevan and the club administrators knew that the 1949-50 season had been one of underachievement. Finishing 11th and losing 14 league fixtures was simply not good enough, not when the strength of the personnel was considered. Crowds had crashed by around 4,500 to an average of 16,351 which, in turn, meant an average reduction of £370 per game. The directors saw one immediate solution in raising the price of a £2 season ticket to £2/10/- (£2.50). This affected 700 holders who expressed their displeasure forcibly at the Annual General Meeting.

Brian, injuries notwithstanding, knew that he had not fulfilled his potential in 1949-50. Something had not been quite right. In all games he had scored 33 tries, good by normal standards but not by his. He had finished only fifth in the try-scoring lists behind Brian Nordgren (57), Lionel Cooper (46), Halifax's Arthur Daniels (36) and Wigan's remarkably prolific loose-forward Billy Blan (34). Sure of his own ability, he was determined to do better. He was so fired up in fact that he is on record as being anxious to beat Albert Rosenfeld's all-time record of 80 tries in a season for Huddersfield set in 1913-14. He really thought 1950-51 might be the year he broke Rozzy's record.

Brian arrived back in England from his trip home to Sydney in August 1950 raring to go. He was not back in time for the Wardonia Cup clash with Wigan on 12 August at Wilderspool, which ended in a 12-7 victory for the Wire. He was in the team for the first league match a week later, however, with both he and his centre Ron Ryder running in hat-tricks in a 55-3 home romp against Hull KR.

Warrington fielded the team which had played at Wembley with the exception of Eric Frodsham, who came in at full-back for Les Jones. 'Cowboy' Jones had decided to retire after 14 years as a Wire. Bevan had plenty of admiration for Cowboy, so-styled because of his bandy legs, who tried to make play for him whenever possible. He would eventually have as much respect for Eric Frodsham, who went on to play in every game of the 1950-51 season. Another notable departure was Albert Pimblett, arguably Bev's best centre partner, who was transferred to Salford on 22 August.

Warrington began the season with a bang. It helped that they had no injuries at all for the first ten games. The team remained completely unchanged with the solitary exception of Bev, who missed two games because of an attack of boils. He returned to the team on 9 September in a 41-17 home win against Swinton. Three more tries included his 200th career try. Four days later Liverpool Stanley were butchered 73-0 in the second leg of the first round of the Lancashire Cup, Bev having missed the 18-5 first leg victory at the newly opened Knotty Ash ground. There were another three tries to add to his total including his 200th for the Wire. The *Examiner* reported: "One of Bevan's efforts left the crowd gasping when he went all out for the corner, jammed on his brakes and then finished the effort less directly to the posts. Two opponents, who had rushed at him with sufficient determination to have thrown him over the wall, themselves finished over the touchline grasping one another!" Harold Palin landed a club record 14 goals.

An away league fixture followed at Liverpool, who this time restricted Warrington to a 23-0 victory. They could not stop Bevan, however, from registering a third consecutive hat-trick. They did considerably better than an unfortunate York side on 23 September though. This time Wilderspool witnessed another massacre - 75-3 - and Bevan ran riot with six tries. He had piled up 18 tries in seven games so far. Admittedly some of the opposition had not been top class, but maybe Rosenfeld's record really was going to be under threat.

Brian notched more tries in a 28-14 victory at Leigh in a second round Lancashire Cup-tie and three days later in a 14-4 success at Rochdale on 30 September, when Great Britain tourists Ryan and Featherstone reappeared. On Wednesday, 4 October Bev found himself on the opposite side to Bob Ryan when he figured in a representative fixture between the returning Great Britain Lions and the Rest of the League at Wigan. Also in the Rest's ranks was scrum-half Gerry Helme hoping to prove a point to the selectors who had left him out of the tour. A crowd of 25,000 contributed £1,552 to the Lord Derby Memorial Fund as the Lions beat the Rest 23-16 with Bevan and his opposite number Tom Danby each scoring twice. Danby had scored a record 34 tries on tour.

On 7 October Warrington played host to Carcassonne, who two days earlier had gone down 22-24 to St Helens on their short tour. Fifteen thousand turned up at Wilderspool, hoping to see the French champions give the Wire a better run for their money than any previous visitors to the stadium that season. Unfortunately the French were severely denuded by injuries and unavailability and were given a good hiding by 46-3. The game was entertaining enough - how could it be anything else with characters about like Bevan and Puig-Aubert, the Carcassonne full-back, as eccentric and enigmatic as Bev himself? It was Puig who scored the sole Carcassonne try after selling Albert Johnson one of the most extravagant dummies ever seen on the ground although Albert had his revenge with a hat-trick. Ally Naughton also bagged three tries. Brian was partnered for the first time by Jock McAvoy, recently signed from Workington Town. The debutant did not strike Jack Steel as match-fit but he did add that "he was given a hard task in partnering the most unorthodox player in rugby league". Steel reported that "the crowd were constantly rooting for a Bevan try and they got their reward, when he scrambled over after a thrilling race."

Bevan had been engaged in a battle of his own with Carcassonne's left-winger Jean Lassegue, described as "a neat winger who frequently hopped off his left foot, went inside and tried to find a way ahead", reminiscent of himself, really. Lassegue had been a rugby union international, capped nine times by France, who had only recently turned to league. He rejoiced in the nickname "The French Buffalo", bestowed on him by British union enthusiasts.

The *Examiner* reported that, "the care-free nature of the Frenchmen and something of their temperament entered into their play. They chattered volubly throughout the match, they gesticulated excitedly when the ruling of the referee went against them and one player did something approaching a flying-trapeze act during a play-the-ball incident, so keen was he to deprive Warrington of possession! They were permitted to bring on a substitute when their left-winger was injured... and for a period in the second half they even had 14 players on the

7 October, 1950. Determination etched in his face, Bev races with the Carcassonne winger Jean Lassegue. Warrington beat the French champions 46-3.

28 October, 1950. More than 26,000 Wilderspool fans were on tenterhooks as Bev juggled with a pass from Ron Fisher, being tackled at right by two St Helens men. Ike Fishwick supports Bev, while Bill Derbyshire and Bob Ryan can be seen in the distance.

field before the incident was noticed and one 'retired'. So the spectators got plenty for their money apart from the actual play."

The contrast between the Carcassonne game and Warrington's next fixture could hardly have been more stark. On Tuesday, 10 October 14,804 excited fans poured into Watersheddings for a 5.00pm kick-off to see Oldham take on the Wire in the semi-final of the Lancashire Cup. Warrington knew it would be hard for they had only just scraped home 8-7 there in the first away fixture of the season. The conditions were dreadful, rain falling continuously and the ball a soggy, slippery, barely catchable piece of leather. It was clear that scoring chances would be few and far between.

A penalty goal from Harold Palin put Warrington ahead but after 28 minutes Jimmy Featherstone was sent off by referee George Phillips, leaving a five-man pack to slug it out for 52 minutes with an uncompromising set of Roughyed forwards. Two-nil was hardly a defensible score but Warrington held it until fifteen minutes into the second half and then Bevan won the game. Bath made a trademark burst down the field, threw the ball wide to the right allowing Helme, Fishwick and Ryder to get the ball out to Bev. A feint threw the defence, Bev changed pace and flew over at the flag and that was that. He had already saved the game just after the interval when he intercepted and knocked down a scoring pass from Billy Mitchell to Alan Davies, who had a huge overlap.

Stuffed by Wigan - again

The 5-0 victory was Warrington's 12th of the season. They had not been beaten in any competitive fixture and only Oldham had really given them a game, albeit twice. Consequently a trip to Dewsbury on 14 October was not viewed with particular trepidation. Bevan had scored in his last nine games, including against Carcassonne and his appearance for the Rest. At Crown Flatt his run came to an end and it was also unlucky 13 for the Wire who went down 7-15. The following two Saturdays brought home victories over Salford (17-2) and St. Helens (19-2), the latter before a crowd of more than 26,000.

Saturday, 4 November was a day of reckoning. It was Lancashire Cup Final day. As usual Wigan had qualified and Warrington faced the ultimate test, yet again. Still, they had beaten them in the Wardonia Cup and on the day that Warrington had suffered their only defeat so far at Dewsbury, Wigan had also gone down for the only time, but even more surprisingly at Rochdale. They were only human and even more crucially, the Wire fans mused, they had recently sold their guiding light, Joe Egan, to Leigh for a world record £5,000. On paper, too, the Wigan team for the final did not look as strong as usual. That was, however, what Huddersfield thought back in May when Wigan, minus no fewer than eight Australasian tourists, murdered them 20-2 at Maine Road to win the Championship. If all else failed, surely the law of averages meant that it was Warrington's turn to win.

Warrington were at full strength for the final. Bevan was in top form - level with Lionel Cooper on 25 tries at the top of the scoring list, nine ahead of Brian Nordgren. A Lancashire Cup record crowd of 42,541 at Swinton expected one

Lancashire Cup final at Swinton, 1950. Bev appears to be going nowhere
as he is confronted by Wigan's Ken Gee and George Roughley.

hell of a game. There was only one team in it and it was not Warrington. Wigan
were simply magnificent. By half-time the game was over at 15-2 to Cec
Mountford's men. Warrington were totally overwhelmed in the end 28-5. Brian
Bevan was the best Wire on the field, probably the only man whose reputation
was left intact. His encounter with Brian Nordgren saw him winning plaudits for
tackling the big New Zealander well in the first half. As the game wore on,
however, Nordgren began to wear him down and he scored two tries himself and
gave another to centre George Roughley, a Warringtonian who was ironically the
man-of-the-match, when he took Bev's tackle before slipping a scoring pass to his
partner. Jack Cunliffe, Johnny Alty and Ted Slevin also touched down while Ken
Gee booted five conversions. All Warrington could produce was a penalty by
Harold Palin and a last-gasp try by Ally Naughton. A few minutes before
Naughton scored, Bev produced a real thrill when he got away in his own half,
kicked past full-back Cunliffe, regathered the ball and hared unchallenged for the
posts. Inexplicably in the act of touching down he somehow managed to hit the
ball with his knee into the crowd. Mortified, he probably never felt the pats on the
back the Wigan players gave him after his great effort.

No doubt many of the Warrington fans, players and officials were past caring
by that stage. There must be some way of beating Wigan when it counted, if only
someone would tell them what it was.

It was back to normal for the remainder of November - easy victories over
Belle Vue Rangers and Barrow (home and away) and seven more tries for Bevan.
The encounter with Belle Vue Rangers at Wilderspool on 11 November yielded a
28-12 victory with Bevan contributing two tries. His second touchdown carried
him past Jack Fish's club record of 215 career tries. Unfortunately no one knew
about it at the time and the remarkable feat went unrecorded. Fish had taken 321

games and almost thirteen years - 1898 to 1911 - to amass his 215 tries. Bevan had eclipsed his record in 184 games.

In the game at Barrow, which was won 26-10, Bevan put on one of his master-classes with another superb hat-trick. The *Warrington Guardian* reported that: "Very few left before the finish because they had been treated to some sparkling rugby and the word 'Bevan' was on everybody's lips. Brian usually does well on this pitch. This time he surpassed himself and was the talk of the Furness district not for that afternoon but for years to come. The Great Bev earned his title quite a while ago and I heard one fellow say if Joe Egan was worth £5,000 the Warrington winger might be exchanged for a ship in Barrow docks. The Bevan tries had been well worth the admission money alone... Then came a Brian Bevan special and it defied all the textbooks on any kind of rugby. He left Toohey standing in a touchline sprint and when everyone of the 12,000 onlookers expected him to kick over Lloyd-Davies' head, he swerved inside, ran obliquely across the field catching Jackson and Lewthwaite on the wrong leg. He finished on the right hand side of the posts. Some try, some player, some applause. It was remarked that to give an indication of the volume of cheering, people near the ground thought Barrow were winning!"

On 2 December, Warrington travelled to Cumberland and met with their second league defeat of the season when they went down to Workington Town 12-8. Town were pressing Warrington and Wigan in the top four and rugby league was for the first time seeing a club from the far north challenging the established order. The following week Warrington atoned by pipping another of the top-four contenders Leeds 6-5 at Headingley. Brian Bevan and Harry Bath were both missing from that encounter because they were engaged on Other Nationalities duty against France at Bordeaux. Leeds were harder hit than Warrington, having to supply Cook, Bartlett, McMaster, Clues and Verrenkamp (as reserve) for the Others. Harry Bath was pressed into service as hooker in the absence of yet another Leeds man, the injured Ken Kearney.

Fracas in France

France gave a polished display to win 16-3 before a crowd of 28,000 with Puig-Aubert at his tantalising best in the loose play and on top kicking form with five goals. The French tackling was remarkable, faltering only once, three minutes into the second half, when Cec Mountford got Bevan away for the winger to leave everyone in his wake as he cut through on his own for a 50-yard try. Yet, it was a game Bevan and his colleagues would have cause to remember for, despite some wonderful rugby, there were some unsavoury incidents.

Arthur Clues and Edouard Ponsinet were two of the finest second-row forwards the game has seen but in this game they sowed the seeds to reap a later whirlwind. Ponsinet was a pretty good boxer but Clues thought he had killed him at one stage. Ponsinet drove the ball up and Clues aimed to take him high. The Frenchman ducked and received a dreadful blow. Clues claimed later that the force of it moved Ponsinet's scalp up one and a half inches. One of the Other Nats players actually vomited at the sight of the injury, while Dave Valentine remarked that he hoped Clues had killed the bugger because of the stick that

Ponsinet had been dishing out. Ponsinet was very badly hurt and he was not going to forget it in a hurry, as future games with the Other Nationalities would prove.

Back in the weekly routine of league football, Warrington had launched themselves on another long unbeaten run. January 1951 saw Bevan in superlative form - three tries against Oldham (won 34-2), four at York (27-12), one against Rochdale (30-20) and another four at Hull KR (26-15). The *Examiner* had plenty to report. On the Oldham game it said: "Bevan's tries were of such vintage that they deserve a paragraph to themselves. I defy anybody to guess just how fast he was running in scoring the first when he finished by hurling himself several yards to get in at the corner... His second try was the result of quick thinking and equally quick action... an inside pass to Bevan did not look particularly dangerous for there were several Oldham players apparently barring his path but an electrifying acceleration took him right through the small gap and a swerve left Ratchford helpless and the winger was round the posts before a nonplussed defence knew anything about it... Then came perhaps the most sensational try of the three. Bevan was served ten yards from his own line. Again his amazing pace took him past two or three opponents and near half-way he kicked over the full-back's head. The ball stuck in a mud patch several yards from the line but so much had Bevan in hand that he was able to slacken speed, pick up again and go on with his nearest opponent some distance away. The crowd cheered wildly."

At York it was reported that "it was obvious from the unstinted applause that people hadn't seen the like of 'The Great Bev' for quite a while. Each time he got the ball the crowd rose to him... when he walked back to his place after slicing open the York defence almost as easily as a knife cutting through one of the city's celebrated sweetmeats, he received an ovation equal to any that has deafened his ears at Wilderspool."

Local reporter Phil Clark trekked to Craven Park, Hull and wrote: "On the restart the crowd were given the chance of seeing Brian Bevan at his best. If Hull KR had a winger possessing the same speed and opportunism as the great Australian, they must certainly have won. His second try was the work of a genius. Taking a pass between the half-way line and the Hull '25', he beat two men and veered over to the left. As he made for the posts, the defenders swept across the field and made a barrier stretching from the posts to the right-hand corner flag where any normal winger would have raced. But not Bevan. He went like a greyhound for the left-hand corner, and touched down before the astounded Hull players could recover. Not a hand had been laid on him and there was not a defender within 20 yards as he touched down."

Chasing Rozzy

By the end of January Bev had scored 48 tries in only 27 games and was way ahead of the other leading try-scorers. His aspirations towards Rosenfeld's 80 tries mark were still tenable. The first three weeks of February, however, proved unfruitful. On 3 February, the Wire struggled to win 7-2 at Belle Vue Rangers, Bev finished try-less and picked up an injury which kept him out of the next two games. They were the start of Warrington's attempt to retain the Challenge Cup, a two-legged first round tie against Hull. Both games were won, Warrington going through on aggregate by 30-12.

Bevan was back on 24 February for a crucial home game against Leeds. It was one of the most exciting matches of the season. Warrington triumphed 24-16 in the end but it was a close thing. Owen Bevan scored a magnificent try after a diagonal run of 35 yards in which he beat several defenders and bluffed several more by hinting that he was going to pass to the wing before hurling himself 15 feet to touch down. Not to be outdone, brother Brian claimed his 10th hat-trick of the season and flagged up his 50th try with his second touchdown. The *Warrington Guardian* reported: "The biggest share in the crowd-pleasing act came from Brian Bevan who even made the great Jim Brough, once England's full-back under two codes, gasp more than once as he took notes in the press seats. I heard the ex-Leeds captain ruminate about the best number twos and number fives he had faced or had on his side and I should imagine that he had never experienced one of the same standard as The Great Bev. They had been saying at Leeds that Bruce Ryan, Brian's opposite number on Saturday, had increased pace and style. He may have done but Ryan's glimpse of his fellow countryman was even more fuzzy than that of the nearby touchline witnesses."

S. H. Yates, of *The Liverpool Echo*, was possibly even more impressed, writing: "If Bevan had not recovered from injury in time to resume in this Wilderspool game, I am inclined to the belief that Warrington would not now be boasting an unbeaten home record. No superlatives can give Bevan a greater share of credit than he deserves. Three times he scored, despite an embarrassing show of regard for his prowess. I say quite boldly that Warrington have not another player on their register who could have done for them what Bevan did, and I doubt if there is a player in the league who could have done so either. The Australian is the modern miracle winger. Whether he is the best ever it is difficult to say. All I can put on record is that I have never seen his superior, and Alf Ellaby never had a greater admirer than myself."

Warrington entertained Featherstone Rovers on 3 March in the second round of the Challenge Cup. More than 16,000 turned up despite the expectancy that the tie would be something of a stroll for Warrington. They were mistaken. Wet weather had reduced the pitch to a mire despite the liberal sanding the groundstaff had applied and Rovers did not adhere to the script. Playing on top of the Wire backs - off-side throughout the entire match, according to Wire fans - the Rovers forwards dominated proceedings and with veteran full-back Freddie Miller landing three goals to Bath's two they led 6-4. Warrington were rattled and a couple of minutes into the second half they were in even greater trouble when Rovers' winger Blackburn flew for the line for what may well have been a winning try. He was a couple of yards from touching down when Bev came from nowhere to make one of the most sensational and vital tackles of his life. Having saved the game, Bevan then went into overdrive to win the game with a stunning trio of tries as the Wire pulled away to win by a flattering score of 18-6.

Around this time the supporters of the club were being given a good deal to think about. Secretary-manager Chris Brockbank decided that he was going to resign from office at the end of the season in order to take a boarding house in Blackpool. He would be a big loss to the club and the game. There was also a continuing debate about the demotion of Harold Palin from the first team following the debacle in the Lancashire Cup Final. Harold was only getting the odd game at prop, while Owen Bevan was given an extended run at number 13. Most shocking though was the announcement in early March that Harry Bath, nearing the end of his contract, was to return to Australia on 6 June and not come back. It did not stop there, either - Brian Bevan was also said to be going back to Sydney permanently. No doubt prayers were being recited in many a local household.

On Wednesday, 7 March, Warrington were due to play Wigan at Central Park in a rearranged league fixture, the original having been snowed off on 30 December. After heavy rain in the morning Wigan unilaterally called the game off, claiming the ground was waterlogged. Chris Brockbank and director Fred Davies were informed and travelled to Wigan to see for themselves the state of the pitch and were not convinced that the game should have been called off. The suspicion, of course, was that Wigan realised that a midweek fixture on an awful wet day would attract a relatively poor crowd. Better to postpone it, and play it later in the hope of a bumper pay day. Warrington were not amused, protested to the RFL and the upshot was a £100 fine for Wigan.

The postponement did have one beneficial effect. Wigan were one point ahead of Warrington at the top of the league at that juncture but had no fixture on 10 March when Warrington beat Liverpool Stanley at Wilderspool. The victory took Wire above Wigan in what was to become a cat-and-mouse contest for the leadership in the closing weeks of the season.

There was more good news later that week. In 'Talking Sport' in the *Warrington Guardian* it was reported that "the brief statement that Brian Bevan had decided not to return to Australia at the end of the season makes good reading. I am sure that Bevan would have suffered financially and so would the club for that matter. It is no idle talk to suggest that people visit rugby league grounds to see The Great Bev".

On 17 March, Warrington visited The Willows for a third round Challenge Cup-tie and edged out Salford 8-4 in wretched conditions which failed to deter a crowd of more than 26,000. Tries from Gerry Helme and Ike Fishwick and a Harry Bath goal did the trick. The draw for the semi-finals, scheduled for 7 April, threw up Wire's worst nightmare - Wigan, yet again. Wigan had even more of a scrape than Warrington had at Salford. They had beaten Huddersfield 2-0, courtesy of a Ken Gee penalty, with 34,981 in attendance at Central Park. Panic set in at the RFL headquarters at Chapeltown Road, for there was no rugby league ground in Lancashire big enough to house the likely crowd. Odsal Stadium would have been large enough, of course, and some people thought the game should be taken there despite the fact that it was in Yorkshire. The other semi-final, Leeds versus Barrow, was assigned to Odsal, which did not go down well with Barrow, but was highly popular with the Loiners. The RFL approached Liverpool FC with a view to hiring Anfield until it was pointed out that 7 April was Grand National Day at Aintree. It was back to plan A and, in the end, Swinton's Station Road was guaranteed a full house.

Warrington had to negotiate an astounding five league matches between the Challenge Cup quarter-final and semi-final. It was not plain sailing by any means although Brian Bevan continued to pass personal landmarks. Against Widnes on Good Friday his two tries went a long way to an 11-5 victory in his 200th appearance for Warrington, but the following day, a 3-5 defeat at St Helens put their position at the top of the table in jeopardy. Another defeat at Leigh on Easter Monday was only rendered bearable when Wigan went down surprisingly the same afternoon at Salford. The next two matches brought an element of redemption. Bev scored both tries in a 10-0 home win over Bradford Northern on 28 March, his second breaking his own club record of 57 tries established in 1947-48. On 2 April he registered his 250th try for the Wire in a narrow victory over Whitehaven at Wilderspool.

Other Nationalities in Wales

On top of having to play in five league games in 10 days, Bevan had another appointment to keep down in Swansea on 31 March. Other Nationalities met Wales in an absolutely wonderful international which finally finished 27-21 in favour of the Others. Bevan was given a hard time by the Welsh winger Terry Cook, who scored two tries to Brian's one. Cook bundled Bev into the ground or into touch a dozen times as the Australian tried to start his bamboozling runs, but commentators attributed that to the poor timing of centre Tony Paskins's passing to Bev. When the Australian did finally get a real chance he amazed the crowd. A reporter described his try: "It was like unleashing a greyhound from a trap, 30 yards covered as it seemed in a few bounding strides, and then the final plunge for the corner effected with an impetus that swept him past even as sturdy and unflinching a defender as Hunslet's Jack Evans."

Challenge Cup semi-final day, 7 April, arrived. Station Road, Swinton was bursting at the seams with a ground record crowd of 44,355 inside. Warrington were the Cup holders, they had vied with Wigan for top spot throughout the season yet Wigan were clear favourites. They had the "Indian sign" on Warrington and some of the Wire followers were clearly faltering in their devotion, for 4,000 unsold tickets were passed on to Wigan who soon shifted them. Warrington had spent the week preparing at Cleveleys, a coastal resort halfway between Blackpool and Fleetwood, however, and were desperate to hang on to the Cup.

The pitch was muddy and a sleet storm shortly before kick-off did not improve matters. The first 20 minutes were torrid as the teams battled each other and the conditions with a ferocity which beggared belief. Most critics wondered how referee Albert Dobson failed to send anyone off. 'Criticus' remarked that "Harry Bath finished with a black eye the like of which I have never seen". Both sides were guilty of overstepping the mark but thankfully the remaining sixty minutes were restricted to gripping football rather than fisticuffs.

Bevan was really only allowed one chance early in the game but was well tackled by Wigan full-back Jack Cunliffe. Warrington did, however, take the lead on 34 minutes when Harry Bath banged over a splendid penalty goal. With Gerry Helme dictating play as only he could and Ike Fishwick outhooking George Curran 32-15, the Warrington forwards played heroically to deny Wigan any glimmer of a try. With six minutes to go Warrington appeared to have laid the

Wigan bogey. At that point disaster struck. Ron Ryder tried to kick to touch when holding the ball seemed a better option. The ball stuck in a mud patch, allowing Wigan possession. 'Knowsley', writing in *Rugby League Review*, described what followed: "There was not a lot of danger apparent when Mountford took Ryder's kick, raced towards touch, and brought Cunliffe into play. Cunliffe was something like 45 yards from the line and between him and his goal were three Warrington players. Many times during the match there had been more menacing situations and nothing had come of them. Fortune favours the brave. Cunliffe raced on, sold a dummy, whose effectiveness must have surprised himself. Brian Bevan, who had put Nordgren out of the attacking picture with tackles that bore the stamp of a master craftsman, and had any amount of speed to spare when compared with Cunliffe, stood flat-footed as Cunliffe sped past. It seemed that he could have put the Wigan man out of play with no great effort. Cunliffe cashed in on the split second hesitation, crowded on all the pace of which he was capable, and down the touch he went... When it seemed he might score himself Frodsham flung himself at him and prevented him from going over. With only a sidelong glance Cunliffe pitched the ball sideways and up, over his shoulder, and there was Nordgren racing up as fast as he could go. He took the ball and carried Bevan with him to touch down for the try that sent all Warrington hopes of a second Wembley in succession crashing to earth. Nordgren, even with the full weight of his opponent's body on top of him, smote the ground with both hands in his expression of glee. The whole Wigan team did a war dance of joy."

Ken Gee's conversion failed but Wigan led 3-2. Warrington stormed back, but unavailingly. Harry Bath made two abortive attempts to drop a goal and it was all over. Wigan had short-circuited the Wire yet again.

On the Wednesday following the semi-final, Brian Bevan was on duty for Other Nationalities against England at Central Park. Seven of the England team were Wigan players and the Others stand-off and captain was another Wiganer in Cec Mountford. They must have felt at home but it was Bev who brought the stands and terraces to rounds of acclamation. By half-time England were 20-2 down and ended up being walloped 35-10. Bev grabbed a hat-trick, the highlight being a 100-yard scoring dash after intercepting a pass from Ken Dean to Jack Cunliffe. Bryn James wrote: "Bevan had a carefree day running and side-stepping in faultless style. His second try was the result of cleverly selling the dummy. Much of his success was due to the brilliance of Trevor Allan, who made dozens of openings for the Warrington flyer and produced the best display of cover defence I have seen from him."

One of the big attractions for the Wigan crowd of almost 17,000 was the appearance of Trevor Allan in the right-centre spot for Other Nationalities. Allan, former captain of the Australian rugby union Wallabies, had cost Leigh a world-record equalling £5,000 a few months earlier. The Australian writer Mike Colman recounted an anecdote of this match almost half a century later: "Allan had tackled his opposing winger and the ball had popped up into Bevan's hands. The freakish winger then set off on the type of darting, weaving run for which he was famous, heading one way and then another on a bewildering run to the try-line. Allan set off to give support. He had gone a few paces before he felt a hand on his arm and heard the voice of team-mate Arthur Clues. 'Stay where you are, mate,' Clues said. 'He'll be back in a minute'."

Just seven days after the heart-breaking semi-final defeat, Warrington met Wigan in a league fixture at Wilderspool. They extracted a modicum of revenge with a 12-2 success before a happy crowd of more than 26,000. Bev and Albert Johnson claimed the Wire tries. Bev's try, his 60th and last for Warrington that season, saw him turn the tables on Jackie Cunliffe but, in truth, it would have been small consolation. Amazingly, the two teams met for a third time within nine days the following Monday, 16 April, before a Central Park attendance of 38,000. To say Warrington under performed would be kind. A 19-2 drubbing reinforced Wigan's superiority complex as the Wire pack, Bath and Owen Bevan excepted, caved in alarmingly. All the Wire had to show was an improbable drop goal from prop Jimmy Featherstone.

The lure of the encounters between Warrington and Wigan, however, seemed almost limitless. In the four competitive fixtures between the two that season the aggregate attendance exceeded 150,000. As the season drew to its climax it seemed that Wigan must finish on top of the league, especially when a tired, battered and under strength - Brian and several regulars were missing - Wire team went down 8-2 at Whitehaven two days after the humiliation at Central Park. With only two games remaining, Wigan were three points clear of second-placed Warrington. It seemed that Warrington had lost whatever chance they had of finishing top of the table and of wresting the Lancashire League title from their arch-rivals.

Warrington's last two games were tricky propositions at Salford on 21 April and Swinton on 23 April, while Wigan were faced with a home fixture against third-placed Workington Town and an away game at Oldham on the same dates. When Warrington sent a side containing 10 reserves to Weaste, it seemed that the management had given up on top spot and the county title. There was general amazement throughout the game when the result came through. The reserves had beaten Salford 19-0 and, to add to the conundrum, Workington had turned Wigan over 14-9, thereby dashing the cherry and whites' Lancashire League aspirations for a week at least.

Monday, 23 April thus became crunch day. Workington Town had already played their final league fixture. They were assured of at least third place but a Warrington defeat or draw at Swinton would present Town with the Lancashire League. A Wire victory would give them the title on superior scoring average. To add spice to the proceedings, a point for Wigan at Watersheddings would be enough to give them the league leadership. Again the Warrington management came up with a surprise. They sent another reserve team to Swinton, adding a little strength with Ally Naughton at centre and sticking Gerry Helme on the left wing. Improbably, the gamble paid off again as the no-hopers won 20-14. Harold Palin, playing at open-side prop, made his last appearance for Warrington and signed off in a blaze of glory and with a haul of four goals. Wigan meanwhile had gambled too, sending a weakened team to Oldham only to go down 2-16. Miraculously, Warrington had taken the county title and pipped Wigan for the Rugby League top spot by a solitary point.

Finishing top gave Warrington a home game against neighbouring Leigh in the Championship semi-final on 28 April, while Wigan played hosts to Workington Town. Brian Bevan had missed the last three league games but was back for the clash with Leigh. It was clear that one of Leigh's main strategies was to bottle up Bev and, despite his trickery, they largely succeeded. Wherever he went he found a posse of tacklers. Concentrating on the Australian, however, resulted in Jackson scoring after using him as a decoy and, with Ike Fishwick beating Walt Tabern 28-12 in the scrums, Warrington ran out winners 15-9. Their opponents in the final turned out to be Workington who again surprised Wigan with a superb 8-5 success at Central Park. Wigan found ample consolation the following Saturday, 5 May, when they beat Barrow 10-0 at Wembley to lift the Challenge Cup.

April 1951 had seen Brian Bevan's hopes of passing Albert Rosenfeld's try-scoring record evaporate. Warrington had played eight games in April and Brian had missed three of them. His tally for the month had been two tries, plus three in the international at Wigan. By the season's close his total of tries was 68, nine more than second top-scorer Lionel Cooper. Brian Nordgren had finished with 42 while the Workington pair of Eppie Gibson and George Wilson had claimed 41 and 40 respectively. Bevan's achievement was, however, a magnificent one. He had come closer to Rosenfeld's 80-try record than any other player, apart from Rozzy himself who had scored 78 tries in 1911-12. Only Johnny Ring (63 tries in 1925-26), Eric Harris (63 in 1935-36) and Lionel Cooper (60 in 1948-49) had previously hit the 60 mark.

The Championship Final took place at Maine Road on 12 May 1951. The crowd of 61,618 was the biggest Workington Town had ever played before. Gus Risman had moulded Town into an honours-challenging club within only six years of its birth and if Warrington were favourites, according to the bookies, the romantics and neutrals were definitely rooting for Town.

Warrington lacked Ron Ryder, who had missed most of the second half of the Leigh game with a ruptured shoulder muscle. So Bill Jackson came in to partner Bevan. The game was a humdinger. Harry Sunderland wrote in *The Sunday Dispatch*: "Yesterday's game turned out to be a thrilling, spectacular final, and I saw more good tries scored in this one match than in any game for years. Some of them had all the best that is in combination play, and the gem of them all was the dextrous back pass flicked from Gerry Helme into Jackson's hands for Warrington's second try, when with Knowelden running wide to the left, Jackson came bursting through on the inside on Helme's right."

The game began disastrously for the Wire. Bill Derbyshire wrecked his shoulder in the opening exchanges and had to have a pain-killing injection at the interval, but heroically played the entire game. Worse still, Albert Johnson broke his left leg after only three minutes and was stretchered off to hospital. Ally Naughton pulled a thigh muscle and was nowhere near as effective as he might have been. Even so, Warrington played some marvellously entertaining rugby. They took the lead after 20 minutes when Austin Heathwood, withdrawn from loose-forward to take Johnson's place on the wing, scored a disputed try from a high kick. Then on 32 minutes Jackson scored a second try, goaled by Bath. Five minutes before the break, Town hit back when Risman linked up from a scrum to put Paskins over.

Warrington's half-time lead of 8-3 was testament to guts and good football, but if they were praying for a miracle their prayers were not heard. In the second half Workington exploited their numerical advantage brilliantly and within 25 minutes had built a lead of 23-8. A last piece of defiance, after some magical passing, put Heathwood in for his second try to make it 23-11, but five minutes from time Town had the final word when Wilson stepped inside Bevan to score his side's sixth try as Workington won by 26-11.

The press were unanimous in their praise for the high quality of the play. None tried to belittle the performance of the underdogs in taking the Championship to Cumberland for the first time. They all acknowledged that Town's victory was a huge fillip for the game at large and, after all, they could only beat the opposition which faced them. There was, however, universal sympathy for the depleted Warrington side which had played manfully under skipper Bryn Knowelden. They may have lost even with a full team for 80 minutes, but no one would ever know.

After the disappointment of Maine Road, Brian Bevan had one last game to play. On 19 May the RFL staged two fixtures as part of the Festival of Britain celebrations. In Llanelli, a Welsh XIII went down 16-29 to an Empire XIII while at Headingley, before a disappointing crowd of 15,000, Brian and his brother Owen figured in Australasia's 23-20 victory over Great Britain. Bev scored his 68th try of the season - a 75-yarder after snapping up a loose ball. Arthur Haddock, of *The Yorkshire Evening News*, declared: "He galloped round Jack Evans like an Olympic man".   By way of diversion he won an invitation 100 yards race before the start. His time of 10.8 seconds, in full rugby kit, kept him five feet ahead of Hunslet's Alan Snowden and Halifax's Brian Vierod, both very quick men. Owen Bevan, who was eliminated in the sprinting heats, had better luck in the goal-kicking contest, tying with Charlie Armitt of Swinton but losing on a shoot-out.

14 April, 1951. Wilderspool rocked as Bev made one of his great dashes
leaving Wigan's Ted Slevin for dead. Brian Nordgren and Jimmy
Featherstone join the chase on the right.
Wire met Wigan three times within 9 days in April 1951,
drawing an aggregate crowd of over 108,000.

Circa 1951, Ron Ryder works a scissors move with Bev against Workington
Town. Internationals Eppie Gibson and George Wilson are the Town defenders.

Season 1950-51

Warrington finished top of the League: P 36, W 30, L 6, For 738, Against 250.
Bevan scored 60 tries for Warrington, plus 8 for representative teams

Date	Opponent	Score	Bevan	Crowd	
19 Aug	**Hull KR**	55–3	3T	13,155	
21 Aug	Oldham	8– 7		12,327	
26 Aug	Bradford N	21–4		7,909	
30 Aug	**Workington T**	30–5	dnp	16,249	
2 Sep	Liverpool St	18–5	dnp	3,000	LC 1
9 Sep	**Swinton**	41–17	3T	15,917	
13 Sep	**Liverpool St**	73–0	3T	10,174	LC 1
16 Sep	Liverpool St	23–0	3T	677	
23 Sep	**York**	75–3	6T	12,217	
27 Sep	Leigh	28–14	1T	17,203	LC 2
30 Sep	Rochdale H	14–4	1T	7,484	
10 Oct	Oldham	5–0	1T	14,804	LC Semi
14 Oct	Dewsbury	7–15		9,704	
21 Oct	**Salford**	17–2	1T	18,332	
28 Oct	**St Helens**	19–2	1T	26,543	
4 Nov	Wigan	5–28		42,240	LC Final (at Swinton)
11 Nov	**Belle Vue R**	28–12	2T	12,118	
18 Nov	Barrow	26–10	3T	12,237	
25 Nov	**Barrow**	27–3	2T	12,722	
2 Dec	Workington T	8–12	1T	13,445	
9 Dec	Leeds	6–5	dnp	16,223	
23 Dec	**Dewsbury**	21–5	1T	12,234	
25 Dec	Widnes	22–4	1T	10,103	
26 Dec	**Leigh**	11–7		22,200	
6 Jan	**Oldham**	34–2	3T	8,651	
13 Jan	York	27–12	4T	7,850	
20 Jan	**Rochdale H**	30–2	1T	11,829	
27 Jan	Hull KR	26–15	4T	6,500	
3 Feb	Belle Vue R	7–2		6,903	
10 Feb	**Hull**	25–9	dnp	14,995	Ch Cup 1
17 Feb	Hull	5–3	dnp	8,000	Ch Cup 1
24 Feb	**Leeds**	24–16	3T	23,728	
3 Mar	**Featherstone R**	18–6	3T	16,006	Ch Cup 2
10 Mar	**Liverpool St**	33–8	2T	11,288	
17 Mar	Salford	8–4		26,327	Ch Cup 3
23 Mar	**Widnes**	11–5	2T	15,858	
24 Mar	St Helens	3–5	1T	18,743	
26 Mar	Leigh	5–12		7,969	
28 Mar	**Bradford N**	10–0	2T	11,671	
2 Apr	**Whitehaven**	14–8	1T	10,668	
7 Apr	Wigan	2–3		44,355	Ch Cup Semi (at Swinton)
14 Apr	**Wigan**	12–2	1T	26,459	
16 Apr	Wigan	2–19		38,000	
18 Apr	Whitehaven	2–8	dnp	7,403	
21 Apr	Salford	19–0	dnp	11,901	
23 Apr	Swinton	20–14	dnp	9,000	
28 Apr	**Leigh**	15–9		24,103	CH Semi
12 May	Workington T	11–26		61,618	CH Final (at Maine Rd)

Representative Matches:

Date	For	Opponent	Score	Bevan	Venue
4 Oct	The Rest	GB (Tourists)	16–23	2T	Wigan
10 Dec	Other Nats	France	3–16	1T	Bordeaux
31 Mar	Other Nats	Wales	27–21	1T	Swansea
11 Apr	Other Nats	England	35–10	3T	Wigan
19 May	Australasia	GB	23–20	1T	Leeds

10. 1951-52 'Dazzling swerve and twinkling feet'

At the close of the 1950-51 season Brian Bevan had enjoyed five highly successful seasons of English rugby league. Bevan was a household word in many sports-loving homes in the north of England. He was probably the most spectacular player in the game and he was already revered as a living legend in and around Warrington. Yet he must have been forcibly reminded just how perilous a rugby league career could be when Albert Johnson had been carted off with a broken leg in the recent Championship final at Maine Road. Albert never played again, his 12 year career with Warrington brought to a sickening end in a simple accident.

Albert, often referred to as 'Jock' or 'Massa', had been a tremendously popular figure at Wilderspool. His debonair, good looks brought him the admiration of female fans and his trickery on the left wing brought him 112 tries for the club, many of them memorably spectacular efforts, in 198 appearances. His sidestep was once measured at nine feet, possibly the widest the game has seen. Bevan's own sidestep was phenomenal enough but shallower and executed at breathtaking speed. There were, however, old Warringtonians who gave the palm for side-stepping to the pre-war winger Tommy 'Tubby' Thompson. Apparently Thompson, not a particularly fast mover, seemed to simply roll around opponents. Partnered by the great Billy Dingsdale, Thompson hardly ever failed to score if given the ball with a solitary man to beat. In the game against Australia in 1929, Tommy scored all Warrington's points (4 goals, 3 tries) in a famous 17-8 victory.

Albert Johnson's misfortune was a salutary reminder that disaster could be just a tackle or fall away. In Brian Bevan's early career in England there were other even more grisly accidents in rugby league. No fewer than four professional players died as a result of playing accidents between 1946 and 1953. Brian found himself playing in commemorative testimonial matches for the victims' dependants on more than one occasion. Thankfully this cluster of fatalities has no real parallels in the history of the game.

Rugby League Review had published its list of stars of the 1950-51 season as usual. Bev was included in the five alongside Jack Cunliffe and Cec Mountford of Wigan, Billy Ivison of Workington and Dickie Williams of Leeds. Sharing the most improved player of the season award with Workington's teenage England cap Eppie Gibson was Warrington's reserve winger Alf Humphreys, who had filled in with great distinction for both Bev and Albert Johnson when required. Humphreys, formerly with Pemberton Rovers and Halifax, had scored some belting tries in 1950-51 but never made the mark some critics expected of him.

On 1 June, 1951 Leslie Hockenhull was promoted from Warrington's assistant secretary to secretary in place of the departed Chris Brockbank, an appointment which came as no great surprise at Wilderspool. Four days later, however, a storm broke over Warrington when Wigan alleged that the Wire had made an illegal approach to their star stand-off, Cec Mountford. Warrington wanted Mountford to be their player-coach. Wigan wanted to retain him because he still had a year to run on his contract and, anyway, where would they find another 'Blackball Bullet', as Mountford was known? The rivalry between the two clubs was intense enough on the pitch and this dispute threatened to turn off-the-field relations extremely sour. The Warrington management was determined to wrest Wigan's top dogs' rating from them. What better way than acquiring the inspirational Mountford, a colleague of Brian Bevan in the Other Nationalities team? New Zealander Mountford was regarded as the fastest stand-off in the game, a fabulous attacking player, who could inject that extra zip into the Warrington back-line. Bevan must have relished the thought of even more running chances with a talent like Mountford in the middle.

On 14 June Mountford announced his retirement as a player in order to take up the Warrington offer of an appointment as team-manager. Warrington were reported to have offered the Kiwi a 10-year contract at £1,000 per annum, an astronomical figure, which provoked Wigan coach Jim Sullivan to remark that he "would have walked to Warrington had he known that such a lucrative and secure position was open". Sullivan was said to be on £11 a week at this time.

On 17 June, the RFL decided that Warrington were not guilty of infringing the by-laws by appointing Mountford as team-manager, but did not refer to the problem of the earlier approach to him as a player. It was all a bit iffy, especially when Wigan refused to accept Mountford's cheque for repayment of a year's income from his contract or to cancel his player registration.

The season began with the annual Wardonia Cup game with Wigan at Central Park on 11 August, not exactly the start to dampen the dispute. Wigan set their stall out by selecting Mountford to play for them despite his managerial position at Wilderspool. A crowd of 16,000 had plenty to talk about before the game, the politics of the situation for a change taking precedence over the actual match. In the event, Mountford did not appear and Wigan won 23-10 without him. Brian Bevan only had one running chance and was upstaged by brother Owen, who scored a splendid try from the left wing, a position he filled for the first four months of the season.

The 1951-52 season promised to be an interesting one. Apart from Warrington's intent to become the game's premier club, there was the exciting prospect of the second post-war Kiwi touring team under Morrie Robertson and there were newcomers to the Northern Rugby League Championship in Doncaster and Cardiff, the latter having signed Wire hooker Bill Gore, while Liverpool Stanley had grandiosely rechristened themselves Liverpool City.

Warrington began the season well enough with an excellent 13-9 victory at Huddersfield on 18 August. A 19-12 home victory over a spirited Hunslet followed with Bevan bringing the house down with two gloriously exciting tries. There was a price to pay for the victory, however, as Eric Frodsham broke his collar-bone and was out of action until Christmas. An extravaganza of open football against Leeds at Wilderspool brought a 28-21 victory and three games had been won within a week, placing Warrington at the top of the league. If hopes had been raised they were soon to be dashed. Bev picked up two tries from kicks at Salford in another riot of scoring but this time Warrington were on the wrong end of a 19-28 scoreline.

The Lancashire Cup arrived, presenting Warrington with an early opportunity to gain revenge on Champions Workington Town. The first leg at Wilderspool, however, was a disaster as Town returned to Cumberland with a 16-6 success. Bevan missed the second leg two days later when Workington gave a strange looking Wire team a 20-3 pasting. Injuries were certainly a problem - Bev, Frodsham, Ryder and Naughton were all incapacitated and the pack was struggling with former Liverpool prop Gilbert Wright and Joe Whittaker, a local who had played with Walker's Brewery ARL, still finding their feet. Harry Bath, who had decided not to sign for an Australian club but was still abroad, was being sorely missed. Meanwhile on 5 September the charismatic, indomitable Harold Palin severed his association with the club who transferred him to Halifax for £500. Les Jones came out of retirement and was allowed to join Liverpool City on a free transfer. Things were in a state of flux as the team struggled to gel.

Waltzing Matilda Try

Although Warrington were stuttering, Brian Bevan was about to enter a period in which he would score in eight consecutive matches. As a young fan, Mike Rowan summed up this rather fallow period with feeling: "No matter what happened elsewhere we still had Bev. The 'Old Man' gave you excitement, thrills and had us spellbound. It mattered little, whether man or boy, girl or woman, was in attendance. He created the same stir. Instinct sensed something was imminent. Bodies jumped up and down, every action was followed with bated breath. We lived the moments with him. Our emotions were interwoven with every one of his fleeting strides. He gave us pride. There was nobody remotely like him."

On 8 September Warrington beat Wakefield Trinity 26-6. Bev had hardly any ball at all but in the last minute he finally found space after Ally Naughton slipped him a pass on the Wire '25'. He was away like a bolt from the blue. Two Trinitarians tried to shove him into touch but only connected with thin air. Full-back Ernie Luckman actually stopped Bev but failed to complete the tackle, allowing him to break free and move straight into top gear. The crowd went wild as he touched down. Somewhere in the run he had side-stepped the referee.

A week later, Warrington were back in Cumberland and victims of another defeat, 13-18, by Workington. Bev scored twice, the second an absolute master-piece. Jack Steel was so enraptured that he drew a plan of the effort for the *Warrington Guardian* and christened it "The *Waltzing Matilda* Try". Warrington had been 13 points in arrears and had to play the last half-hour without Naughton. An amazing rally almost brought an astounding victory. Steel described Bevan's try thus:

"The Town's backs passed well enough to suggest a score but when Eppie Gibson went down to a tackle he attempted to pass to 'Happy' Wilson waiting near the touchline. Brian not only accepted the pass but shot between centre and winger at a terrific rate which surprised the Workington cover defence. Billy Ivison, always on the alert for any eventuality, came across in a despairing effort to cut off the Australian but all he saw was a flash of primrose and blue.

Risman, ten yards from touch, awaited the next Bevan move. Would he continue along the side-line or turn inside? Bevan chose the latter course but

Risman's right hand was not long enough to grab the winger's jersey ... And yet another blue and white jerseyed player positioned himself between foe and line. It was Australian Johnny Mudge, who had raced back to close the gap between his captain and Bevan. Split-second thinking and Bevan had Mudge moving the wrong way and, when the forward attempted to retrieve himself, off Bevan went on the other leg and only an earthquake could stop him. To complete the dance which he had led the defence Bevan put the ball down, turned completely round, faced the dejected defenders and walked calmly back to his place."

Steel declared that "The *Waltzing Matilda* Try" "left onlookers breathless for several seconds and then the roar of applause almost awoke the beloved patron saint John Peel from his resting place."

Another couple of tries followed as Swinton were despatched 26-17 at Wilderspool but on 29 September, before the best crowd of the season so far - 22,546 - Warrington went down 13-19 to St Helens. It was the first time the Wire had lost a home league match since Easter 1950. The Bevan boys had a good time, however. Owen scored a try and two goals and Brian's two tries had the crowd in raptures. Jack Steel wrote: "We witnessed a try which only Brian Bevan could score. Warrington supporters were tickled to death by Brian's first-half try when he outpaced McCormick and left Stott appearing like a well-known pre-war petrol advertisement caricature. His second effort was really worth double winning money. Off he went on his 70-yard dash to the line, kicking accurately as he was in danger of being hemmed in, and don't those kicks appear to bounce advantageously? Brian collected the ball at Powderhall speed and the rest was easy."

Bevan scored superb tries in each of the next three games in October but all ended in Wire defeats. At Oldham on 6 October they went down 12-20. Bob Ryan missed this game because he was on duty in the first Kiwi test at Odsal but his replacement was Harry Bath, who had finally returned to England. The New Zealanders came to Wilderspool the following Saturday and won a splendid match 19-13, their first victory over Warrington after losses in 1907, 1926 and 1947. Ike Proctor, a Maori signed from Leeds, played his first game for Warrington against his compatriots, as centre to Bevan. The next match saw almost 22,000 pack into Wilderspool on 20 October for another wonderfully contested encounter with Wigan. Warrington almost pulled off a surprise victory but were edged out 12-8. However, four defeats in a row, no matter how heroic or unlucky, was not Championship form.

Bev's try-scoring run came to a halt with two in a 29-5 defeat of Liverpool City on 27 October, a game which was notable for the debut of young full-back Eric Fraser. Fraser scored two tries himself to kick-start a career which would see him become the captain of Great Britain.

Boulevard battle

On Saturday, 3 November, Warrington scraped a 5-4 home win over Salford. Bevan was an absentee because he was in the Other Nationalities team in an international against France at Hull. There was enormous interest in this clash, which was declared an all-ticket game and produced a sell-out 18,000 crowd.

France had returned triumphant from their first tour of Australia, where they had beguiled the public of New South Wales and Queensland with sorcerers' rugby league. They were arguably the best international side in the world. Brian Bevan knew how entertaining the French could be but he and his colleagues - nine Australians, a Scot, an Irishman and a Kiwi - also had a pretty good idea that the sparks would fly, if memories of Bordeaux the previous season were rekindled.

The game erupted immediately and the legend of the 'Battle of The Boulevard' was born. It was a brute of a match. Brian Bevan was up against Raymond Contrastin, nicknamed 'the bulldozer' and one of French rugby league's great wingers. The two may as well have been spectators and were probably glad to be, in view of what went on in the middle of the pitch.

Edouard Ponsinet clearly had only one thing on his mind - revenge. Two minutes into the game he poleaxed Arthur Clues, who was carted off to spend the night in hospital with concussion and a severely bruised face. Ponsinet was merely penalised by referee George Phillips. Ponsinet was again penalised when Others' skipper Lionel Cooper staggered rubber-legged away from one of his tackles, although this time the Frenchman was cautioned. After 70 minutes Phillips finally gave Ponsinet his marching orders after second-rower Jeff Burke of Leigh had been knocked senseless and had his nose broken into the bargain.

Alfred Drewry, in *The Yorkshire Post*, wrote: "Something will have to be done to prevent this developing into an interminable sour serial. The clubs who had players injured - Clues, Cooper, Burke, Henderson and Paskins on one side, Puig-Aubert and Comes on the other - will have something to say about it... When the first concern of a man with the ball is to guard against the probability of a brutal assault you cannot expect much good football."

Other Nationalities won the game 17-14. It was Bevan's fellow wingman, Lionel Cooper who decided the issue. He scored a glorious hat-trick, while his centre Pat Devery landed four goals. Drewry reported that "the spectators were lucky to see three flashes of majesty by the incomparable Cooper. All his three tries were splendidly taken; the last, for which he beat four men in 15 yards with his left foot no more than six inches inside the touchline, was sheer magic."

Cooper had certainly been on the top of his form. After the 'Battle of The Boulevard' his try total for the season stood at 26, the same as Barrow's flyer Frank Castle and Bradford Northern's New Zealander Jack McLean, ten more than Bevan, who also trailed behind Huddersfield's other winger Dick Cracknell on 23.

On 17 November, Bev returned to club football when Rochdale Hornets were the visitors to Wilderspool. He must have thought he had gone a good way to closing the try deficit on Cooper when he raced over for half-a-dozen touchdowns, five in the second half, as Hornets were routed 30-10. It must have been with some amazement when he learned that as he was bagging six tries, Cooper was collecting 10 - and kicking a couple of goals for good measure - in Huddersfield's 48-3 thrashing of Keighley at Fartown. No other player had ever scored as many tries as Cooper in a league fixture - not even The Great Bev.

The following week Bev was on hard rations as Warrington went down 2-11 at Hunslet. It was to be Owen Bevan's last game for the club. Owen had played on the left wing in 16 of Warrington's 17 fixtures so far that season. He was no

Albert Johnson but he had made a pretty good fist of the job, scoring 10 tries and kicking 22 goals to top the Wire scoring chart. It came as something of a surprise when he asked to be transfer-listed and was offered for sale at £2,000 on 11 December 1951. On 28 December, he was signed by Leigh. It was reported that in order to gain his release from Warrington, Owen had to pay back half his signing-on fee. He played for Leigh for the remainder of the season playing 16 games, and scoring eight tries, helping them almost reach Wembley only to go down 2-6 in the Challenge Cup semi-final to Featherstone Rovers. Owen subsequently returned to Australia where he made a solitary appearance for Sydney St. George in 1954.

On 1 December, Brian missed a 26-11 home win over Belle Vue Rangers, a game in which Laurie Gilfedder, a future test forward, made his debut in the centre. Aged only 16 years and 199 days, Gilfedder became the youngest player ever to represent Warrington. Bev was engaged at Abertillery on Other Nationalities duty against Wales, running in two tries in a 22-11 victory.

The following week Brian was back running rings around Rochdale Hornets with four tries in a 42-0 romp at the Athletic Grounds. Making his debut on the other wing was Roy Lambert, a £2,500 signing from Dewsbury. Lambert scored a good try after a typical blind-side break by Gerry Helme, but may have been a little leg weary, having played less than 24 hours earlier in Wales's 3-15 defeat by New Zealand in a floodlit international at Odsal.

On 15 December Bev again racked up four tries against a hapless Liverpool City who were crushed 57-10 at Wilderspool. Harry Bath had a good time, helping himself to a try and nine goals, although former Wire favourite, 'Cowboy' Jones, the City full-back, must have wished he had been elsewhere as 13 tries went past him. Lambert made a good impression with another couple of scores and some of his cross field runs were reminiscent of Bev's meanderings.

The Christmas and New Year period presented Warrington with four tough fixtures and Brian's scoring rate dropped dramatically. On Christmas Day, Widnes came to Wilderspool and gave the home men a torrid time before losing 3-7. Bev got the crucial score, a first half try, which had the crowd on its feet. From a scrum in Warrington's own '25', Ike Fishwick heeled and the little maestro Helme shot down the blind side to halfway, fired the ball to Bev as full-back Sale made the tackle and watched him streak down the touchline before turning into the posts for a try fit to win any match. Boxing Day brought a hard-earned 3-3 draw at Leigh and three days later Huddersfield were beaten 13-8 at Wilderspool. Bevan and Cooper had a tremendous tussle, each scoring a try on a very heavy ground.

New Year's Day, 1952 attracted a crowd of almost 21,000 to Central Park. It was a rotten afternoon, a gale was blowing, hail fell during the match and the pitch was a quagmire apart from two strips down the touch-lines. As usual Wigan were near the top of the league, having dropped just nine points, and had won the Lancashire Cup for a record sixth consecutive season. Warrington, despite their recent good form, were not expected to win. Wigan's scrum-half Tommy Bradshaw was playing his last game for Wigan, his tussles with Helme having always been enjoyable titbits in these encounters. For the first time at Central Park a white, plastic-coated, ball was used - the RFL were encouraging its use. Under the circumstances, the spectators were glad about the innovation, although Bevan and other players believed that it was more slippery and lighter than they were used to.

A terrific game ensued, although open play was not the order of the day. Harry Bath kicked a penalty to start the scoring and the only other score of the first half was a try by the increasingly popular Lambert at the corner flag. Five-nil might as well have been 25-0 in the conditions. Bevan had only one chance after the break. Late in the game he broke clear down the comparatively firm touchline. Jack Cunliffe barred his way and, when most of the crowd expected him to kick past the full-back, Bev surprised everyone by shooting inside only to be swallowed up by the squelching mud. The only points of the second half came to Wigan via a Jack Hilton try and Warrington were 5-3 winners. The scoreline flattered Wigan who had lost at home to the Wire in a league match for the first time since 9 November 1946.

Warrington were quickly brought down to earth, however, with comprehensive defeats in Yorkshire at Wakefield (0-15) and Leeds (3-22). Second-rower Ted White had made his debut in the game at Headingley on 12 January, a match which should have been an historic occasion for Warrington. The BBC had begun to show an interest in covering live rugby league, having shown the second test against New Zealand at Swinton on 10 November, 1951. They had wanted to show the Leeds versus Warrington game as the first ever televised league fixture but Leeds had balked at the prospect in fear of losing gate money and instead the distinction went to the Wigan versus Wakefield Trinity fixture, although bizarrely only the first half was shown.

Television debut

Brian Bevan was soon to make his television debut, however, for the third game the BBC covered was the British Empire XIII versus New Zealand at Chelsea on 23 January. The game was not a success. The New Zealanders had just completed their tour of France and had been away from home since September. They did not really relish this strange Wednesday afternoon fixture in London. Only 6,800 people attended, probably because of the lack of local promotional activity, and the Empire team won easily 26-2. Bevan scored a sensational second-half try in combination with his centre Trevor Allan, but Lionel Cooper stole the show with a hat-trick.

Back in the league Warrington recovered form to defeat bogey team Workington Town 21-8 and Oldham 14-4 at Wilderspool. The latter game on 2 February brought Bev his 300th career try but all sporting events were eclipsed in the public consciousness four days later when King George VI died. A more memorable try followed at Whitehaven three weeks later. The Wire won a hard game 13-2 and the *Warrington Guardian* reported that "Bevan's 70th- minute try was unanimously voted as the best ever seen on the ground. Quickfire passing by Sheridan, Helme, Proctor and Naughton paved the way, Bevan receiving the ball on his '25'. Would-be tackler number one barely touched him, two coming up in support grabbed empty space as he sped between them, then rounded Fearon on the outside and, as McKeown came across to tackle, Bevan accelerated across the full-back's front to cover the last 20 yards into the centre of the field and on under the posts unopposed. The tremendous and ungrudging ovation which resulted was tribute in itself to a masterpiece no other winger could have scored."

Unrestrained admiration

The People's reporter said: "It is rare that a Whitehaven crowd shows unrestrained admiration for a member of an opposing team, but the distinction was accorded to Australian winger Brian Bevan, when he scored Warrington's second try at the Recreation Ground. This lithe speedster, who had previously been balked of half a dozen tries chiefly because of colleagues fumbling the final pass when he had sliced the defence, was cheered and clapped for some time after he had dashed 85 yards for the finest try ever seen on the ground. He impressed as a potential match-winner every time he was in possession, smiled and bowed his acknowledgement of ovations, which greeted his spectacular wing dashes, with obvious embarrassment."

The following Saturday Bevan ran in four more tries in a 26-9 home victory over Dewsbury in the second round of the Challenge Cup, his fourth being almost a replica of the Whitehaven effort. The Wire were still pressing for a top four place but as usual the fans' thoughts turned toward Wembley now that the third round beckoned. Warrington drew a stinker - Workington Town away. A row erupted when it was realised that the Workington soccer team were due to play a Division 3 North game against Oldham Athletic at Borough Park, their shared home with Town, on the afternoon scheduled for the cup-tie, 15 March. It was not until 12 March that the matter was resolved when a meeting between Workington Town, Workington AFC, the RFL and the Football League agreed that the soccer match would kick off at 2pm with the Challenge Cup-tie starting at 4.45pm, giving barely an hour to sort out the pitch, clear the ground and admit the all-ticket rugby crowd.

The late start meant that the results from the other three Cup-ties were known just as the Borough Park game kicked off. It had been shocks all round. Featherstone Rovers had stunned Wigan 14-11 before a record Post Office Road crowd of 14,340 - a thousand more than the town's population. Leigh had put out big-spending Leeds 9-5 at Hilton Park in front of 29,000. A few miles down the Cumbrian coast, a Willie Horne-inspired Barrow had won 10-2 at Whitehaven, where 14,464 had crammed into the Recreation Ground. It was added spice that the winners of the Town-Wire game would undoubtedly be favourites to win the Cup.

If Brian Bevan harboured thoughts of a second Wembley visit, they were rudely dispelled. Town took an early lead when Johnny Lawrenson landed the first of four goals and, after 13 minutes, full-back George Wilson, deputising for Gus Risman, finished off a lovely move with a try. By half-time it was 8-0 to Town after Lawrenson had also touched down. Twice Bevan made glorious efforts to score but was stopped by Billy Ivison and then by his opposing winger, George Huddart. In the second half he would surely have scored had he not put down Helme's pass after the half-back had conjured a rare opening. Town were good value for their ultimate 14-0 victory and went on to lift the trophy. Half a

Bev scored exactly 50 tries against Rochdale Hornets in his Warrington career.
Here he bangs down one of them just before Hornets' international
second-rower Derrick Schofield arrives.

century on in the era of Super League one thing is certain: we will never again see a semi-final grouping of the likes of Featherstone Rovers, Leigh, Barrow and Workington Town. More is the pity.

Warrington's next games were against Halifax. In the preview to the game at Thrum Hall on 22 March, the *Halifax Courier & Guardian* writer declared that "probably the outstanding figure [in the Warrington team] is the Australian Brian Bevan, the man with the dazzling swerve and twinkling feet". In the event Bevan hardly saw the ball but Warrington won 20-16 to maintain their position in the dog fight for the top four. A week later in the return fixture at Wilderspool Bev failed to get on the scoresheet for the third consecutive game and things were looking bleak. 'Winger' reported in the *Halifax Courier & Guardian*: "Twenty minutes from the end Halifax were three points in front and looked capable of holding this narrow lead. The visitors, indeed, were attacking at the time, when Bevan, taking advantage of a defensive mistake, ran through the Halifax ranks to send Ryder in for a try which was the signal for the transformation which followed." Bevan's effort opened the floodgates as Warrington leapt from 2-5 behind to win 19-5.

April 1952 began catastrophically for Warrington. Their hopes of a top four position nose-dived with a 13-3 defeat at St Helens, followed by a 41-0 humiliation at Barrow, where Willie Horne, scorer of 17 points, put on one of his master classes. There was still an outside chance of fourth spot, however, as Warrington went into the usual hectic Easter schedule. Three victories in four days, at Widnes and home against Barrow and Leigh, saw Bev back to form with a try in each match.

The game against Leigh on Easter Monday was a special occasion for Brian for he came face-to-face for the only time in his English career with brother

Owen. The crowd of 23,847 was the largest to attend Wilderspool that season. They were rewarded with a hell of a match, won 12-11 by Warrington with a mazy try from Lambert converted by Bath 15 minutes from time. The fraternal battle between the Bevans ended with honours even. Brian had put Warrington into a 5-4 lead when he scored the game's first try. *The Examiner* reported: "Ryder brilliantly cut through during a passing movement and sent Brian Bevan away with a well-judged pass. The winger had not much room in which to work but he rounded his brother Owen... left Ledgard mesmerised with a beautiful side-step while on top speed, and went behind the posts for a great try."

Owen evened the score by putting Leigh ahead when Warrington passing broke down, allowing centre Harry Green to pick up and send Owen over at the flag with Brian helpless to intervene. Twelve days later Owen signed off in a style which would have done his more famous brother proud. In his last game in England, a 45-17 home victory over Liverpool City, he bagged four tries for Leigh.

Anti-climax

Warrington's season ended in anticlimax. The last league fixture of the campaign took them to mid-table Swinton on 21 April. Warrington needed a win to give them a glimmer of a chance to finish fourth, provided both Huddersfield (at home to Hull) and Oldham (at Hull KR) lost five days later. The equation never added up. Warrington lost 4-6 in a strangely tame encounter, Harry Bath kicking two goals to Albert Blan's three. Huddersfield and Oldham murdered the Humberside clubs anyway.

Warrington thus finished sixth in the Rugby League Championship although they had surprisingly ended up only two points behind Wigan to finish as runners-up in the Lancashire League.

Brian had one more game to play. The last game of the European Championship between Other Nationalities and England was scheduled for Central Park on Wednesday, 23 April. Bev and Harry Bath were in their accustomed green jerseys for a match which drew a crowd of almost 20,000. Surprisingly, Other Nationalities had not yet won the Championship outright in their short, but colourful, existence but a win against England would rectify that. It was not to be, however, for England rampaged through the first half to take a 24-4 lead and with Arthur Clues limping with an injured leg from early in the game, it seemed a lost cause for the Others. The second half saw an astonishing comeback by the Greens who ran in four good tries - two to Bev and two to Trevor Allan - to reduce the deficit to 24-18. It was unfortunate that Harry Bath missed five of eight kicks at goal although he was the outstanding forward on his side. Just as it seemed the Others would steal an improbable victory, full-back Johnny Hunter was taken off with a damaged shoulder and England reasserted themselves to win 31-18. The wingmen had a beano, the standard of their play being scintillating. Both the England wingers, Dick Cracknell and Frank Castle, scored a brace of tries to emulate Brian Bevan. Bev's tries brought his tally for the season to 51, well down on the previous season's record-breaking total. John North wrote in *The Daily Dispatch*: "Others fought gamely to the end, especially

Bevan ... who provided many thrills." The result left England, Other Nationalities and France tied on four points each. The title went to France on points difference.

The only winger not to score tries in the Wigan international had been Lionel Cooper, a disappointment for the strapping Aussie, who had been simply awe-inspiring all season. Lionel finished the 1951-52 campaign with 71 tries - an even better return than Bev's in 1950-51. Also finishing with bigger tallies than Bev were Bradford's New Zealander Jack McLean with 60 tries, a player with a style akin to Cooper and with the sublime benefit of playing outside that great centre Ernie Ward, and Barrow's blindingly fast left-winger Frank Castle on 52 tries.

Warrington's season had been less successful than expected. The team had fallen from top of the league to sixth and for the first time since 1946-47 Brian Bevan and his team-mates had not picked up a major winners' medal. The average league crowd at Wilderspool had slipped from 15,237 to 14,317, which in the circumstances was probably not too bad, thanks to the team's near invincibility at home. Their away form had been their undoing. Financially there was a £1,704 loss on the season, the first since the war, with gate receipts falling by a massive £9,479.

On a personal level, even though Bevan had again topped the half century in all games, including 46 for the Wire, there was a feeling that he could be even more of a menace with a steady centre partner. He had suffered somewhat from playing alongside no fewer than seven centres in 1951-52, Ally Naughton missing most of the season through injury. Alan James, in *Rugby League Review* on 24 July 1952, wrote: "It is quite fair to say that of the passes Bevan gets, two out of three give him very little chance of doing anything but getting half murdered."

Season 1951–52

Warrington finished 6th in the League: P36, W24, D1, L11, For 622, Against 396
Bevan scored 46 tries for Warrington, plus 5 for representative teams

Date	Opponent	Score	Bevan	Crowd	
18 Aug	Huddersfield	13–9		16,418	
22 Aug	**Hunslet**	19–12	2T	15,479	
25 Aug	**Leeds**	28–21		19,364	
29 Aug	Salford	19–28	2T	11,487	
1 Sep	**Workington T**	6–16		13,866	LC 1
3 Sep	Workington T	3–20	dnp	15,000	LC 1
8 Sep	**Wakefield T**	26–6	1T	12,041	
15 Sep	Workington T	13–18	2T	12,341	
22 Sep	**Swinton**	26–17	2T	15,411	
29 Sep	**St Helens**	13–19	2T	22,546	
6 Oct	Oldham	12–20	1T	13,197	
13 Oct	**New Zealand**	13–19	1T	18,889	
20 Oct	**Wigan**	8–12	1T	21,960	
27 Oct	Liverpool C	29–5	2T	1,402	
3 Nov	**Salford**	5–4	dnp	7,821	
17 Nov	**Rochdale H**	30–10	6T	11,026	
24 Nov	Hunslet	2–11		9,000	
1 Dec	**Belle Vue R**	26–11	dnp	9,956	
8 Dec	Rochdale H	42–0	4T	1,428	
15 Dec	**Liverpool C**	57–10	4T	8,600	
22 Dec	Belle Vue R	12–5	1T	2,049	
25 Dec	**Widnes**	7–3	1T	15,842	
26 Dec	Leigh	3–3		12,159	
29 Dec	**Huddersfield**	13–8	1T	17,738	
1 Jan	Wigan	5–3		20,773	
5 Jan	Wakefield T	0–15		9,068	
12 Jan	Leeds	3–22		20,411	
19 Jan	**Workington T**	21–8	1T	15,109	
2 Feb	**Oldham**	14–4	1T	13,400	
9 Feb	**Liverpool C**	28–4	1T	10,345	Ch Cup 1
16 Feb	Liverpool City	6–6	1T	750	Ch Cup 1
23 Feb	Whitehaven	13–2	1T	7,473	
1 Mar	**Dewsbury**	26–9	4T	17,698	Ch Cup 2
8 Mar	**Whitehaven**	54–5	dnp	13,208	
15 Mar	Workington T	0–14		19,720	Ch Cup 3
22 Mar	Halifax	20–16		12,543	
29 Mar	**Halifax**	19–5		9,307	
2 Apr	St Helens	5–13	1T	13,054	
5 Apr	Barrow	0–41		8,235	
11 Apr	Widnes	26–4	1T	15,775	
12 Apr	**Barrow**	23–9	1T	18,283	
14 Apr	**Leigh**	12–11	1T	23,847	
21 Apr	Swinton	4–6		6,000	

Bevan's Representative Matches:

Date	For	Opponent	Score	Bevan	Venue
3 Nov	Other Nationalities	France	17–14		Hull
1 Dec	Other Nationalities	Wales	22–11	2T	Abertillery
23 Jan	British Empire XIII	New Zealand	26–2	1T	Chelsea
23 Apr	Other Nationalities	England	18–31	2T	Wigan

11. 1952-53 'A host in himself'

Despite the presence in the game of such crowd-pleasers as Brian Bevan, Lionel Cooper and many other three-quarters capable of scoring 30 or more tries in a season, despite the machinations of half-backs of genius such as Willie Horne, Gerry Helme and Cec Mountford and despite the creativity and forcefulness of great forwards like Joe Egan, Arthur Clues, Harry Bath and Ken Traill, many people in rugby league at this time were worried about the way the game was played. The early 1950s had seen the deterioration of variety at the play-the-ball. Players had become increasingly proficient at retaining possession and legislators were concerned that prolonged bouts of possession by one team was spoiling the game. This trend had been illustrated by a very dull Challenge Cup final between Barrow and Wigan in 1951.

The International Board had resolved to alter the play-the-ball law and New Zealand and Australia had played the new rule in their competitions in 1952. The old law had allowed for acting half-backs to be two yards behind the tackler/tackled player with the remainder five yards behind the play-the-ball. The new law allowed the acting half-backs to be one yard from the play-the-ball and the remainder were on-side as long as they did not get in front of the acting half-backs. Just how this arrangement was supposed to alleviate the problem and open out play beggared belief. The New Zealanders certainly did not take to it and reverted unilaterally to their own version of playing the ball in mid-season. The French and Australians were also unenamoured.

Nonetheless, the 1952-53 English season opened with the new law in force. The annual Wardonia Cup game drew a crowd of 19,569 to Wilderspool on 16 August. Wigan won 13-9, so at least something remained constant. Bevan did not score, but there was a marked tendency for kicks to be employed for him to chase, a welcome tactic which promised to bring him more chances to avoid the spotters. The new play-the-ball rule, however, was less welcome. Warrington complained to the RFL, declaring that it "completely spoiled the game". They were not too pleased either that injuries to skipper Ally Naughton and Gerry Helme would keep them out action for many weeks.

The first league programme of the season, on 23 August, rather perversely, brought an increase in crowds on the previous season's figures as curious fans turned out to sample the new law. Just short of 150,000 witnessed the 15 games, including 14,718 for Warrington's 26-2 home victory over Workington Town. It was a good start for the Wire and a good start for Bev. *The Examiner* noted: "In the second half he gave the defence such a toasting that several times two and even three opponents went racing over to stay his progress. Sure enough, however, Bev found a way of circumventing them all. He came running, swerving, side-stepping across the field and mesmerised the whole Cumbrian back division, somehow managed to dodge the last line of defence and scored the try of the match."

This season was to be full of landmarks in Bev's career. The second league game of the season, a decidedly bad game at Bramley, was his 250th for Warrington. The next, a first round, first leg Lancashire Cup-tie at Salford, brought him his 300th and 301st tries for the club, as Warrington scraped a two-point advantage for the second leg. The new play-the-ball law did not seem to be putting the brakes on either the team or Bev. The first seven games were all won and Bev scored nine tries in the first six.

At Belle Vue on 13 September, Warrington won at a canter 47-18, but the crowd had not seen any fireworks from Bev in the first half. He made amends early in the second half: "accepting a back pass near touch at halfway, he went inside and was half-stopped by a tackle round his pants but he broke free and went careering across the field, as the opposing centre and wing on the opposite side of the field converged in the hope of hemming him in. He swerved outside again and made them turn and follow. Again as he was half-tackled, he broke inside and just managed to struggle over. It was a magnificent effort and the cheers which greeted it were loud and prolonged."

Brian failed to score for the first time on 20 September, when Leeds were defeated 29-22 at Wilderspool, Harry Bath plundering three tries and four goals. The defences left much to be desired with Bevan, paradoxically, being almost redundant. Jack Steel lamented: "It does seem remarkable that a player who must be worth at least £10,000 to the club hardly got a chance to show his unusual talents. I have to agree that Bevan is an extraordinary player whose emphasis is on the unorthodox. But blank scoresheets as far as he is concerned will not satisfy the cash-paying customers."

The following Saturday, Bev bagged a couple of tries as Warrington were soundly beaten by Huddersfield at Fartown. It was the start of a particularly tough programme for the Wire, one which exposed the team's limitations against the better combinations. There was good news on 29 September, however, when the RFL finally allowed Cec Mountford to be registered as a Warrington player, as his playing contract with Wigan had now expired.. On 4 October he lined up alongside Gerry Helme for the first time in a home game against a bouyant Bradford Northern. Perhaps, at last, Wire's stand-off problem might be solved.

The game clashed with Great Britain's first test against Australia at Headingley, the first live television transmission of an Ashes test. Warrington provided Ryder, Featherstone and Ryan to the test cause, Bradford supplying Ward and Traill. Mountford must have been happy with a 12-9 victory on his playing debut, but Wire fans knew they had been lucky. Bev had scored a runaway 75-yarder when everyone at the ground, except Matt Coates, the referee, saw him knock-on. Bev had even glanced back quizzically at Coates as if waiting for the whistle, which was never blown.

The Australians lost the first test 19-6, but beat Bradford Northern 20-6 in midweek. They were anxious to put on a good show when they came to Wilderspool on Saturday, 11 October, having won only once in eight previous encounters against the Wire. Unfortunately, Warrington, facing a Lancashire Cup semi-final the following Tuesday, elected to put out a weakened team against the Kangaroos. The tourists won as they pleased 34-10, their first success on the ground since 1911. Bev scored a try against his compatriots after Gerry Helme opened the way for him.

A massive Fartown crowd holds its breath as Bev chases after his greatest rival, fellow Australian Lionel Cooper. On this occasion, 27 September 1952, Huddersfield won 32-13. Bev scored twice, but Lionel failed to trouble the scorers.

The 21,478 spectators may have felt short-changed but even more - 26,000 - paid for admission four days later when St Helens, now under Jim Sullivan's inspiring management, came to Wilderspool for the Lancashire Cup semi-final. Saints, the undoubted team of the season, had hammered the Aussies 26-8 - the only club team to beat the tourists - and were destined to become Lancashire League Champions, Challenge Cup finalists and League Champions. Sullivan had signed a five-year contract for Saints and was to found a dynasty there almost as successful as the one he had left at Wigan. In effect, Saints became the new Wigan.

Warrington gave St Helens a hard enough game, but were clearly inferior. Even so, five Harry Bath penalty goals kept them in with a chance at 10-14 with quarter of an hour left, at which point Bath was sent off by referee Ron Gelder on the advice of a touch judge. At that point Bevan appeared to have at last got away and was heading for glory when a flying tackle by Stan McCormick pulled him to the ground by his flapping shorts. Jack Steel wrote ruefully: "Bevan was watched like a band of detectives surrounding a spy-ring." A further try saw Saints through to the final 17-10.

Four at Fartown

Worse followed for Warrington. On 18 October they lost their third home game within a week when Oldham, another rising team, crushed them 28-0. Bevan was fortunate to be missing. He was busy running in four tries for Other Nationalities in their 31-12 defeat of England at Fartown. In the *Yorkshire Sports* the headline proclaimed "Bevan Star Man Of Fartown's Big Match", as the great man equalled the record for tries scored in an international or test match. His opposing winger Frank Castle and the England full-back Jimmy Ledgard must have had nightmares

95

recalling how he repeatedly toyed with them. 'The Veteran' wrote: "Bevan's success was the outstanding feature of the match. He was a host in himself". Winning pay for the Greens was £10. Bevan had certainly earned his tenner.

Returning to league action on 25 October, Bevan faced up to Oldham in the return fixture at Watersheddings. Harry Bath for Other Nationalities, Ron Ryder and Bob Ryan for England had also played in the Fartown international but if some at Warrington regarded their absence as a mitigating factor in the previous week's humiliation, there was no excuse for another lamentable display. This time the Roughyeds won 27-2, full-back Bernard Ganley adding six goals to the eight he had landed in the first encounter. The dismissal of Oldham's hooker Jack Keith only accentuated the poverty of Warrington's performance.

Another home defeat followed on 1 November when Wigan overcame Wire 17-10, all Warrington's points coming from Eric Frodsham's boot. Bev this time had a bit of a nightmare, missing three chances he would normally have gobbled up and being overshadowed by Dai Bevan, the Wigan right winger, who scored two dramatic tries. More worrying than anything was the fact that Warrington had not scored a solitary try in their last four matches.

It was therefore something of a relief that a trip to Knotty Ash was next on the fixture list. Warrington beat Liverpool City 28-2 with Bevan scoring five of their six tries, three of them length-of-the-field affairs. His first try had taken him past the 1,000 points mark for the club but, oddly enough, Warrington's remaining try, by Roy Lambert, was the outstanding event of the match - a try as outlandish as some of Bev's own specials.

It was back to the doldrums the following week, beaten 7-25 at lowly Rochdale Hornets, Bev scoring the only try for a dispirited Wire. International duty caused Bev to miss Warrington's next defeat - 19-8 at home to St Helens on Saturday, 22 November. The following day he and Harry Bath were parading their skills at the Stade Velodrome in Marseilles. In view of the bad blood exhibited, not to mention spilled, in the last couple of Other Nationalities versus France games, the French selectors had the wit to leave out Eduoard Ponsinet, the 'Ogre' of the Boulevard. The game could ill afford another riotous assembly. After trailing 6-10 at half-time, Other Nationalities took advantage of France's loss of a forward to overrun their opponents 29-10, with Bev crossing for two tries while Harry Bath landed four goals.

Warrington's next game was at Leeds on 6 December. Leeds fans and the game at large were in the early stages of assessing the merits of Lewis Jones, who had cost the Headingley club a world record signing-on fee of £6,000 a month earlier. Brian Bevan, 20 times cheaper, must have wished he had made his name as a rugby union player. There was no doubt about Jones's genius, however, as his long and brilliant career proved. He was straight out of the Bevan mould, or as near as damn it - eccentric, electric, instinctive, unpredictable, a crowd-puller. Whenever the two were on the same pitch, the fans were sure to get their money's worth. On this occasion Jones was the happier bunny. He scored a try and five goals, a couple of them from amazing distances, as Leeds thumped the Wire 34-12 in a fog-shrouded arena.

At this stage things were looking bad for Warrington. They had won only half their 14 league matches and were just in the top half of the table. The players held a clear-the-air meeting and, for a while, the team's fortunes revived. Bev scored a couple of tries in an easy home victory over Dewsbury, but made a much more vital contribution in the following match at Workington on 20 December. With four minutes remaining Town led by 8-5 when Helme flicked a back pass out to Bev from a scrum. The winger was immediately into his stride, side-stepping past three defenders before appearing to break clear. A desperate flick of his heels by Tony Paskins, however, sent Bevan crashing earthwards only for him to sling out a superb pass to Ally Naughton, who in turn sent Jimmy Featherstone over at the corner for a try which stole an 8-8 draw for the Wire.

On Christmas Day Warrington travelled to Naughton Park and, despite being hopelessly beaten for possession, earned an 8-0 victory over Widnes, with tries from Bevan and Mountford both coming from kicks on a muddy pitch. Boxing Day brought a crowd of almost 20,000 to Wilderspool, only for Leigh to beat the home men 9-6 in an exciting encounter. New Year's Day, however, saw a welcome 14-5 Wire victory over Wigan at Central Park. Bev played a blinder with two majestic touchdowns. It was debut day for Warrington's latest signing, Widnes's 1950 Great Britain tour prop, Danny Naughton, brother of Ally. He had cost the club £1,775 but he would prove a good buy. Harry Bath had been sent off with 20 minutes to play but Warrington's new spirit saw them through.

Two days later Huddersfield attracted a crowd of 18,293 to Wilderspool and a marvellous exhibition of rugby league ended in a 27-7 victory for Warrington. Lionel Cooper was absent and Warrington scored seven tries, but surprisingly Bev did not figure among the scorers.

By the time Warrington next took the field a fortnight later, the RFL had abandoned the contentious new play-the-ball law. Before Christmas, Hull had circulated all the clubs asking for support to revert to the old rule and had received plenty of encouragement. There had been a marked fall-off in crowds at many grounds and the play-the-ball rule took most of the blame. On 31 December, Halifax requested that an Emergency General Meeting be held to take action and on 10 January, 1953 it was agreed that the new law should be thrown out. There had been other factors in the decline in the gates, a few voices argued - the rise in admission due to the increase in Entertainments Tax, which had shot up from 10% to 25%, for a start. Not only did higher admission prices deter spectators, but the tax was absolutely crippling to sporting organisations. That and the spectre of rough play were probably the two issues that were exercising the minds of those running the game.

No stopping Bev

While the play-the-ball alteration had been maligned for bringing scrappy forward barging into the game and a surfeit of penalty kicks, it had not appeared to stop Brian Bevan from scoring tries. After the victory at Wigan he had scored 30 tries in 23 games, including international matches. He was engaged in a battle royal for the leadership of the try-scoring charts with Brian Nordgren (32), Lionel Cooper (31), Dai Bevan (29), Jack McLean (27) and Peter Henderson (25), all wingers and not an Englishman among them.

The revised rule did not hamper Bevan either. The first game under its auspices on 17 January saw him race over for four tries in a 39-10 home win over Belle Vue Rangers. There was no joy for him or the team in the following two games - a predictable 5-17 loss at St Helens and a more surprising home reverse to Swinton.

Even so, there was much more optimism in the Warrington camp than had been evident in the dark days of October and November. The Challenge Cup draw, televised live for the first time by the BBC on 9 January from Odsal, gave Warrington an interesting tie against local amateurs Orford Tannery, who had defeated Llanelli 31-6 in the last qualifying round. Both legs of the tie were played at Wilderspool and Orford were despatched 46-2 and 46-8. Bevan made hay with five tries in the first leg and a hat-trick in the second. They catapulted him to the top of the try-scorers for the first time in 1952-53.

On 21 February, Warrington travelled north to Cumberland for a league fixture at Whitehaven. The composition of the team - no Bevan, Frodsham, Ryder, Mountford, Helme or Fishwick - left no one in any doubt that their priority resided with the Challenge Cup. A 11-10 defeat ensued. The game that counted was next Saturday when the other Cumbrians, Workington Town, travelled south for a Challenge Cup second round tie at Wilderspool.

Cup-holders Town had, of course, dumped Warrington out of the competition the previous season. Their season had not been at all successful, and they were looking for another long run in the Cup to restore confidence, pride and a healthier bank balance. Warrington were favourites, most of the crowd of 19,723 expecting victory for the home team. For a long time it seemed an unlikely prospect. Gus Risman gave Town the lead with a 37th-minute penalty and there was no further score until the 67th minute when, after a prolonged siege on the Workington line, a scrum went down. Hooker Ike Fishwick struck for Gerry Helme to fire a sharp pass to the onrushing Ally Naughton, who swept head down between two defenders to touch down beneath the bar. Bath converted and the game was as good as over. Gilly Wright made doubly certain with another converted try just three minutes from time. It had been an amazing match. Warrington had almost unlimited possession but could not break down Town's stubborn resistance. Brian Bevan had been plied with chances, had worked his magic over and over again, but the heroic Town defenders had somehow kept him off the scoresheet.

Bev did not have such trouble the following week, when Warrington gained revenge on Rochdale Hornets with a 40-5 jaunt at Wilderspool. His haul was four tries and he could have had seven or eight with a bit of luck.

Cup fever was back in town by now. Seven of the remaining teams were praying for a third round home tie with basement club Hull Kingston Rovers. Wigan were the lucky ones. Warrington were presented with a toughie in Leeds but at least it was on home ground. The tie brought an expectant crowd of 25,423 to Wilderspool. At half-time Warrington led 7-2, thanks to a try from Alf Humphreys, now established as the regular left-winger following Lambert's departure to Castleford, and two Bath goals. It had been hard work for Warrington and when Leeds's Bert Cook kicked his second penalty goal in the 41st minute, there were palpitations in the home support. It was Bevan who banished them with a stupendous effort, dubbed "the ballet dance try" by The *Examiner*: "What a try it was. When he accepted the ball near touch on the members' side at half-way there seemed no immediate danger for, as he turned in, there were six or seven defenders lined out across the field forming what looked a complete barrier. But Bevan twisted and twirled past man after man. Once he seemed almost to be stopped only to accelerate again on his way across the field. Then he found Turnbull bearing down on him from behind, so he 'invited' him infield, side-stepped round him, as he had done with the rest, and flung himself over at the left-hand corner for one of the most sensational tries even in his extensive repertoire. In short, it was a replica of the one he scored at Wigan several seasons ago and it is a wonder the roar of the crowd was not heard there."

It was all over for Leeds now. Three more tries by the Wire, including a wonderful solo from Cec Mountford, playing like his old self at last, and a second from Bev, brought the final score to 25-8.

Bernard Cain of Warrington remembers

Unfortunately I missed the famous try at Central Park in 1948 as I was doing some pre-season training. Therefore the one I would nominate as his best was against Leeds at Wilderspool in the third round of the Cup on 14 March 1953. He got the ball by the players tunnel, made about 20 yards up the touch-line, then went off the right foot, then again, and again, passing, I would say, six or seven players in a zigzag, which ended in the left hand corner, with Drew Turnbull wrapped round his legs. Look at the Leeds team he did this against - Cook; Turnbull, McLellan, Ward, Broughton; Verrenkamp, Stevenson; McMaster, Wood, Gwyther, Poole, Moore, Clues.

The Sporting Chronicle *heading said: "After Bevan Wonder Try It Was All Warrington." Wires won 25-8 and went on to meet Saints at Swinton in the semi-final. Bev scored another great try from a typically pinpoint kick from Ally Naughton but Warrington went down 9-3. I was so sure we would get to Wembley that I had already bought tickets for my wife and me. So we saw the infamous final when Saints were booed off after losing to Huddersfield.*

The Challenge Cup quarter-finals had drawn a post-war, and possibly all-time, attendance record of 146,633 - no worries about the play-the-ball law when it came to blood and thunder Cup-ties. At Odsal 69,429 had watched Huddersfield beat Northern 17-7, a record for any game other than a major final or semi-final. Leigh's ground record had also been broken when 31,326 saw them go down 12-3 to St Helens, while, most unusually, the round's lowest gate - 20,455 - had been at Central Park where Wigan had accounted for Hull KR 25-6.

Saints too good

Warrington's luck in the Cup draws ran out in the semi-final. They came out of the bag with hot favourites St Helens and their match at Station Road, Swinton was declared all-ticket. Huddersfield and Wigan were to meet at Odsal in the other semi-final.

On 21 March, Warrington travelled to Barrow minus seven rested first-teamers, including Brian Bevan and went down 17-30. Bev's deputy was Jim Challinor who scored a try on his debut. Unfortunately Warrington's weakened team took some of the gloss from an important occasion for the Furness club, as the game was Willie Horne's testimonial match.

Despite a dismal day, a crowd of 38,059 packed into the Swinton ground for the Challenge Cup semi-final on 28 March. The bookies made St Helens and Huddersfield joint favourites for the Cup at 13/8 with Warrington the 9/2 outsiders. Saints were top of the league, Warrington 14th. Remarkably, Saints had won every single away game they had played in the league and lost only two at home. Warrington had managed only six away victories in 14 outings. Moreover Saints had already beaten the Wire three times that season. Even so Mountford's men were confident that they could upset Jim Sullivan's superteam.

The Station Road pitch was heavy after prolonged overnight rain and some more before kick-off. A military band had not improved matters underfoot. After two minutes silence for the late Queen Mary, Warrington, playing with the wind in their favour, set out to prove the pundits wrong. They certainly took the game to St Helens and had the better of the first half. Bev twice went close with brave efforts and it was he who broke the deadlock after half an hour. 'Red Rose', in *The Rugby Leaguer*, described the score: "Warrington had split the Saints ranks with a spectacular movement - Helme and Mountford passing quickly before Albert Naughton flashed down the centre and put in a diagonal kick to the right. Bevan was there first and waited until the ball had crossed the line before touching down. There was a howl from the St Helens supporters who claimed that Bevan had knocked on."

Knock-on or no knock-on, the score stood and Warrington led 3-0. A minute before the interval, Ike Fishwick conceded a penalty which Saints' scrum-half George Langfield potted from an easy position. The second half seemed to be a continuous siege in the Warrington quarter but St Helens simply could not find a way through a dreadnought defence and wasted the chances which did fall to them. It appeared that even with such a slender lead the Wire might just hold on, although there was consternation among their supporters when Warrington received a string of penalties deep in their own territory and elected to take taps instead of pushing their opponents back with kicks to touch and the possibility of more possession from the scrums.

Warrington were only nine minutes from Wembley when Saints struck the killer blow. They had been creating field position for a drop at goal and eventually the opportunity presented itself for Langfield to coolly send the ball flying between the posts. Three minutes later, it was all over when Ron Ryder tried to clear his line with a kick only to have it charged down allowing Saints' centre Don Gullick to pounce for a try, converted by Langfield. Warrington had gone down 9-3 to the best team in the land and given everything in their bones. It was still a bitter pill to swallow for Brian Bevan who had now experienced three semi-final defeats within six years.

Two days later, the disappointment among Warringtonians was reflected in the paltry crowd of 4,637 at Wilderspool for the visit of Salford. A ferocious encounter ended in a surprise 13-10 victory for Salford with the winning try from

Tom Danby coming eight minutes from time. Bev scored both the Wire tries, his 50th and 51st of the season.

The Salford game marked the first of 10 Warrington had to contest within 27 days in the customary end-of-season pile-up. In view of their setback against St Helens, they could perhaps have been forgiven for losing heart and impetus. They were never going to get back into the race for the top four and there appeared little to play for. However, seven straight games were won and Brian Bevan struck one of the richest veins of tries in his career. Five of those seven victories saw Bevan score at least three tries. He had three against Whitehaven on Easter Saturday and four against Liverpool City the following Tuesday, the last touchdown being his 350th for Warrington.

There was also a bit of a sideshow involving Brian during this latter fixture. The *Warrington Examiner* reported: "It was a pity that there had to be an unpleasant flavour to this good Eastertide for Warrington. This came in the shape of a private war waged on the wing between Bevan and his opposite number, White. There were a number of incidents between the two, and before the game was over both of them had been cautioned by the referee. But, in fairness to Bevan, it must be said that the offensive in the war came from the City man."

Amazingly, in this log-jam of fixtures Warrington were without a game for 11 days between 7 and 18 April. Quite remarkably, by today's standards, they arranged a friendly at Wigan on Saturday, 11 April. Just short of 10,000 attended and saw Wigan win 20-12. Bevan did not play in the game, nor did Ally Naughton and Gerry Helme, who were helping England to defeat France in Paris.

Bev was in international action himself on 15 April alongside his team-mates, Mountford and Bath, in Other Nationalities' game with Wales. The trio had not far to travel because Wilderspool was the venue. It was the first international fixture ever staged at the ground and the destiny of the European Championship depended on the result. A win for Bevan's team would confirm them as champions and he would at last get a winners' medal for the tournament. On the other hand, a wide margin in favour of their opponents would secure the Jean Galia trophy for the Welsh.

There was a disappointing turnout for this piece of local history with a crowd of only 8,449 - 300 fewer than Wire's next home game against Bramley. In fairness, however, there had been continuous rain all day which must have deterred many. Those who did attend enjoyed a thrilling spectacle despite the rain and a treacherous pitch. The Others led 13-7 at half-time and scored again soon after the break and were seemingly home, if not dry, at 16-7. A tremendous fightback by the Welsh, however, stunned the Others and a late try by centre Norman Harris, converted by skipper Jack Evans, snatched an 18-16 victory for Wales. It was not enough to deprive Other Nationalities of their first European Championship and Bev finally got his hands on that winners' medal after Jean Galia's widow had presented his captain Lionel Cooper with the Jean Galia Memorial Trophy.

Bev's contribution to a super game was summed up thus: "Bevan revealed his great pace from the few chances he had. He gave the crowd a thrill with a typical forty yards run in the closing minutes but unfortunately kicked too deep. Earlier he had knocked on in trying to gather the greasy ball when he had prospects of a run from his own 25, and only the full-back ahead. How the crowd groaned!"

At this late point in the season, Bevan had scored 53 tries for Warrington plus six in internationals. With five league matches remaining there were hopes that he might break his club record of 60 tries set in 1950-51, but no one seriously considered the prospect that he would surpass his best overall tally of 68. It was an even more remote possibility that he could get anywhere near Lionel Cooper's massive 71 tries scored in the 1951-52 season.

Thirteen tries within four days in the next three games turned those suppositions upside down. On 18 April Warrington won 33-11 at Salford. Bev ran in a hat-trick, his 50th for the club.

Two days later he bagged another in a 30-5 victory at Swinton. Jack Steel was moved to write: "A most unimpressive Swinton team was taught many lessons in classical rugby and, in these days of extreme partisanship, it was pleasing to witness spontaneous handclapping by almost everyone in the crowd when Bevan's swerve, side step and super speed beat at least half the home team without his being touched although he started his effort on the half-way line. Off he set on his great run rounding Birkett, whose clutching hands grasped nothing but thin air. The middle men hadn't time to get back but three men awaited near the touchline hoping to send the winger into touch. A split second and the cover defence, if you could call it that, was on the wrong leg because a deep side step had taken Bevan well inside the side line. With a wide gap thus created Bevan was through and it was then just a matter of seconds - a try under the posts. There was a roar when he started, a deafening cheer as he strode magnificently to the line and handclapping even as he walked to his position on the '25' - 125 yards or so of glorious endeavour."

He went on: "If Warrington had 90 percent of the play Bevan caused many of the thrills and humour. His unorthodox tactics delighted the crowd in more ways than one and he narrowly missed bringing his total of tries to six. That he should score three and miss others was due to a tricky ball which caused so many Swinton mistakes. Oh, if only Brian could play the ball correctly!"

Records all the way

On 22 April, Warrington massacred Bramley 71-10 at Wilderspool. Bevan was unstoppable. His second try broke his own club record and his seventh and last took him past Lionel Cooper's milestone mark of 71 tries in the previous season. Only Abe Rosenfeld could now claim to have scored more tries in a season than Bev's 72, a statistic which remains unchanged almost half a century later. His seven tries also equalled his own club record for tries scored in a match. They brought his tally for the season for Warrington to 66, his best ever. It was the fourth time he had broken the club record.

It was not only Bev who was breaking records. Harry Bath had been kicking magnificently and he booted 10 goals against Bramley, the first of which broke Harold Palin's club record of 146. By the season's close, Harry had extended the Warrington record to 162 goals. He also finished as the league's leading goalkicker with 170 in all games and the leading points scorer with 379. Old

Moggy Palin was still going strong though, having landed 102 goals for Halifax and Keighley. His Warrington record may have been eclipsed but he had set a Keighley club record by landing 81 goals.

The day after the Bramley match, Warrington went to Odsal. Bev was directly opposed to the rumbustuous former All Black winger Jack McLean, who had scored 13 tries in Bradford Northern's last five games and was Bev's nearest challenger in the race for the leadership of the try-scoring chart. The prospect was mouth-watering. In the event, a fantastic game ensued. George M. Thompson of *The Yorkshire Observer*, one of the sport's most distinguished reporters, was simply bewitched. He wrote: "I have seen most of Odsal's biggest and most thrilling games, but I cannot recall one being anywhere near so exciting or so accomplished as this one - a thriller from the start to the finish, with the luck of the result going to the home side in a match which neither deserved to lose". Bradford won 24-23 and nine tries were scored but astonishingly neither Bevan nor McLean touched down - Sod's Law, probably. Wire's left-winger Ronnie Herbert did not mind, with three tries as Northern concentrated on stopping Bev.

Warrington's season finally ended on 27 April with a 25-7 defeat at Barrow, their 15th in 36 league fixtures. A final league position of ninth was probably as much as they could have hoped for after their disastrous pre-Christmas form. There was, however, a great deal of optimism for the future. The second half of the season had seen much better performances and the Cup run had been a real tonic. There wasn't too much wrong with the attacking prowess of the team which had scored 155 league tries in 1952-53, a figure bettered only by St Helens (161) and Huddersfield (157). The reliance on Bevan as a strike weapon was, however, a little worrying, his nearest challengers in the Warrington side were Ally Naughton and Alf Humphreys, who had both claimed 17 tries. If Warrington fans needed any inspiration they need only look at the progress of the 1953 Championship finalists, St Helens and Halifax, who had risen from 20th and 21st in the table in 1951-52 to first and second respectively.

Brian Bevan's achievement in totalling 72 tries in 1952-53 was all the more remarkable for being performed with a team which won nothing and finished so low in the league. The mind boggles as to how many tries he might have scored with a more successful team. Certainly Rosenfeld's record would have never come under greater threat.

Rugby League Review again acknowledged Bev as one of its 'Stars of the Season', this time listing six instead of the customary five. His fellow "Oscar" winners were Tommy Lynch (Halifax), Stan McCormick (St Helens), Jack McLean (Bradford), Drew Turnbull (Leeds) and Dave Valentine (Huddersfield). Bev's late-season surge had seen him finish 13 tries ahead of McLean (59) in the try-scoring charts, followed by Cooper (50), Nordgren (47), Henderson (46) and Dai Bevan (40).

Brian Bevan's powers of evasion were recognised as unparalleled, but just how fast he may have been was always a moot point. There were lots of really fast men in rugby league in the post-war period. Many of the wingers were genuine sprinters, who won prize money in professional athletics meetings. Some people believed that Barrow's Frank Castle was the quickest man in the game, while

Peter Henderson, Huddersfield's Empire Games sprinter, had his own supporters for that title... and there were plenty of others.

One man who was an expert in judging sprinters was Matthew Clamp, organiser of many professional sprint meetings in this period. In an article in *The Rugby Leaguer* on 25 April, 1953, Clamp said: "Brian Bevan is the fastest and most phenomenal runner to take to a rugby field and taking into consideration the buffeting he gets week by week at football, is amazing." The article continued: "Mr. Clamp thinks that if Bevan had a 'prep' course of training by professional experts... then Warrington's wingman would be a match for any man in the world... Every effort on the football field is distinctly different from a track effort, and my own opinion is that Brian Bevan is the only man correctly timed, who, with professional training, could have been as fast and maybe faster than McDonald Bailey."

This was some compliment to Bev when one considers that McDonald Bailey had won more Amateur Athletics Association titles than any other athlete and had equalled the world record for 100 metres (10.2 seconds) in 1951. Bev would have been fascinated when Bailey famously but briefly turned to rugby league with Leigh, signing for them on 23 July, 1953. He would have been equally disappointed not to have faced the great Trinidadian sprinter, who gave up the game after a solitary appearance in a specially arranged friendly for Leigh against Wigan on 16 December 1953.

Season 1952–53

Warrington finished 9th in the League: P36, W20, D1, L15, For 733, Against 486
Bevan scored 66 tries for Warrington, plus 6 for representative teams

Date	Opponent	Score	Bevan	Crowd	
23 Aug	**Workington T**	26–2	1T	14,718	
27 Aug	Bramley	11–6	1T	4,748	
30 Aug	Salford	19–17	2T	15,000	LC1
3 Sep	**Salford**	30–8	2T	14,535	LC1
6 Sep	Dewsbury	19–11	1T	2,279	
13 Sep	Belle Vue R	47–18	2T	4,761	
20 Sep	**Leeds**	29–22		19,075	
27 Sep	Huddersfield	13–32	2T	18,644	
4 Oct	**Bradford N**	12–9	1T	17,288	
11 Oct	**Australians**	10–34	1T	21,478	
14 Oct	**St Helens**	10–17		26,000	LC Semi*
18 Oct	**Oldham**	0–28	dnp	13,231	
25 Oct	Oldham	2–27		15,390	
1 Nov	**Wigan**	10–17		16,405	
8 Nov	Liverpool City	28–2	5T	1,212	
15 Nov	Rochdale H	7–25	1T	7,092	
22 Nov	**St Helens**	8–19	dnp	12,890	
6 Dec	Leeds	12–34		16,455	
13 Dec	**Dewsbury**	35–10	2T	7,437	
20 Dec	Workington T	8–8		5,829	
25 Dec	Widnes	8–0	1T	9,056	
26 Dec	**Leigh**	6–9		19,750	
1 Jan	Wigan	14–5	2T	20,797	
3 Jan	**Huddersfield**	27–7		18,293	
17 Jan	**Belle Vue R**	39–10	4T	11,113	
24 Jan	St Helens	5–17		20,527	
31 Jan	**Swinton**	8–10		7,387	
7 Feb	**Orford Tannery**	46–2	5T	10,258	Ch Cup 1
14 Feb	Orford Tannery	46–8	3T	5,537	Ch Cup 1(at Wilderspool)
21 Feb	Whitehaven	10–11	dnp	5,905	
28 Feb	**Workington T**	10–2		19,723	Cup 2
7 Mar	**Rochdale H**	40–5	4T	10,900	
14 Mar	**Leeds**	25–8	2T	25,423	Cup 3
21 Mar	Barrow	17–30	dnp	10,729	
28 Mar	St Helens	3–9	1T	38,059	Cup Semi (at Swinton)
30 Mar	**Salford**	10–13	2T	4,637	
3 Apr	**Widnes**	15–3	1T	17,506	
4 Apr	**Whitehaven**	52–8	3T	10,309	
6 Apr	Leigh	17–8		8,838	
7 Apr	**Liverpool City**	34–5	4T	4,957	
18 Apr	Salford	33–11	3T	8,113	
20 Apr	Swinton	30–5	3T	5,450	
22 Apr	**Bramley**	71–10	7T	8,759	
23 Apr	Bradford N	23–24		18,372	
27 Apr	**Barrow**	7–25		8,955	

* Warrington received a bye in the second round of the Lancashire Cup

Bevan's Representative Matches:

Date	For	Opponent	Score	Bevan	Venue
18 Oct	Other Nationalities	England	31–12	4T	Huddersfield
23 Nov	Other Nationalities	France	29–10	2T	Marseilles
15 Apr	Other Nationalities	Wales	16–18		Warrington

Gerry Helme

Albert Naughton

Four great backs who starred alongside Bevan.

Albert Pimblett

Ray Price

12. 1953-54 'All the record books rewritten'

A lot of water passed under a lot of bridges in Warrington's 1953 close season. A week after the club's final game of the 1952-53 season - an embarrassing and heavy home defeat by Barrow - the sporting nation was gripped by one of history's greatest FA Cup finals, when Stanley Matthews finally took a winner's medal after Blackpool had defeated Bolton Wanderers 4-3 at Wembley. Later that summer, England wrested back cricket's Ashes from Australia after a barren spell of 20 years as the country thrilled to the deeds of Alec Bedser, Len Hutton, Ray Lindwall and Keith Miller.

Brian Bevan would no doubt have been dismayed at the outcome, but maybe his thoughts also strayed home when he read about the novelty of an American team of gridiron footballers touring Australia as rugby league players. They did not play any test matches but, in their first game, they drew a crowd of 65,453 to the Sydney Cricket Ground, where Sydney beat them 52-25.

On the wider stage, Tenzing and Hillary became the first conquerors of Everest on 29 May, East Berlin experienced a popular rising in June which brought Russian tanks onto the streets and, on 27 July, the Korean War armistice was signed.

The major focus of the summer, however, in Great Britain and the Commonwealth was on the coronation of Elizabeth II on 2 June, an event made accessible to millions through television.

The mood in the country was certainly brightened and Warrington fans also shared the glow of optimism for the coming season. They had seen their team improve markedly in the latter part of 1952-53, and were expecting a real challenge for honours. Brian Bevan had much to look forward to. August had seen an influx of Australians at Wilderspool - despite the international ban. Len Horton, a winger, Ron Dixon, a half-back and Peter Groves, a forward, swelled the Australian contingent to five, although ultimately only Horton would make any real impression.

Bevan also had the prospect of a joint testimonial with Bob Ryan to contemplate. Gerry Helme and Albert Johnson's benefit year had just ended with each receiving the considerable sum of £762. A successful testimonial would go some way to compensating for Bev's comparatively poor contract conditions. It was his misfortune to have come to England before he had made a name for himself in his homeland. Had he waited a couple of years he would undoubtedly have been several thousand pounds better off. The Warrington club made a generous opening contribution of £700 to the testimonial fund.

The Warrington directors were able to report a profit of £503 on the previous season, a remarkable achievement in view of the drop in average home league crowds from 14,317 to 12,301. A staggering £6,303 had been paid in Entertainments Tax, a burden which was increasingly hamstringing clubs. It was particularly galling for enterprising organisations like Warrington RLFC when the previous April, the Chancellor of the Exchequer had abolished the tax for cricket and amateur sports clubs, including rugby union. Even so, the club continued to invest money in ground improvements, adding extra cover to the popular side.

Bevan might continue to get wet on his serpentine runs but fewer spectators would.

Brian Bevan always maintained that the Championship-winning team of 1947-48 was the best Warrington team for which he played, and man-for-man that may well have been true. However, he and Warrington were about to embark upon the most successful season the club had experienced since its foundation in 1879. By the time the 1953-54 season closed, Bev would have rewritten all the record books and Warrington would have three of the four major cups in their trophy cabinet.

At the close of the 1952-53 season, Brian Bevan had amassed 385 tries in his career in England, 22 of which had been scored in representative matches. The only men who had scored more in the entire history of the game were Albert Rosenfeld (386), Eric Harris (399), Johnny Ring (415), Eric Batten (426) and Alf Ellaby (446). All, like Bev, were right-wingers but all had played for much longer in acquiring their mammoth totals. Indeed, Eric Batten, captaining Featherstone Rovers at the age of 39, was still adding to his tally, having made his debut for Wakefield Trinity as far back as 1933. It should be noted that no accurate figures existed for career aggregate try totals in 1953. Consequently, many landmarks set by Bev went unnoticed or were reported erroneously at the time.

Despite the optimism prevalent at Wilderspool the season began with unpropitious omens. The day after taking part in a public practice match on 1 August, Harry Bath was rushed into hospital to have an appendectomy which kept him inactive for a month. A week later Wigan defeated Warrington 30-20 at Central Park to lift the Wardonia Cup for the third consecutive time before a sweltering crowd of 16,134. Bev was among the Wire try scorers but was thought by some onlookers to be a bit slower than the previous season - an annual optical illusion.

The season proper began on 15 August - unusually early - when more than 12,000 braved a wet afternoon to see Wire defeat Salford 17-4 at Wilderspool. It was Bevan, back at full speed, who put them on the road to victory with a splendid try following a kick from Ally Naughton. In doing so, he equalled Albert Rosenfeld's career total of 386 tries. The next game, four days later saw him leave Albert's mark behind as he grabbed both his side's tries in a 12-7 home defeat of Barrow.

Even Bevan could do nothing, however, when Warrington went to Craven Park in Hull for their first away league fixture. Supporters who did not travel were astonished when they heard the result - 17-5 to lowly Hull KR, who were captained and coached by their old favourite Bryn Knowelden. The game had been a disaster from beginning to end. The players boots bag had been thrown out of the train at Manchester along with other parcels and post. They were despatched on the following train, but caused a twelve minute delay to the kick-off. No one would have been more perturbed by this chain of events than the meticulous Bevan. There were other mitigating circumstances too. Second-rower Ted White was taken off before the interval having suffered a broken ankle and Ron Ryder showed amazing guts to return after a 20 minute absence to play out the game with a broken jaw. Further injuries to Gerry Helme and Gilly Wright meant that at one point Warrington only had nine effective men on the field.

This catalogue of injuries threatened to disrupt Warrington's ambitions, but a masterstroke by the club management two days after the Hull KR fiasco proved a catalyst for the success which was to follow. Jimmy Featherstone had been on the transfer list at £2,500 for months. The fee had been reduced to £2,000 and Belle Vue Rangers had offered to sign him. A deal was struck in which Warrington secured the services of Rangers' Welsh international stand-off Ray Price. Price proved to be the vital cog in the machine which was to drive the Wire to undreamed of heights. His partnership with Gerry Helme certainly ranks with the very best half-back pairings the game has seen. Price was a lethal mix of belligerence and footballing nous, a stand-off who played well beyond his apparent physical attributes, feared no opponent and brought out the best in his team-mates. Bev and his colleagues were quick to appreciate the benefits of his introduction.

Price made his debut on 29 August in a 16-4 home win against Rochdale Hornets, a game which saw Harry Bath back after his appendix operation. Victories in the league at Barrow and home and away over Belle Vue in the Lancashire Cup followed. A calamitous result at Leeds brought Warrington crashing to earth on 12 September, however. The Loiners won 43-14 before an ecstatic 19,240 Headingleyites.

Yet the star turn was not mercurial scrum-half Jeff Stevenson, eight goal full-back Ralph Morgan or the rampant Arthur Clues, grandly though they all played. It was Bev who scintillated despite his team's ineptitude. Tom North wrote rapturously: "No matter how long I live I doubt whether I shall see many tries as spectacular as the two which Bevan notched. It would be wholly inadequate to call them 'picture' tries. They were more than that - real masterpieces by a master craftsman. It isn't that often that the close-packed ranks of opposition supporters acclaim the wizardry of an 'enemy'. But they did at Leeds and when Bevan crossed for the first of his two tries 19,000 Headingley sportsmen roared their praise. But even that full-throated acclamation was dwarfed by the storm of cheering that greeted Brian's second and even more spectacular effort. It continued for long after the event which caused it and, in the dying minutes of the game, the very sight of Bevan with the ball was enough to start the cheering all over again. In fact I got the impression that the Headingley crowd - though naturally anxious for the Loiners to chalk up a convincing win - were almost equally anxious for Bevan to score one or two more, if only for the thrill of seeing him in action."

The following Saturday Wigan were the visitors to Wilderspool. Warrington fielded a debutant in the former Fylde and Lancashire RU hooker Frank Wright, but many of the crowd were just as interested in Billy Boston who was a spectator, having signed for Wigan a month or so previously, Warrington having been one of the clubs disappointed not to have captured him. Billy must have wondered what all the fuss about Bevan was, for Warrington's maestro never got a touch of the ball for the first 32 minutes, presented Brian Nordgren with a try after a misunderstanding with Cec Mountford and, when he did finally get a chance to run in the second half he was immediately buried by three desperate defenders. Boston soon recognised Brian's genius, however, and in later life always acknowledged Bev as the best winger he ever encountered. A remarkable game ended in a 13-9 victory for the Wire thanks to five Harry Bath goals, which cancelled out Wigan's three to one try tally.

On the following Thursday, Harry Bath was again the match-winner in an enthralling second round Lancashire Cup-tie against Oldham at Wilderspool. Warrington trailed 7-11 just seconds from time when left-winger Jim Challinor squeezed over at the corner in a welter of bodies for a try, which allowed Harry Bath to pilot home a breathtaking touch-line conversion, seeing the Wire victorious by 12-11.

Two days later Warrington had a much easier passage, winning 19-5 at Whitehaven and cementing a spot in the top four. It was Bev's 300th appearance for the Wire and he celebrated with two typical touchdowns, his 373rd and 374th for the club.

There was another brace for him on 30 September when Warrington travelled to St Helens for a Lancashire Cup semi-final. They were not enough, however, to prevent Saints from progressing to the final against Wigan. Stand-off Peter Metcalfe was the match-winner for Saints with two tries and three goals but the turning point came midway through the second half when Wire lost the inspirational Ray Price, after they had appeared well capable of holding onto a 10-7 lead. Saints eventually won 17-10 in a tremendous Cup-tie which fully satisfied the 23,184 spectators.

400 up

Warrington gained revenge on Hull KR on 3 October, hammering them 42-13 at Wilderspool. Bev ran in a hat-trick, one an extraordinary solo effort and another, his third, which 'Criticus' described as: "one of the most amazing tries ever seen on the ground". For a change Bev did not create this score out of nothing, merely majestically finishing a mesmeric combined action. Eric Frodsham began the movement when he fielded Bryn Knowelden's kick-off over his own line. The move was carried on by Mountford, Bath and Helme before Bevan was unleashed to apply the *coup de grâce*. It may have been simple for Bev, but it was also significant for it was his 400th career try, taking him past the total of another of the immortals - fellow Australian Eric Harris, alias 'the Toowoomba Ghost'.

Unfortunately, the victory came at a heavy cost for Warrington. Cec Mountford, who had been filling in for Ray Price at stand-off after playing most of the season at left-centre, was stretchered off a quarter of an hour before the end and taken to Warrington Infirmary with an injury to his left knee ligaments, which was so serious it ended his illustrious playing career.

October 1953 was a busy month for Bev. On the Wednesday following the Hull KR fixture he was in the Other Nationalities team for the international against Wales at Odsal, the second half of which was televised by the BBC. The Greens had turned into Whites for the cameras, wearing England jerseys as a contrast to the scarlet shirts of the Welsh. Wales put up a strong fight in the first half but trailed by 9-5 when the televised action began. Thereafter it was one way traffic despite Welsh hooker Tommy Harris's 29-17 advantage over Wally Ellean in the scrums. Lionel Cooper ran in a characteristic hat-trick as the Others ended up winners by 30-5. *Rugby League Review* reported: "The general opinion was that the football was better than the commentary. For future televised RL matches it might be a help if the commentator (Alan Dixon) could be provided with an abacus. All the time there was also a feeling the speaker was uncertain of his players with the exception of Brian Bevan. Eddie Waring's introduction was good and more use should have been made of his wide knowledge of the game and players." Bev's main contribution was a run from his own half which brought him a try witnessed by a million or more viewers, besides the Odsal crowd of 14,646, most of whom had paid half-a-crown for the privilege.

It was back to league fare for Bev on 10 October and another sizzling hat-trick in a 28-13 victory at Castleford. Jim Challinor, on the other wing, scored the other three Wire tries. Bev had started the season rather slowly but 10 tries in his last four games for Warrington and one for Other Nationalities had shot him to his accustomed place at the top of the try-scoring lists with 21, just ahead of his nearest challengers Drew Turnbull of Leeds, Stan McCormick of St Helens and George Wilson of Workington Town.

His next engagement was in Bordeaux for Other Nationalities' fixture against France on 18 October. It was to be some game. The Others were missing star men Pat Devery and Tom McKinney through injury and the unavailable Harry Bath, who had recently taken over the Britannia Hotel in Buttermarket Street, Warrington. After leaving out Edouard Ponsinet in the previous season's encounter, the French selectors decided to play him in the Bordeaux fixture, no doubt believing lessons had been learned all round. No such luck!

Arthur Clues had neither forgiven nor forgotten his vendetta with Ponsinet. Vengeance was the only thing on his mind as the game kicked off. A couple of minutes into the game Arthur instructed scrum-half Neville Black to hoist an up-and-under toward Ponsinet. He then went hell for leather straight in Ponsinet's direction with murderous intent. Ponsinet was not prepared to die just yet and amazingly decided to leg it round the cycle track with Big Arthur in hot pursuit. Arthur always joked that by the time they got back into play Brian Bevan had scored the two tries which won the match - a considerable exaggeration. He also maintained that in later years Ponsinet and he always exchanged Christmas cards.

Clues and Bevan often roomed together on trips abroad. Clues was unequivocal in his admiration of Bevan. He was simply "the greatest winger I have ever seen. Out of this world". He did not appreciate Bev's habit of chain-smoking in their room, however. He understood though why, after scoring his long distance specials, Bev would return to his position coughing, spitting and cursing.

Brilliance at Bordeaux

The game at Bordeaux was one of Bev's greatest triumphs. He regarded it as "the hardest international match in which I have played", according to one report. Allan Cave wrote in the *Daily Herald*, "International rugby league opposition stands in as much fear of Brian Bevan as England's soccer foes dread Stanley Matthews, and Bev is the man who beat France in yesterday's Bordeaux international."

Bill Fallowfield, Secretary of the RFL, most unusually wrote about Bev's performance in the match programme for the following international, England versus France at Odsal on 7 November. The Others had won the French encounter 15-10 and Fallowfield noted: "Something must be placed on record about this game because it proves conclusively that Brian Bevan must indeed take his place among the Rugby 'immortals'. Surely there has never been a better attacking wingman in the whole history of the Rugby game... The Empire boys, even in the eyes of the French officials, started as odds-on favourites. Opinions rapidly changed when the French team went into action. Their tackling was superb and defence impenetrable. For 20 minutes every movement of the visitors was nipped in the bud. Then Bevan got the ball! A rapid succession of side-steps left three would-be tacklers trailing on the ground and then Brian, having perfectly demonstrated his elusiveness, gave us an equally effective demonstration of his speed with a diagonal run of forty yards in which he outpaced all opposition to score in the opposite corner. France counter-attacked and at half-time were leading by 10 points to 5, and on the play looked like retaining this lead. Twenty minutes after half-time Bevan again had the ball. There was no possible chance to score - or so we thought. From a standing start near the touch-line Brian side-stepped again and again into the thick of the French players and then with a prodigious spurt he bounded clear to gain what must have been the best individualist's try ever scored on the ground.

Five minutes from the end York's nippy little stand-off Johnny Robinson broke clear after a planned move from the base of the scrum to give his side victory - on the whole, a rather lucky win. Dropped passes by the French three-quarters frittered several chances away. But, irrespective of who won or should have won, it will be remembered as 'Bevan's match'. He was rightly referred to by the French Press as the *Roi du Terrain* (King of the Ground)."

There was no winning pay for Brian on his return to league action with Warrington on 24 October as the Wire went down 7-9 at Borough Park to their bogey team Workington Town. Gus Risman, now 42-years-old, kicked a penalty goal in the dying seconds to inflict only the third league defeat of the campaign on the Wire. A 15-9 home win over Leeds followed with Bev again failing to trouble the scorers. November, however, saw him claim a succession of crucial tries as Warrington struggled to win fixtures, which on the form book appeared more or less routine victories.

On 7 November Warrington went to Belle Vue. Rangers had won only two games all season and only 1,082 spectators turned out for another probable thrashing. However, a dour day and a dour defence restricted Warrington to a solitary try. Inevitably it was a flash of genius from Bevan which undid Rangers. Syd Phillips made the initial break and then, wrote Jack Steel, "We saw the uncanny rugby league brain of Brian Bevan at work. He came inside and in the twinkling of an eye he had slipped through a loophole and had Rangers players pursuing him like a pack of hounds. It was a try from the overcast sky".

Warrington won 9-2 and repeated that scoreline the following Saturday against Hull at Wilderspool. Again it was a hell of a struggle for the Wire. Hull were trailing 2-6, all the points being from penalty goals, and had been hammering relentlessly on the Wire line for a winning score. With less than a minute

Other Nationalities versus England at Wigan, 28 November, 1953. Tony
Paskins slings a pass to Bev as he is tackled by England full-back Ted Cahill.
Paskins partnered Bev in 10 representative matches - more than any other player.

Other Nationalities versus England, 28 November 1953:
Back row: Ellean, Bevan, B. Wilson, Clues, Mossop, Valentine, Mudge.
Front row: Dawson, Phillips, Cooper, Robinson, Paskins, Devery.

remaining Harry Bath hoofed a clearing kick upfield just to relieve the pressure. The ball came to earth only for a Hull defender to lose possession, Bev arrived from nowhere, punted on, snapped the bouncing ball up and shot diagonally from the centre-field to the left corner flag for a try which sealed the game and sent the Warrington fans mad with delight. Perhaps it was Bev's way of paying them back for their contribution of almost £60 which had been collected that afternoon for his joint testimonial with Bob Ryan.

On 21 November Warrington had a third consecutive close shave. At Salford they lost the physical battle but won the game 10-8. For much of the game they played with 11 men. Dan Naughton was sent off, Harry Bath was on and off the field between injuries and loose-forward Reg Hughes carted off with concussion. This time Bev did his damage early on in the game giving Warrington the lead with a tremendous 75-yarder.

A memorable month for Bev ended at Central Park, Wigan on 28 November, when Other Nationalities met England in a game which decided the European Championship, both teams having already beaten France and Wales. This was the last four-cornered European Championship to be played, Wales being put into a 15 year cold storage before resurrection in 1968. By half-time England, orchestrated majestically by skipper Willie Horne and gorging on a massive scrum advantage from hooker Harry Bradshaw, were out of sight with a 21-7 lead. The Others fought back hard in the second half, but finally lost 30-22. Bev scored twice after the interval, firstly finishing off an overlap and then providing one of his specials for the last try of the match. He was, however, overshadowed in the newspaper headlines the following day by Swinton's Peter Norburn, the England right-winger, who had scored four tries on his international debut.

On 5 December Bev waltzed past a bewildered Castleford defence for two tries in a 36-12 home victory over the Yorkshire visitors. The victory, coupled with a defeat for table-toppers Halifax at Leigh, gave Warrington the league leadership for the first time in 1953. They had lost more games than both Halifax and St Helens, but their position at the top of the league was clear evidence of their burgeoning prowess. They had won their last six games and were to extend that run to 14 straight victories. During this run Bev appeared in 13 matches, failing to score in only two and racking up 20 tries.

The Christmas Day derby with Widnes at Wilderspool, played for the first time with a morning kick-off, saw him in prime form. Four scintillating tries took his career total onto 417 - two more than Johnny Ring had scored in his monumental career with Wigan, and briefly Rochdale, between 1922 and 1933. Only Eric Batten and Alf Ellaby were still ahead of him.

A series of crunch matches followed, and the Wire came through with flying colours. First up was another derby at Leigh on Boxing Day. A crowd of 12,360 was something of a disappointment, even though it was a wretched day with a muddy field and constant fine rain. Amazingly, there had been objections from some clubs that the Boxing Day gates were bound to be hit, particularly in Yorkshire, by the BBC's televising of the amateur county match between Yorkshire and Lancashire at Hunslet. In the event an aggregate of 136,171 attended the 15 league fixtures played. The Leigh crowd certainly enjoyed a fine game, despite the conditions. Again it was left to Brian Bevan to decide the issue.

The last minute arrived with Warrington leading precariously 10-6. At that point Ally Naughton broke from his own half and performed what had become something of a party piece. He kicked ahead for Bevan to chase. There was no stopping the Australian as he was first to the rolling ball, which he punted on again and flew over for the match-clinching points.

1954 - Year of Years

New Year's Day 1954 took Warrington to Wigan seeking a 10th consecutive victory and their first league double over the home side since 1938-39. The 22,000 spectators must have thought that Wigan were about to thwart them when the cherry and whites led 12-5 at one point. Injuries to Wigan players helped the Wire's cause, but it was not until late in the game that they finally got on top. The second half produced a real virtuoso performance from Bevan, who had to atone for allowing Wigan's Ernie Ashcroft to score a try after mistiming an attempted interception. With the score at 12-7 it was Bev who scored Warrington's equaliser. Ron Ryder set him free around his own '25', allowing him to evade Jack Fleming. It seemed that Don Platt and Nat Silcock had him wrapped up, but although both came to grips with him, neither could hold him and he went onto score to the great joy of the travelling fans. Bath's conversion made it 12-12. Ken Gee failed to land a penalty which could have won the game for Wigan and Bev was the man who made them pay. Again Ryder made the running, putting in a short kick before being clattered. Bev followed up, and began a dribble that was worthy of Stanley Matthews before touching down for the winning try which Bath converted.

The following day was apparently mission impossible. Warrington played champions St Helens at Knowsley Road. Saints had had a week off, they had been undefeated at home for over a year and had beaten Warrington in their last eight encounters. They had won their last 15 matches, remaining unbeaten since late September. Moreover, injuries ruled out the Wire centres Naughton and Ryder, their replacements being Len Horton, with just one first team appearance with Warrington, and 'A' teamer Arnold Stevens, who was making his debut.

A foggy day obscured the 18,000 spectators' views, but another nerve-tingling game ensued. Warrington were murdered 37-18 in the scrums, but defended like demons, the only scores of the first half being a penalty goal to each side. As usual it took a Bevan special to break the game. Jack Steel described the try: "A tall figure - it proved to be White - drew McCormick and then passed to Bevan. The winger must have sensed that this was the winning opportunity, for he fairly flew along the touchline. But when one might have thought that Bevan would have kept within inches of the line, he moved inside and through the growing mist. He looked as if he was going straight at Moses. We all thought the full-back would flatten the Australian in his tracks, but after that split second of uncertainty there was a gap of thin, foggy daylight between the two and that gap widened as all Warrington fans roared their approval."

Bath's conversion gave the Wire a 7-2 victory and restored them to the league leadership. Top-four contenders Workington Town were next on the executioner's list. They came to Wilderspool on 9 January and went down 15-7.

This time Bev scored early - another kick-and-chase effort - and could have had a hat-trick. He did score hat-tricks in the following two games, at home against Bramley (won 53-5) and at Rochdale (won 19-7). The game at the Athletic Grounds on 23 January brought up Bev's 399th, 400th and 401st tries for the club.

Bewildered Bramley

Against Bramley, the Wire had amassed 40 points without any score from Bev, a most unusual occurrence in such a runaway game. Just as everyone had resigned themselves to a blank Bevan afternoon, three tries were suddenly registered by the man. It was just like the late bus. None comes for ages and then three arrive at the same time.

For the first he merely added the *coup de grâce* to a wonderful length of the field movement. The second came from a typical interception, a grand run and a final dash past a mesmerised full-back.

As for the third, "it was not of this world", according to an awe-struck Bramley director. 'Criticus' described it thus in the *Warrington Examiner*: "Bevan beats two, three and even four opponents so easily that we have perhaps come to expect it every time. Well, he beat several again but how he managed to evade a challenge not an arm's length away on his left, and at the same time keep his foot off the touch-line literally inches away on the right, will remain a mystery. Indeed, it seemed an impossibility to keep in play, but he somehow contrived to sway his body away from his inside challenger, to push back off his left foot and straighten up with one and the same movement, then to accelerate like a flash to run on, outside of the last defender who had set himself to drive him inside.

His body at one moment seemed like a human corkscrew and if I ever saw a variety stage tight-rope act on a football field, then this was it. How the crowd roared - and well they might!" Warrington eventually won 53-5, Harry Bath booting ten goals and scoring a try.

After 14 consecutive victories Warrington travelled to Hull, themselves top-four challengers, on 30 January. In those days such a trip necessitated an overnight stay for Warrington. There was much interest in Warrington's latest debutant, the Lancashire, England and Great Britain winger, Stan McCormick who had been signed from St Helens. With Bevan on one wing and Stan on the other, the opposing sides were certainly going to feel the strain. On this occasion, however, it was Warrington who felt the strain. The Hull pack was simply unstoppable, hooker Tommy Harris ran in three tries and Warrington went down 10-24, despite Bev's two tries, one of which was created by McCormick.

The business end of the season had now arrived. Warrington were drawn against Bramley in the Challenge Cup first round - the last to be staged over two legs. The first leg at Wilderspool on 13 February saw a mighty effort from Bramley, who held the Wire to a mere five points until losing their hooker deep into the second half. Two devastating late tries from Bev eventually killed them off 17-0, but it had been a poor show by Warrington. In the return at the Barley Mow four days later, Bramley again had more of the play but this time

116

Warrington made the most of every chance, running in eight tries in a 30-5 triumph. Stan McCormick scored the first two with an interception and then a solo effort, both of which Bevan would have been proud had he scored them himself. Incredibly Bev then scored the remaining six, three of them following kicks. A genuine hat-trick - three consecutive tries by one player - is rare enough. A double hat-trick may possibly be unique.

Bev's half-dozen tries at Bramley brought his total for the last 10 games to 25 and he had scored in every one of them. On 20 February he failed to score in a 14-2 home victory over Oldham and Jack Steel remarked that: "Oldham marked Bevan in more ways than one". It was a tough game against a team Warrington would be visiting two weeks hence in the Challenge Cup second round. The Warrington forwards stood up well before a very physical Oldham pack and the 17,271 crowd went home happy in the knowledge that Warrington could make real progress in the Cup given a similar performance at Watersheddings. Gerry Helme and Brian Bevan were perhaps less happy. Gerry had several teeth knocked out and Bev had unaccountably lost the ball on one occasion when running clear for a try.

Before the Oldham cup-tie Warrington had a massive game to negotiate. St Helens were the visitors to Wilderspool on 27 February, and they were hell-bent on avenging their Knowsley Road defeat eight weeks earlier. A crowd of 29,107 saw a humdinger, a real blood and thunder affair. There were only two tries in the game, both in the first half, and young centre Jim Challinor was heavily involved in both. He scored the first after Gerry Helme had brilliantly bamboozled the Saints into ganging up on Bev, who never got the ball. Instead, Challinor was sent flying 40 yards for the touchdown. With Wire leading 5-4 Challinor then capitalised on smart play by Helme and Frodsham, shook off two tackles and punted to the line, enabling Bev to outpace Gordon Ratcliffe and George Parsons to score the decisive try. Warrington won 12-8 and 'Criticus' was moved to write: "better Warrington teamwork than this has not been seen since their Championship days".

In the concluding minutes of the game the crowd were treated to an unedifying but riveting sight, as Saints centre Duggie Greenall and Ray Price battered hell out of each other 40 yards behind play. A spectator ran on to the field and clouted Price, another ran on to intervene and the police ran on to cart both trespassers away. The two players then nonchalantly trotted back to rejoin the rugby match, Ron Gelder, the referee, and his touch-judges, apparently not having noticed anything untoward at all.

On 6 March, Watersheddings heaved with a capacity, all-ticket attendance of 21,000 for Warrington's second round Challenge Cup-tie with Oldham. Only one try resulted from the 80 minutes. Needless to say, it fell to Bev and it was arguably the most important he ever scored for the club. Certainly, it was one of the most dramatic and memorable, as all those present would testify. At one stage in his career Bev found scoring against Oldham as easy as shelling peas. He had already amassed 25 in 16 games against the Roughyeds, but most of them had been chalked up against teams which did not remotely measure up to the calibre of the Oldham side of 1954. They had managed to prevent Bev from scoring in their last three altercations with him.

Watersheddings lived up to its name that Saturday afternoon. Fans had to wade through slush, snow and water outside the ground, the pitch quickly became a morass and rain bucketed down. Ten minutes into the second half Oldham led 4-2, thanks to two goals from full-back Bernard Ganley. Under such conditions such a lead might be insurmountable.

That try at Oldham

Jack Steel's report in the *Warrington Guardian* was a minor masterpiece. Under the headline " 'Give it to Bevan' and Oldham did just that," he purred:
"Wonderful, wonderful Brian Bevan,
How Oldham's defence was at sea
Once he sailed away,
It was Warrington's day
As the crowds yelled BEVAN,
Glorious Bevan
Wonderful Bevan for me
The greatest ever Rugby League player, whose displays have exhausted almost every superlative in the 20th century dictionary, causes me to become lyrical, though the parody on the famous song may be as much off the beat as Tin Pan Alley is to Hans Andersen's mythical tales.

Apologies, therefore, to the composers of the popular number for major alterations but with Warrington (and other) sports-folk singing Bevan's praises, it becomes somewhat difficult to find something original to apply to this terrific figure of the professional handling code.

Wonderful Bevan ... What more can I say after that amazing score which made all the difference between a second round exit, a Wembley visit and possibly three trophies in the Wilderspool Stadium boardroom? That try, which only the Australian COULD have scored, was worth more than £10 to his club for every one of those eighty-odd yards he stepped out to the posts.

Bevan could not have timed the effort better if he had been clutching a stop-watch, because Oldham did look as if they were going to hold on to that two points lead. They did not appear quite so virile as they had done in the first '40'. Yet even the most primrose-and-blue-spectacled fan had to agree that when these two teams trooped off this pitch (it was equally as black and sticky as a coal by-product!) the home supporters had really something to crow about.

And, after 50 minutes had ticked away, Warrington supporters - the real kind who had paddled through snow, slush and mud in and around the stadium... - were becoming a little subdued. Yes, the shouting was to a larger degree the prerogative of the locals, until IT came.

Oldham were passing the ball neatly without really much incisiveness, and when Barrow came from the right to the left in an effort to try something new, he sent out a pass, which as events turned out, changed the whole complexion of the match.

Partly held, he tried a lobbing sort of throw to O'Grady close to the touchline. Whether the ball, slippery from the very first seconds of this match with an 'edge', handicapped the right centre in his effort, I don't really know. What I did see was Bevan placed between the pair and the ball fall, more or less, into his lap as he STOOD in a crouching position.

Oh! shouted the Oldham officials and from that split second 42,000 eyes (and those belonging to the small contingent who gate-crashed) were on Bevan. The often-linking-up Ganley was getting back into position as Bevan went through the gap. Just what would he do? Would he carry on along the wing and defy the full-back's desperate bid to head him off or force him over the side?

We, with pulses working overtime and hearts missing an extra jump, hadn't to wait long. Bevan moved inside, had forward Little almost on his tail, though the no. 12 was outside the clutching distance. Then Ganley made his effort and missed. The roar increased for it was impossible to stop a score under the posts.

Though the ovation was spontaneous, even from the Oldhamers, I traced a streak of relief in those Wire cheers. Warrington's section felt that this was IT - the real winner - though Bath's conversion made things still brighter.

Before I move off from the effort which changed the atmosphere, I cannot help but think that had Little made a do-or-die dive he may have touched Bevan's legs and brought him down. The slippery mud would undoubtedly have assisted the forward's momentum.

And, lastly, over to the Warrington players who were either left trailing or standing in their tracks. Once the ball was safely placed over the line, they charged from all quarters towards the scorer. It was amusing - more like a mad rush for the last bus home."

Bevan's reaction to the adulation was typical. 'Criticus' wrote in the *Warrington Examiner*: "Naturally he was 'mobbed' by his delighted colleagues as he walked back nonchalantly pulling up his knee-pads, and looking as if a magnificent effort such as he had just provided was the most commonplace thing in the world."

The match was won 7-4 and there was unbounded delight when a home tie with mid-table York was pulled out of the bag for the third round. Things could not get much better - top of the league and an almost certain passage into the Challenge Cup semi-finals.

Warrington were to get the rudest of wake-up calls the following week. If there was over-confidence in the camp it was well and truly shaken out by the events of 13 March. Warrington had only to turn up at Knotty Ash for the ritual slaughter of Liverpool City, the league's rubbing rags. City, winners of only two league games thus far, produced one of the biggest upsets imaginable winning 5-2 and deservedly on the day. The players had started on £7 to win but, at half-time with a 3-2 lead, their directors had upped the pay to £12 if they held out. The City heroes eventually got £13 a man as the Supporters' Club chipped in with an extra £1 each.

Bev did not get a look-in. As his colleagues constantly dropped passes and made wrong decisions, he was shackled by the unknown Bill Adair. It was a humbling experience for all concerned. Moreover, it ultimately cost Warrington their position at the top of the league.

The York cup-tie took place the following week before a crowd of over 19,000. A 26-5 victory ensued and Bev scored a try from another Ally Naughton

6 March, 1954, Challenge Cup second round. Snow is banked up along
the touch-lines as Oldham winger Terry O'Grady attempts to catch
a determined Brian Bevan.

Challenge Cup, second round, 6 March, 1954. Oldham winger
Terry O'Grady gets to grips with Bev. Forwards Ted White (Wire) and
Syd Little (Oldham) look on. A classic Bevan interception try won
this match for Warrington.

1954 Challenge Cup semi-final. Warrington beat Leeds 8-4 at Swinton. Jim Challinor works a reverse pass with Bev as Gordon Brown attempts to thwart the move. Challinor played centre to Bev 181 times, almost 100 more than anyone else.

kick but, for a change, it was his defence that drew the plaudits, as he bravely took down his opposing winger, the powerful Brian Smith, who regularly attempted to run through him.

On 3 April, Warrington met Leeds at Swinton in the Cup semi-final before a crowd of 36,993. Wire were the favourites but a team containing the likes of Lewis Jones, Jeff Stevenson and Arthur Clues were capable of beating anyone. Besides, Station Road was a bogey ground for Warrington, who had lost there twice in Lancashire Cup finals and thrice in Challenge Cup semi-finals since the war. In the end, there were only four points between the teams as Warrington won 8-4 although they were much the superior team. After only eight minutes they had taken a lead they never lost. Jim Challinor came bursting through the Leeds defence, feinted towards Bev and deceived a couple of defenders into going for the winger. The rest was easy as Jim sailed away for 30 yards to the line before touching down. Bath extended the lead to 5-0 with a penalty and five minutes from half-time Bev flew to the line after taking an awkward pass from Bob Ryan. He was denied a second try minutes later after beating four or five tacklers when Leeds winger Drew Turnbull came from the opposite side of the field to crash him into touch at the corner, as fine a tackle as one could wish to see.

Warrington paid a price for their victory. Second-rower Ted White had suffered an ankle injury in the early stages of the game but heroically played to the final whistle. X-rays showed he had played on a broken ankle and his season was over.

Bev's try in the semi-final had been his 442nd, bringing him level with Eric Batten's total and within striking distance of Alf Ellaby's all-time record. Within a fortnight the record did fall to Bev although there were no tries for him in Warrington's 7-7 draw at Oldham on 8 April and he was absent from an easy victory over Belle Vue two days later.

The Easter programme revealed Bev in all his glory. Three games in four days brought him nine tries as he left Ellaby's record in his wake. Good Friday, 16 April, took Warrington to Naughton Park where they despatched Widnes 21-5 before a crowd of more than 15,000. Bev scored three tries to take his total to 445 but again the victory was costly as second-rower Syd Phillips suffered a fractured collar-bone which ended his season.

Easter Saturday brought Whitehaven to Wilderspool where they received a 43-7 trouncing in front of 14,726 spectators. Bev was irresistible. His second of four tries finally eclipsed the great Ellaby's monumental record. Jack Steel was again voluble in his praise:

"Bevan is more than a day's tonic. He's the fellow who provides more chatter, discussion and 'off the record' conversation than happens at any Eastertide Trades Union Conference and, paradoxically, the Australian talks very little. Therefore, when the referee took his name the crowd chuckled at the mild reproval. But Whitehaven would have been delighted if he had been given the afternoon off for he danced around them as if they were raw amateurs instead of seasoned professionals. Bevan scored four spectacular tries. All of them were of exceptionally high standard. For one he ran 85 yards juggling [Whitehaven centre] Smith's pass and the crowd yelled 'TRY' even before he got to the halfway line. But for sheer artistry, uncanny action and split-second thinking, I preferred the effort in which he nipped out of a 'box' of opponents and showed as much skill as the owner of a seaside Puzzle Garden leading his patrons out of the maze of twists and turns and back to full daylight again. For another try he went inside as McKeown grabbed the air and for the other went streaking through like a centre forward chasing a through pass."

Unfortunately for Warrington they suffered yet another injury blow from the clash with Whitehaven. Skipper Ally Naughton had played despite a bruised calf sustained in the game at Widnes. The injury was aggravated and Ally did not complete the game and he missed the concluding fixtures along with White and Phillips. Eric Frodsham took over the captaincy.

Leigh gave Warrington a much tougher test at Wilderspool on Easter Monday. There were 22,658 at the ground hoping for a morale-boosting victory prior to Wembley five days later. Their wish was fulfilled as Wire won an entertaining match 21-15 and Bev scored two excellent tries, his first, the 450th of his career, following good approach work by Price and Challinor. The second was just pure Bevan - mystifying footwork which completely befuddled four would-be tacklers.

First, Wembley

Warrington's opponents in the Challenge Cup final at Wembley on 24 April were Halifax, who were to pip the Wire to top place in the league table by a solitary point. Only twice, in 1902 and 1903, had the game's top two teams met in the Challenge Cup final and never, as yet, in the Wembley era. It was hard to pick a favourite although Warrington did have a score to settle, because 50 years earlier Halifax had defeated them 8-3 in the 1904 Challenge Cup final at Salford. What was certain was that this Halifax team would be a desperately hard nut to crack. Their pack was one of the best the game had produced and the quality of their defence was amazing. In the whole of the 36-match league programme they conceded only 41 tries - five fewer than Bev scored for Warrington in the entire league programme during the season.

The press were so unsure of the outcome that many characterised the final as one that may well be decided by Brian Bevan. As far as they were concerned the two teams were so evenly matched that it would take a touch of genius to break the game. *The Rugby Leaguer* summed up the situation succinctly: "Blue and White soundness v Primrose and Blue soundness, plus the brilliance of Brian Bevan".

It did not turn out like that at all. If any side had the ability to bottle up Bev it was the Thrum Hallers. Their pack's cover defence was nigh impenetrable and in Dai Bevan they had arguably the best defensive winger in the game, a formidable obstacle to his Australian namesake. His centre Peter Todd was regarded as one of rugby league's hardest tacklers.

The teams at Wembley were:

Warrington: Frodsham (captain); B Bevan, Challinor, Stevens, McCormick; Price, Helme; Naughton, Wright, Lowe, Bath, Heathwood, Ryan

Halifax: Griffiths; Daniels, Lynch, Todd, D Bevan; Dean, Kielty; Thorley, Ackerley (captain), Wilkinson, Fearnley, Schofield, Clarkson

The final turned out to be a huge let-down. No tries were scored. Griffiths kicked two penalties for Halifax in the first half and Bath landed a pair in the second half. Bath missed seven kicks and Griffiths four. The 4-4 draw was the first ever at Wembley and the first in a Challenge Cup Final since 1910. The press put their own boot in. Jim Sullivan, writing in the *News of the World*, said: "The only thrill of a monotonously forward-controlled second half was a 50-yard diagonal dash by Brian Bevan". Alfred Drewry of the *Yorkshire Post*, wrote: "Bevan had one 60-yard run which started on the right touchline and died near the other; Lynch made one splendid run to clear his lines - and that takes care of the three-quarter moves worth mentioning". Phil King in *The People* droned: "A dull and uninspiring Wembley! Halifax and Warrington played like two groups of tired businessmen".

With Halifax leading 4-2 midway through the second half and defending their advantage with suffocating play-the-ball manoeuvres, sections of the crowd gave vent to their frustrations by slow handclapping and, when Ron Gelder blew for time, the feeling of anti-climax was all-pervading. No one had won the Cup and the public address announcer merely informed the 81,841 people present that "the game will now take place on another ground". It was all very unsatisfactory.

Brian Bevan had not had a bad game. It was not his fault that his genuine running chances amounted to only two. He had plenty of bad ball and spent much of his time over the touch-line, a victim of Dai Bevan's attentions or overwhelmed by a posse of Halifax forwards. 'Airedale' wrote in *The Rugby Leaguer*: "How Brian Bevan tried - and how a note of expectancy rose from the terraces every time he had the ball. This occurred to no other player with such uniformity and illustrated the regard in which Bev is held as a match-winner by the fans".

Even so Brian, his team-mates and the Warrington fans must have been mightily relieved to have got away with a draw. Two minutes from time Gerry Helme, having a rare bad day, had given away a penalty at a scrum, allowing Tuss Griffiths the opportunity to win the Challenge Cup for Halifax. It was one of those kickable-missable shots but the total silence as Griffiths connected with the ball turned to cheers from the Halifax supporters as the oval flew straight and true, only to suddenly veer past a post at the very last gasp. On such trifles are Cup finals won and lost, or, in this particular case, drawn.

The 1954 Challenge Cup final was not televised but the RFL allowed the BBC to make a film of the game. Tantalisingly, a video, issued in 2000, *Century of Rugby League* contains a fragment of the film. For those who never saw the maestro in action, it is an all too brief representation of what they missed. It does not show footage of Bevan going for the line. In fact he is seen racing back to his own line to field a kick from Ken Dean which he takes in full stride about ten yards in from the right touchline on the goal-line. He looks to the left, but decides to go to the right - the short side. By now he is well inside his own in-goal area and Tommy Lynch, the tough-tackling New Zealand centre, has arrived on the scene. Bev seems to slip onto one knee with Lynch all over him. It is a situation where any normal player would be happy to settle for a five-yard scrum.

Not Brian Bevan. Somehow, almost imperceptibly, he shakes Lynch off and proceeds to run flat behind the goal-line, skirts behind Frodsham, Challinor and the referee, suddenly steps onto the field of play proper and sails past the flailing dive of second-rower Albert Fearnley five yards from Warrington's line, all the time hurtling parallel with the goal-line towards the left wing. Loose-forward Des Clarkson tries to cut him down, but cannot live with the speed of the winger and flounders behind as Bevan at last straightens up having covered around sixty yards with the ball but is still only fifteen yards from his own goal-line. He has Stan McCormick flying outside him on the left wing but does he do the obvious things - either pass to Stan or die with the ball having done as much as could reasonably be expected? No, he puts his right boot to the ball, bisects Jack Wilkinson and Derrick Schofield and tears upfield after the kick.

The clip then ends. What is so riveting about this minuscule footage is the sheer effrontery of Bevan's play. There is precious little logic, in a rugby league sense, to anything that happens. Bev takes practically all the supposed wrong options, but such is his supreme confidence in his own ability and pace that the whole episode appears to be bread and butter to him. It is even more amazing when it is remembered that the action took place in the era of unlimited tackles, when kicking away possession could mean a hard time for the kicker's side. Of course, Bev probably expected to catch up with the ball before anyone else.

The replay of the Challenge Cup Final had been set for Wednesday, 5 May but first Warrington had a date with St Helens at Wilderspool on 1 May in the Championship semi-final. A cloudburst around noon flooded the pitch and made handling hazardous in the first portion of the match. Nonetheless, a good, hard, entertaining game ensued with Warrington clearly the better team. The only scores of the first half were two penalties from Harry Bath, but within minutes of the restart the result was in little doubt as Warrington claimed the afternoon's only try. Saints' winger Steve Llewellyn came racing down the right wing before cross-kicking around halfway. Eric Frodsham, a former Saint, fielded the ball more or less at the centre spot and found Stan McCormick, another ex-Saint, in support. Mac went between two hesitant defenders and linked with Bev. Away he went, calmly beating two tacklers before roaring past full-back Glyn Moses for a try which electrified the 23,888 onlookers. Bath converted Bev's 67th try of the season, added a further penalty and Wire had won 11-0.

Halifax had beaten Workington Town in the other semi-final and thus set up another clash with the Wire in the Championship final, which was to be staged at Maine Road on 8 May, just three days after the Challenge Cup Final replay at Bradford. It would be the first time that the top two sides in the league had ever met in the game's two major domestic finals. Both Warrington and Halifax had won their respective county championships and had been presented with their winners' medals after the Championship semi-finals. Unfortunately, the RFL blundered by sending the Lancashire League medals to Thrum Hall and the Yorkshire League medals to Wilderspool. Bev and his colleagues would have to wait until the encounter at Odsal, when an exchange of medals would be arranged.

Then, Odsal

Cec Mountford took his team to Ilkley for a few days prior to the replay. Rest, relaxation and a dose of tactical talking might just swing the final Warrington's way. Bev was probably a little distracted. His wife Doreen had only just come home from hospital having undergone surgery. He could really have done with time at home. Still, it could not be helped. He just had to get on with preparing for the biggest game he would ever play. Physically Warrington were well prepared for the exertions to come. The events which soon followed would prove whether they were psychologically ready.

Bev later recalled the journey from Ilkley to Bradford. As the team coach crossed the moors and hit the West Riding conurbation, he and his team-mates became aware of a huge volume of traffic. It seemed that all the north of England had decided to meet at Odsal Stadium that dull Wednesday evening at 7.00p.m.

No one - not the clubs, not the RFL, not the police, not the traffic authorities - had foreseen the migration of biblical proportions which took place on 5 May.

When a few minutes before seven o'clock, Brian Bevan left the dressing rooms at the top of the dark, vast slopes of Odsal's massive bowl, following next in line to his skipper, Eric Frodsham and alongside Halifax's Welsh international winger Arthur Daniels, he could hardly believe his eyes. Descending the path which led precipitously through the crowd to the pitch, his eyes were met by probably the biggest mass of humanity he had ever seen crushed into such a space. Top class rugby league players of the 1940s and 1950s were used to playing before massive crowds, but this was something else entirely. The Sydney Cricket Ground? Forget it. Wembley Stadium? Forget that too. Odsal's record crowd up to that evening had been the 69,898 for the Warrington versus Leeds Challenge Cup semi-final of April Fools' Day 1950. Bev had played in that game, of course, and had not scored but had gone away deliriously happy with his side's 16-4 passage to Wembley. Perhaps he considered it a good omen.

History records the attendance at Odsal for the Fax-Wire showdown as 102,569. That is merely the figure for those who paid. The most reasonable guess for the crowd, given the overwhelmed turnstiles, the broken-down fences and the men taking money in buckets at gaps in the perimeter, was more like 120,000 and possibly even higher. There were only 8,000 seats available and 3,000 of those were ringside seats around the playing area. Otherwise it was a case of find a spot and hope no one started a surge. Thankfully, miraculously, no one did and the whole fantastic event passed off without serious mishap.

Both teams made one change from their Wembley line-ups, both altering the left-centre berth. Warrington replaced Arnold Stevens with Ron Ryder, who had been on the transfer list for the last month, unhappy at being shifted from one position to another. Halifax had lost Peter Todd to injury and brought in a youngster from Warrington in Billy Mather.

A crowd of such gigantic proportions could have differing effects on the participants. It could inspire them or unnerve them. Fortunately, on this occasion, inspiration seemed to be the order of the day. The seething mass of spectators was treated to an infinitely better game than had been provided at Wembley. There was an abundance of controversial decisions, much good football and a game which was in the balance until the final whistle.

Crucially Warrington scored first and scored early. After eight minutes Bath moved towards the right wing taking the defence with him to cover the threat from Bev. At just the right moment Bath turned the ball inside to the onrushing Gerry Lowe, who made 20 yards before throwing out a pass that looked suspiciously forward to Challinor, who crashed over at the corner for an unimproved try. There was no further scoring until just before the interval. In the last five minutes of the half Warrington came under severe pressure. Halifax's speedy second-rower Derrick Schofield broke from his own half, kicked to the Wire line and looked likely to score after a 40-yard chase only for Brian Bevan to thwart him by booting the ball dead. It was a close shave but not as close as a Tommy Lynch try disallowed for a forward pass and an Arthur Daniels effort which was denied when Frodsham and McCormick bundled him into touch at the corner flag. In the 39th minute, however, the pressure told when Griffiths landed a simple penalty for offside. Warrington's 3-2 lead at half-time was, however, a somewhat meagre return for their general dominance.

Sixteen minutes into a terrific second half Harry Bath extended the lead to 5-2 with a 40-yard penalty, having missed with four previous kicks. Five minutes later Griffiths replied with a similar effort and it was 5-4 to Warrington. Warrington had the ascendancy and the biggest thrill of the game came 13 minutes from time. Gerry Helme, who had so nearly lost the Challenge Cup for his side at Wembley, decided the final with one of the greatest tries of his career. David Nicholls of the *Daily Express* described it thus: "The mighty roar of 103,000 fans swelled in crescendo across the packed terraces and rolled out across the Yorkshire moors as Helme, starting inside his own half, passed groping, frustrated men on his way to the line. He veered away to the left, turned back inside, found two customers for a dummy, turned outside again, ducked and scuttled in at the corner under a barrage of tacklers. What a try!"

Helme's try made the final score 8-4, but Warrington had a heart-stopping shock in the last minute when Daniels was again denied a try after jumping for and claiming Stan Kielty's cute kick over the Wire line. As he came to ground, Stan McCormick and Eric Frodsham somehow managed to prevent him from grounding the ball, or at least referee Ron Gelder thought so. "Robbed!" roared Halifax fans. "Justice!" was the Warrington retort.

The breaks had gone Warrington's way, but Wire had undoubtedly been the better team. Helme's performance had been magnificent, earning him the Lance Todd Trophy for the second time, while the Warrington pack, out-scrummaged 15-29, had taken all that the Halifax juggernaut could throw at them and returned it with interest.

Bev had won his second and last Challenge Cup. His remaining decade in the game would not see Warrington as finalists again. He had not scored in two finals and a replay but in each game he had provided excitement aplenty. Of his performance at Odsal, the *Daily Herald's* Allan Cave said: "Brian Bevan... gave the crowd their money's worth, although Halifax's Dai Bevan saw to it that he did not score. The less famous Bevan tackled the other with rare gusto and efficiency".

Finally, Maine Road

Three days later, the two sides trooped out at Maine Road, Manchester to contest the Championship Final. This time the whole game was televised by the BBC, who had paid £150 for the privilege, £50 more than their original bid. This time there was no world record crowd - just a rather disappointing 36,519. The comparatively low crowd was perhaps caused by the live broadcasting of the game or, just as likely, the limit to the fans' finances. They would certainly not have been put off by the prospect of a game as thrilling as the Odsal affair.

Warrington were bidding for an unprecedented club record of three trophies in a season. They were also aiming to become the first peacetime winners of the League and Cup double since Swinton had performed it in their All Four Cups season of 1927-28. Brian Bevan was taking part in his fourth Championship Final, all at Maine Road, and hoping for a winner's medal to go with that of 1948.

The teams at Maine Road were the same as at Odsal with the sole exception of the return of Todd for Mather in the Halifax ranks.

The game began badly for Warrington, who fell behind after only three minutes to a try in Brian Bevan's area of the field, although he was in no way to blame. Jack Wilkinson knocked on about 10 yards from the Wire line but Eric Frodsham gathered the ball and advantage was allowed. Crafty Stan Kielty then performed one of his party-pieces by driving forcefully into the full-back and relieving him of the ball. The next thing anybody knew he had shifted the ball to prop John Thorley, who rampaged over for a try converted by Griffiths. The 5-0 lead Halifax established was the most daylight seen between the teams during this three-match epic.

The gap was soon reduced to more normal proportions, however, when Bath succeeded with penalties in the 10th and 24th minutes. A long, straight penalty from Griffiths after 27 minutes concluded the first half scoring. The 7-4 lead was probably less than Halifax deserved and Warrington's task was a big one for the second half. A third Bath goal after 51 minutes placed the game on a knife edge. Des Clarkson hit a post with a penalty for Halifax before Warrington finally grabbed the lead at 8-7 with a simple Bath goal after Kielty was penalised in the 64th minute.

127

Three minutes later Brian Bevan seemed to have secured the match for Warrington. Gerry Helme had begun the move with another sparkling run, carried on by Stan McCormick, who sidestepped daintily but devastatingly down the left flank. Mac seemed to hesitate as the Halifax cover converged on him and then booted the ball across the field. Bev was onto the ball like lightning, taking a favourable bounce and racing to the posts with no challengers. Yet, referee Arthur Hill ruled him offside, a decision which perplexed Bev, many of the crowd and countless television viewers. In the *Manchester Evening Chronicle* the following Monday, Bev penned the following: "No prize money offered for guessing my big moment in the serial story of 240 minutes' football against Halifax. It could only be Saturday's try that was not a try. What do I think of it? Quite simply it seemed as good as many another one I have scored in my career... When I looked over my shoulder a few yards from the line I realised something had gone wrong, but carried on to ground under the post. Friends say that on TV they had a lengthy camera shot of myself with the ball under the posts. I'm told I looked the most disappointed man ever to have been on the screen. I certainly felt that way."

Bernard Cain of Warrington remembers

One of Brian Bevan's greatest tries was the one he scored at Maine Road in the 1954 Championship Final against Halifax, apart from the fact that it was disallowed, that is.

I was in direct line with Stan McCormick and when he glanced across, seeking Bevan, so did I. Bev was definitely three or four yards behind McCormick when he kicked across. The ball went fairly high, a kind bounce followed and Bev was on to it cleanly and behind the sticks. I suppose the referee assumed that Bev could not have got there so quickly - no one else would have - but we who saw him every week knew differently. I can see Bev now, standing beneath the crossbar, one arm raised in protest, and he was not a player who appealed without reason, as were none of the stars in those halcyon days.

Many, many times in an ordinary league game, the crowd quiet, the ball would reach Bev. Then the whole crowd would hum in anticipation as the tempo increased in a second as he shot away, even if he was eventually stopped. The threat was always there.

Once I was talking to Bill Kindon, the ex-Leigh and Lancashire left wing. He was moaning about the tough Christmas Leigh were facing - Workington, Wigan and Wire. He was due to mark Ike Southward, Billy Boston and Bevan. We asked who he dreaded most. Guess who! He said, in effect, they were all difficult, but at least you could maybe hold the first two if you took them low. But Bevan? You are lucky if you can get near his legs, he said.

Regarding some remarks I have heard down the years about suspect defence, just check how many of the top men had a field day against Bev. I recall one day seeing him track Vollenhoven right across from the opposite wing and bring him down in full flight. Nordgren, Cooper, Castle were all great left-wingers who he always coped with. And, of course, they all out-weighed him - but who didn't?

There were more anxious minutes for Warrington as the game went into its death throes. Kielty failed twice with drops at goal and, as at Wembley, Griffiths had a chance to win the game with two minutes to go. Thirty-five yards out and 10 yards from touch proved too difficult, however, the ball sailing inches wide again.

Bev later expressed sympathy for Halifax, who after all had scored the only try of the game, but he was in no doubt that the Wire deserved their victory - defence as well as attack wins games and Warrington's defence over the three matches had been breached just once. They had out-Halifaxed Halifax. The civic reception at Warrington Town Hall was a riot of joy as Warrington paraded the three trophies for which they had striven so valiantly.

Less than three weeks later the Warrington-Halifax saga was re-activated. The two clubs had been invited to play a couple of exhibition games in Ireland by the Marist Fathers of Milltown. The Warrington players had originally been promised a trip to France at the season's end but the jaunt to Ireland was equally welcome. Warrington were without their crackerjack half-backs, Price and Helme, who were more strenuously engaged in Australia with the 1954 Lions. Ally Naughton and Ted White were, however, fit for the trip and reserves Alan Brocklehurst, Roy Glover and Billy Sheridan also joined the party.

Harry Sunderland, the famous Australian journalist and rugby league propagandist, donated "The Dublin Copper Kettle" as a trophy for the winners of the second game at Dublin. The first game on Thursday, 27 May was staged before a crowd of 10,000 at Windsor Park, Belfast, Halifax winning easily 34-15. Bev, for a change not plagued by Dai Bevan, who was unable to get leave from his teaching post, scored Warrington's only try of the first half when he "beat several Halifax men to the ball in a mêlée near the Yorkshire goal and scrambled across the line".

The following evening the two teams met at Dalymount Park, Dublin and again Halifax were victorious 23-11. The crowd of 15,000 were well pleased, one Irish correspondent reporting: "They saw more open football and slick passing than they would normally expect in a whole season of Irish club rugby". Bev made "some scorching runs" and after 50 minutes "dazzled with a 40-yard run which put him between the posts".

The general consensus was that Halifax took the Irish games more seriously than Warrington. They won Harry Sunderland's kettle but how they would have preferred to have the Challenge Cup and Championship trophy.

Brian Bevan enjoyed his sojourn on the Emerald Isle but must have wondered why he and his team-mates were paid only £4 for their time and efforts.

Season 1953–54

Warrington finished 2nd in the League: P36, W30, D1, L5; For 663, Against 311
Bevan scored 62 tries for Warrington, plus 5 for representative teams

Date	Opponent	Score	Bevan	Crowd	
15 Aug	**Salford**	17–4	1T	12,290	
19 Aug	**Barrow**	12–7	2T	10,023	
22 Aug	Hull KR	5–17		5,597	
29 Aug	**Rochdale H**	16–4	1T	10,256	
3 Sep	Barrow	5–0		11,869	
5 Sep	**Belle Vue R**	28–7	2T	11,400	LC1
8 Sep	Belle Vue R	17–14		3,000	LC1
12 Sep	Leeds	14–43	2T	19,240	
19 Sep	**Wigan**	13–9		18,046	
24 Sep	**Oldham**	12–11		15,524	LC2
26 Sep	Whitehaven	19–5	2T	6,678	
30 Sep	St Helens	10–17	2T	23,184	LC Semi
3 Oct	**Hull KR**	42–13	3T	12,590	
10 Oct	Castleford	28–13	3T	6,416	
17 Oct	**Swinton**	23–8	dnp	14,350	
24 Oct	Workington T	7–9		12,285	
31 Oct	**Leeds**	15–9		16,109	
7 Nov	Belle Vue R	9–2	1T	1,082	
14 Nov	**Hull**	9–2	1T	10,132	
21 Nov	Salford	10–8	1T	7,252	
28 Nov	**Liverpool City**	30–6	dnp	7,424	
5 Dec	**Castleford**	36–12	2T	9,479	
12 Dec	Bramley	19–6		2,953	
25 Dec	**Widnes**	23–7	4T	10,599	
26 Dec	Leigh	13–6	1T	12,360	
1 Jan	Wigan	17–12	2T	22,048	
2 Jan	St Helens	7–2	1T	18,000	
9 Jan	**Workington T**	15–7	1T	16,115	
16 Jan	**Bramley**	53–5	3T	9,556	
23 Jan	Rochdale H	19–7	3T	14,200	
30 Jan	Hull	10–24	2T	16,000	
13 Feb	**Bramley**	17–0	2T	10,789	Ch Cup 1
17 Feb	Bramley	30–5	6T	2,048	Ch Cup 1
20 Feb	**Oldham**	14–2		17,271	
27 Feb	**St Helens**	12–8	1T	29,107	
6 Mar	Oldham	7–4	1T	21,000	Ch Cup 2
13 Mar	Liverpool City	2–5		2,748	
20 Mar	**York**	26–5	1T	19,118	Ch Cup 3
27 Mar	Swinton	15–9	dnp	7,800	
3 Apr	Leeds	8–4	1T	36,993	Ch Cup Semi (at Swinton)
8 Apr	Oldham	7–7		7,257	
10 Apr	**Belle Vue R**	42–6	dnp	12,387	
16 Apr	Widnes	21–5	3T	15,527	
17 Apr	**Whitehaven**	43–7	4T	14,726	
19 Apr	**Leigh**	21–15	2T	22,658	
24 Apr	Halifax	4–4		81,841	Ch Cup Final (at Wembley)
1 May	**St Helens**	11–0	1T	23,888	CH Semi
5 May	Halifax	8–4		102,569	Ch Cup F Replay (at Odsal)
8 May	Halifax	8–7		36,519	CH Final (at Maine Road)

Bevan's Representative Matches

Date	For	Opponent	Score	Bevan	Venue
7 Oct	Other Nationalities	Wales	30–5	1T	Odsal
18 Oct	Other Nationalities	France	15–10	2T	Bordeaux
28 Nov	Other Nationalities	England	22–30	2T	Wigan

130

Warrington's Great Season

Wembley 1954. Bev follows Eric Frodsham onto the Empire Stadium pitch for the try- less final against Halifax, who are led out
by Alvin Ackerley.

Wembley 1954. Halifax centre Tommy Lynch crunches Jim Challinor, but not before he releases Bev. In turn Bev will be stopped by his opposite winger Dai Bevan (extreme right), who made a huge impression on Bev as a defender.

The programme from
the Odsal replay

131

After the Odsal Replay, 1954. Bev, second from right, celebrates with his team mates. Skipper Eric Frodsham holds the Challenge Cup.

Bev runs laterally to avoid the attentions of Halifax defenders Tommy Lynch (3), Peter Todd (4) and Stan Kielty

Warrington 1953-4 with the Rugby League Championship Trophy, Rugby League Challenge Cup and Lancashire League Trophy
Back: E. White, S. Phillips, R. Ryan, G. Lowe, J. Challinor, A. Stevens, A. Humphreys, B. Bevan, H. Fishwick. Sitting: W. Sheridan, A. Heathwood, D. Naughton, S. McCormick, A. Naughton, C. Mountford, E. Frodsham, R. Ryder, H. Bath, F. Wright. Front: R. Price, G. Helme.

13. 1954-55 'Talk about winged feet'

The 1953-54 season had been one long triumph for Brian Bevan and for Warrington - records, trophies, medals all the way. Bev had again finished as the league's top try-scorer. His total of 67 was 15 ahead of the runner-up Jack McLean of Bradford Northern. Leeds's Drew Turnbull (41), Lionel Cooper (40) and St Helens's Steve Llewellyn (37) completed the top five. Harry Bath had jointly topped the goal-kickers with Peter Metcalfe of St Helens on 153 successes. In finishing at the head of the try-scorers for a fifth time Bev had equalled the record of Eric Harris of Leeds. The pair held the record until Martin Offiah finally broke it in 1995-96.

Rugby League Review, awarding its 'Oscars' for the last time before its imminent closure, included Bev yet again in its 'Stars of the Season' alongside his team-mate Bob Ryan, Ted Cahill (Rochdale Hornets), Lewis Jones (Leeds), Stan Kielty (Halifax) and Peter Metcalfe. Bev's centre partner, Jim Challinor was declared one of the 'Discoveries of the Season' with Billy Boston (Wigan), Eric Lockwood (Wakefield Trinity), Joe Mullaney (Featherstone Rovers) and Brian Smith (York). Warrington, unsurprisingly, were 'Team of the Season' while Ally Naughton was nominated as the year's 'Unluckiest Player'.

Much was expected of Warrington in 1954-55 and equally Bev was expected by a myriad of fans to carry on performing miracles. A correspondent of *The Rugby Leaguer*, previewing the 1954-55 season in the edition of 7 August, posed a disturbing thought, however, writing: "What Warrington would do without his services is a position which nobody at Wilderspool cares to discuss. He shows no signs of losing his terrific form but he simply cannot keep it up forever".

How comforted the writer would have been had he had the gift of clairvoyance. He was not to know that Bev was only halfway through his Wilderspool career.

He was now 30-years-old, had been a resident of Warrington for eight years and his life had changed. He had two infant daughters, Jennifer and Jeanette, and he had given up his job as a compositor and become an insurance agent. Physically, according to the official statistics, he had put on a solitary pound since 1946, now weighing in at 11 stones 10 pounds, but mysteriously had lost an inch-and-a-half from his 5ft 10in of 1946.

There were changes at the club, which had made a profit of only £425 on a turnover of almost £40,000 the previous season. That had been achieved despite average league crowds of 13,724, a rise of 1,423 on the 1952-53 season. During the off-season, Bev's former centre partner Ron Ryder joined the newly formed Blackpool Borough as player-coach under the managership of Chris Brockbank. Also off to the seaside went Ike Fishwick and two Wire reserves in Ray Perkins and Bill Wilkinson. On 2 June there was a big shock when Bev's fellow beneficiary, Bob Ryan, was transfer listed at £5,000. In a wider context, there was much rejoicing in the country a month later, when food rationing was finally abolished after more than 14 years.

Even as the season started, there were arguments raging in the press as to who the fastest player in the game was. These were fuelled by the sensation caused by

MacDonald Bailey's failed venture as a rugby league player and the sudden emergence of Wally McArthur, an Australian Aboriginal, who had made an electrifying start with Rochdale Hornets. 'Homer Genn', one of Bev's most avid supporters, succinctly put the question into perspective. He wrote: "Personally, I couldn't care less. There may be, and no doubt are, other wingers who may be equally as fast as Bevan, but where is the winger who possesses, as does Brian Bevan, the ability to see moves ahead, the deceptive body swerve, sidestep and amazing acceleration and an alert football brain? Brian Bevan is, in my opinion, the outstanding player of rugby league football in this age or any other age ... Long may he reign and run."

Whether Bev was or was not the fastest man in the game was irrelevant. He was best judged by the number of tries he continued to score and they showed no signs of drying up. Wigan were the first side to suffer. In the Wardonia Cup game at Wilderspool on 7 August, Bev was on top form opposite his old adversary Brian Nordgren. Noggy did not do too badly himself with a try and four goals but Bev outshone everyone with four scintillating touchdowns in a 27-14 victory. Jack Steel stated the blindingly obvious when he wrote: "We at Warrington think that the best way to win a game is to let Bevan have the ball".

The following week, he got plenty of ball in the opening league match at home against Hull. With Jim Challinor excelling inside him, Bev flew in for three more tries as Hull went down 29-8. Warrington then faced two tough away games within a couple of days of each other. At Barrow on Thursday, 19 August they were defeated 12-10 in an exciting encounter. Almost criminally, Bev only had one chance. A fine passing movement swept from the left and ended up with Bev 10 yards from the Barrow goal-line. By that time there was seemingly nowhere for him to go, as he faced three defenders with practically no space in which to manoeuvre. No matter, Bev wafted ghost-like past all three to score an outrageous try which levelled the scores at 10-10. Bath's conversion missed and Willie Horne eventually won the game for Barrow with a penalty goal.

Tries and testimonials

Two days later at Thrum Hall, another thrilling game took place. Despite a tremendous storm which spoiled the playing surface the two teams excelled. This time, Halifax emerged victorious 5-0 thanks to a penalty from Schofield and a clever try from Dean. As usual, Bev got little change out Dai Bevan. Two defeats in the first three games was not too good a start, but the Wire had been playing fine football, crucially without the missing tourists Price and Helme, for whom Ken Kerrigan and Eric Frodsham were deputising.

There was good news for Bev when it was announced that his testimonial fund had raised £1,528 for himself and Bob Ryan to share. Bev was certainly giving value for money, scoring in the next 11 games for Warrington, another of those purple patches he produced so frequently. In this period he touched down 23 times and added another five hat-tricks to his record. He began by terrorising Belle Vue Rangers on 25 August. Amazingly some Wire supporters had been catcalling him in the first half because he seemed a bit lackadaisical. His response was emphatic - four tries, two of which only he could have scored, as Warrington won 57-5.

Hat-tricks followed in the next two fixtures at home to Swinton and at Workington Town. Apart from Bev's eye-catching running, the Swinton game was notable for the use of an orange ball with which Warrington were clearly unhappy. Their 28-11 victory was somewhat laboured despite the score. The game at Borough Park on 4 September saw Bev at his incomparable best. He had often bewitched crowds in Cumberland but his performance in a super 29-18 victory over Town was truly exceptional.

A report by guest writer 'Cumbrian' in the *Warrington Guardian* eloquently described Bev's afternoon, starting with his second try: "Deep in the Warrington quarters, Challinor flicked an inside pass to Bevan, who, with three opponents no more than an arm's length away, would have done well to get only a few yards without being tackled. At least, that's what it looked like. But Bevan skirted them as if they had been mere shadows, then set off on one of those famous cross-country efforts by which regular followers of the game have come to know him so well. Swerving, dodging, side-stepping, he bamboozled a host of opponents. One second he looked certain to be stopped, but the next he was off again, apparently never slackening pace as he continued his triumphant course.

Opponents grabbed at him, but grabbed only shadows, others measured their length on the turf and looked positively nonplussed, while the flying winger went on and finished on McCormick's wing with as fine a try as is ever likely to be seen on Borough Park, or any other ground for that matter.

As he walked back, opposing players shook his hand or patted his back, and the crowd just roared and roared. The cheers continued while Bath prepared to place the ball for the kick at goal, and they were continued when he had succeeded. Bevan must have felt proud on this occasion if he has never done so before, for such a spontaneous tribute by supporters of the opposing side has surely never been given before.

'That try would have brought the Medes and Persians to their feet,' said one onlooker. 'It will be talked about for many a day.'

Within five minutes Bevan again did the unexpected. Helme put in a dashing run on the left touchline before kicking over the head of the Town full-back. The ball bounced nearly a route march from Bevan's usual position, but he was there to dribble over and score... Bevan's first try in the first half was a simple affair: swift passing and a walk-in at the corner."

The Workington game had seen the welcome return of Ray Price and Gerry Helme. Price had been playing a wonderful game until he was stretchered off just before the interval with a badly sprained ankle which caused him to miss the next nine games. Stan McCormick, too, suffered an ankle injury but managed to score a try almost literally on one leg.

Incredible

David Nicholls wrote in the *Daily Express*: "Bevan's Day will be the talk of Cumberland through many a long winter evening. Brian Bevan put on another of his incredible try-scoring acts as Warrington beat Workington Town 29-18 at Borough Park. A try looked as remote as the distant mass of Skiddaw when

Bevan got the ball on the edge of the Workington '25'. But away he went, twisting, side-stepping and striding out with deceptive pace across field.

Three would-be tacklers were handed off, four others groped desperately for the elusive shadow of the Australian ghost. But on went Bevan to a touchdown in the left corner. The stand rose, and 11,000 Cumbrians cheered the man who had scored **against** their own side. Fellow Australian Harry Bath added the final tribute with a goal from the touch-line."

On 11 September, Warrington visited Widnes in the first round of the Lancashire Cup. They were expected to win easily as Widnes were in a trough. Bev had never been in a Lancashire Cup-winning side. In fact it was his only missing honour. He scored twice but Widnes spoiled his party by winning 16-13.

Warrington were climbing the table, but were behind the West Riding trio of Bradford Northern, Halifax and Huddersfield, as well as local rivals Leigh and Wigan. A sketchy win at Swinton was followed by Warrington's first encounter with the rugby league's newest club, Blackpool Borough, on 25 September at Wilderspool. Six of the Borough team were ex-Wires, but they had lost all eight fixtures so far. In one of those dire displays with which Warrington were capable of shocking the world of rugby league, they would certainly have presented Blackpool with their first victory had it not been for Brian Bevan. In the end the Wire scraped home 22-15 on the back of Bev's genius and another hat-trick. He was, on the day, the only thing with which Borough could not deal.

A 17-17 draw at Rochdale cost Warrington a point, with a try conceded at the death, before Hull KR were routed 32-11 at Wilderspool on 9 October. Jimmy Honey, making his debut, had been signed from St Helens for £1,000 to cover the absence of Price but again it was Bev who stole the show with his sixth hat-trick of the season.

Going home?

A bombshell then struck readers of *Rugby League Review*. It was the news Warringtonians dreaded. The article on 14 October 1954, was headlined: "BRIAN BEVAN FOR AUSTRALIA" and was written by the respected Australian writer George Crawford. It ran: "Is Warrington's champion winger Brian Bevan having his last season in England? We in Australia are speculating on this. Bevan's brother Owen... telephoned recently to inform me that Bevan would be returning to Australia at the end of the current season.

'We don't know yet whether Brian will stay in Australia or go back to England,' he said. 'All we know is that he's coming home. It is inevitable that Australian clubs will bid strongly for Bevan, whom we have come to acknowledge as the greatest winger the game has seen'."

Stories like this periodically surfaced during Bev's career. Within a fortnight, however, Bev officially announced that he was not going back to Australia and most of Warrington could again sleep soundly. It was reported that he would be much better off in England as he was one of the country's best-paid players, receiving a signing-fee at the start of every season.

On 16 October Warrington travelled to Knotty Ash and to yet another potential banana skin. Without Bevan they may well have slipped up again. It helped Liverpool City that the ground conditions were a leveller, but their spirit and resolve were a sore trial to Warrington. Wire led 5-0 at the break, courtesy of their two tricky wingers. Stan McCormick provided the spark punting hard straight down the field, having noticed City's full-back was out of position. For once, Bev was able to shake of the attentions of Bill Adair and shot off after the ball. Obligingly, a few yards from the line it sat up and Bev crossed the line, as Adair crashed into him. Adair drove Bev on to his back but he had the ball down for a crucial score. Both sides scored one try in the second half. Warrington's was again the result of McCormick and Bevan prising open the tight Liverpool defence. Bev had put in one of his typical corkscrew runs before being finally grassed a few yards short, but not before he had popped up a scoring pass to Challinor and Warrington were home 8-3.

A week later, Warrington faced a vital home clash with Bradford Northern. The team had a novel half-back pairing in Honey, a real flyer over short distances, and Alf Arnold, a new scrum-half signing from St Helens Rugby Union club. Conditions were deplorably muddy, yet a pulsating game entranced a crowd of more than 10,000. Warrington led 12-0 at the break but Northern hit back furiously and it took a late Bevan try to clinch the match 15-10, the wingman taking Challinor's pass to race away before kicking long, shooting past two defenders, and catching up with the ball before toeing it over the line to ground yet another match-winning try.

Gerry Helme and Albert Naughton had been missing from the Bradford victory because they were in Great Britain's party for the inaugural World Cup competition in France. Both were to return as heroes three weeks later, having helped Britain to lift the trophy. Helme in particular had been an inspiration. While they were in France, Warrington won three matches to maintain their drive for a place in the top four.

On 30 October a very satisfactory 18-2 victory was recorded at Whitehaven. 'Cumbrian' was again happy to extol the virtues of Brian Bevan: "It is a tribute to Bevan that nowhere outside Warrington has he more admirers than at Whitehaven. He put in several of his inimical, baffling runs. Only one brought a try - a real classic - but the others were all so entertaining and he richly deserved the ovation he received from the crowd."

Salford gave Warrington a close shave the following Saturday, 6 November, and were the first team to prevent Bev from scoring since Halifax had done so back on 21 August. An 18-15 home victory was hard earned, particularly as Warrington had to play half the match minus Jimmy Honey, whose shoulder was dislocated. There were plenty of tries for Bev the next week, however. He roared over for half a dozen in a 39-12 drubbing of Liverpool and could have had a few more. Australians scored all but three of Warrington's points, Len Horton scoring a couple of tries and Harry Bath booting six goals. Jim Challinor was the sole English scorer with a try. Jim had now developed a nice line in snaffling tries by using Bev as a decoy. Not even Bev's performance could steal the headlines that week-end, for while Warrington were dealing with Liverpool, Great Britain were beating France 16-12 at Parc des Princes in Paris in the final of the World Cup, a game controlled by Warrington referee Charlie Appleton.

The Australian and New Zealand World Cup teams travelled to England following the tournament. They were heading for California to play two exhibition matches on their way home, testing the water for the development of the game in the United States. Two games involving the Antipodeans, both under floodlights, had been arranged in the north of England prior to their departure for the USA: a Rugby League XIII versus Australasia at Odsal on Wednesday, 17 November, and Australia versus New Zealand at Leigh on 19 November.

Brian Bevan was selected to play for the Rugby League XIII against the combined Kangaroos and Kiwis. There were five Australians - Bev, Paskins, Cooper, Bath and Clues - in the side and two New Zealanders, Joe Phillips and Tommy Lynch. Five Englishmen and a Scot, Dave Valentine, the captain, were also included. Three of the victorious World Cup team - Valentine, Gerry Helme and Don Robinson - added interest to the make-up of the side.

Something to talk about

In the afternoon, the teams were afforded a civic reception by the Lord Mayor of Bradford and before the game the World Cup was paraded around Odsal by members of the Great Britain team. A cold and misty night kept the crowd down to just above 17,000. Lionel Cooper scored the first try, crashing over at the corner, but straining a thigh muscle in the process. It was the first and only time that the RL XIII would lead. The Australasian team, comprised of nine Australians and four New Zealanders, and led well by full-back Clive Churchill, had a decided advantage in teamwork and spirit. They eventually ran out 25-13 winners. "Even so," wrote Leslie Temlett in the *Yorkshire Evening Post*: "It was from Warrington's Australian flyer, Brian Bevan, that the two greatest thrills and the two best tries of the match came. What gems they were! Bevan at his best. The men from Australia and New Zealand, to whom Bevan, despite his Australian birth, is but a name and a legend, will go home with something to talk about."

The following afternoon, Bevan was privileged to attend a unique reception at the Queen's Hotel, Leeds. It was given by the Rugby League Council and involved the Australian and New Zealand teams, who had never before been in England at the same time, as well as members of the Rugby League XIII and the Great Britain World Cup squad. Among the distinguished guests were five former Lions captains in Jonty Parkin, Jim Brough, Gus Risman, Ernest Ward and Dickie Williams, as well as 78-year-old former Secretary of the RFL, John Wilson.

The game at Odsal marked the end of an era because it was the last time that Brian Bevan and Lionel Cooper ever appeared on the same pitch. Cooper and Bevan formed a mutual admiration society, which would only end in their deaths. Lionel had decided to retire at the end of the season, by which time he would have passed his 32nd birthday. He had plenty of good football left in him, for at that point in the season he had already amassed 33 tries, second only to Bev, who was on 35. New Zealanders Peter Henderson (24) and Brian Nordgren (22) were the nearest challengers, along with Leigh's World Cup winger Frank Kitchen (22).

By the time the World Cup was completed, the complexion of the top-four struggle had changed. Oldham had hit the top, a point ahead of Warrington, who were closely followed by three more Lancastrian clubs in Wigan, St Helens and Leigh. From then until the season's end Warrington and Oldham would engage in a dogfight for the leadership of the competition.

The Wire had not been beaten in the league since 21 August. On 20 November they met Hull at The Boulevard with an unbeaten 12-match run to defend. It looked like unlucky 13 as the Airlie Birds built an early 7-0 lead, but a try from Bev put them back into the picture and, when the game had to be won in the last 10 minutes with Warrington holding a 15-12 lead, it was Bev who sealed the victory. Ally Naughton put in a shrewd kick which Bev collected in his own half, booted forward and left everyone behind for a killer try, making the final score 20-12. It was one of Warrington's best performances of the season. Bev was, however, outshone by Harry Bath, who scored a try and landed four fabulous goals with a heavy, soddened ball from a mud-bound pitch.

The following week it was again Bath who provided the goods. His four penalty goals matched four from St Helens's scrum-half Joe Ball, as Warrington earned an 8-8 draw at Knowsley Road before a crowd of 17,593. Then, on 4 December, Warrington had the narrowest of escapes against a resurgent Rochdale Hornets at Wilderspool. In atrocious conditions, Hornets took a 7-0 lead into half-time and seemed well capable of holding their advantage. Bev was seen limping off in some discomfort at the break and returned with his right foot strapped, but it was the miracle man who turned and finally won the game. A penalty got Warrington onto the scoreboard before Bev was finally given a chance to run. Frodsham started the move which Price carried on before setting the winger free 60 yards out.

Only Ted Cahill, albeit a limpet-like tackler, stood between him and a try. Bev's injury dematerialised and, after making as if to turn inwards, he flew outwards past the flailing arms of Cahill's half-tackle and sped to the corner flag for a fine try. Bev, again feeling the injury, hobbled back to the congratulations of his team-mates. With four minutes to go, Warrington still trailed 5-7 and Bev's troubled gait seemed to indicate that there was not much point in plying him with the ball. Suddenly, however, a chance arose. Bath and Syd Phillips brought the game out of Warrington's half and Bev was put in possession. He zipped past opposing winger Wilf Roach and outpaced a couple of coverers. Cahill this time failed to lay a finger on him, as he skated past him to score the try which gave his team a truly dramatic 8-7 victory.

Jack Steel wrote: "Fish, Rosenfeld and Bevan... and the greatest of these is Bevan. Apologies for switching the words of a time-honoured axiom (Faith, Hope and Charity) but the belief is that Bevan by his extra-ordinary elusiveness IS the greatest winger of all time. At least that is what the 6,985 onlookers thought after the famous Australian had scored two wonder tries and set Wilderspool alight on Saturday... Many times I've seen Wilderspool roar its approval of the mighty deeds of this great player but never have I witnessed such an enthusiastic scene from barely 7,000 souls. Hats, scarves, gloves were used in a spontaneous 'wave' to acclaim the man who turned defeat into victory."

On 11 December, Bev literally walked over for a try - all of two yards - in Warrington's 23-3 victory at Blackpool but missed the next two games with that troublesome ankle. That victory, coupled with Whitehaven's holding of Oldham to a 2-2 draw, took Warrington to the top of the league, one point ahead of the Roughyeds, who had played two matches fewer. Bev was back for the home match against Leigh on 27 December, a game crucial to the top-four placings. A 25,757 crowd went home content with Warrington's 27-12 victory, Bev scored a good try and his ankle appeared mended. Warrington had now gone 19 league games without defeat. Wigan at Central Park on New Year's Day would be a big obstacle to making it 20, but Warrington had apparently laid the Wigan bogey over the last couple of years.

When Bev met Billy

There was tremendous interest in the clash - 28,778 attended - not least because this was the first time rugby league fans would have the opportunity to compare the merits of Bev and Billy Boston, although the two were both right wingers and therefore not directly opposed. Mike Rowan vividly recalled the occasion: "The jeers of the Wigan faithful wound me up no end as the game wore on. Billy Boston was the new kid on the block and had established himself as the best of British. For years the Old Man had reigned supreme and was regarded as the master but the lads at Central Park hailed Bill as the new Messiah. As it turned out Boston scored in magnificent fashion early on with a long range effort, leaving McCormick and Frodsham for dead. Quite naturally the pie-eaters were in their glory, rubbing it in, but, alas for them, yon man with the bald head got two.

Talk about winged feet. Bevan had the speed of a greyhound and the movement of a panther, as he took a pass from Jim Challinor and beat three men to get in at the corner. Cutting across to head him off was Boston but to no avail. In later years on video Billy recalled him as: 'bald, droopy shoulders, no teeth, big pads on his knees. As soon as he got the ball he was gone like a whippet. I've never seen anything as good in my life. You'd never put a hand on him normally.'"

Actually on this occasion Billy put more than his hands on Bev who was carried off in agony! Many of the Warrington fans were incensed at their favourite's misfortune but he soon recovered. No one was to know, of course, but they were witnessing the first clash of the men who were ultimately to be rugby league's two most prolific try-scorers. Bev might have finished 2-1 up on tries but his side lost 6-18, allowing Oldham to regain the league leadership.

A week later another huge fixture pitched Warrington against St Helens at Wilderspool. There was another massive crowd of 23,932, bringing the aggregate for the last three matches to more than 78,000. Bev was shackled by Saints' own young sensation Frank Carlton and never got a running chance but was happy enough with Wire's 18-14 victory. This set up nicely what was possibly the most crucial league fixture of the season - Oldham at Watersheddings on 15 January. Victory there would again knock Oldham from the top spot. There was good news too as reinforcements were coming. Cec Mountford had declared: "People are tired of seeing Warrington play without the ball". He therefore signed Tom McKinney, a 1954 tourist and the only Irishman ever to represent Great Britain in tests, from Salford at a reputed cost of £3,500, a record fee for a hooker. McKinney was in the team at Watersheddings.

Oldham had lost only one league game all season, at Salford on 25 August, and had reached the Lancashire Cup final, losing to Barrow. They were undefeated in their last 19 league matches and were on a princely £17/10/- (£17.50) to beat Warrington, a result of their win bonus system. Snow and bitter cold gave Watersheddings an Arctic appearance. All other games except Leeds versus Featherstone were postponed. Nevertheless, the vile conditions failed to deter more than 15,000 hardy souls from trekking up the hill from Oldham town centre. They were rewarded with a thrilling encounter.

In the first minute a scrum went down 15 yards from the Oldham line. McKinney struck like an adder, Helme scooted round the blindside and shot a long pass to Bev, who rounded Terry O'Grady as if he was not there, to give Wire an immediate advantage. By half-time, however, O'Grady and his centre, Alan Davies, had both scored tries down Bev's wing and Oldham led 8-5. Moreover, Jim Challinor was well and truly crocked, missing the last 10 minutes of the half and spending the entire second half limping on the left wing. Oldham dominated the second half, but failed to score again. Warrington had just two chances to add to their own score. Bath took the first to land a penalty to bring the score to 7-8.

Eighteen minutes had gone when the second chance arose out of the blue. Len Horton took a ball from Bath near his own '25', beautifully beat a couple of defenders and raced to halfway before hoofing the ball almost to the Oldham posts and just to the right of them. A group of Oldhamers raced for the ball, but out of the wide blue yonder came a figure running faster than all of them. It was Bev. In high glee he dropped like a thunderbolt from heaven on to the ball for a try which won the game 12-8. Mike Rowan recalled: "Oldham defenders were nonplussed as their peculiar nemesis won the race to register a change on the scoreboard. Peculiar? Yes, but not in a derisory way. It was just that in a moment of absolute delight the highly charged-up Bev provided a comic interlude by hugging himself and doing a jig. When his mates got to him they felt like doing a conga. Yet again he had shown himself to be the matchless match-winner. We were glowing with pride. 'There's no one like him,' we reminded ourselves. Oldham men agreed. He had pulled off a great win against the odds. Only the very best were capable of that. Once again this insignificant looking man was the hero. On a bitter, freezing cold day he had us all aglow inside."

Geoff Smith of Warrington remembers

Just one of many wonderful memories I have of Bev was when, as a teenager, with a few of my mates, we travelled by train to Oldham. It was a freezing cold day and only the exuberance of youth got us there. All other soccer and rugby matches were off except at Watersheddings.

Such was the importance of the match that Oldham were on a double bonus scheme and on a long winning run. This was in the 1950s when Oldham were a great team.

When the tons of straw and braziers were cleared from the pitch, a confident looking Roughyeds team ran out but they were in for a bonus-stopping shock in the shape of the great Brian Bevan. Warrington ended up winning a hard fought, low-scoring game in which they got only two tries. The first try came when Bevan took a blind-side pass from a scrum on the halfway line. With his great balance and blinding speed, he ghosted between the opposing winger and fullback to score a brilliant try.

His second try just begged the question, where did he come from? The Wire centre Len Horton broke clear on the left touch-line and, with 70 yards to go, gave the ball an almighty hoof. It settled over the try-line. Horton was in a neck and neck race with the Oldham fullback. From the right touch-line and many yards further back, Bevan had set off on an incredible angled run, to beat them both by a good 10 yards to touch down for the try.

Nothing, not even adverse ground and weather conditions, affected his electrifying, balanced running. Brian Bevan - a great, great athlete.

The yo-yo syndrome at the top of the league had dumped Oldham from the top and instead of that huge bonus they received just £5 a man for losing. Salt was rubbed into the wound the following Saturday, 22 January, when they went down at Workington while Warrington despatched Whitehaven 30-3 at Wilderspool, giving them a three-point lead at the top although Oldham had two games in hand. The victory enabled Warrington to become the first team to score 500 points in the league that season. Unbeknown to anyone, it also marked a monumental milestone in Bev's career. He scored three tries, all through sheer pace, the third of which was his 500th. The chaotic state of record-keeping had made it impossible for statisticians to pinpoint the achievement. Instead, they would mistakenly celebrate the feat some seven weeks later.

On 5 February, Warrington played their great rivals Halifax at Wilderspool and won easily 24-3. Bev was missing due to a bout of influenza and, ironically, his replacement Jimmy Honey scored two tries against Dai Bevan. Wire were back on the winning trail, five consecutive victories had followed the defeat at Wigan. The Challenge Cup had paired them with Bradford Northern at Odsal on 12 February, a tricky tie but one which they were expected to win. The bookmakers had made them 13/2 second favourites for the Cup, Oldham being 6/1 favourites, despite being paired with Wigan.

Out at Odsal

Northern had covered the pitch with straw, which was just as well, because a couple of inches of snow had fallen and more continued to fall in the freezing bowl during the match. It presented a very different picture to Warrington's last appearance at Odsal in the Challenge Cup replay back in May, 1954. This time there were only 14,302 spectators dotted around the snow-clad slopes. Shocking weather had appeared to dog Warrington throughout the season, yet they had so far managed to avoid postponements, an advantage that would be clearly demonstrated as the campaign drew to its close. The glut of postponements had prompted once again the age-old call for a summer season. And another familiar cure-all had been rejected on 31 January, when a Rugby League Council vote to set up two divisions had actually been won 19-12 (Warrington voted in favour) but failed to obtain the necessary two-thirds majority. Arguments were also still raging over the play-the-ball rule and the televising of matches. *Plus ça change...*

Brian Bevan probably wished he had caught the 'flu a little bit later, as the Odsal ice-field provided him with one of the worst days of his playing career. In the first minute Northern's loose-forward Ken Traill put in a long touch-finder which Bev spilled as he was tackled. Bradford gained possession and Traill's sublime long pass sent centre Len Haley between Bevan and Horton for a try at the corner, magnificently goaled by reserve full-back Bill Seddon, who soon added two penalties for a 9-0 lead. Wire had overwhelming possession throughout, but their only scores were two goals by Eric Frodsham. Bev had a couple of glorious chances to save the match, but fell to the treacherous surface and to fantastic tackling by the inspired Odsalites. Bradford's 9-4 victory was the shock of the round but the 1955 Challenge Cup mirrored that of 1952 when shocks abounded. Ultimately, the unlikely pairing of two teams from the north-west, Barrow and Workington Town, at Wembley provided the romance sadly missing from the Challenge Cup in the 21st century.

Warrington had to put their disappointment behind them. They still had the Championship and Lancashire League in their sights. Bev was quickly back in the try-scoring groove, adding a dozen in the next five matches. Two in a 31-3 romp at Belle Vue, Warrington's last ever appearance at the Zoological Gardens (a rampant Ally Naughton scored the other five Wire tries), was followed by four in a 35-9 thumping of Workington at Wilderspool on 12 March. This was a momentous day for Bev and his Warrington worshippers for the whole rugby league world believed that he had finally scored his 500th try when he ran in a routine 25-yarder about half an hour into the game. The 15,264 witnesses certainly raised the roof in recognition of the great man's historic achievement, even if it was in reality his 504th. He did, however, score his 1,500th point for Warrington with his fourth try.

A week later, Wigan came to Wilderspool and upset the Warrington applecart with a 13-9 triumph before a crowd of 21,629. Bev scored the sole Warrington try, although Wiganers swore he bounced the ball in touching down. The game saw Bev lined up for the last time opposite Brian Nordgren, who gave up the game soon after to pursue his career as a barrister. Noggy's 312 tries in 294 appearances for Wigan was ample testimony to his prowess, as Brian was all too ready to acknowledge, having sampled plenty of the New Zealander's punishing power and pace in their many confrontations.

On 26 March, Warrington met Oldham at Wilderspool in what was, at that juncture, thought to be the crucial game of the season. Warrington were just one point ahead of Oldham, but still Oldham had those two games in hand. Defeat by the men from Watersheddings would probably mean the loss of the Lancashire League title and a best place of second in the league. It was the proverbial must-win-game. As usual the weather was atrocious. It had been raining heavily since Friday night and continued throughout the game. Under the circumstances the play was wonderful and, on balance, Oldham had the better of it. It was, however, another Brian Bevan extravaganza. Warrington were leading 7-4 when Oldham attempted to move the ball from their own '25'. Wrong move - Bev was in between Ken Jackson and Dick Cracknell before they could blink for an interception try, which gave his side a 10-4 interval lead.

Early in the second half a similar situation arose and this time Frank Stirrup tried to put Cracknell away. Wrong move again - Bev repeated the dose and Oldham were surely beaten. They still had not learned their lesson, it seemed, for yet again they tried to bring the ball from their own '25', and spilled it for Helme

to grab. He pushed it out to Naughton who kicked for the corner and Bev was first to the ball for a stunning hat-trick, his 10th of the season. Warrington had won 18-4, thanks mainly to the usual suspect.

Three more victories in seven days took Warrington to their final league fixture on 11 April, the Easter Monday derby at Leigh. Victory there would have given the Wire both the county title and the league leadership - as things turned out even a draw would have sufficed. Leigh were desperate for the points too because they were fighting for a play-off spot. Their 14-5 victory over the Wire threw everything into the melting pot. Intriguingly it was Leigh who decided the destination of the prizes five days later when they went to Oldham. Oldham seemed to have the game and the Lancashire League won but a late goal by Leigh full-back Jimmy Ledgard dramatically stole a 15-15 draw and presented the trophy to Warrington on a superior scoring average.

Oldham could still pip Warrington for the rugby league's league leadership, however, if they picked up a point from their final game against Hull, who were to finish 19th, at Watersheddings on 18 April. A formality turned into a disaster for Oldham who went down 5-18. Wire were thus presented with another gift. Oldham had finished on 60 points, the same as Warrington, but again their points average was inferior. The Championship semi-finals were scheduled for Saturday, 23 April, when Oldham disposed of Leeds 25-6. Warrington, on the other hand, had to wait to find out who their opponents would be. It had appeared likely to be Wigan but they were beaten by Rochdale Hornets in their last fixture and Halifax came with a late run with seven consecutive victories to steal fourth spot, again on scoring averages. Their fixture backlog was so severe that the semi-final had to be pushed back to Wednesday, 27 April to see if they could pip Wigan.

Retaining the Championship

Consequently Warrington had the good fortune to meet a side which had played six times since Warrington's last game, and who had also played nine games in 18 days, the last coming only 48 hours earlier. However, this Warrington side was not going to fall into the trap of over-confidence. Certainly the 22,311 crowd arrived expecting a stern struggle, in the recent tradition of Wire-Fax meetings. They got one, too. Warrington won 17-9 to progress to their fifth Championship final of the post-war period. They would have to play better though to beat Oldham and certainly they would have to get the ball to Bev, who did not get a solitary running chance against the Thrum Hallers, even though this time Dai Bevan was not on the field.

Prior to the final, Bev and his team-mates were called in for extra training - there was a gap of 17 days between the semi and the final - and on the Thursday before the game they were taken to Cleveleys for relaxation.

Ray Price had been out since 2 April with a cracked wrist and missed the final. Oldham were lacking Arthur Tomlinson, their fearsome second-rower, who had received a 10 match suspension, and fielded half-back Frank Stirrup at full-back, despite having the opportunity to reintroduce Bernard Ganley, who had been injured for quite some time. If goal-kicking were to enter the equation they might regret his omission.

The normal conditions for Warrington matches in 1954-55 followed them to Maine Road on 14 May. 'Criticus' described matters thus:

"The Northern Rugby Football League Championship final of 1955... will be remembered as the match which produced football of a quality which we had no right to expect, under conditions as weird as one could imagine. Heavy rain on Friday, and on Saturday morning, had left the Maine Road playing pitch soaking wet and spongy. Then, before the interval, came a deluge of rain and hailstones, which continued while the players were off the field, and continued for some minutes after they returned. Parts of the field, near the goalposts, resembled miniature lakes, and the rest of it, except near one touch-line, was little better. How the players managed to master the conditions and produce such grand football must forever remain a cause for wonder. Before long numbers on jerseys were obliterated by mud and wet, and many of the players looked more like nigger minstrels. All were heroes under the circumstances, and it seemed a pity after such a thrilling struggle from beginning to end that one team had to lose."

The teams, for a game which attracted a drenched crowd of 49,434, were:
Oldham: Stirrup; Barrow, Cracknell, Davies (captain), O'Grady; Daley, Pitchford; Ogden, Keith, Jackson, Winslade, Little, Goldswain.
Warrington: Frodsham; Bevan, Challinor, A. Naughton (captain), Horton; Honey, Helme; D Naughton, McKinney, Lowe, Phillips, Bath, Ryan

Four minutes into the game Oldham produced a delightful passing movement, which ended in Roland Barrow hurtling over at the corner with referee Alf Hill pointing for the try, only to be overruled by the touch judge as the corner flag went down. Bev was unlucky when he chased after a kick from Honey, only for the ball to trickle into touch just before he got to it and then he turned saviour by bundling Terry O'Grady out of play just in time.

It was certainly against the run of play when Warrington took the lead after 24 minutes. When the ball was jolted out of an Oldham player's hands in a tackle in their own '25', Bath was first to it. "He twice cleverly changed direction in the course of a short run", wrote 'Criticus', "before serving Challinor on his right, and he in turn passed to Bevan. With a despairing effort full-back Stirrup actually got a grip on the winger, but in trying to put him down could do no more than swing him round, and the impetus helped Bevan over."

It was not one of Bev's greatest tries, but it was one of his most important scores. Oldham came again and Bev once more saved his line by throwing O'Grady into touch. After 35 minutes Warrington finally cracked. Oldham captain Davies was taken into touch near the Warrington line but his side won the scrum and Frank Pitchford scurried sharply down the blind side between the packs and Bev, who made the tackle all right, but was too late to stop the scrum-half from touching down. The teams waded to the dressing rooms locked at 3-3.

A change of kit at least enabled the players to feel more comfortable, but within minutes of the restart most were again bedraggled and virtually unrecognisable. After five minutes Harry Bath raised his arms high in the air and applauded himself, as he saw his wide-angled 45-yard kick sail between the posts after Oldham had been penalised at a play-the-ball. Warrington clung to this slender lead as if their lives rode on the outcome. They were the better team in the second half and hearts jumped into mouths, when Bev almost sealed the match late on but was buried, along with the corner flag, over the touchline by a three-man tackle, as he dived for glory. A few minutes from time Bath did seal Warrington's victory at 7-3 when he landed another mammoth 40-yard penalty after Ally Naughton had been obstructed. Harry had done it again - he had clinched Warrington's second consecutive Championship with his mighty kicking. *The Rugby Leaguer's* headline said it all: "Bath And Bevan Were The Winners".

It had been a magnificent match. There was widespread sympathy for Oldham, who had finished as runners-up in three competitions, but as Bev and his happy colleagues collected their winners medals from the Earl of Derby, they could not have imagined that it would be Warrington's last Championship final victory.

Bev had finished runner-up to Lionel Cooper in the try-scoring stakes in 1954-55, his Championship final try bringing his total to 63, three behind the now retired Cooper, whose fellow Fartown winger Peter Henderson finished third with 45. Bev had scored his tries in only 38 games, Cooper playing one more match.

The *Manchester Evening Chronicle* had inaugurated a Player of the Year competition in various Kemsley run newspapers in Lancashire with votes cast by readers. Bev won the trophy, which was presented to him before the Championship semi-final against Halifax. He had polled 15,102 votes, ahead of Jim Ledgard (14,638) and Gerry Helme (14,517). The presence of six Wires in the top twenty was a clear indication of the club's high standing in the game.

Brian Bevan's own unique standing in the game received further recognition in the May 1955 edition of the popular *Rugby League Gazette*. Their correspondent 'J.E.B.' issued the first 'World Ratings', a practice taken up in more recent times by *Open Rugby*. His top five wingmen read: 1. Brian Bevan (Warrington), 2. Raymond Contrastin (France), 3. Vincent Cantoni (France), 4. Noel Pidding (Australia), 5. Frank Kitchen (Leigh).

PLAYER OF THE YEAR

Bev won the *Manchester Evening Chronicle* Player of the Year Award in 1954-55. This portrait appeared on the back page of the newspaper's Championship Final Souvenir issue of 14 May, 1955.

Below are the full results of the poll for the Player of the Year, and the World Ratings by 'J.E.B.' for 1954-55, from *Rugby League Gazette*.

BEVAN TOPS THE POLL

THE Manchester published " Evening Chronicle " has recently conducted a ballot to find the " Rugby League Player of the Year," and the final voting has revealed the tremendous interest that followers of the game have in ballots of this kind. Whilst it is agreed that the paper is essentially a Lancashire paper and that the final placings strongly reflect this fact there can be little doubt that the selection of BRIAN BEVAN as the " Player of the Year " would meet with the approval of Rugby League enthusiasts everywhere.

We publish here the final placings in the " Evening Chronicle " ballot and a picture of the trophy, which is to be awarded to Brian Bevan

BEVAN (Warrington) ..	15,102
LEDGARD (Leigh) ..	14,638
HELME (Warrington) .	14,517
NORDGREN (Wigan) ..	14,399
BOSTON (Wigan)	13,675
VALENTINE (Huddersfi'd)	13,513
BATH (Warrington) ..	13,484
HORNE (Barrow)	12,500
ASHCROFT (Wigan) ...	11,937
PLATT (Wigan)	10,641
WOOD (Liverpool)	10,286
A. NAUGHTON (Warr'n)	9,729
CHALLINOR (Warrington)	9,545
KITCHEN (Leigh) .	9,146
A. DAVIES (Oldham) ...	8,814
PRICE (Warrington)	8,343
COOPER (Huddersfield) ...	8,020
CHISNALL (Rochdale) ...	7,306
GREENALL (St. Helens) ...	7,111
GANLEY (Oldham)	7,046
L. JONES (Leeds)	6,939

Courtesy of " Evening Chronicle "

WORLD RATINGS by "J.E.B."

EVERY sport in the world, with the exception of Rugby League, has for a number of years now issued a list which gives the world ratings of the best men of that particular sport.

Over the past two years I have watched our sport at many venues with a view to issuing the following list which in my opinion records five players in each position who are our world's best.

All of the men named are playing to-day, all are past and present internationals. I have chosen them for their consistency of play, sportsmanship and team spirit (in club and country sides)

You will notice I have included LEWIS JONES in the full backs. I have in mind his marvellous displays in this position during the Australian tour of last year.

FULL BACK
1 J. LEDGARD (Leigh)
2 P. AUBERT (France)
3 C. CHURCHILL (Australia)
4 L. JONES (Leeds)
5 D. H. WHITE (New Zealand)

CENTRE THREEQUARTERS
1 C. TEISSEIRE (France)
2 E. ASHCROFT (Wigan)
3 C. EASTLAKE (New Zealand)
4 P. JACKSON (Barrow)
5 M. SULLIVAN (Huddersfield)

OFF HALF
1 R. WILLIAMS (Hunslet)
2 A. JIMENEZ (France)
3 W. HORNE (Barrow)
4 W. SORENSON (New Zealand)
5 G. BROWN (Leeds)

HOOKERS
1 J. EGAN (Leigh)
2 T. McKINNEY (Warrington)
3 J. AUDOBERT (France)
4 K. KEARNEY (Australia)
5 A. ACKERLEY (Halifax)

WING THREEQUARTER
1 B. BEVAN (Warrington)
2 R. CONTRASTIN (France)
3 J. CANTONI (France)
4 N. PIDDING (Australia)
5 F. KITCHEN (Leigh)

SCRUM HALF
1 G. HELME (Warr'n'ri'n)
2 K. HOLMAN (Au'lr'l'a)
3 J. CRESPO (France)
4 A. TOOHEY (Barrow)
5 S. KEILTY (Halifax)

FRONT ROW FORWARD
1 J. KRAWZYK (Australia)
2 D. HALL (Australia)
3 M. SCOTT (Hu'l)
4 J. THORLEY (Halifax)
5 A. PRESCOTT (St. Helens)

SECOND ROW FORWARD
1 D. ROBINSON (Wakefield)
2 G. DELAYE (France)
3 R. WATTS (York)
4 N. SILCOCK (St. Helens)
5 A. CLUES (Hunslet)

LOOSE FORWARD
1 D. VALENTINE (Huddersfield)
2 P. DIVERSI (Australia)
3 A. ATKINSON (New Zealand)
4 K. TRAILL (Bradford Northern)
5 J. WHITELEY (Hull)

147

Maine Road, Championship final, 1955. The Oldham defence cannot stop Bev from scoring one of his most crucial tries in helping Wire to a famous 7-3 victory.

Jim Challinor puts his arm round Bev's shoulders as skipper Ally Naughton raises the championship trophy after Warrington had beaten Oldham 7-3 in the final at Maine Road on 14 May 1955.
Other Warrington players (from left): D. Naughton, L. Horton, T. McKinney, G. Helme, R. Ryan, E. Frodsham, S. Phillips, H. Bath, J. Honey, J. Challinor, B. Bevan, G. Lowe

Season 1954–55

Warrington finished top of the League: P36, W29, D2, L5, For 718, Against 321
Bevan scored 61 tries for Warrington, plus 2 for representative teams

Date	Opponent	Score	Bevan	Crowd	
14 Aug	**Hull**	29–8	3T	13,057	
19 Aug	Barrow	10–12	1T	8,490	
21 Aug	Halifax	0–5		11,216	
25 Aug	**Belle Vue R**	57–5	4T	11,114	
28 Aug	**Swinton**	28–11	3T	13,208	
4 Sep	Workington T	29–18	3T	10,918	
11 Sep	Widnes	13–16	2T	9,582	LC1
18 Sep	Swinton	23–16	1T	6,096	
25 Sep	**Blackpool B**	22–15	3T	9,466	
2 Oct	Rochdale H	17–17	1T	11,478	
9 Oct	**Hull KR**	32–11	3T	11,883	
16 Oct	Liverpool City	8–3	1T	3,661	
23 Oct	**Bradford N**	15–10	1T	10,180	
30 Oct	Whitehaven	18–2	1T	4,395	
6 Nov	**Salford**	18–15		9,398	
13 Nov	**Liverpool City**	39–12	6T	4,666	
20 Nov	Hull	20–12	2T	8,000	
27 Nov	St Helens	8–8		17,593	
4 Dec	**Rochdale H**	8–7	2T	6,985	
11 Dec	Blackpool B	23–3	1T	2,007	
18 Dec	**Barrow**	24–0	dnp	10,565	
25 Dec	Widnes	10–0	dnp	8,396	
27 Dec	**Leigh**	27–12	1T	25,757	
1 Jan	Wigan	6–18	2T	28,778	
8 Jan	**St Helens**	18–14		23,932	
15 Jan	Oldham	12–8	2T	15,087	
22 Jan	**Whitehaven**	30–3	3T	11,158	
29 Jan	Hull KR	16–8	1T	8,267	
5 Feb	**Halifax**	24–3	dnp	16,876	
12 Feb	Bradford N	4–9		14,302	Ch Cup 1
5 Mar	Belle Vue R	31–3	2T	1,636	
12 Mar	**Workington T**	35–9	4T	15,264	
19 Mar	**Wigan**	9–13	1T	21,629	
26 Mar	**Oldham**	18–4	3T	13,863	
2 Apr	Salford	26–10	2T	6,015	
8 Apr	**Widnes**	10–4		18,570	
9 Apr	Bradford N	13–8	1T	8,715	
11 Apr	Leigh	5–14		13,179	
27 Apr	**Halifax**	17–9		22,311	CH Semi-final
14 May	Oldham	7–3	1T	49,434	CH Final (at Maine Road)

Bevan's Representative Matches:

Date	For	Opponent	Score	Bevan	Venue
17 Nov	Rugby League XIII	Australasia	13–25	2T	Odsal

1955-56: Playing with and against Billy Boston. The two great wingers together for Other Nationalities, and on opposing sides for their clubs.

Other Nationalities 33 England 16 at Wigan, 12 September 1955.
Back row: Price, McKinney, Kelly, Clues, Thorley, Bath, Bevan
Front row: Lynch, Banks, Valentine, Moses, Boston, Jones.

2 January 1956, Central Park, Wigan. A memorable clash before almost 25,000 fans saw Wire gain a famous 14-6 victory. Bev is shown in his own battle, trying to halt Billy Boston.

14. 1955-56 'Towards the distant posts'

The 1955-56 season began problematically for both Brian Bevan and the game at large. Bev was about to embark on his 10th season in England and had now turned 30 years of age. *The Rugby Leaguer*, in its first edition of the season, ran an article headed "CAN BEVAN KEEP IT UP?" It asked: "Will, or can, the amazing Brian Bevan... retain that super form which has placed him in a category of his own? For the past two or three seasons, we have heard experts, both professional and amateur, declare the Warrington No. 2 was a trifle slower, but Bevan, who has not only belied textbooks and accepted forms of attack, has also shown wise men to be entirely wrong."

The article continued, "The question is indeed very hard to answer, and only time will supply the reply. It must be taken into account that Bevan has had a great deal of trouble upon his shoulders during the close season. His young wife was taken suddenly seriously ill with an unusual complaint, and after being critically ill, she has made a slow recovery. At the time of writing she has not been restored to complete health... Happily, relatives have been able to give assistance in caring for their two children, but Bevan, like most outstanding figures, whether in sport or otherwise, is inclined to be highly strung. The trouble of the past [close] season may lie heavily on his shoulders, but all RL followers sincerely hope to see this lithe and speedy winger making defences look silly for quite a while to come."

As usual the rugby league establishment was shooting itself in the foot as the game struggled to decide what it really wanted. The play-the-ball problem would not go away. It was decided to try the rugby union method of releasing the ball at a tackle in the pre-season charity games and in the county cups. Unsurprisingly, the clubs mutinied over this, Wakefield Trinity cancelling their game with Castleford and the whole daft plan was aborted, when, at an International Board meeting in New Zealand, a new play-the-ball rule was adopted. This allowed the acting half-backs to be as near as they wished to the men playing the ball, while all other players had to be three yards back. It was also decreed that a new, smaller ball was to be used.

Another big problem arose when Belle Vue Rangers were excluded from the league fixtures after experiencing troubles in finding a satisfactory alternative to the Zoological Grounds. To many it appeared that the RFL did not want Rangers to survive - they were simply allowed to die. It left a bad taste in the mouths of many. The upshot was that all the Lancashire clubs plus Batley, Bramley, Dewsbury and Doncaster lost two fixtures and it was necessary to decide the league placings on an untidy percentage basis.

Warrington had a few problems of their own. Stan McCormick, unhappy at being switched around, was listed at £1,500 and there was a feeling that the three-quarters needed strengthening, especially as Jim Challinor was going to be rarely available because of his National Service duties in the RAF. Left-wing certainly proved to be a headache because no fewer than 10 players were eventually used there during the season. Fans were perturbed at the lack of signings, although there had been a major coup in the capture of Wigan schoolboy half-back prodigy

Jackie Edwards on his 16th birthday. He had cost an astronomical £1,000, a record for a player at that age. However, he was one for the future, if not the present.

The season began on 13 August with a resounding 19-10 victory at Wigan in the Wardonia Cup and if Bev's shoulders were bowing under his personal stress it certainly did not show, as the crowd of 14,593 were treated to another display of his genius. He scored twice, Tom North in the *Warrington Guardian* writing: "The first of Bevan's amazing tries came soon after the start of the second half after Frodsham had linked with the three-quarters. A kick to the right saw Bevan racing in but Platt was there calmly waiting to collect the ball as it reached him. It didn't quite! The leather was just about to enter his hands when in shot Bevan and, before anyone realised what had happened, he had swept up the ball and touched down... and what a peach of a try his second was. Honey gave Bevan the ball and in 30 yards he beat Ralph and Platt and simply shot past Armstrong to score under the posts."

No change there then! Unfortunately, there was also no change a week later in the first league fixture. Warrington lost 13-18 at Halifax and Bev again finished try-less opposite the miserly Dai Bevan, although he very nearly snatched a possible late equaliser only to be crashed into the corner-flag.

On 27 August, Warrington went to Central Park, this time for a Lancashire Cup first round tie. More than 23,000 attended on a boiling hot afternoon. It proved to be one of the most memorable games Bev ever played in and many Wire fans ever saw. With 25 minutes remaining Wigan led 15-0 - not a catastrophic deficit in 21st century rugby league terms, but 99 per cent unrecoverable in the 1955-style game. Even the best teams could not pull back so many points, particularly against a side like Wigan. Somehow Warrington did turn the game around. Frodsham converted tries by Bath and White and the score became 15-10, at which point Warrington had a stroke of luck which dramatically unnerved the already fading Wiganers.

Ray Price shattered the defence with a blistering 35-yard break, kicked ahead and deftly regathered, as he raced to the line. He would have scored himself but decided to waft a pass out to Bev to make sure. The pass was definitely forward, but was deflected by a Wigan player straight into Bev's pouch. Instead of blowing for a forward pass, referee Alf Howgate waved play-on and Bev only had to step over the line to score. Bath failed with the kick and Wigan still led 15-13 with only a minute remaining. The killer-blow was delivered when Bath made a mid-field surge and the ball found Honey out of position on the wing. Honey produced an electric burst to clear the opposition with Bev flying up on the inside in support and only full-back Don Platt to beat. The crowd was beside itself as Honey ignored Bev, kicked over Platt and descended on the ball for a truly breathtaking try, which won the game 16-15 in the most pulsating finale imaginable.

Inexplicably, three days later it was a case of after the Lord Mayor's carriage as Warrington, minus Bev, went down 12-8 away to Dewsbury, who would finish next to bottom of the league. When Bev returned for the home game against Blackpool Borough he produced a master class in scoring four tries opposite the redoubtable Wally McArthur. He was among the scorers too as Warrington won at Rochdale in the second round of the Lancashire Cup, and then easily accounted for Swinton in the league. The new play-the-ball rule, combined with good weather and firm grounds, suited Bev and there was a general feeling that the game as a spectacle had improved. Certainly the number of points scored had risen.

Last hurrah for the Other Nationalities

The International Championship, albeit in a modified form, had been reinstituted following its suspension because of the 1954 World Cup. Wales had been deemed too weak and Welshmen were now eligible for Other Nationalities. Consequently, Bev found himself in a dream three-quarter line when the Others met England at Wigan on Monday, 12 September. His centre partner was New Zealander Tommy Lynch, while the left flank paired Lewis Jones with Billy Boston, and what a combination they made. The game started in glorious sunshine, but towards the end of the first half a cloudburst deluged the crowd of 18,000 and made the pitch treacherous for the remainder of the game. It did not make an iota of difference to the Others who imperiously swept England aside 33-16.

Lewis Jones - six goals and a try to his credit - played immaculately. He put Boston in for possibly the easiest hat-trick of his career and simply mesmerised the English team. Billy's second try was his 100th. He had registered the century quicker than any player in history – in his 68th game. Even Bev could not match that, having taken 84 games. Bev did, however, score two tries himself and provided the highlight of the game. Mike Rowan recalled: "At the onset of the torrential downpour the crowd scattered like ants in an effort to find cover. Trapped in the boys' pen, we had nowhere to run. The *Wigan Observer* claimed that: 'Bevan lifted the game above the ordinary' with one moment of pure unadulterated Bevanism. The big Barrow centre Denis Goodwin approached the Other Nationalities' line and may well have scored himself because of his massive frame. It remains pure conjecture because he passed the ball wide towards Terry O'Grady. 'Thank you,' said Bev, and away he went from close to his own line. Full-back Jimmy Ledgard was some yards off when I swear I saw the genius of Brian Bevan come into its own. Very sure-footed, Brian stepped inside and headed towards the distant posts. Ledgard, unable to control his own momentum, went sliding on his backside. Poor Jim! I don't know how he felt as he slid towards the Douglas Stand, left to ponder the helplessness of his situation. What prompted the Aussie to swerve when he did? According to the textbook, he ought to have been closer before taking evasive action. There again, the man used to alter scripts, that is if he ever read them. It was sheer instinct. It was also comical to see water spray either side of Ledgard."

If the crowd at Central Park had found the weather a trial, the fans at Blackpool for Warrington's game at the seaside two days later would have laughed them to scorn. They experienced something like a monsoon. It was so bad that it was agreed to dispense with the half-time interval, a decision of which Bev apparently disapproved. He had only touched the ball once and, although saturated, he had not a mark on his kit. Blackpool pressed Wire all the way and when the referee, Norman Railton, blew for time Warrington had won 12-7. Or

153

had they? Everybody in the press box thought the game must have been abandoned because only 70 minutes had been played. Railton was adamant that the game had been completed, but later admitted that when he had fallen he may have nudged his watch in wiping his hands. The Blackpool manager, Chris Brockbank appealed and the RFL ordered the game to be declared void, a most unusual occurrence.

Even allowing for the dreadful weather at Blackpool, Warrington's performance had not been good and three wins and two losses in the league was not what had been expected. Briefly it got worse. On Saturday, 17 September, they were beaten 18-3 at Oldham, who picked up their first league win of the season, both teams struggling to strike the form which had taken them to the Championship final a few months earlier. The following Thursday, with high hopes of a place in the Lancashire Cup final, Warrington went down 11-6 at Widnes in the semi. They could have won had Bath not missed six penalty attempts with Frodsham also missing one and they were certainly not helped by the loss of Bev's centre partner, Jimmy Honey, with a knee injury after 20 minutes. The injury was so bad it ended Jimmy's career.

On 24 September a ray of sunshine appeared when Warrington, with seven reserves in the side, delighted a 13,000 Wilderspool crowd by defeating Halifax 24-9. Brian Bevan at last got on the scoreboard in his clashes with Dai Bevan and he did it twice, one try being awarded for obstruction after Tuss Griffiths impeded him over the line. The other was pure Bevan, a typical interception, the *Halifax Courier & Guardian* reporting that: "Brian Bevan stole his first try on Dai Bevan's wing in the last eight league and cup clashes between the clubs, when he took Palmer's pass, which the latter intended for his wingman."

October opened badly with yet another league defeat in Yorkshire, this time 20-32 at Leeds before a crowd of almost 22,000 contented Loiners. The reverse was a turning point, however. Warrington struck another of those long winning runs which had been a feature of their post-war endeavours. Fifteen straight wins were reeled off. Bev missed the first, an excellent 32-19 success at Barrow, along with Price and McKinney, who were both on test duty against New Zealand at Swinton. Warrington had at last entered the transfer market and signed the fiery Bill McFarlane from Leigh. He made his debut at centre at Barrow but was soon shifted to loose-forward.

The 27-11 home win against Huddersfield on 15 October was a special occasion for Bev. He rattled up four tries. His third, from yet another Ally Naughton kick-through, was his 500th for Warrington. He could have had another but was held over the line by Peter Henderson, who prevented him from grounding the ball, "probably the first occasion we have ever seen this happen to the Australian", according to Jack Steel. Bev's next game four days later was also special, although he may not have realised it at the time. Bev was in the Other Nationalities team which met France at Leigh under floodlights. Harry Bath captained the side in place of the injured Dave Valentine and Tom McKinney and Ray Price were also in the team.

The game was the last ever played by the Other Nationalities, because the International Championship was abandoned after this season. It was Bev's 16th international for them, the try he scored bringing his total to 26, a phenomenal rate without equal at this level. Ironically, the French were beaten 32-19 in a fine match and Other Nationalities won the International Championship. Harold Mather in the *Manchester Guardian* remarked that: "It was easily the best and most exciting struggle... since the World Cup matches in France last year." Billy Boston, on the left wing, scored two tries but, according to Mather "was below his best form, but on the other wing Bevan frequently wandered into the centre in search of the ball, which otherwise reached him only rarely. When he did get it the French immediately were aware of it!"

On 22 October Wire scraped home 15-13 against Oldham at Wilderspool before a crowd of 17,499, thanks to a monster last gasp penalty goal from halfway by Harry Bath. A more convincing performance followed on 29 October when Warrington won 24-8 at Workington. By now the Borough Park fans knew what to expect of Bevan and he did not let them down. Most of the crowd must have thought that Town manager Jim Brough had lost his marbles in playing a 17-year-old trialist from rugby union, Michael Jackson, opposite the bewildering Bevan. The poor lad certainly received an education from the maestro, who scored a fabulous hat-trick, employing his full repertoire.

There was no try for Bev the following Saturday, 5 November, when Warrington beat the New Zealanders 22-15, watched by a crowd of 14,462. It was not for want of trying. He was clear four times in the first half, only for capriciously bouncing balls to elude him twice, while he also knocked on in the act of scoring and was surprised by a sensational cover tackle by the Kiwi centre Ron McKay. In almost the last act of the game he chased a long kick to the in-goal and threw himself full-length to claim a try only for the referee to rule the ball had gone dead. For Bev it had been a fairly novel experience - so much bad luck in one game was not normal.

Floodlit Trophy winners

His next game was another novel experience. Warrington had been selected as one of eight teams to take part in a televised competition sponsored by the commercial television company ITV. Each team received £400 and the games were staged in London. None of the games could be transmitted to the north of England, however, because the technology was not yet available to commercial television. Warrington met Wakefield Trinity at Loftus Road, home of Queens Park Rangers FC, on Wednesday, 9 November and won 33-9. Their large points difference ensured that they progressed to the final the following week. Warrington had taken the opportunity to give Jackie Edwards his first-team debut but the star performer was young left-winger Billy Kilbride, who scored three tries to Bev's two.

There was a hat-trick, however, for Bev when it really mattered three days later, as Leeds were obliterated 35-6 at Wilderspool in the league. Harry Bath booted seven goals in a welcome return to kicking form. He had struggled most of the season to adjust to the new type of ball.

Bath was the star turn on 16 November, when Warrington went south again to Loftus Road to meet Leigh in the ITV Floodlit Cup Final. He rattled up 22 points (eight goals and two tries) as Leigh were eventually overwhelmed 43-18. Bev and

Bill McFarlane also claimed a couple of tries each.

At this stage in the season Warrington were running around sixth-eighth in the league table, behind pace-setters St. Helens and Wigan and Yorkshire clubs such as York, Bradford Northern, Keighley, Halifax and Featherstone Rovers. Bev on 28 tries was behind Billy Boston on 31 in the leading try-scorers list, with Jack McLean, in his last season, third on 24. It was also reported that Bev (6,601 votes) was running second to Billy (6,644) in the *Manchester Evening Chronicle*'s Player of the Year poll. There was plenty of time yet, however.

Warrington settled back from their trips to the capital into a concentrated effort to storm the league table. A victory at Fartown on 19 November was hailed by Jack Steel as one of the club's best on an opponent's ground since the war. Bill McFarlane was taken to hospital after just five minutes, Huddersfield scored from the first scrum and Warrington were soon 0-11 down. Len Horton then put Bevan over for a try and by half-time it was 10-11. Bev provided an amusing interlude running fully 15 yards with the ball held on his back like a haversack before Mick Sullivan dealt with the menace. This was the first game in which Bev and Sullivan had faced each other as wingers. It had always been tough but fair against Cooper. Now it was a bit different. Sullivan was more like Bev in size but he was one hell of a tough customer to play against. Jack Steel noted that Mick bumped and bored his illustrious opponent over the touchline at every opportunity - "sometimes unnecessarily". Mick could also play a bit, of course, and he bagged a couple of tries. With only 80 seconds remaining the Fartowners led 16-15 and a scrum went down 20 yards from their line. McKinney won the heel and the ball was flashed to Horton, who dashed to the line and was clattered by two defenders, who claimed he had failed to touch down properly. The referee disagreed and Bath's conversion sealed a famous 20-16 victory.

On Wednesday, 7 December, Bev, Ally Naughton, Ray Price and Harry Bath played in a televised match for a Rugby League XIII against the New Zealanders at Odsal. The Kiwis had already lost the test series to Great Britain, although the third test had yet to be played. It was a bitterly cold night and only 3,643 spectators braved the conditions. Left-winger Jack McLean, remarkably playing in his only representative match in England, opened the scoring after just six minutes with a typically barnstorming try against his countrymen. In the *Daily Express*, David Nicholls wrote: "Bevan had to wait until two minutes from the end for the try the fans had been ready to cheer from the start. Then Brian popped up in midfield, far away from his usual touchline beat, to grab eagerly at a pass from centre Duggie Greenall and go slithering over near the posts." Bev's team won 24-11. Astonishingly Warrington referee Charlie Appleton awarded just one penalty in the 80 minutes.

Swinton's Gordon Haynes, a former Orford Tannery ARL player, was the loose-forward for the Rugby League XIII. Being a local man he arranged to travel to Bradford with Ally Naughton, Harry Bath and Brian Bevan. Mike Rowan recorded that "In the days of no motorways the journey took a considerable time along the A roads and B roads. Gordon sat alongside Bevan for the journey going, shared the dressing room, played the game, had a drink and made the same trek home. Yet in all that time Bevan never spoke a word. Three days later both Swinton and Warrington played home games. As was his custom on his return,

Haynes parked his car at the back of the pub next to his house on Knutsford Road. He walked in the bar to enjoy a drink with the Warrington lads. There on his own was Brian Bevan. 'Hello, Gordon', he greeted the surprised Haynes. Not one word in hours together just three days before yet on their own Gordon said, 'You know, he was garrulous. I couldn't believe it. He really was a one-off'."

It was always that mixture of shyness and absolute tunnel vision, inextricably intertwined, which made Bev the man such an enigma for ordinary mortals.

Warrington continued their winning streak until 27 December, when they lost 7-11 on a mud-heap at Leigh. Fifteen successive victories, including 13 in the league, had lifted Warrington to second place in the table behind St Helens, with Halifax and Bradford Northern completing the top four. Bev's scoring rate, however, had slumped, having managed just four tries in the last seven games. He finished the old year with a return to form with two of his very best vintage in a hard-earned 18-13 win at Rochdale Hornets, twice leaving three Hornets buzzing with bemusement in his wake.

All the Bs

On 2 January 1956, Warrington went to Wigan for the third time that season. The Wire were seeking a third victory at Central Park, having also beaten the cherry and whites 13-4 at Wilderspool on 26 November. Four out of four - surely not! A great deal of spice was added to the fixture, and probably a few extra thousand on the gate, when it was announced in the morning papers that Billy Boston was swapping to the left wing for Wigan, in order to protect the inexperienced Bobby Chisnall from the wiles of Brian Bevan. Billy B versus Brian B - the prospect was an immediate attention-grabber. It even interested the folk on the other side of the Pennines and it had nothing to do with them! 'Veteran', in the Bradford *Yorkshire Sports*, wrote: "The Wigan-Warrington match this week drew 24,387, something like the accustomed crowd at Central Park for such an important clash - here enhanced by a Bevan-Boston clash that was worth going from anywhere in the league to see. Here we had the grip on the public imagination of great personalities."

Mike Rowan's memories of the encounter remain fresh: "Billy gave notice of his intent when he bowled his opposite over early in the game. Boston was well aware that his sheer physical presence and its impact would ensure the Australian had a torrid time. As Wigan made the early running Billy, on a second occasion, swept past Bevan to the loud partisan cheers of the home crowd.

Soon afterwards Ted White's lobbed kick to the line was too high. As a result Bev had to wait for the downward flight of the ball so that Boston's flying tackle grounded him. How the crowd yelled! We feared the worst, remembering the clattering that Billy Boy had given him 12 months before. 'Yon man's gone! Billy's the lad!' were the jibes. Wiganers took to baiting Bevan and in some quarters there was sadistic delight at his physical discomfort. When Brian did eventually pull off a textbook tackle on Boston, ironic cheers followed. Brian responded by clasping his hands high above his head. Then he waved to the jeering hordes. How they loved it and they catcalled even more, adding V-signs in his direction.

157

We juveniles suffered with him even though Warrington had control of the game. Normally we would have been very happy to be winning at Wigan but now there was something personal and intense at stake. On the day the Wire got four tries to two and Bath only kicked one goal. So Warrington were the better outfit. Nevertheless, the Wigan followers were not ready to do their famous walk - well, not yet. They were enjoying their moments. Our moment came in the second half.

There was nothing on as the Warrington threes handled the ball along the line until Len Horton's reverse pass had Bevan in full stride. His eccentricity did the rest. A body wobble and lightning acceleration had them all at sea. Boston was left trailing. After only a few strides he literally stopped dead having given up the ghost. Like many over the years, he accepted the inevitable and asked, 'What the **** happened?'

Full-back Don Platt might just as well have been standing with us. He was neither use nor ornament. As the flying Australian ace covered the last 50 yards to the Kop the enormity of what had happened hit the Wiganers like a belt in the mouth. The baiting stopped. Well, theirs did. It was our turn now! It was especially delightful to return the Winston Churchill salute.

Ray Price made a mistake with a kick and Boston gathered to race 40 yards to half way. The movement carried on to Chisnall and Ashcroft and the last-named handed it to Billy who crossed the line. So it ended one-all in the three-points stakes. I suppose honours were even but no one present could forget the spectacular run by the 'Elder Statesman of Scorers'. 'He ain't number one yet, mate!' How we dished back the jibes. 'Don't you lot forget it'.

Really, we were lucky to see two outstanding figures in direct opposition. It never happened again but our philosophical years were a long way off. For the time being we were just thrilled to bits that our hero had accomplished such a brilliant score against such a brilliant opponent."

There was a welcome break from league warfare for Warrington on 14 January, when they played host to their old friends from Albi. A horrible day and a dreadful, muddy pitch did not stop the Frenchmen from playing their usual flamboyant game, which was much appreciated by a crowd of 10,142 - bigger than any of the league games that dismal afternoon. Celestin Ayme, the Albi left-winger, gave Bev a hot time, constantly collaring him and showing himself to be a clever and forceful attacker. Eric Fraser on the Wire left wing stole some more of Bev's thunder by scoring 13 of his side's points in a 16-5 victory.

Defeat at struggling Whitehaven amid more mud the following week was a blow to Warrington's confidence and Bev was again well policed, this time by Syd Lowden. Jack Steel ruefully remarked: "As the final whistle for full time went Bevan made his fastest run of the afternoon beating man after man to the hot bath. And he fully deserved it for never at any time during the match had he been fully employed."

But it was back to normal service on 28 January when Dewsbury were beaten 30-4 at Wilderspool. Bev celebrated his 400th appearance in the primrose and blue with his 75th hat-trick for the club.

There was great excitement when the news came that Warrington had been drawn away to table-toppers St Helens in the first round of the Challenge Cup on 11 February. The winners would clearly be the favourites to lift the trophy and

Warrington were confident it would be them. In order to ensure that the game was played – it was threatened by frost and snow - St Helens covered the pitch with 115 braziers, mounted on metal sheeting, which were kept burning through Friday night until the following day. Their efforts were rewarded with a crowd of 24,230, who saw a typically tough cup-tie. Unfortunately, Warrington were not tough enough. Saints, with a pack of super-fit and super-fast forwards, were too good and dumped Wire out of the competition 15-6. Bev was superfluous to requirements, Jack Steel complaining: "For the world record try-scoring champion to handle the ball three or four times during the game - and then when he was hopelessly placed - leaves nothing to the imagination". Bevan's role was that of defender for the most part and he did as well as anyone, Steel particularly noting that he dealt with the galloping giant, Alan Prescott "as if he had been pole-axed".

Warrington regrouped and resolved to win what remained to them - the Championship and the Lancashire League. One of the best ways to achieve their aims was obvious to all and sundry - start getting the ball to Bevan again. The plan was simplicity itself, but it worked. Warrington won the next six games and Bev got back on track with a dozen tries. He began with four against Workington Town, who down the years lived in dread of the ball reaching him. On 3 March, Warrington had to replay the match at Blackpool which had been declared void back in September. Borough gave them another gruelling match before succumbing 18-11.

It was 15-11 with only seconds remaining when Stan McCormick, playing his last game for the Wire, did what he had so often done before over the past couple of years - wandered from his own wing to Bev's and set the Australian loose. Bev received the ball near the right touchline on halfway and proceeded to beat and bamboozle most of the Blackpool players in a series of forward spurts, followed by sidesteps off his right foot. The final touchdown was between the posts and the left corner-flag. Jack Steel christened it the 'Staircase Try' and produced another of his diagrams for the *Warrington Guardian*. It ranked among the best that Steel or anyone else had ever seen the maestro produce - an ineffable masterpiece. What a shame that there had only been 931 paying customers to relish it.

There were more the following Saturday - 26,088, to be precise - when Warrington hoped for some measure of revenge against St Helens at Wilderspool. They got it too with a comprehensive 17-4 victory, the forwards completely reversing the pattern of the cup-tie. Bev's late try broke the Saints' resistance and gave Wire fans the conviction that their team might just tip the Knowsley Road men off their perch at the top of the league.

Salford were the next victims, hammered 41-10 at Wilderspool. Bev claimed four tries, but missed several more through an inability to master a new orange ball, which afflicted almost everyone on the field. He was given a rest the following week when Keighley were beaten 39-18 in a hastily arranged friendly. He was back, however, on 30 March, Good Friday, scoring his 50th try of the season in an 18-10 victory at Widnes. The following day he was again among the scorers, profiting from a Billy McFarlane punt through, as Warrington completed a stirring double over St Helens at Knowsley Road. The result brought Warrington level with Saints at the top, both having won 24 of their 30 league matches. Saints, however, still had the Challenge Cup in their sights and consequently more games to negotiate.

A dropped point in an 11-11 draw at home to Leigh on Easter Monday could have been disastrous but ultimately proved to be a point won rather than lost, when Saints suffered a 40-8 thrashing at Oldham two weeks later. Victory over Liverpool City at Wilderspool on 5 April brought silverware in the shape of the Lancashire League Championship, Warrington winning the trophy five points ahead of runners-up St Helens. Wire had taken the Lancashire League three seasons in a row and Bev now had his sixth winners medal from the competition.

On 14 April, Warrington demolished a makeshift Barrow 37-0 in their final league game. Bev was rampant, scoring three tries. "His third try was magnificent in the truest sense," wrote Jack Steel, "the sort spectators long to see, but seldom have the opportunity. He gathered the ball about 40 yards out, accelerated so amazingly that two opponents within arm's length could do nothing about it, and, as he moved infield, was knocked down by a third. But he was up in a flash and threaded his way past three or four more bewildered opponents to score wide of the left upright after starting from the right touchline."

Warrington's great end-of-season run - they had dropped only one point in 10 games since their defeat in the Cup - had taken them to the leadership of the league. The top four places which, because of Belle Vue's demise were decided on a percentage system, were filled by: Warrington 80.88%, Halifax 80.55%, St Helens 79.41% and Hull 70.83%.

Disaster at the hands of Hull

If the semi-finals went with home advantage, yet another Warrington-Halifax clash would ensue. Certainly there was very little betting on Hull to win at Wilderspool. The Boulevarders arrived for the Championship semi-final on 21 April and, before a stupefied crowd of 20,068, left with a 17-0 victory. The old Wire favourite Roy Francis, now the Hull coach, had definitely done his homework on Warrington. He had declared that "our boys had only five men to worry about - Bath, Price, Helme, Naughton and Bevan". The Hull pack mastered Warrington's so comprehensively that Bath, Price and Helme failed to spark and one reporter wrote: "The man Hull feared most was that Stanley Matthews of rugby wings, Brian Bevan. What happened? He didn't get his first pass until the 32nd minute and then he faced such a battery of heavyweights Houdini himself would have done a disappearing act into the dressing-room. Brian improved on that. He beat three before being dragged down. In the second half he got two passes. Both looked hopeless but he swerved and jigged his way to within inches of the line before being bulldozed into touch. For the rest of the game Brian watched his team fumbling away gift chances."

Prior to the Hull debacle, Warrington had stood on the threshold of history. If they had beaten Hull and gone on to win the Championship, they would have been immortalised as the first team to take three consecutive titles. The manner of the defeat dumbfounded the onlookers, who, in reality, saw a team in the throes of decline. Hull had also destroyed a proud Warrington record. Since Castleford beat them 27-13 back on 14 January 1939, Warrington had not lost at Wilderspool to a side from Yorkshire. Indeed since that 1939 loss there had been 72 Yorkshire visitors to Wilderspool and only Hunslet, with an 8-8 draw on 8 December 1945, had returned home unvanquished.

Thus the 1955-56 season ended disappointingly for Warrington. They had finished top of the pile but the signs were there that changes were on the way and they may not be for the better. Many of the team were getting on in footballing terms, particularly in the forwards. New blood was going to be needed, if standards were to be maintained. Despite their lofty position in the league Warrington's attendances had actually gone down. In 1954-55 the average home crowd for league matches was 13,754. In 1955-56 it dropped to 12,322. The club still made a profit of £349 on the season, but to remain a major power much more would be needed.

Brian Bevan had, remarkably, maintained his own standards. His 57 tries for the season placed him behind Bradford's Jack McLean who had topped the charts with 61, an outstanding performance from a man in his last season. Billy Boston had finished third with 49, followed by St Helens's Frank Carlton (42), Barrow's veteran Jim Lewthwaite (41) and Steve Llewellyn, Saints' other winger, on 40.

Once again, however, the spectre of Bev leaving Wilderspool had reared its frightening head. Reports had circulated in the *Sydney Sun* in April that Bev was keen to return home. Jerry Brien, a former pre-war Wests, St George and New South Wales stand-off and an Australian test selector, was reported to have been on a visit to England during which he met Bev. He said: "I had a two hour talk with Bevan and his wife. Both are keen to get to Australia but Brian will not give up the substance for the shadow. He showed me all his medals and trophies but said he would trade the lot for the honour of wearing an Aussie jersey. Bevan is signed on each year for only one season, so he can leave here in a matter of weeks. He would welcome a proposition from any club."

Happily, nothing came of it and Bev turned his attentions to other matters. On 4 May, he figured in Dave Valentine's benefit match at Fartown. The 1954 Great Britain World Cup-winning captain led his famous team – the only time they played on home soil - against a British Empire XIII, captained by Arthur Clues. Lionel Cooper was again charging up the touchline, only this time as a touch judge! The Empire XIII emerged 47-41 winners with Bev scoring a hat-trick, the *Huddersfield Daily Examiner* noting that "Bevan delighted with some tortuous runs". Such occasions must have reinforced Bev's regrets at never having represented his own country.

Warrington embarked on a tour of France a week later but Brian, injured at Fartown, was missing from the party, which played fixtures at Bayonne (won 18-6), Toulouse (lost 10-7), Albi (lost 36-16) and Villeneuve (won 28-9) within seven days.

Season 1955-56

Warrington finished top of the League: P34, W27, D1, L6, For 712, Against 349
Bevan scored 53 tries for Warrington, plus 4 for representative teams

Date	Opponent	Score	Bevan	Crowd	
20 Aug	Halifax	13-18		13,291	
27 Aug	Wigan	16-15	1T	23,161	LC 1
30 Aug	Dewsbury	8-12	dnp	4,982	
3 Sep	**Blackpool B**	30-10	4T	9,183	
6 Sep	Rochdale H	26-12	1T	14,261	LC 2
10 Sep	**Swinton**	30-13	1T	10,971	
14 Sep	Blackpool B*	12-7		2,821	
17 Sep	Oldham	3-18	1T	16,432	
22 Sep	Widnes	6-11		16,468	LC Semi-final
24 Sep	**Halifax**	24-9	2T	13,051	
1 Oct	Leeds	20-32	1T	21,913	
8 Oct	Barrow	32-19	dnp	6,899	
15 Oct	**Huddersfield**	27-11	4T	12,571	
22 Oct	**Oldham**	15-13		17,499	
29 Oct	Workington T	24-8	3T	5,541	
5 Nov	**New Zealand**	22-15		14,462	
9 Nov	Wakefield T**	33-9	2T		ITV Trophy
12 Nov	**Leeds**	35-6	3T	13,160	
16 Nov	Leigh**	43-18	2T	3,173	ITV Trophy Final
19 Nov	Huddersfield	20-16	1T	10,130	
26 Nov	**Wigan**	13-4		14,320	
3 Dec	Swinton	18-7		6,000	
10 Dec	**Whitehaven**	17-12	1T	5,977	
17 Dec	**Rochdale H**	25-16	2T	8,752	
24 Dec	Salford	24-0		4,741	
26 Dec	**Widnes**	15-0	1T	10,808	
27 Dec	Leigh	7-11		7,666	
31 Dec	Rochdale H	18-13	2T	8,522	
2 Jan	Wigan	14-6	1T	24,387	
21 Jan	Whitehaven	4-14		3,144	
28 Jan	**Dewsbury**	30-4	3T	9,655	
11 Feb	St Helens	6-15		24,230	Ch Cup 1
25 Feb	**Workington T**	41-8	4T	10,112	
3 Mar	Blackpool B	18-11	1T	931	
10 Mar	**St Helens**	17-4	1T	26,088	
17 Mar	**Salford**	41-10	4T	10,599	
30 Mar	Widnes	18-10	1T	12,850	
31 Mar	St Helens	13-7	1T	25,242	
2 Apr	**Leigh**	11-11		16,709	
5 Apr	**Liverpool City**	25-9		7,695	
9 Apr	Liverpool City	25-7	2T	2,166	
14 Apr	**Barrow**	37-0	3T	12,318	
21 Apr	**Hull**	0-17		20,068	CH Semi-final

* The game against Blackpool Borough on 14 September was declared void as
Blackpool claimed only 70 minutes had been played. It was replayed on 3 March.
** At Loftus Road, London

Bevan's Representative Matches:

Date	For	Opponent	Score	Bevan	Venue
12 Sep	Other Nationalities	England	33-16	2T	Wigan
19 Oct	Other Nationalities	France	32-19	1T	Leigh
7 Dec	Rugby League XIII	New Zealand	24-11	1T	Odsal

15. 1956-57 'Then the wheels fell off'

For Warrington followers and for Brian Bevan the season of 1956-57 was not exactly Armageddon, but it came close.

It did not start too badly for Bev, who ran in four tries in the Wigan sevens at the beginning of August. His performance may have consoled him after some of his fellow countrymen, the Australian cricket team, had just been humiliated a few days earlier and a few miles down the road at Old Trafford. Surrey's Jim Laker had performed his epic feat of taking 19 wickets for 90 runs, as Peter May led England to a fourth test victory and the Ashes were retained. The triumph generated one of those national feel-good factors.

However, 10,000 Warrington fans immediately lost that feel-good factor when their team lost the Wardonia Cup on 11 August. Sure, it was only 16-15 to Wigan, Bev scoring the last try of the game, but Jack Steel wrote: "There was much consternation and argument over Bevan's first-half display. He could not get the better of Eric Ashton. In fact the lanky left-winger, who also slammed over two good goal-kicks, looked faster than Bevan. To see the Australian tackled three times and all in the space of 60 seconds is something I have never recorded."

Even more worrying for the Wire management and supporters was the pedestrian pace of their pack. The side clearly needed new blood. Eric Frodsham, a great servant to the club, had broken his wrist playing against Liverpool at the back end of the previous season and had played his last game for the Wire. Stan McCormick, to Liverpool City and Gerry Lowe, to Keighley, had also been transferred before the 1955-56 season had ended. Matters were made worse when Jackie Edwards and Bill McFarlane suffered serious injuries on the May tour to France and were not able to play any first-team matches at all in 1956-57. Ray Price too suffered pre-season injury and missed the first half-dozen games.

Some of the gloom lifted when an astonishing signing was made. Warrington surprised the sporting community at large, and the rugby union world in particular, by capturing Robin Thompson, the Ireland second-rower and captain of the 1955 British Isles team in South Africa. There was a local connection. Thompson's brother was a doctor, who was in a Warrington practice. It also showed the directors were taking action. They needed to, for they were desperately hoping that Thompson could be groomed to replace Harry Bath, both as a pack leader and inspiration. Harry had decided that he was going to return to Australia at the season's end.

Thompson made his debut in the opening league fixture on 18 August, performing creditably in a 16-8 home win over Whitehaven. He figured with Bath and Challinor in a handling move, which sent Bev hurtling from half-way for a cracking try. Two more Bevan tries at Liverpool in a third consecutive victory indicated that perhaps, after all, nothing had really changed. This was followed by another massive signing from rugby union. Martin Regan, the Liverpool, Barbarians and England stand-off, joined Warrington on 27 August. Warrington were certainly hogging the headlines.

Regan, a native of St Helens, showed himself to be a good footballer on his debut on 29 August, when his presence helped to swell the crowd to 15,451 for the visit of Halifax. It was an inauspicious occasion for the Wire, however, who went down 14-17, to suffer their first home league defeat by a Yorkshire club since 1939. First Hull in the previous season's Championship semi-final, now Halifax. Before the season's end Leeds, Hull again and Bradford Northern would all shatter Warrington's erstwhile home invincibility against White Rose opponents, as matters took increasingly ugly turns. Bev had very nearly rescued his side late in the Halifax game with a tremendous run which was halted inches from the line when Scottish winger Drew Turnbull came from nowhere to nail him.

There was a try from a Naughton cross-kick for Bev on 1 September, when Warrington beat Rochdale Hornets 31-8 in the first round of the Lancashire Cup. It was reported that "Bevan, who was now attempting the kick and follow-up more than at any time in his career, supplied two or three thrills of his own special kind," but added ominously that "There are quite a lot of people who think that the extra yard is not in Bev's legs so far this season."

Papering over the cracks

Tight victories at Featherstone and at home against Blackpool, and 35-5 in a friendly against Albi at Wilderspool papered over some of the cracks. A magnificent Lancashire Cup-tie against Barrow then enraptured a crowd of almost 17,000, Wire winning 5-2 to progress to the semi-finals. Unfortunately, the wheels then fell off, as it were.

On Saturday, 15 September Bev missed the game at Leeds. He was lucky. Ally Naughton and Harry Bath were sent off and Leeds buried Warrington 32-9. The following Thursday 26,281 fans crammed into Wilderspool for the Lancashire Cup semi-final against St Helens. Warrington put up a brave show, going under 17-9, but lost debutant prop Alan Robinson with a broken leg after only 15 minutes, while Ally Naughton suffered a fractured jaw which kept him out of the next seven games. Two days later, the crowd had gone down by more than 17,000 as Warrington went down 15-11 at home to Salford. Bev scored from a kick through by Horton, but was admonished by the *Examiner* for rambling over the field too much and twice being missing from his wing when tries might have accrued. A big defeat at Hull followed which, more significantly, was Danny Naughton's last game.

On 3 October, Bev represented the Rest of the League in a test trial against Great Britain at Odsal. In view of the dark atmosphere surrounding Warrington, the game probably came as something of a relief. Harry Bath captained the Rest and Ray Price was stand-off. Tom McKinney was the Great Britain hooker. A good, open game finished in a 26-23 victory for Britain. Bev, beautifully served by Lewis Jones, displayed brilliant finishing power with three tries, while Billy Boston ran in four for Britain. Ray Price, in no mood to let Martin Regan take his number six jersey at Wilderspool, terrorised Great Britain's Dave Bolton and went on to win the test jersey himself for the upcoming Ashes series.

Warrington defeated Huddersfield 20-7 on 6 October, a good performance, but Bev failed to impress. A *Warrington Guardian* report ran: "Bevan may not have got many chances but after writing for years in such glowing terms about the world's best winger, I find it hard, but not harsh, to say that some of the edge has gone off his attacking ideas. Without the stopwatch I wouldn't like to wager on the argument that he has lost a yard or two, but he appears to have done so and the uncanny anticipation is not there as it used to be."

On 20 October, Warrington plummeted to an 18-5 loss at Blackpool and dropped to ninth in the table. The old order crumbled a bit more as Syd Phillips made his last appearance in the primrose and blue before transferring to St Helens. The following week the Australian tourists visited Wilderspool. They went down 21-17 to the Wire, who scored three tries from interceptions, none of which, for a change, involved Brian Bevan. Bev's next game was also against the Aussies, two days later, for a Rugby League XIII at Leigh. This time he was on the losing side, the Australians being good value for their 19-15 win, although it took two Gordon Clifford penalties in the last five minutes to decide the issue. Bev was well held by his opposing winger, Des McGovern, who scored a couple of super tries to put the old master in the shade.

November opened with a disappointing defeat at Swinton, but the nation was probably more concerned with events in Egypt, where an Anglo-French force was engaged at Suez, and in Hungary, where a revolution erupted against the Soviet Union. Brian Bevan had his own problems. His toe was cracked, a possible explanation for his uncharacteristic form. It meant a six-week break in his season. By the time he returned the troops had withdrawn from Suez, the Soviets had crushed the Budapest revolt and Alan Prescott's Great Britain had beaten Ken Kearney's Australia 2-1 in the Ashes series.

Bev made a couple of appearances for the reserves, after a gap of 11 years. He was clearly not entirely happy and Eddie Waring was quick to spot a story, running the following in his *Sunday Pictorial* column on 15 December, 1956, under the banner: "Will Bevan stay?"

"What is Brian Bevan's future? Will the world's greatest Rugby winger stay at Warrington and win back his place in the side? There are rumours of a Bevan transfer and I know more than one club who would like him. What does Brian himself think? After two games with the reserves he is now fit for first team action. He told me: 'I just want to play first-grade football whether it's here or in Australia'."

The past few months had patently been a dreadful trial for Bev - indifferent form, a lack of tries, playing in a declining team and niggling injuries had all conspired against him.

When Bev did return to the Warrington ranks it was for the home game against table-toppers Oldham on 22 December. As a test of his resolve and fitness it could hardly have been harder. Equally, it could hardly have turned out better. Warrington won 12-2 with easily their best performance of the season thus far. As for Bev, Jack Steel was again lyrical: "Bevan's back in town! The maestro of swerve and side-step again called the tune to a fiddling Oldham defence and also took a bow from that critical section which had gone along, not to praise him, but to bury him among the fallen stars. If some Warrington people are still ready to forecast the date of Bevan's retirement, Oldham supporters are still apprehensive when he is around. He provided the right type of elusive run on a surface as slippery as a skating rink, to score a try which put the right type of spirit into the rest of the team and more or less demonstrated to Oldham that they were fighting a losing battle. In that try-movement which sent Bevan past Ganley like the ghost of Christmas yet to come, the Oldham two-point lead was wiped out... Bevan is far from being a back number."

On 29 December, Wilderspool witnessed a heart-stopping game in the mud which ended in an 8-8 draw against St Helens, who played the last 55 minutes without injured centre Duggie Greenall. Warrington had led 8-0 and it was not Bev's fault that they failed to nail a magnificent Saints thirteen. He brought down flying Frank Carlton when he appeared clear and saved a try with a tackle on Todder Dickinson, "which beggars description".

Not a happy New Year

Things had appeared to be looking up for Warrington. Prior to the Saints game they had won their last four games, were moving up the table and Bev's successful return had put welcome new heart into the supporters. If they were hoping for a happy New Year, however, they were sadly mistaken. Three of the worst defeats in the club's history opened January 1957. New Year's Day saw a 37-2 massacre by Wigan at Central Park. Bev hardly saw the ball and was involved in an altercation with Wigan skipper Ernie Ashcroft, who was sent off for the first time in a career stretching back to 1942.

On 5 January, an irresistible St Helens played all over Warrington at Knowsley Road, winning 33-7. Yet even in such a drubbing Bev's genius was undimmed. The *Rugby Leaguer*'s St Helens correspondent was moved to pay the Australian the following singular tribute: "Write off the notion that Bevan is blighted. The way he went hunting for the ball, looking for work, showed that his heart is still the dauntless and courageous organ of old. Moreover, the way he chased and caught Howard, who was pausing slightly to look for help, suggested that he was indeed faster than at any time this season. If Warrington fans do not give Bevan the encouragement he needs after going through sorrow and tribulation they are indeed an ungrateful lot. Has there ever been a better man in any particular position in the Warrington team since the First World War? Thousands of miles from home, bumped, bounced and blasted, week-in-week-out, Bevan has never faltered or hesitated to face whatever fate has in store. If only we had a man of his class and courage in every team in the league, what a game this Rugby League would be."

On 12 January, Warrington suffered the indignity of a 42-7 home defeat by Leeds, the Loiners' first victory at Wilderspool for 20 years. Tom McKinney played his last game for the Wire and was transferred to St Helens for £2,000 a few days after the rout. Astonishingly, a week later Warrington recovered sufficiently to defeat second-in-the-table Barrow 22-13 but defeats at Oldham and Workington, both of which Bev missed, plunged the team to 16th in the league.

The game at Workington proved to be Gerry Helme's last game for Warrington. Ironically, he was drafted in at left wing. Alf Arnold had become first choice scrum-half and Gerry had just been listed at £1,000. There was to be no transfer for this truly great scrum-half, however. Instead he went into retirement, save for a brief flirtation with Keighley in January 1958. The old order was certainly changing. It changed some more after Warrington's home first round Challenge Cup-tie against Bramley on 9 February. Harry Bath booted four goals in a 14-2 victory, and then decided to go back to Australia without seeing out the season. It was a body blow for all concerned at Wilderspool, for Bath had been one of the outstanding forwards in the history of the game. He joined the St George club in Sydney, where he enjoyed three hugely successful playing seasons, adding 510 points, in 60 games, to the 1,857 he had amassed as a Wire. Subsequently, he became one of the most influential coaches of the second half of the 20th century. Team-mate Ally Naughton took over Harry's licenseeship of the Britannia Hotel.

The Cup-tie against Bramley was the sixth successive match in which Brian had failed to score, a sequence unprecedented in his career in England. The following week, he provided the antidote, winning the home game against Featherstone Rovers practically on his own. Warrington crept home 9-5 thanks to an inimitable Bev hat-trick, his first of the season for the club.

On 23 February, Warrington travelled to Headingley for a second round Challenge Cup-tie. In view of the heavy towellings they had received from Leeds in the league, they may have been happy to find a snow-covered pitch. They were now a team which needed any help they could get. The terrible conditions did not deter a crowd of almost 25,000. For Warrington, there was nothing else to play for apart from the Challenge Cup, a novel post-war experience. The game typified their season, as the luck ran against them completely. By half-time Leeds were 10-0 up and Warrington's Robin Thompson and Frank Wright were on their way to hospital. In the second half Alf Arnold suddenly collapsed and Warrington for a period played with only 10 men. Leeds eventually won 28-6 and went on to lift the Challenge Cup with a 9-7 victory over Barrow at Wembley.

Bev did score a try against Leeds, but it was the last of the season for him. At Whitehaven the following Saturday he injured his knee in a very simple fashion which resulted in him missing Warrington's final 10 fixtures.

It was probably very much in the public mind that Bev was finished at the top level. How long could the man go on? He was approaching 33-years-old and the injuries he had suffered in 1956-57 were proof that he was not indestructible, whatever his admirers thought. He had missed 18 of Warrington's games, far more than ever before. Common sense indicated that even if the knee injury was rectified, he was hardly likely to regain the blinding pace and brilliance of past days. Would he want to soldier on as a mere mortal?

Warrington did not only have Bev to worry about. Their season had been a stinker. They had dropped from top of the league in 1955-56 to 10th in 1956-57. Their average home league attendance had fallen to 10,083 – more than 2,000 down on the previous season. There were, however, a couple of rays of sunshine on the financial horizon. Warrington, like many clubs in this period, had established a weekly soccer lottery, which had about 9,000 members. The lottery was a vital counterweight to the loss in income from gates. The treasurers of all clubs finally received the news they had prayed for in April 1957, when the Chancellor of the Exchequer, Peter Thorneycroft, abolished the iniquitous Entertainments Tax, which it was reckoned would save £100,000 per annum for the game's professional rugby league clubs.

When Brian Bevan's season ended at Whitehaven's Recreation Ground on 9 March, he had scored 14 tries for Warrington, plus three for the Rest of the League. For the first time since his arrival a decade earlier there was no entry under B. Bevan in the highest reaches of the try-scoring charts. In his absence 'Bouncing' Billy Boston led the way with 60 tries, followed by Barrow's Jim Lewthwaite (51 in his last season), Halifax's Johnny Freeman (48) and Oldham's John Etty (43). There was no Warrington representation in the top 20 try-scorers, Laurie Gilfedder, on 22 tries, being the first man to displace Bev at the head of the Wire try-scorers since 1946-47.

Season 1956-57

Warrington finished 10th in the League: P38, W21, D1, L16; For 571, Against 565
Bevan scored 14 tries for Warrington, plus 3 for representative teams

Date	Opponent	Score	Bevan	Crowd	
18 Aug	**Whitehaven**	16-8	1T	5,030	
22 Aug	Salford	12-11		7,233	
25 Aug	Liverpool City	34-13	2T	1,356	
29 Aug	**Halifax**	14-17		15,451	
1 Sep	**Rochdale H**	31-8	1T	10,629	LC 1
5 Sep	Featherstone R	17-13	1T	8,400	
8 Sep	**Blackpool B**	25-21	2T	10,294	
13 Sep	**Barrow**	5-2		16,737	LC 2
15 Sep	Leeds	9-32	dnp	15,654	
20 Sep	**St Helens**	9-17		26,281	LC Semi
22 Sep	**Salford**	11-15	1T	8,945	
29 Sep	Hull	14-38		11,228	
6 Oct	**Huddersfield**	20-7		12,186	
13 Oct	Bradford N	16-11	1T	5,531	
20 Oct	Blackpool B	5-18		2,726	
27 Oct	**Australians**	21-17		15,613	
3 Nov	Swinton	6-14		7,000	
10 Nov	**Rochdale H**	11-10	dnp	8,890	
17 Nov	Barrow	3-19	dnp	6,554	
24 Nov	**Workington T**	28-5	dnp	8,133	
1 Dec	Rochdale H	13-7	dnp	5,739	
8 Dec	**Swinton**	34-14	dnp	8,673	
22 Dec	**Oldham**	12-2	1T	8,748	
29 Dec	**St Helens**	8-8		18,314	
1 Jan	Wigan	2-37		20,284	
5 Jan	St Helens	7-33		14,510	
12 Jan	**Leeds**	7-42		11,840	
19 Jan	**Barrow**	22-13		8,612	
26 Jan	Oldham	0-18	dnp	13,799	
2 Feb	Workington T	7-11	dnp	4,415	
9 Feb	**Bramley**	14-2		9,373	Ch Cup 1
16 Feb	**Featherstone R**	9-5	3T	8,684	
23 Feb	Leeds	6-28	1T	24,032	Ch Cup 2
2 Mar	Whitehaven	16-14		4,750	
16 Mar	**Liverpool City**	27-5	dnp	5,754	
30 Mar	**Hull**	12-13	dnp	8,870	
4 Apr	Widnes	6-8	dnp	6,607	
6 Apr	**Bradford N**	17-18	dnp	7,220	
10 Apr	Halifax	7-6	dnp	6,779	
13 Apr	Huddersfield	28-8	dnp	9,804	
19 Apr	**Widnes**	19-5	dnp	11,746	
20 Apr	**Wigan**	40-7	dnp	15,700	
22 Apr	Leigh	10-24	dnp	6,394	
27 Apr	**Leigh**	27-15	dnp	8,496	

Bevan's Representative Matches:

Date	For	Opponent	Score	Bevan	Venue
3 Oct	Rest of League	Great Britain	23-26	3T	Odsal
29 Oct	Rugby League XIII	Australia	15-19		Leigh

Occasionally commercial opportunities arose for Bev. In 1957, for example, he featured in a long-running advert for Dextrosol. The image used was from Warrington's victory over Widnes at Wembley in 1950. The Great Britain captain, Alan Prescott replaced Bevan in the advert in 1959.

Below: Bevan promoted his business in this 1958 advert in the Warrington match programme.

16. 1957-58 'Back and serious'

If Warrington fans were glad to see the back of the 1956-57 season, they were no less pleased to see the end of the 1957-58 campaign. The club fell three places further down the league to 13th, their worst showing since the war. It was even more disappointing because their fixture list was easier than previous years. Their poor performances of 1956-57 had cost them their plum fixtures against the top Yorkshire clubs, apart from Leeds, who were drafted into the Lancashire League for the season. Financially, the loss of games against the likes of Halifax, Huddersfield and Hull was a blow to a club, which had lost £2,692 on the previous season and was dependent on recurring success on the field.

There was, however, a ray of sunshine. Brian Bevan was far from finished. He returned to action having effectively had six months' rest and recuperation. He was raring to go and even the most cynical of pundits were astounded by his form and accomplishments in 1957-58. The long rest seemed to have revitalised the 'old man'.

Another 'old man', in rugby league terms, Ray Price had caused Warrington a headache. Ray had gone with Great Britain to Australia in the summer for the second World Cup. He had been badly injured in the first warm-up game at Perth and took no further part in the tour. He had returned home to Wales and announced his retirement. The loss of the lion-hearted stand-off was yet another grievous blow to a side reeling from the loss of so many key personnel in such a short time.

The season began on 10 August at Central Park, where 15,209 saw Wigan retain the Wardonia Cup with a 15-14 win. Bev gave notice of his return to form and fitness by scoring both Wire tries, one a direct dash and the other a classic concoction of swerve, deception and acceleration, so stunning that "even the hard-headed Wigan popular side applauded unstintingly and stayed on until the final whistle".

The first league fixture at Bramley would in years gone by have been a formality for Warrington. This time, the Barley Mow witnessed a mighty struggle which Warrington eventually won 21-16. Bev scored a lovely try, finishing off a wonderful nine-man move but was upstaged by his centre partner Jim Challinor, who bagged the remaining four Wire tries.

Bev left no one in any doubt that he was back and serious by scoring in Warrington's first six competitive matches, a total of 12 tries, including three hat-tricks. True enough, the opposition was not too stern - perennial strugglers Liverpool City accounting for three of those occasions. The tries had to be scored nonetheless and he could do no more than score them. On 7 September, Warrington met good opposition for the first time in Featherstone Rovers, who beat them 27-20 in a thrilling game at Wilderspool. Although his team lost, it was another red letter day for Bev. He nabbed three tries, the second of which was the 600th of his career. Rovers' full-back Jackie Fennell, one of the best defenders in the game, is probably still wondering how Bev got round him.

Warrington were having real problems with their pack, which had undergone major reconstruction. The giant second-rower Josh Gaskell was signed from St

Helens to bolster a set of forwards which bore no resemblance to Wire packs of recent vintage. Aspiring players such as Maurice Gallagher, John Hudson, Peter O'Toole, Peter Storey, John Manniex, Arthur Fryer, Gaskell and, of course, Robin Thompson were bound to struggle to emulate their illustrious predecessors. Billy McFarlane had returned after a season's absence, and Frank Wright and Ted White were still available, but there would be no return to the top ranks until the pack could match the best.

Alan Marchant remembers

When I was a boy I went down to Wheldon Road with my dad to see Castleford play Warrington. Bevan was playing. He always reminded me of an undertaker. He looked so frail and seemed as white as chalk. He was not getting much of the ball but then about quarter of an hour from time he scored a fantastic try. I am not kidding but he sidestepped eight of our players and put the ball down under the posts. I remember he went off his right leg every time. There were bodies all over the pitch - laid out as if they had been shot. It was unbelievable.

I later joined Featherstone Rovers as a scrum-half. Early on in my career I remember working at Glasshoughton Colliery. I was called to the office one day and told I had to report to Post Office Road as I had been drafted in to play at Warrington. When we were in the dressing rooms at Wilderspool I broke my boot lace - I think it was the nerves - and we did not have any spares. Billy Williams told me to go next door to the Warrington dressing room and ask for one. When I went in I saw this colossal pile of bandages and strapping. I had never seen as much. I asked: "What's all that for?" Somebody piped up: "It's for him over there" and pointed at Bevan. I have still never seen anyone with as much strapping as he used to put on.

Before the match, we were all forcibly warned about Bevan's skill at intercepting. He always seemed to be at it. I remember going round the blind-side of a scrum early in the game and half-letting the ball go before I remembered not to. I got away with it, but a lot of players did not. When he intercepted he always seemed to knock the ball upwards, then got a grip on it and away he went. Anyway, Bevan did not score that day and Rovers won 27-20. I think it was the first time they had ever won at Wilderspool.

Warrington put up two gutsy shows in four days at Watersheddings, but lost both times, 12-18 and 15-17, to Oldham, the current champions. The first encounter, in the second round of the Lancashire Cup, was illuminated by a try worthy of Bevan himself, but this time it was scored by teenage stand-off Jackie Edwards, who eluded man after man in a 40-yard mystery tour. The second game could have been won, but for a totally unexpected mistake by Bev. One of his most uncanny gifts was his ability to gauge what a ball would do when it had been kicked. One of his golden rules was to get to the ball quickly, but not too quickly. He was acutely aware of how quirky an oval ball could be. On this occasion, Ally Naughton placed a perfect kick to within a couple of feet of the Oldham posts, where it stopped dead. Bev beat three Roughyeds in the chase, but somehow overran the stationary ball, allowing one of his pursuers to gratefully clear the

172

danger. In view of Bev's past successes against Oldham, perhaps they deserved this belated piece of good fortune.

On 12 October, Bev got another shock when Warrington lost 8-10 at Salford. He was playing opposite Wally McArthur, the Australian Aborigine, who was unquestionably one of the fastest men to have played rugby league. Both men scored tries, Bev's a corker 30 seconds from time, which make shift kicker Ally Naughton failed to convert. McArthur's try was the first of the match, disputed because almost everyone thought it was a forward pass - except the referee. It was, however, a tackle which made everyone present gawp with astonishment.

Jack Steel declared: "The best tackle I have ever seen was effected on Bevan by a player who thousands of people have been led to believe is somewhat shaky on defence... Bevan, who had been well watched... suddenly shot into the middle with a characteristic burst. Salford defenders... were scattered around like fallen tin soldiers. Twenty-five yards to go, then 20, 15, 12 - and then it happened. McArthur 'took off' in approved jet plane fashion, hitting Bevan with such force that he was brought down in his tracks. The tackle was so effective that Bevan, with uprights and bar in his sights, temporarily 'blacked out' as if he had crashed into a wall. The crowd was equally as shocked as Bevan and they only realised the full significance of McArthur's save when three Salford men suddenly appeared in FRONT of the prostrate Bevan. After a huge gasp, and another, the spectators yelled for McArthur. He certainly got the cheers which had been purposely kept for Bevan."

Warrington continued to struggle, scraping a home win against Workington Town, once again a real power, but going down ignominiously at Keighley. Austin Heathwood reappeared at Lawkholme Lane after a year in retirement. His return, plus the recent introduction of Ally Brindle and Harry Major, indicated that the directors were still intent on bolstering the side's forward power.

Wigan overwhelmed

There was much rejoicing, however, when Wigan, lacking Boston, Bolton and their recent £9,500 world-record signing Mick Sullivan, all on test duty in France, were overwhelmed 21-5 at Wilderspool on 2 November. Brian Bevan reminded the 13,491 spectators that he could still turn it on with a couple of tries scored within the space of five minutes. Percy Kay wrote: "He went like the wind for one try, and the other was a sheer delight - a momentary change of pace which had Cherrington absolutely nonplussed, then racing round him on the touch side where there seemed barely room, but through which Bevan went like a shot".

Workington Town certainly felt that Bev was still as dangerous as ever, for the following week at Derwent Park they shifted their own local hero Ike Southward from right to left wing to counter the threat Bev posed. Southward, often aided by Town forward Doug Holland, took his role seriously. Bev was tackled mercilessly. Four times he was held without the ball and Warrington never received so much as a penalty. There was uproar, however, when Bev retaliated by holding Ike down yards from the ball in a Workington passing movement. Bev was cautioned by referee Matt Coates, much to his disgust. A try three minutes from time by Jim Challinor snatched a 10-10 draw. Ironically, when asked to name the greatest rugby league players he had come across for his biography in 1995, Ike Southward named Brian Edgar as the best forward and Brian Bevan as the finest back.

Try number 600?

On 16 November, Warrington defeated Bramley 29-17 at Wilderspool before a meagre crowd of 4,321, yet the occasion was one of Bev's most memorable. He was given a constant supply of ball and scored four tries, all of which had to be worked for. The public had erroneously been informed that Bev had so far scored 596 tries in his career (the record-keepers were eight adrift of the real total, for he had already scored 604). So when Bev received a long ball from fellow Aussie winger Len Horton and flew for the corner flag for his fourth try, the crowd erupted. Everyone believed he had touched down his 600th try. The applause went on for minutes, Bev was swamped by his team-mates and, when the game ended shortly afterwards, both teams formed a guard of honour to the dressing-rooms for the great man. He was presented with the match ball in recognition of the feat.

In his *Warrington Guardian* column, "Talking Sport", the following Friday, Jack Steel wrote: "What did Bev think about it all? He was a little overawed by the scenes at the finish when players on both sides lined up to allow him the honour of the order of the first bath. He just nodded his head in approval... He was still sitting in a corner splashing away fully a quarter of an hour after the finish of the game and I caught him in a really reflective mood. He merely remarked in reply to my congratulations that he would be able to sleep better that night. 'And I'll certainly not score another hundred', was the further comment of the player whose exploits will live as long as rugby league is played."

That was Bev - try-scorer extraordinary but no prophet!

Warrington fell 16-12 at Rochdale on 23 November. Bev's opposing winger Norman Short, stole two passes intended for the Australian to score two fine tries - the biter bit, many Hornets' fans would claim. Bev lit up a wretched Wire performance, however, with a characteristic try which brought the score to 12-14 with quarter of an hour left. It was described thus: "It looked as if Warrington would wilt but we saw Bevan in all his glory... Heathwood, who had made one or two nice breaks, went away nicely on the right and Bevan was in possession. That's the signal for panic stations at Rochdale. From half-way Bevan sprinted near the touch-line and had the waiting Jones completely foxed. There was room enough along the chalk line but Bevan moved inside with a deft step on the right foot. The speedy Short caught up to Bevan snatching at his collar. Unfortunately, he did not take into account Bevan's flying hooves and slipped to the ground. The Australian recovered his balance and went on to defy a vain last despairing dive by a Hornets forward. You must have heard the claim 'left three men grovelling in the mud'. Well, here it was in reality and how the Rochdale crowd, made so partisan by some of the referee's decisions, roared in approval of a wonderful try."

On 30 November, Wilderspool was agog with excitement reminiscent of the glory years. St Helens were the visitors and the attendance was 18,522, Wire's largest of the season. Saints had lost only one of their 16 league fixtures and topped the table. The major cause of the excitement was, however, the first appearance at the ground of St. Helens' latest capture, 'The Flying Springbok', Tom van Vollenhoven. Comparisons with Bev would immediately be drawn, even though their ages, physiques and styles of play were totally different. Spice was added to the affair with the appearance of Ray Price at stand-off for Saints, in partnership with another blossoming legend, Alex Murphy. Price's return to football had not gone down well with members of the Warrington directorate.

No one gave Warrington much of a chance, but how close they came to a surprise victory. Bev pushed Warrington into an 8-0 lead after 23 minutes when he chased a Naughton kick to the corner. Two Saints defenders dillied and dallied - something Bev would never do with a try on offer - and he touched down under their noses. With 10 minutes remaining Saints trailed 8-11 when van Vollenhoven was put away deep in his own '25'. A lame Horton tried to stop him but was brushed off as van Vollenhoven strode to half-way, where he kicked rather weakly into midfield. Warrington skipper Eric Fraser somehow contrived to lose the ball as it bounced. It shot up in the air and van Vollenhoven snatched it to hare away to the side of the posts, for a well-taken and spectacular, if somewhat fortuitous, match-winner. Ironically Ray Price landed the easy conversion and Warrington had lost 13-11.

The following week, there was a crowd of only 917 for Warrington's game at Blackpool and Wire reverted to their lackadaisical selves, just winning 18-14. Another sketchy win followed at home to Salford, when a young stand-off of exceptional pace and promise, Bobby Greenough, made his debut. There were complaints that Bev was so severely rationed for passes that he probably thought there was still a war on. His inside men seemed forever intent on kicking impossible balls for Bev to chase.

By the time Christmas arrived, he had scored 22 tries, which was pretty good for a supposed has-been in a mediocre team. He had scored as many as Billy Boston, but fewer than Billy's team-mates Eric Ashton (24) and Mick Sullivan (27). Way out in front, however, was Halifax's sensational left-winger Johnny Freeman, who had rattled up 38 in only 20 matches - a rate as rapid as anyone in the game's history had achieved. Unfortunately, a bad injury sustained at Batley on 21 December put Freeman out of the game for a year, and robbed him of the chance to really threaten Albert Rosenfeld's record of 80 tries in a season.

Touched by a red hot poker

Between Christmas week and the beginning of February 1958, Warrington hit a dismal vein of form. Only two games out of 10 were won and they plummeted to 15th in the table. The ever-dependable Bob Ryan, who had begun his Wire career even before Bevan, was brought back from semi-retirement to bolster the pack. The veteran Widnes hooker Jack Hayes was also induced to give up retirement in the quest for more possession from the scrums. Despite his team's wretched performances in this period, Bev continued to pile up the tries. His 30th of the season, in a 12-8 defeat at Leeds on 25 January, brought the house down. Gaining possession near the '25', "he did not hare for the line but ran as if he had been

Thrum Hall, 22 February 1958. Challenge Cup second round. Warrington surprised Halifax with a 17-12 victory. Bev admires a tackle by Jim Challinor on Halifax's giant centre Geoff Palmer. On the extreme right is Keith Williams, who in later life became the Vicar of Batley. Williams once scored 8 tries in a match for Halifax, a feat even Bev never achieved. This match was the author's first sight of Brian Bevan.

suddenly touched by a red hot poker. He defied the slippery ground to swerve and weave past three men. Another Leeds man grabbed chilly air and then Bevan turned to the posts with two men hanging on as he plunged over".

The first round of the Challenge Cup arrived on 8 February, but Warrington's tie at Batley, along with six others in Yorkshire and one in Cumberland, was wiped out by snow. When the game was played the following Wednesday afternoon, Warrington won easily 27-6 and three days later a good home win over Barrow was recorded. The crowd, for such attractive opposition, was a mere 3,352. The conditions were pretty dire, but even the Wire die-hards were losing faith in their side. Bev had never played before so few spectators at Wilderspool.

The crowd at Halifax in the next round of the Challenge Cup was more like the old days at 14,620, but Warrington were definitely second favourites. They rose grandly to the occasion, however, winning 17-12, Bev just making the line for their second try after Alf Arnold had skipped through a static defence.

As usual, visions of Wembley suddenly appeared. Warrington were in the third round. Admittedly the tie was a tough one - Workington Town, away. On the afternoon of the match, 8 March, the Cumbrian weather threw everything it could at the 16,415 souls, 1,500 of them Warringtonians, who attended Derwent Park - a ground record. There was hail, snow, a mind-numbing wind from Siberia and even a little sunshine. The much-maligned Wire pack, which had done so well at Thrum Hall, played magnificently against a mighty Town six. For an hour they held everything that Town and the elements launched against them, as the game remained scoreless. Warrington had hard luck in the first half when Greenough's kick to the line was touched down by the flying Bev, only for referee Ron Gelder to rule out the score. He had just one more chance in the second half, when he got away only to be brought to earth by a desperate cover defence. A brave effort by Warrington came to nothing as Town notched the only 11 points of the game in the final 15 minutes.

Bob Ryan never played again after the Workington cup-tie, leaving Bev as the longest-serving player on the books. And there was more distressing news on 12 March when the popular Warrington club chairman Fred Davies died. The team bounced back surprisingly well to win five of the last eight league matches with Bev in something like his old form, piling up 13 more tries onto his monumental total.

At Featherstone on 22 March, again in Arctic conditions, he led the Rovers a merry dance in a 22-3 victory. He only touched down once but had the crowd spellbound with one run which took him 50 yards and mesmerised half-a-dozen opponents before he was brought down a couple of feet from the posts. His try was less spectacular but more singular, as Jack Steel noted: "He is not a broad sort of chap when it comes to measuring up physiques yet this time he edged in at the corner in a sideways movement as if he was moving down a narrow passage".

Easter was a profitable time for Bev. Three vintage tries at Naughton Park on Good Friday, 4 April, were a major factor in Wire's 21-17 victory, but his two tries against Leigh at Wilderspool on Easter Monday were the only highlights as Warrington dithered to an 8-13 defeat. The following Saturday, 12 April, Warrington entered the last few minutes of their home game against Whitehaven with a lead of 36-10 having grabbed eight tries. Bev's centre partner Laurie Gilfedder had notched three and Bobby Greenough on the left wing scored a couple, but Bev remained try-less. Then Alf Arnold slipped Bev a pass almost on the Wire goal-line.

According to the *Warrington Guardian*, he "sailed past two tired Cumberland forwards and was at half-way in five seconds. The fast moving McMenemy had edged over quite nicely, intent on a cutting-off movement. But Bevan kept him at more than an arm's length. Then just as McKeown thought that Bevan might go inside and become the victim of a sandwich tackle, the Australian rounded the full-back by a deft turn of direction. Nothing but an earthquake or false handling of the ball could have stopped a score. It was a try which brought along friend and foe to shake Bevan's hand and, to supplement the great ovation from the reserved enclosure, the fans on the popular side clapped and cheered in a rapturous outburst".

On 22 April, Bev figured on the right wing for a Rugby League XIII which took on France at Headingley. He was partnered by Leeds's Australian captain Keith McLellan while the left wing pairing comprised Lewis Jones and Tom van Vollenhoven. Voll was the star of a highly entertaining game which the Rugby League XIII won 19-8. He scored two tremendous tries and Bev helped himself to a stunner too, his 41st of the season. Full-back Garfield Owen banged over five goals, when an off-target Jones handed over the goal-kicking. The game ended riotously, however, with a couple of boots-and-all brawls in the last 15 minutes. The French seemed to have it in for scrum-half Jeff Stevenson, who was the victim of their flying feet. As Stevenson was the smallest man on the field and a local hero, it was not surprising that the French were booed continuously for quarter of an hour, and all the way back to the dressing-rooms.

Warrington's season ended on 30 April with a 61-16 rout of Rochdale Hornets at Wilderspool. They amassed 15 tries, of which Bev claimed five. It was Bev who performed the last rites of the campaign. His fifth try in the last seconds of the game was, as usual, well summed up by Jack Steel: "The Bevan effort shook us all, especially that section who keep saying 'this is the Australian's last year'. And then are disappointed if he doesn't turn out! Bevan slipped into a passing movement, juggled as only he knows how, and then, after all the oohs and ahs from the crowd, went on his merry way, giving a backward glance just to show that it is usually easy - the unorthodox Bevan way. Four times previously he had used his top speed gear to score."

It was as if he was leaving a reminder that he was still around and capable of running riot from time to time. Bev finished the season with 46 tries, an outrageous figure for someone for whom the obituarists were sharpening their pencils. The problem with Bev was that he had been so phenomenally coruscating for so long that any diminution in his powers was enough to fuel the rumour machines of the doom merchants. He may not have been quite as good as he had been but he was still far too good for almost every other winger.

Bev had still managed to finish third in the try-scoring lists - hardly a sign of a has-been. He was only four tries adrift of the leader Mick Sullivan and one behind second-placed Ike Southward. These two fine wingmen were the current world record transfer fee holder (Sullivan, £9,500) and the man who would be the next (Southward, £10,650 in March 1959). Below Bev were Bradford Northern's Malcolm Davies (45), Billy Boston (43), Eric Ashton (41), Tom van Vollenhoven (40) and Halifax's Keith Williams (40). If Bev was past it he was in exceptionally good company. Moreover, Bev was the only one, apart from Davies, who had been playing with a team outside the top six, which made his achievements even more meritorious.

His season was, however, apparently insufficient to qualify him for inclusion in *Rugby League Gazette*'s world ratings, published in April 1958. Having been rated best winger in the world three years previously, Bev was now excluded from the top 10. The rather eccentric ratings of 'J.E.B.' placed the still injured Johnny Freeman as number one right-winger, despite the fact that he invariably played on the left. Behind Freeman followed Guy Husson (France), Billy Boston, Raymond

178

Contrastin (France) and van Vollenhoven. The five top-rated left-wingers were Ian Moir (Australia), Frank Carlton (St Helens), Mick Sullivan, Bill Wookey (Workington Town) and Vincent Cantoni, a third Frenchman. Still, everyone is entitled to an opinion.

Despite Bev's resurrection, Warrington's prospects were not particularly rosy. The average home crowd had dropped down to 7,571. Support towards the end of the season had fallen away alarmingly, the last two home games against Whitehaven and Rochdale having pulled in just over 4,000 each and even the Leeds fixture had only produced a crowd of 4,843 on 29 March. The large outlay on rugby unionists Martin Regan and Robin Thompson had not reaped the expected dividends, both being plagued by injuries, and there remained an urgent need to fortify the pack. Warrington had plenty of pace and potential in the backs - Eric Fraser and Jim Challinor returning heroes from the 1958 Lions tour, for example - but, without the necessary fire-power up front, life would continue to be a struggle.

Four Warrington forwards

Owen Bevan

Jim Featherstone

Harold Palin

Bob Ryan

179

Season 1957-58

Warrington finished 13th in the League: P38, W19, D1, L18; For 669, Against 529.
Bevan scored 45 tries for Warrington, plus 1 for representative teams

Date	Opponent	Score	Bevan	Crowd	
17 Aug	Bramley	21-16	1T	5,073	
21 Aug	**Liverpool City**	36-6	3T	6,444	
24 Aug	**Keighley**	20-17	1T	7,627	
31 Aug	**Liverpool City**	50-19	3T	6,457	LC1
4 Sep	Liverpool City	18-9	1T	1,121	
7 Sep	**Featherstone R**	20-27	3T	9,021	
10 Sep	Oldham	12-18		15,402	LC 2
14 Sep	Oldham	15-17		12,594	
21 Sep	**Bradford N**	16-8		8,534	
28 Sep	St Helens	2-14	dnp	7,116	
5 Oct	**Blackpool B**	19-6		7,278	
12 Oct	Salford	8-10	1T	7,445	
19 Oct	**Workington T**	10-5		7,300	
26 Oct	Keighley	7-14	dnp	3,933	
2 Nov	**Wigan**	21-5	2T	13,491	
9 Nov	Workington T	10-10		5,358	
16 Nov	**Bramley**	29-17	4T	4,321	
23 Nov	Rochdale H	12-16	1T	4,247	
30 Nov	**St Helens**	11-13	1T	18,522	
7 Dec	Blackpool B	18-14	1T	917	
14 Dec	**Salford**	20-16		5,697	
21 Dec	Barrow	15-25		5,772	
25 Dec	**Widnes**	28-2	2T	5,945	
26 Dec	Leigh	2-8		7,577	
28 Dec	**Oldham**	14-15	1T	13,463	
1 Jan	Wigan	13-22	2T	14,267	
4 Jan	Whitehaven	12-28	1T	3,993	
11 Jan	**Swinton**	32-6	1T	5,151	
18 Jan	York	12-17	dnp	4,676	
25 Jan	Leeds	8-12	1T	12,583	
1 Feb	**York**	7-31		6,025	
12 Feb	Batley	27-6	1T	2,000	Ch Cup 1
15 Feb	**Barrow**	16-14		3,352	
22 Feb	Halifax	17-12	1T	14,620	Ch Cup 2
8 Mar	Workington T	0-11		16,415	Ch Cup 3
15 Mar	Bradford N	19-5	1T	3,850	
22 Mar	Featherstone R	22-3	1T	4,600	
29 Mar	**Leeds**	13-28		4,843	
4 Apr	Widnes	21-17	3T	9,192	
7 Apr	**Leigh**	8-13	2T	8,608	
12 Apr	**Whitehaven**	39-10	1T	4,118	
19 Apr	Swinton	14-17		4,500	
30 Apr	**Rochdale H**	61-16	5T	4,119	

Bevan's Representative Matches:

Date	For	Opponent	Score	Bevan	Venue
16 Apr	Rugby League XIII	France	19-8	1T	Leeds

180

17. 1958-59 'I had him covered... Then he just wasn't there'

The 1958-59 season saw Warrington rise from 13th to ninth in the league. The progress was not spectacular, but at least there was progress. As for Bev, he was spectacularly successful, again topping a half-century of tries and passing more and more personal landmarks. By this time in his working life he had embarked on a new career. The Warrington match programmes of the period carried an advertisement urging customers to "Try Bevan's for ladies' and gents' outfitting, children's and babies' wear, drapery and hardware" at 18, Lindi Avenue, Grappenhall, helpfully adding that the business was near the bus terminus.

There was an important new change in rugby league too. The English Rugby Football League decided at last to fall in with the other nations by ordering a scrum to be formed if the acting half-back was caught in possession after a play-the-ball. This would encourage more passing and prevent the creeping barrage of interminable play-the-balls in which the acting half-back, or even the man playing the ball, merely drove forward a yard or two at a time. In theory it meant more opportunities for men like Brian Bevan, who had more chance of the ball reaching them when they could do most damage.

More than 10,000 people were present at Wilderspool for the Wardonia Cup game on 9 August. Wigan led 8-0 at half-time, fell behind 8-21 and then came with a rush to win 29-21, leaving Wire fans in some trepidation as to what the rest of the season held. Bev scored the try that levelled the score at 8-8 after a mazy dash by Edwards, but was outshone by Wigan winger Terry O'Grady, who went over for three tries.

There was a better outcome from the opening league fixture when Huddersfield were beaten 27-17 at Fartown. Huddersfield had Athol Brown, a Rhodesian winger, making his debut opposite Bev. South Africans and Rhodesians had become the new Australians and Kiwis, as far as English clubs were concerned. The international transfer ban had been extended, cutting off signings of top Australian and New Zealand players and depriving English crowds of personality players. Consequently, southern Africa became a hunting ground where English scouts hoped to unearth another van Vollenhoven. Brown proved to be no Voll, but shared in a piece of history as Bev scored two typical tries, his 599th and 600th for Warrington. Bobby Greenough, on the left wing, did even better with a late hat-trick, the last try courtesy of interpassing with Bevan.

On 20 August, there was much disbelief when Warrington went down 26-23 to Liverpool City at Wilderspool. Alf Arnold suffered a burst blood vessel in his eye and was taken to Manchester Eye Hospital after only 17 minutes. Even so, Warrington took a 10-2 lead, but were eventually overwhelmed by the City pack. This game saw Len Horton make his last appearance in the primrose and blue.

Bev scored two tries, one a wonderful swerving, side-stepping affair reminiscent of his greatest days, in a 20-16 home win over Keighley on 23 August. Two days later, he was given the captaincy for the game at St Helens, where Warrington put up a decent show only to lose 15-7. Bev took quite a baiting from the Saints support - the crowd topped 18,000 - but had the

181

The 1958 Wardonia Cup ended in a 29-21 victory for Wigan. Here Bev looks for an inside pass from Laurie Gilfedder as Wigan winger Bobby Chisnall tackles. Gilfedder partnered Bevan 27 times as a centre but made his name as a second-rower.

satisfaction of quietening them by scoring his side's only try. Jackie Edwards put in a good kick to Bev's wing, which full-back Fearis and winger Johnson rushed to cover only to collide and send each other sprawling. Bev was also brought to his knees, but grateful to the gods, when the ball popped into his lap. Up he shot and over the line. Most unusually, in his excitement he touched down immediately instead of moving nearer the posts.

Billy McFarlane played his last game for Wire at Knowsley Road, transferring back to Leigh, although not in time to play for them in the first round of the Lancashire Cup at Wilderspool on 30 August. Another disappointment, a 16-10 knock-out, was all a crowd of more than 10,000 received.

Warrington entered the transfer market, much to the relief of the Wire faithful, when they signed Nat Silcock, a 1954 Great Britain tourist, from St Helens. Formerly a second-rower of outstanding pace, he was now a prop-forward and much reliance was placed on him to shake up the Warrington pack. His arrival coincided with a three-match winning run, Widnes, Leeds and Bradford Northern being the victims. Bev had a good afternoon at Odsal on 13 September, the *Examiner* noting: "Brian Bevan showed he still has enough pace left to beat most defenders. He got a couple of opportunist tries that bore the stamp of the master tactician, his first resulting from a hare-like dash up the wing which left would-be-tacklers floundering hopelessly."

Bev shows Voll

A week later St Helens attracted 16,745, again the season's biggest home crowd, to Wilderspool. It turned out to be Alf Arnold's last game for the club and ended in a 15-29 defeat. It was a hell of a game, however, as Mike Rowan recalls: "From the moment the game started Saints took charge and were 19-2 in the ascendancy after twenty minutes or so. From a scrum on half-way Murphy ran between Arnold and Edwards and flew round Eric Fraser to score a fabulous solo behind the posts. Saints appeared in a different league... It seemed so easy that I feared the worst. For half an hour Saints dominated. Then Greenough, playing centre to Bevan, got on the end of a handling movement to reduce the arrears. Then just as only happens on cinema screens, the script changed.

People watched in sheer admiration as Saints received a startling visitation from the admirable old stager, who just defied the years. At first Johnson had bumped the eccentric Australian, showing no respect. Dave Johnson could pick 'em up and was a fast man in his own right... In the innocence of youth he seemed to be somewhat contemptuous of the guy opposite. Appearance and movement he learned to his cost were, oh, so deceptive with that bald old man. Corner him and he struck like a snake.

As Ken Large touched a long high pass the ball fell behind him and Johnson. Before anyone else could react Bevan gathered the ball waist high and away he went. With a magnificent side-step he went by Fearis, the last line of defence. Johnson did turn and gave chase but it was all to no avail. We made the rafters roar because following the conversion the half-time whistle blew and Warrington were back in it. The Wire pulled back 13 points in as many minutes on either side of the interval and our pulses raced in anticipation. The next effort came from... well, you know who.

Writers struggled to find adequate words to describe the circumstances. New superlatives are always difficult to trace if one has seen magic before, but on this occasion the principal players in the action compelled the scribes to at least try.

Alf Arnold for once got the better of Murphy and his inside pass to Brian Bevan had the wingman sweeping away. A series of side-steps and our hearts pounded as an awareness hit the onlookers of the obstacle that barred his way. It was like the *Gunfight at the OK Corral*. There was no cold and calculating trepidation - the action was too rapid - but an instant gasp arose as Tom Van Vollenhoven came across. A few sets of false teeth fell from jaws and hearts and lungs nearly collapsed... as we waited the outcome...

A week later Alan Prescott paid tribute and described van Vollenhoven's reactions: 'I had him covered. I set myself to take him and then he just wasn't there.' He had heard of it but had never seen the prowess of Bev in all its glory. In fact he never saw it even then but the roars of the crowd told Tom that his adversary had swept past him with consummate ease. So, gentlemen, add van Vollenhoven to the list of bewildered numbers.

Jack Steel obviously shared in the delight of Bevan's supporters for he declared, 'He didn't know whether it was a Springbok or a Kangaroo.' St Helens reporter, Tom Ashcroft noted that there were two Saints men hanging on as his speed eventually gave out. Ashcroft also described it as a wonderful effort but not a wonderful try. He said that referee Railton was unsighted as Bevan went down in the ruck and lost possession. 'There was no demonstration, however, for the veriest Saint-ites took the view that the effort deserved the scoreboard adjustment.'

Tom van Vollenhoven, to his eternal credit, led the applause...BB's feat became part of the Aussie's folklore. Whether the reaction to the score was sheer ecstasy or a knife plunged in the heart, no one could deny such artistry. What hit people was the difference in appearance of the two men. Blond Vollenhoven, of superb athleticism, looking every inch the marvellous wingman that he was and then Bevan, who resembled anything but the image one would conjure up for the undisputed 'King of Tryscorers'...

Warrington missed further chances but St Helens did not. In fact Tom registered a good touchdown of his own. Saints deservedly won... but the day belonged to the veteran on the flank. Oh, how our chests stuck out as we left the ground. Basking in reflected glory we were chuffed to little mint balls. 'Who's this Voll then?' we gloated. 'Up yer jacksey!'"

That try, fittingly, brought Bev the 2,000th point of his career.

Warrington fielded two newcomers at Salford the next Saturday in hooker Paddy Lannon (ex-Liverpool City) and the 1954 Great Britain tourist, Terry O'Grady, on the left wing. O'Grady had been signed from Wigan, having lost his place to Mick Sullivan. It was Bev, who took the eye at The Willows, however, running in two typically opportunistic tries in a 22-16 win. Bev was also amongst the scorers against Oldham, who proved too strong, winning 20-13 at Wilderspool before a crowd approaching 15,000. Then on 11 October, Warrington ran riot at Headingley. Leeds lost their hooker, Bernard Prior, early on and conceded 11 tries to a rampant Wire who triumphed 47-17. Bev had a field day with three tries in a virtuoso performance. His third try was the 650th of his career but it was his first which captivated the 16,153 fortunate witnesses. Jack Steel reported: "Hereabouts we saw a touch of Bevan's genius. Ten yards from half-way he got a Challinor pass and set off at an astonishing pace though crouching in Indian-runner fashion. Two big forwards would have scalped him had they been able to head him off to the side-line. A third opponent grabbed at nothing at all while Dunn, a yard or so from touch, merely saw a streak - it was all over. Bevan finished up on his arc of triumph on the popular side to receive a grand hand from the amazed home folk."

At the close of the game, swarms of autograph-hunting youngsters surrounded Bev and hundreds of adults, stayed to cheer the great man back to the dressing-rooms. The Loiners had seen so many displays of pure artistry down the years that it was almost as if they regarded him as one of their own.

Bev chalked up another hat-trick the following week, but Warrington went down 20-21 at Blackpool. Warrington's up-and-down form continued when York were defeated 26-17 at Wilderspool, with Bev pilfering one of those exciting interception tries that were so much his speciality. Warrington may have been inconsistent, but that fault did not apply to their right winger, who had scored in each of the last seven fixtures - 14 tries in that spell. Bev's form was good enough to give him joint leadership of the try-scorers. By 8 November, he had scored 19 tries and was level with van Vollenhoven, Garry Hemingway (Leeds) and Keith Williams (Halifax). Amazingly, their nearest challenger on 18 tries was the Barrow hooker, Len McIntyre, who was followed by his team-mate and one of Bev's oldest rivals, Frank Castle on 17.

November had started badly for Warrington with a defeat at Hull KR, when Bev must have thought he had been 'sent to Coventry', so little ball did he receive. The next game, however, a 30-4 rout of Workington Town at Wilderspool, marked the beginning of an eight match winning run. Bev profited accordingly with another 10 tries, the first another long-distance classic in a 37-8 win at York on 22 November. He was absent when Huddersfield were beaten 19-14 at Wilderspool the following week, thanks to an immaculate kicking performance by Eric Fraser, who landed eight goals. Bev was on right-wing duty for a Rugby League XIII against France at St Helens, local hero Tom van Vollenhoven being on the left wing. The two master wingers, however, hardly got a sniff of a try all afternoon. The French team, 26-8 winners, were altogether too smart for the home side, ripping them apart for six tries with exhilarating handling and running. Their wingers Maurice Voron and Andre Savonne ("the Bison of Vaucluse"), scored three times between them and gave Bev and Voll a torrid time, courtesy of the incisiveness of their middle backs.

Back in league action, Bev continued to alter scoreboards as Warrington's winning run continued. A stupendous interception try at Rochdale was followed by more tries against Hull KR, two against Rochdale at home, a hat-trick at Liverpool and two at home against Leigh. The 35-13 home victory over Leigh on Boxing Day was Bev's 500th appearance for Warrington and he celebrated with two crackers which delighted the crowd of 10,540.

During December Warrington, having played a few more games than their rivals, actually entered the top four alongside Swinton, Oldham and St Helens but it was to be their high point of the season. A home defeat to Swinton and losses at Wigan and Whitehaven obstructed their victory trail as the year turned, and then a three-week break for diabolical weather caused further disruption. Returning to action on 24 January 1959, Warrington defeated Blackpool far less convincingly than a 25-8 scoreline indicated. Bev, however, was in prime form, snapping up three tries, including one of those classic interceptions, and having two others disallowed.

Booed and misunderstood

Warrington had begun to descend from the lofty heights of the top four. Another trio of games was lost in the run-up to the Challenge Cup-ties. Workington beat them 32-15 at Derwent Park on 31 January in a canter on a mud-covered surface. Wire were dire, but Bev reminded the Cumbrian crowd of his greatness. He scored two superb tries from his only two chances, while Town's own right-winger Ike Southward did even better with five tries from five running chances. It was, however, Bev's second try which stole the entire show. At half-time Bev had been booed from the field, having been involved in a minor fracas with Harry Archer, Town's burly stand-off, who was playing his first game since returning from the Australian tour the previous summer. Archer had nearly taken Bev's head off with a high tackle and this caused a ruckus. However, the boos turned to cheers when Bev claimed yet another amazing try on Cumbrian soil. The *Examiner* reported: "Bevan's try... will be long remembered by Workington supporters. Faced with a solid wall of defenders near the touchline on the Workington '25' line, he veered inside until just opposite the posts. There he was staggered by an attempted tackle, but recovered in a trice and shot like an arrow from a bow through a narrow gap to touch down near the posts."

Defeats at Oldham and at home to Wigan dropped Warrington to ninth in the league table, just three places above their first-round Challenge Cup opponents

Keighley, who were due at Wilderspool on 21 February. The team's confidence was eroding, as was that of the supporters, who had been alarmed even further by some comments appearing in the press attributed to Brian Bevan. Apparently Bev had been rumoured to have been unhappy both with his remuneration at Wilderspool and at the training regime the coaches were using. He was again supposed to be ready to move on. On the eve of the Keighley cup-tie Jack Steel set matters straight in an article headlined "Brian Bevan Explains". He wrote: "There was a dramatic moment in the Warrington RL Club's dressing-room last night after the players had returned from the field after their final training session before tomorrow's cup-tie. Brian Bevan called for silence and gave his explanation about recent statements which have been attributed to him.

Afterwards Brian told me, 'The Warrington club have dealt with me quite fairly about money matters. I have no quibble on that score. Although I'm a professional footballer and money is a vital matter because of the risks I have to take and as insurance for myself and family, I'm not money-mad. I would play for Warrington for nothing in tomorrow's cup-tie just to show what I think about the club. Rugby League is my life and I'm never happier than when playing it - though sometimes I may not appear to be so.

The training at Warrington is very good but I think the present attitude of youth towards training of any kind - these are general terms - is not what it was when I was a youngster. I want to play for Warrington for years to come. I know that some people consider me a veteran but, honestly speaking, I have never felt better in my life. I will be at Wilderspool tomorrow and will try my hardest to help the team towards victory.

I am sorry that some misapprehension may have been caused but I'm happy at Wilderspool, and will continue to play hard for my place and the club as long as it is humanly possible to do so. As for the supporters, well, there have been times when I have been criticised but those are outweighed by the hundreds of times they have cheered me to the echo.'

Manager Ces Mountford said, 'Warrington training is really stiff. It is harder than when I was at Wigan. Some of the players think the schedule is too tough. We are not making any changes. We have had some unlucky breaks but our luck is bound to turn.'"

Wire's luck did turn, but only for long enough to despatch Keighley 26-7 from the Cup. Bev showed his commitment with another two tries and a third disallowed and skipper Eric Fraser landed his 100th goal of the season. The crowd of 7,423 was below Warrington expectations for a cup-tie and the crowds at Wigan (31,614 against Leeds) and at Oldham (23,000 versus St Helens) demonstrated just how far behind Warrington had fallen in the crowd-pulling stakes.

The following week, Keighley extracted revenge with a 24-15 victory at Lawkholme Lane in the league, despite falling behind to a Bevan interception try in the first five minutes. It did not augur well for the second-round Challenge Cup-tie at Leigh on 7 March. More than 14,000 saw Warrington put up a stern, but unavailing, fight. Their cause was not helped when second-rower Jack Arkwright was sent off just before the interval. All Warrington had to show for a hard afternoon's labour was an Ally Naughton try a few minutes from time as

Leigh won 13-3. Coach Cec Mountford's woes were compounded when he was ordered by the RFL to give a written apology to referee Eric Clay for his comments made after the game.

Warrington's form in the league perked up following the Challenge Cup reverse with five victories in the next six games. Bev's form in this period was sensational as he piled up 15 tries, including four hat-tricks. The Good Friday - 27 March - derby win against Widnes brought Bev a couple of relatively simple tries, the first of which, courtesy of Silcock and Greenough, saw him pass the 2,000 points mark for Warrington. The crowd for this game, 11,972, was the third highest of the season at Wilderspool, but paled into insignificance compared to the all-time league record of 47,000 plus which turned up a few miles away for the Wigan versus St Helens clash at Central Park. On Easter Monday, Warrington hammered Leigh at Hilton Park with Bev's third try being his 50th of the season. Then in a 26-15 home victory over Barrow on 11 April he passed another milestone, when the first try of his hat-trick took his total number of tries for the club to 650.

At that point, with only two games remaining, Bev was top of the try-scoring chart, two ahead of Tom van Vollenhoven. With extra games to play, however, Voll finally finished at the top with 62 tries, with Bev tied in second place on 54 with Billy Boston. This was an astounding performance by Brian Bevan, considering that Tom and Billy played for teams which finished first and second in the league. Bear in mind too that both were more than 10 years younger than Bev, who was now pushing 35, and that physically they were far better endowed. Voll had the great good fortune to play with a truly wonderful Saints side in 1958-59, a champion team which rewrote history by becoming the first to score more than 1,000 points in league fixtures alone. Boston was a member of an almost equally prolific scoring team, which richly deserved to win that season's Challenge Cup. What might Bev have achieved playing at Knowsley Road or Central Park at this stage in his career? The mind boggles.

Wire's season petered out tamely with defeats at Barrow and at home to Bradford Northern, games in which Bev might just as well have been a spectator. The latter game attracted another post-war low attendance for Wilderspool of only 2,910. Financial alarm bells were ringing in the boardroom because the season had seen a further reduction in average home attendances, the figure falling from 7,571 to 7,215. Warrington were unhappy that the RFL had agreed to allow the BBC to televise 10 live matches during the season. Along with other clubs, they felt that crowds had fallen as a result. In January 1959 they had formally objected to the agreement but their protest had been rejected.

Only an attractive, honours-challenging team could bring back the good days and financial stability to Wilderspool. Meanwhile Warrington fans at least still had their grand old man to provide entertainment and thrills - but for how much longer?

Season 1958-59

Warrington finished 9th in the League: P38, W22, L16; For 780, Against 585
Bevan scored 54 tries for Warrington

Date	Opponent	Score	Bevan	Crowd	
16 Aug	Huddersfield	27-17	2T	7,986	
20 Aug	**Liverpool City**	23-26		3,490	
23 Aug	**Keighley**	20-16	2T	4,525	
25 Aug	St Helens	7-15	1T	18,253	
30 Aug	**Leigh**	10-16		10,586	LC 1
4 Sep	Widnes	17-13		10,574	
6 Sep	**Leeds**	32-15		8,480	
13 Sep	Bradford N	26-16	2T	3,676	
20 Sep	**St Helens**	15-29	2T	16,745	
27 Sep	Salford	22-16	2T	6,363	
4 Oct	**Oldham**	13-20	1T	14,627	
11 Oct	Leeds	47-17	3T	16,153	
18 Oct	Blackpool B	20-21	3T	2,490	
25 Oct	**York**	26-17	1T	6,239	
1 Nov	Hull KR	11-15		6,691	
8 Nov	**Workington T**	30-4		6,151	
15 Nov	York	37-8	1T	4,557	
22 Nov	**Huddersfield**	19-14	dnp	5,324	
29 Nov	Rochdale H	13-5	1T	4,177	
6 Dec	**Hull KR**	19-9	1T	3,995	
13 Dec	**Rochdale H**	19-0	2T	3,290	
20 Dec	Liverpool City	44-8	3T	1,144	
26 Dec	**Leigh**	35-13	2T	10,540	
27 Dec	**Swinton**	5-15		9,330	
1 Jan	Wigan	16-24	1T	23,142	
3 Jan	Whitehaven	2-19		3,901	
24 Jan	**Blackpool B**	25-8	3T	4,376	
31 Jan	Workington T	15-32	2T	5,376	
7 Feb	Oldham	8-19	1T	11,736	
14 Feb	**Wigan**	5-18		11,914	
21 Feb	**Keighley**	26-7	2T	7,423	Ch Cup 1
28 Feb	Keighley	15-24	1T	3,420	
7 Mar	Leigh	3-13		14,324	Ch Cup 2
14 Mar	**Whitehaven**	42-8	3T	3,656	
21 Mar	Swinton	18-22	3T	4,000	
27 Mar	**Widnes**	11-7	2T	11,972	
30 Mar	Leigh	23-4	3T	8,475	
4 Apr	**Salford**	27-21	1T	5,839	
11 Apr	**Barrow**	26-15	3T	3,674	
18 Apr	Barrow	14-21		3,849	
25 Apr	**Bradford N**	6-14		2,910	

Bevan's Representative Matches:

Date	For	Opponent	Score	Bevan	Venue
22 Nov	Rugby League XIII	France	8-26		St Helens

18. 1959-60 'He showed me a thing or two'

As the 1959-60 season began, the Warrington directors were spending a lot of money on improvements at Wilderspool. The popular side cover was extended so that 6,000 people could be sheltered and a huge bar was constructed in its bowels. Other bars, tea rooms and the boardroom were refurbished. This was all well and good, but many fans, as always, were more interested in seeing new signings. However, there was no sign of any new players as the campaign got under way at Central Park on 8 August with another defeat before a crowd of 18,701 as the Wardonia Cup was lost to Wigan by 31-22 for the fourth consecutive year. Bev scored characteristically when he nipped between Keith Holden and Mick Sullivan for yet another interception try.

The opening league game at Hull KR on 15 August had the pessimists wringing their hands after a 13-4 half-time advantage was overturned, and Rovers ran out 18-13 victors, thanks mainly to full-back Cyril Kellett's 15 point haul. Dennis Karalius, the former St Helens second-rower, made his debut in this match. He had cost around £3,000 and was the Wire's only major signing of the season.

Coach Cec Mountford had been given sole responsibility for team selection after being at Wilderspool for eight years. Previously, the team had been picked on a majority vote of the directors and the coach. The poor beginning to the season obviously did not faze the little New Zealander, for his team confounded the carpers with a characterful run of eight straight wins, Bev scoring tries in the first seven as he quickly fell into the old routine. Even so, stand-off Bobby Greenough took the scoring honours with 10 tries in the first six fixtures and was rewarded with the right-wing berth for Lancashire.

After easy home victories over Liverpool and Bradford, Warrington sprang a surprise with a 10-6 success at Oldham on 25 August, Bev sneaking in at the corner for a crucial try. Four days later, they returned from Workington having despatched Town 33-12 in the first round of the Lancashire Cup, with Bev having to wait until the last five minutes to streak over for his only score. York were the next Wire victims, hammered by 40-5 at Wilderspool. Bev crossed twice for legitimate tries but had another three ruled out. A second-round Lancashire Cup-tie at Leigh on 9 September seemed a tough proposition but, after Leigh lost their second-rower Derek Hurt in the early minutes, there was no stopping Warrington, who advanced to the semi-finals 29-2. Ally Naughton, in his testimonial season and playing loose-forward, scored a hat-trick.

Three days later, Warrington almost came unstuck once again at Knotty Ash when Liverpool City held them to 16-19. Bev provided the thrill of the encounter, however, when he took a pass from Jim Challinor near his own line, shot clear of the cover and left future Great Britain full-back Ray Ashby clutching thin air on the half-way line before racing away to score at his leisure. The Wire may, forgivably, have been saving themselves a little for the more arduous task of taking on Wigan at Central Park in the semi-final of the Lancashire Cup on 15 September, three days later. The tie aroused tremendous excitement, a crowd of 30,637 being reminiscent of the early post-war days.

Although no one knew it at the time, the game marked another important milestone for Brian Bevan. He was making his 527th appearance for Warrington, thereby breaking the club record held by Jack 'Cod' Miller. Miller, a former Lancashire and test prop-forward, had played his 526 games between 1926 and 1946. The two great men had actually played together once - on the occasion of Bev's debut back in November 1945. Few, if any, of the 30,000 folk present at Central Park that day in 1959 would have put money on Bev playing almost another 100 games in the primrose and blue - but that is what he went on to do.

Bev failed to score in the semi, having bagged nine tries in his last seven games, but he did play a significant part in a tie which many people regarded as one of the most exciting games ever seen at Central Park. Wigan looked likely to run away with the game when, after nine minutes they led 10-0. Full-back Jack Cunliffe, an even older stager than Bev, and centre Eric Ashton claimed tries, both of which Ashton converted. Wire hit back before the break when Terry O'Grady scored after some fine passing. Fraser's conversion took the score to 10-5. After 52 minutes Warrington levelled the scores when Silcock made a try for Edwards, again converted by Fraser. The tension was now tangible. Bev was proving a menace and at last got a clear run, shooting down the touch-line, swerving inside past Mick Sullivan and then being engulfed by a cracking tackle from Cunliffe. The danger seemed over, but Denis Karalius suddenly appeared in support and Bev popped out a deft inside pass for the second-rower to crash over. Warrington led for the first time at 13-10.

Wigan were not done, however, and Ashton wrecked the Wire's left-wing defence before throwing an inside pass to Keith Holden, who scored wide out. Central Park exploded as the Wiganers anticipated victory but Ashton's conversion attempt failed narrowly. At 13-13 with 30 seconds remaining, no-one was leaving the ground and thoughts were turning to the replay at Wilderspool. Jim Challinor had other ideas. From 25 yards out and to the right of the Wigan posts, he let fly with a drop at goal, the first he had ever attempted at first team level. Referee Matt Coates raised his white handkerchief in the air to signal the goal and Challinor was buried by ecstatic team-mates. Warrington had won a heart-stopping affair 15-13 and had reached their first Lancashire Cup Final since 1950.

Four days later, Warrington had another tough fixture when the Australians came to Wilderspool. It was to be Bev's fourth and final appearance for the club against the Kangaroos and it was certainly an occasion to remember for him and the 17,112 spectators. Warrington fell behind to a penalty by Australian skipper Keith Barnes, but took the lead when Bev profited from a brilliant Greenough break to race over at the corner. O'Grady and Edwards scored further quick tries and Warrington led 11-2. The Aussies were clearly second best and when second-rower Brian Hambly tottered to the touch-line after 10 minutes, bleeding, concussed and broken-nosed, to be taken away, their cause seemed lost.

After 20 minutes, however, Jim Paterson entered the field in Hambly's jersey and, by coincidence, sporting a plaster over a cut to his nose. Warrington had sportingly allowed him to substitute for Hambly, although it was against the International Board rules. Referee Ron Gelder never actually noticed that the substitution had been made, believing Hambly had returned. RFL Secretary Bill

Fallowfield subsequently made sure substitutes were not allowed in any other tour games. The substitution probably saved the Kangaroos who trailed 15-16 at the break. They pulled away to lead 25-16, with loose-forward Johnny Raper leading the revival with a hat-trick. Bev, who had been the victim of much blatant obstruction, then scored a gem of a try side-stepping three tacklers, each intent on doing him serious mischief. The crowd went mad with delight. They would have been even more demonstrative had they known that the try had been the 700th of Bev's career. A try from Greenough, converted by Fraser, brought the score to a nerve-jangling 25-24 and then Fraser missed a penalty which could have won the match.

As the last scrum of the game went down well inside the Australian '25' and fairly central, the Warrington players appeared to be preparing to set up Jim Challinor for a repeat of his match-winning drop goal against Wigan. They expected to get the ball despite the fact that Australia's scrum-half Barry Muir had been getting away with murder all afternoon, according to the Wire fans, with his scrum-feeding. He did it again. The ball was swept away down the short side via stand-off Ron Boden, to left winger Ken Irvine, who raced almost the length of the field for a try which sealed a 30-24 victory for the Australians. Breathless stuff.

If Brian Bevan was a legend in England, Ken Irvine was to become almost as big a legend in Australia. Irvine, just 19 in 1959, went on to become the most prolific try-scorer the Australian game has seen, claiming 212 first-grade tries for Norths and Manly in 242 games between 1958 and 1973. He scored many more for representative teams including 33 tries in 31 tests. He was also possibly the fastest man to have played rugby league. In 1963 he set a world professional record for the 100 yards of 9.3 seconds. Yet his recollection years later of his encounter with Bev is an eloquent testimony to the real Wizard of Oz: "I was totally overawed... Normally I played on the right wing, as Bevan did. But that day Brian Carlson was in the Australian side and I played where I was told - and it was on the left wing, opposite Bevan. I was stunned. Here was this scrawny, bald-headed bloke, who looked 40 if he was a day... He had strapping on him everywhere - elbow pads, kneeguards, the lot. Without wanting to sound disrespectful, he looked like a broken-down trotter... I couldn't believe the way he looked and I must admit that it did cross my mind that maybe he wasn't as good as everyone made out he was... He showed me a thing or two. He may have looked past it, but he still had speed and he was smart and deceptive."

Of his winning try, Irvine said: "By the time I got the ball I had about 90 yards in front of me but no defenders. Bevan had been drawn in by the extra man (Boden), and I raced away. As I walked back past him he said to me, 'That's the way to run, son'. It was a game I'll never forget - an introduction any young bloke would cherish. I don't know how old he was but he still showed me up. He scored two tries down my wing. He still had it. I scored the winning try but on the wings I know who finished in front on the day."

By a sad and strange quirk of fate, Ken Irvine and Brian Bevan died within a few months of each other in 1991.

Returning to league action on 26 September, Warrington went down 37-19 at Featherstone, one of the teams vying for a top-four place. Bev scored a simple (for him) try from his only pass of the game. The following Saturday, Warrington got back on the winning path with a 16-6 victory over Wigan before a Wilderspool crowd of almost 19,000. Wigan were unlucky to have stand-off Dave Bolton injured early on and a passenger for most of the game, but Bev was at his lethal best. Left-winger Terry O'Grady scored Wire's first try but Bev grabbed the other three. Phil Clarke wrote: "The third try showed Bevan at his unorthodox best. He took Edwards' reverse pass, cleanly swept inside Griffiths and was then confronted by Ashton racing over to cut him off. An average winger would probably have veered for the corner. Not Bevan. He raced towards Ashton, stepped neatly in and out of a tackle and touched down near the posts."

Warrington won their three league matches, at Salford and Dewsbury and at home to Oldham, leading up to the Lancashire Cup Final. The 27-8 victory over Oldham, second in the league, was a real morale-booster. Bev scored a first-half try but it was skipper Eric Fraser's nine goals which won the headlines.

Winning the Lancashire Cup - at last

The Lancashire Cup Final at Wigan on 31 October pitted Warrington against St Helens, the game's outstanding team. Champions Saints were again top of the league, having won all 12 of their games. Like Warrington, they had won all three of their Lancashire Cup-ties on opponents' grounds and the only blemish on their campaign record had been a 15-2 defeat by the Australians three weeks previously. Both Saints wingers, Springboks Tom van Vollenhoven and Jan Prinsloo, had already scored 21 tries - Bev was on 16 - and their full-back Austin Rhodes topped the goal-kickers with 81. At half-back they had the one and only Alex Murphy, lightning quick in mind, legs and mouth, while the pack at full strength consisted entirely of test men. It was without doubt a formidable side and the bookies thought they would win.

Warrington, however, were not a lost cause by any means. They were unbeaten in the Lancashire League, were fourth in the league table and had at last developed the habit of winning on opponents' grounds. Their pack, nowhere near as distinguished as Saints' in terms of representative honours, had been transformed into a durable, die-hard set of dreadnoughts. The backs, Jackie Edwards apart, were all past, present or future internationals. And, there was Bev. He wanted a Lancashire Cup winners' medal. He had everything else on offer but after 13 Lancashire Cup campaigns he had just two runners-up medals. Indeed Warrington had not won the trophy since 1937.

The meeting of Wire and Saints generated enormous interest as soon as the finalists were known. For some intangible reason the anticipation was almost on a par with a trip to Wembley. More than 10,000 Warrington fans made the journey to Wigan, where a crowd of 39,237 gathered. Drizzle persisted throughout the game and the surface of the pitch was treacherous. The teams were:

St Helens: Rhodes; van Vollenhoven, Greenall, McGinn, Prinsloo; Murphy, Smith; A. Terry, McKinney, Prescott (captain), Briggs, Huddart, F. Terry
Warrington: Fraser (captain); Bevan, Challinor, Gilfedder, O'Grady; Greenough, Edwards; Silcock, Lannon, Brindle, Arkwright, Major, Naughton

Lancashire Cup Final, 1959. The try which won the Cup. St Helens's fans still swear that Tom van Vollenhoven booted the ball away from Bevan's grasp. The score-books say he did not.

28 November, 1959. Bev strides over the Blackpool Borough line for what was thought to be his 700th career try. It wasn't, but that did not prevent the Wilderspool crowd from celebrating their hero's perceived achievement.

193

There was disappointment that one of the anticipated titbits was not to materialise when both Karalius brothers, Dennis (Wire) and Vince (Saints), withdrew with knee injuries. While St Helens supporters were naturally desperate for their heroes to win, Warrington fans and a large part of the neutral rugby league fraternity seemed to have a strange emotional investment in Brian Bevan's quest for that elusive medal. By the time referee Matt Coates signalled the end of 80 minutes everyone in Central Park was drained by the drama which enveloped the occasion.

The conditions militated against an open game, handling was difficult and mistakes abounded. None of that mattered, however. The ferocity of the defences was awe-inspiring. There were potential match-winners all over the field, but this was an afternoon when tackling was the staple diet. All the scoring was accomplished in the first half, the second 40 minutes a mixture of tenterhooks, jarred nerves and heart failure, as each side risked life and limb to break the other's resolve.

Saints took the lead when Rhodes landed a penalty in strange circumstances. He had hit the bar from long-range, the ball bouncing back into play, where Warrington players somehow contrived to concede a second penalty by playing the ball forward in an offside position. Rhodes then potted the goal from an easy position. Eric Fraser had no such luck, missing a couple of relatively easy shots. After half an hour, however, the whole game turned on its axis. Alex Murphy took a long drop-out from Saints' '25', which Terry O'Grady fielded well inside the Wire half. The winger ripped infield, sidestepped a trio of defenders in a 40 yard surge and fed Bobby Greenough just inside St Helens's territory. Bobby shot outside Prinsloo, "as if he had been chased by night-shift steel-rolling staff equipped with white-hot metal", and kicked ahead just before Rhodes crashed him down. Wire fans yelled for obstruction but the action rolled on. Van Vollenhoven and Prinsloo were rapidly converging on the ball but out of the blue there was Bev, tapping the ball before them into the in-goal area. A wild welter of arms and legs homed in on the slippery ball. Voll booted the ball dead with his right foot but not before Bev had dived headlong to get his fingertips to it for a fantastic try.

Van Vollenhoven, Prinsloo and the ball flew into the ring-side crowd, Bev flew up from the mud, arms reaching skywards in triumph, the Wire players flew down-field to embrace Bev and referee Coates pointed for the touchdown. Even today Saints fans swear blind that Bev never got a touch of the ball. Bev swore he did, Voll believed he did not. Wire fans did not care - the try was on the scoreboard and that was all that mattered. Bev certainly scored better tries, but he never scored a more dramatic or a more crucial one. As Bev jigged back in delight to his own half, Fraser's magnificent conversion from near touch made up for his previous misses and Warrington led 5-2. Before half-time, Rhodes kicked a second penalty when Edwards was penalised for not retiring at a scrum, and the scoring was complete.

The second half seemed to last forever as Saints battered away at the Wire defence. There was no way through what St Helens star forward Dick Huddart described as "a brick wall across the field" and the *Warrington Guardian* termed "the unyielding wall of Wilderspool". The Wire forwards were unbreakable, every man a tackling machine. Jack Steel was really impressed: "Confidence oozed out of the Warrington pack's muddy ear holes in equal quantities to slimy mud from boot-lace holes, and sweat from their brows... They had matched the Saints in tight and loose play".

Just before time Bev got away and was streaking for the line when Alex Murphy, summoning up a tremendous head of steam, bundled him into touch at the corner flag. It did not make any difference. The day belonged to Bev, who was swallowed up in the ensuing pitch invasion, hoisted onto the shoulders of the adoring Wire invaders and paraded in triumph to the presentation of the Cup and medals. There was a volcanic roar when Bev received his medal from Mrs Brockbank, wife of Chris, the old Warrington manager, who was now president of the Lancashire County Rugby League. Bev also received a kiss and a hug from the president's wife, who clearly understood the significance of the occasion to the great Australian wingman.

Bev had now done it all and won everything. The last day of October, 1959 was one of the best of his life. Ally Naughton too had at last completed his set of winning medals. He had suffered a bad groin injury, however, in the last ten minutes of the encounter and was to miss the next dozen games.

On 7 November, Bev was among the scorers in a 30-2 home win over Whitehaven, left-winger Terry O'Grady taking the honours with a hat-trick but the following week neither winger got a look-in as an inspired York team trounced Warrington 27-2. O'Grady was over for another hat-trick on 21 November, when Dewsbury went down 48-12 at Wilderspool. Left centre Laurie Gilfedder also scored a double hat-trick (three tries and three goals) while Bev's stand-in centre Martin Regan brought the three-quarters' points tally for the match to 39 with a haul of six goals and a try. Bev amazingly drew a blank. There may have been some excuse for Bev. He was under pressure from all and sundry to score what was mistakenly believed to be his 700th try and it just would not come.

700 tries and a broken jaw

When it finally did arrive against Blackpool Borough at Wilderspool on 28 November, there was great rejoicing. Ten minutes into the game Jim Challinor presented him with an easy run-in and the celebrations started. Later on he produced an old-time special. After receiving a long pass from Gilfedder, he left two defenders trailing at half-way and comprehensively bamboozled full-back Lowe before rushing to the posts and into a crowd of excited schoolboys, who mobbed him. The Wilderspool tannoys blasted out *Waltzing Matilda* at half-time and full-time in tribute.

The following week Warrington were visitors to Blackpool and scraped a 12-5 victory. They were indebted to Bev for both their tries and only a couple of late Fraser penalty goals made the game safe. A much better performance on 12 December brought a 24-10 home victory over Barrow. Bev was imperious, scoring three tries and giving his old adversary Frank Castle a hard time. Jack Steel wrote: "The daddy of the lot was - and still is - Bevan. He went left, right, and skipped over a fallen foe for a try so adroitly that the crowd yelled, 'Which way did he go, Castle?' It was the nippiest thing I have seen from the Australian for some time".

The next few weeks proved that Warrington had gone off the boil since their famous victory in the Lancashire Cup. On 19 December, a 7-0 loss at Whitehaven cost them their unbeaten record in the Lancashire League and, on Christmas Day, Widnes forced a draw at Wilderspool. A sketchy win at Leigh on Boxing Day was followed by a catastrophic 34-5 defeat at Wigan before 25,760 fans on New Year's Day. Bev had scored a brilliant try, but fell victim to a high tackle from test stand-off Dave Bolton. Bev's jaw was shattered and he did not play for another six weeks. Some pundits thought the injury might have been enough to make Bev consider retirement.

By the time Bev returned to action, the law-makers had changed the rules again, abolishing the tap penalty and advantage at the scrum. Warrington had slipped from the top four down to ninth and the personnel of the Warrington playing staff was undergoing change. Martin Dickens, the former Leigh loose-forward, Barrow second-rower Roy Robinson and ex-Wire prop Gilly Wright (a free transfer from Blackpool Borough) had joined the club, while the reliable Ted White had moved to Salford. Bobby Greenough had not played for almost three months and had been listed at a world record transfer fee of £12,000, while a new name had begun to appear in the first team, Welsh centre or second-rower Malcolm Thomas.

The specialist dealing with Bev's jaw injury suggested that he should have some support for his gums when he played again - Bev wore dentures. So Bev resorted briefly to using a gum-shield like a boxer. Judging by his obsession with protecting his joints with strapping and padding, it is a little surprising that he had never thought of this precautionary wheeze before. He may have argued that he did not run with his mouth.

Bev made his reappearance on 13 February 1960 at Widnes in the first round of the Challenge Cup. Warrington's hopes of a good run in the tournament were scuppered by a fine performance from the unfancied Chemics, who won 14-0 before a crowd of almost 12,000. The following week Huddersfield beat the Wire 12-2 at Fartown, with Bev hardly seeing any ball in either game. He was afforded extra match practice, along with Bobby Greenough and Harry Major, in the reserves against Leigh 'A' on 27 February, and scored his first try since New Year's Day.

On 5 March, Warrington played hosts again to St Helens before a crowd of 14,329, despite the presence of the BBC television cameras. Wire, who had been crushed 40-6 at Knowsley Road in Bev's absence on 9 January, were not expected to extend their illustrious foes but were unlucky to lose 19-16. Bev was back in the groove, running in two snappy tries and "making Prinsloo look like a tortoise", according to Jack Steel, who added, "It was the Bevan wiles which did the trick. Here he was just demonstrating that he is the past master at hesitation and acceleration - plus".

Bev claimed another brace in a 37-5 defeat of Salford, but a draw at Odsal and a crucial home defeat by Featherstone effectively killed off Warrington's dreams of a place in the top four. Wire's season fizzled out in April with four defeats in seven games but Bev continued to pile up the points with another 10 tries, four of which were produced in a vintage performance in a 30-12 victory over Hull KR at Wilderspool. He was Wire's only try-scorer in an 27-8 hiding at Workington on 23 April, but reminded Cumbrians of his greatness with a run from his own line in which he beat man after man only to be stopped five yards from the Town goal-line. A week later against the same opposition, in the final game of the season, the result was reversed 30-8. Bev lit the game up with two tries, the second, his 40th of the season, resulting from a length-of-the-field combination with Jim Challinor, which almost raised the stand roofs.

Bev's 40 tries placed him third in the league's try-scoring lists behind van Vollenhoven on 54 and Boston on 47. To some it appeared that he would go on for ever and ever until the final amen. When questioned about retirement he reckoned he had a couple of seasons left in him. After all, Gus Risman had gone on until he was gone 43. 'Enthusiast' in the *Rugby Leaguer* of 29 April 1960 was a little less gung-ho than Bev, writing: "Bevan cannot go on for ever. Will he be content to remain with the club to the end of his playing days, or will he go to another club as a player-coach? I cannot give the answer to that query, but I can say this: that Bevan cannot go on losing that extra yard, as we have seen of late. If he does so then he will be getting tackled harder and more often than has previously been the case. Bevan's dodging, side-stepping and swerving have got him out of many tackles, which would certainly have shaken him up had they happened. Bevan, however, keeps on scoring... and he's a much better winger than many of the young players we see on the field these days."

A month later, having apparently done the ground work for Bev's obituary, 'Enthusiast' declared Bev to have been Warrington's player of the year!

Another classic try from Bev late in his career with Warrington

Season 1959–60

Warrington finished 7th in the League: P38, W22, D2, L14; For 650, Against 482
Bevan scored 40 tries for Warrington

Date	Opponent	Score	Bevan	Crowd	
15 Aug	Hull KR	13–18		7,910	
19 Aug	**Liverpool City**	26–8	2T	5,617	
22 Aug	**Bradford N**	35–6	1T	6,759	
25 Aug	Oldham	10–6	1T	11,580	
29 Aug	Workington T	33–12	1T	3,119	LC 1
5 Sep	**York**	40–5	2T	8,104	
9 Sep	Leigh	29–2	1T	13,952	LC 2
12 Sep	Liverpool City	19–16	1T	1,640	
15 Sep	Wigan	15–13		30,637	LC Semi-final
19 Sep	**Australians**	24–30	2T	17,112	
26 Sep	Featherstone R	19–37	1T	5,900	
3 Oct	**Wigan**	16–6	3T	18,940	
10 Oct	Salford	15–7		7,467	
17 Oct	Dewsbury	29–11		1,800	
24 Oct	**Oldham**	27–8	1T	10,359	
31 Oct	St Helens	5–4	1T	39,237	LC Final (at Wigan)
7 Nov	**Whitehaven**	30–2	1T	9,384	
14 Nov	York	2–27		4,081	
21 Nov	**Dewsbury**	48–12		7,182	
28 Nov	**Blackpool B**	30–12	2T	8,156	
5 Dec	Blackpool B	12–5	2T	1,070	
12 Dec	**Barrow**	24–10	3T	4,782	
19 Dec	Whitehaven	0–7		2,550	
25 Dec	**Widnes**	9–9		6,404	
26 Dec	Leigh	12–10		7,887	
1 Jan	Wigan	5–34	1T	25,760	
2 Jan	**Swinton**	12–19	dnp	8,708	
9 Jan	St Helens	6–40	dnp	16,255	
16 Jan	**Rochdale H**	16–0	dnp	5,800	
23 Jan	**Huddersfield**	11–7	dnp	8,253	
13 Feb	Widnes	0–14		11,820	Ch Cup 1
20 Feb	Huddersfield	2–12		6,023	
5 Mar	**St Helens**	16–19	2T	14,329	
12 Mar	**Salford**	37–5	2T	7,640	
19 Mar	Bradford N	5–5		1,550	
26 Mar	**Featherstone R**	6–12		7,444	
30 Mar	Swinton	6–5		3,012	
9 Apr	Barrow	17–13	2T	2,874	
15 Apr	Widnes	13–15	1T	8,877	
16 Apr	**Hull KR**	30–12	4T	7,184	
18 Apr	**Leigh**	10–12		10,237	
23 Apr	Workington T	8–27	1T	3,147	
26 Apr	Rochdale H	4–15		2,655	
30 Apr	**Workington T**	30–8	2T	5,751	

The Warrington team which won 15-7 at Salford on 10 October, 1959. The same team beat St Helens in the Lancashire Cup Final at Wigan three weeks later.
Back: Challinor, Naughton, Silcock, Arkwright, Brindle, Major, Bevan, O'Grady.
Front: Lannon, Gilfedder, Fraser, Edwards, Greenough.

Bev with Terry O'Grady, who joined Warrington from Wigan in 1958. In 1961, the pair had scored 1,000 career tries between them. No club has ever fielded two men whose combined totals reached 1,000 tries, apart from Warrington. O'Grady's final total was 267 (1951-62).

International action

19 September, 1959. Bev shakes hands with Australia captain Keith Barnes before Warrington's 24-30 defeat. Ironically, Bev never represented his country while Barnes, born in Margam, Wales, won lasting fame in his adopted Australia.

Below: 22 November 1958, Rugby League XIII 8 France 26 at St Helens. Geoff Gunney sends Bev on a run but this time there was no try for him.

19. 1960-61 'You can't beat an old master'

Warrington's efforts in the 1959-60 season had given the club and its supporters a fillip. The team had finished in seventh position in the Northern Rugby League, the highest since 1955-56. Crowds had started to improve too, the average league attendance at Wilderspool rising from 7,217 to 8,170. A clutch of young players had been recruited towards the end of the season, including local amateur international forward Henry Delooze and centre Joe Pickavance from St Helens RU. On the debit side, the unfortunate Robin Thompson had decided to retire, injury having kept him out for the entire 1959-60 season and on 22 June the talented Jackie Edwards had gone on the transfer list at £10,000. Overall, however, the outlook was definitely brighter as Bev contemplated his 15th campaign in English rugby league.

However, the season did not start well. Champions Wigan easily retained the Wardonia Cup, beating Warrington 31-8 at Wilderspool before a crowd of 10,776. Wire were desperately poor. Jack Paul wrote in the *Sunday Express*: "It was left to evergreen Aussie ace Brian Bevan to raise the biggest cheer. He did it with a 50-yard scoring burst the first time he got the ball... but that was two minutes after half-time AND he had to get it with an interception." Wigan full-back Fred Griffiths scored 19 of Wigan's points but was left for dead by Bev, prompting the Wigan correspondent of the *Rugby Leaguer* to lament rhetorically, "Brian Bevan, who must hold the record of scoring most tries against Wigan over the seasons, foxed the South African, but what full-back hasn't been beaten by the speedy Bevan?"

The opening league match at Huddersfield on 13 August ended in a 7-0 defeat. Bev, again starved in the first half, very nearly won the match in the second. He was clear away to the posts on one occasion only to be recalled for putting his foot in touch and was denied another match-winner, when full-back Frank Dyson kicked the ball away just as he was about to touch down a long kick-through.

Four days later Oldham came to Wilderspool and at half-time a lamentable display by Wire had their fans believing they were in for a lacklustre season. The second half produced a remarkable transformation as Warrington suddenly found that relentless support play, hard tackling and team spirit could defeat even the best of opponents. The 11,010 fans left Wilderspool in a happy frame of mind, having seen their team win 25-9. An increased crowd of 13,056 turned up three days later for the league visit of Wakefield Trinity, the Challenge Cup-holders. A glorious Wire performance began with Bev touching down a Nat Silcock kick at the corner in the first minute and ended with a repeat performance following a kick from Ally Naughton. In between these two tries, Warrington put on a brilliant performance to win 26-5. A try by Bobby Greenough was the real highlight. It began with Bev side-stepping half-a-dozen bemused Trinitarians before serving Naughton. Ally was eventually boxed in, but put up a high kick over the line, upon which Greenough pounced as the crescendo from the crowd reached its deafening climax.

On 22 August, Warrington faced a tough encounter at Hunslet. It was made even more problematic when the team coach broke down crossing the Pennines, but a fleet of taxis finally took them to Parkside. Unperturbed, Warrington put on one of their best performances in Yorkshire for some time to run out 18-8 winners. Jackie Edwards produced a clever try for Bev. Alfred Drewry of the *Yorkshire Post* wrote: "Racing out toward the right flank, Edwards bluffed the Hunslet defence into expecting a reverse pass to Bevan, held on long enough to beat them, and then with split-second timing sent Bevan away for a try with an orthodox inside pass. Hunslet had no-one who could think as quickly as that".

Easy victories over at Liverpool in the Lancashire Cup and at home over Workington Town followed to keep up the Wire momentum, but then the side hit a bad patch. On 6 September, they met Leigh at Wilderspool in the second round of the Lancashire Cup, hopeful of retaining the trophy they had so manfully taken the previous year. They looked to be semi-final bound at half-time with an 8-0 lead but faded on a mud-covered pitch to a 9-8 defeat, Leigh scrum-half Brian Fallon scoring all his side's points.

Three of the next four league games were lost - at Wakefield and Halifax and at home to a fast-improving Swinton. Bev was having a lean time in the try-scoring department, just picking up a couple in a 38-5 home victory over Liverpool on 17 September.

The third World Cup was held in England between 24 September and 8 October, and consequently no league fixtures on Saturdays were held. Warrington had three men - Fraser, Greenough and Challinor - in the Great Britain squad, which won all three of its matches to lift the trophy. The Australian and New Zealand squads had been interested spectators at Thrum Hall on Monday, 19 September but had seen a truly awful try-less game in murky conditions as Warrington lost 8-4 to Halifax. Bev had practically no chance to impress his watching fellow countrymen and as the tournament got under way, his try tally from 10 games was only seven, well behind Billy Boston, who led the charts with 15. Bobby Greenough and Leeds's South African winger Wilf Rosenberg were tied behind Billy on 13.

One of the crowd at Halifax had been George Crawford. Crawford, a famous rugby league writer for the Sydney *Daily Telegraph*, had made a point of visiting Thrum Hall to watch Bevan, who he had last seen play almost 15 years ago back in Australia. On 3 September, 1961 in *Rugby League News*, he recalled his visit to Thrum Hall: "Halifax was studded with placards, 'Bevan Here Today'. That was the sole advertising for the match. The match started at 6pm and mill and factory hands still grimy from their day's work packed the Halifax ground. Mist and fog had already descended on the ground and street lights outside struggled ineffectively in the gloom. Visibility was so limited that players on the opposite side of the field to where I sat looked like ghosts flitting about in the fog and mist.

There was Bevan in typical conditions under which England develops its great League players. Bevan presented a sight I shall never forget. He was frail, bald-headed, cheeks sunken in his toothless jaws. He wore shin pads and huge knee-guards. He was strapped up in tapes, bandages and pads. That is his customary football attire. He looked more like a comic strip character than a great football star. How on earth could this fellow be such a great player, I wondered. But I did not take long to realise.

When in action this frail, strapped-up fellow transformed miraculously into a ball of dynamite. The sole strategy for the match was Warrington trying to get the ball to Bevan and Halifax cutting it off from him. I realised then that from the time this fellow made his name in English football each of his tries had been scored with determination and football genius. Not a single try was scored in this match which Halifax won 8-4 [but] Warrington never gave up hope of Bevan getting yet another try to bridge the gap. Unable to get the ball to Bevan because the Halifax men were cutting it off, Warrington tried other means.

Warrington five-eighth Jack Edwards kept glancing at the clock on the ground as the minutes ticked away. He began grubber-kicking to Bevan's corner. Bevan, dashing over the mushy surface, just failed to reach those kicks on the corner. A minute from the end Bevan dived at one of them and just missed by inches.

A lad, about nine years of age sitting next to me, buried his face in his hands and in his broad North England dialect said, 'Lor' master, should that 'appen agin ah should die. It's Bevan, ye know'."

Allowing for the fancifulness of some of Crawford's report on what was one of the most tedious games ever to have been played at Thrum Hall and his misfortune in being seated next to the only Cockney kid in the whole of the West Riding of Yorkshire, Crawford's words were a fine indication of the legendary status Bev had created for himself on both sides of the globe.

Back to the top

The break provided by the World Cup appeared to reinvigorate the drooping Wire players, for after its conclusion they strung together a winning sequence of nine games. At that point Warrington were 11th in the table, the top four consisting of Leeds, Wigan, Wakefield Trinity and Halifax. By Christmas Day Warrington stood on top of the league.

Bev scored tries in eight of those nine victories, beginning with his 700th try for Warrington in a 30-3 romp at Liverpool City on 15 October. Unfortunately, the game was disfigured by an almighty brawl two minutes from time, which brought the wrong kind of headlines to the sport, particularly as the previous Saturday had seen similar unruly scenes at Odsal during the Great Britain versus Australia World Cup match. Club chairman, Dr Tom McLelland, a former Ireland RU international forward, declared: "It was disgraceful. Certainly Warrington directors will not stand for anything like this again. We shall notify our players that we shall not put up with it." Ironically, Bev had recently been complaining in his column in the *Liverpool Echo* that the game was in danger of falling into disrepute with too much off-side play at the scrums, fighting, double-tackling and off-the-ball tackles.

Warrington's winning run was characterised by a mean defence, only four tries being conceded in the nine games, while a bonus of two shillings (10p) per point scored and a £200 bonus for finishing in the top four was incentive enough to encourage plenty of open play. The run came to an end on Boxing Day, when more than 14,000 attended the home derby against Leigh. Warrington went down

3-4, Greenough scoring after only two minutes. The loss of hooker Martin Dickens after only 15 minutes was, however, too much of a burden for Warrington. Dickens's leg was broken, ending his season. Ironically, Dickens had taken over the hooking job after Paddy Lannon had also suffered a broken leg in the Lancashire Cup-tie at Knotty Ash back in August. For the remainder of the season, third-choice Bill Harper took over the hooking duties.

Warrington opened 1961 with a visit to Central Park on Monday, 2 January. There was a bumper crowd of 28,257, most of whom were very happy to see Wigan leading 5-0 at half-time, through a Fred Griffiths try and goal. Seven minutes into the second half, Laurie Gilfedder booted a 40-yard penalty for Warrington and, after 60 minutes, the Wire equalised. Wigan were moving the ball near half-way when their stand-off Dave Bolton lost possession. Gilfedder hacked the ball forward, but Eric Ashton was back to cover as the ball rolled toward the Wigan line. Somehow he failed to gather it. No matter, Billy Boston arrived on the scene... only to make another mullock of securing it. As the two Wigan superstars slipped to ground up charged a gleeful Brian Bevan from the opposite wing, hardly able to believe his luck. He casually picked the ball up and strode the remaining yard for possibly the easiest try he ever scored and certainly one of the strangest. A section of the Wigan crowd had been baiting Bev for the past hour, and it must have given him immense satisfaction to have rendered them mute, as he calmly walked back to his own half. With 10 minutes remaining, Greenough's converted try brought Warrington a famous victory.

The next few weeks brought little joy, however. On 7 January 16,345 piled into Wilderspool to see if the Wire could topple St Helens in a crunch top-four encounter. They could not. Saints established an 8-0 interval lead through tries by Rhodes and van Vollenhoven and a Rhodes goal. Voll's try resembled Bev's at Wigan as Harper's pass to winger Atherton near the home line was not gathered, allowing the South African to score one of the softest tries of his career. Warrington pulled back to 5-8, thanks to a try and goal from Gilfedder. With just a few minutes remaining, Bev got away and flew for the line only to be grassed a yard short by Saints' 17-year-old full-back Frankie Barrow.

Bev and his team-mates had an unusual experience the following Saturday when they travelled to Oldham. South-west Lancashire was swathed in fog as the team coach left Warrington just after noon for a 2.30 kick-off. Because of the dreadful visibility it was not until 4 pm that they arrived at a sun-kissed Watersheddings, the game having been called off with 11,000 people in the ground! Many had watched an amateur game on the adjacent field instead. Unbelievably, the fog on the return journey was even denser. Bev and his fellow Wires did not arrive in Warrington until 1.30am on Sunday, or at least that was the tale.

Another home defeat against Featherstone Rovers followed on 21 January, and Warrington had slipped down to seventh in the table. There was more bad news when pack leader Nat Silcock announced that he intended to emigrate to Australia in April.

Warrington's luck turned at Barrow on 28 January, when with the scores locked at 2-2 after 78 minutes and playing a man short, Jack Arkwright having been sent off just before the interval, a dramatic victory 5-2 was snatched by a

Bobby Greenough try. Yet the following week, an even more dramatic game took place at Knowsley Road before almost 15,000 spectators.

The game was crucial to both sides' top four aspirations with third-placed Saints two places ahead of Warrington. Eden Thomas encapsulated the match in a few paragraphs: "You can't beat an old master. So thought the crowd at Knowsley Road when that artist of the Rugby League, Brian Bevan, scored the try which put Warrington on the victory path. Warrington had a 2-0 lead after 15 minutes' play when shortly afterwards Bevan got a pass from Brindle 35 yards from the St Helens line. Bevan accelerated and headed towards St. Helens full-back Rhodes.

Rhodes didn't panic and thought he could allow Bevan enough room to lead him into a touch-line trap. As Bevan approached Rhodes, however, he threatened to come inside. Swerving outside again the veteran winger proved he still has the speed and skill to teach youth a trick or two. Rhodes made a desperate effort to save the situation but was beaten.

Then in the second half, with St Helens menacingly near at 5-4, Bevan added the finishing touch to round off another Brindle breakaway, and enabled Warrington to pull away again. True, the chance was well presented, but the cool Bevan made no mistake in getting the ball down.

The closing few minutes were fought out in a typical derby climax, with an excellent passing movement from St Helens to send Vollenhoven over for a try. St Helens spectators cheered wildly, but then many went suddenly silent as they realised that only a superb touch-line goal could provide that one point victory. Rhodes made a gallant effort, but his shot was not quite strong enough.

And spectators left the ground with the picture once again of a highly delighted Bevan leaping high into the air along with several team-mates as the final whistle blew."

Warrington's next engagement was a much easier affair - Doncaster at Tattersfield in the first round of the Challenge Cup. Warrington had never met the Dons before, so the journey for both the team and the visiting supporters was a novel one. Warrington had been installed as joint second favourites for the Cup with Wakefield Trinity at 5-1, St Helens being the favourites at 5-2. Bottom-of-the-league Doncaster were listed at 10,000-1. The crowd only amounted to 1,448 on a cold, windy and wet afternoon and Warrington coasted to a 39-0 victory. They did, however, witness a near perfect exhibition of wing-centre play from Bev and Jim Challinor. Both scored four tries, the other coming from Terry O'Grady, while Eric Fraser added six goals. Bev set down another couple of historic milestones. Firstly, early in the second half, Challinor burst from his own half, dummied outside to Bev, continued his run and then threw inside to Bev, who raced to the posts for his second try of the match and the 750th of his career. And secondly, Bev's third try brought him his 100th career hat-trick, a monumental achievement, still unparalleled in the history of the game and unlikely ever to be matched.

Bernard Mahoney remembers
In 1961, Warrington were drawn away to Doncaster in the first round of the Rugby League Challenge Cup - the first time the two clubs had met. As the teams

came on to the field they had to pass through part of the crowd. There were hoots of derision and catcalls when Bev appeared - balding, bandaged, bandy-legged and looking as if he had just got out of a sickbed. Little did they know! With his first touch he raced 75 yards to score under the sticks. His second was even better - a 90 yard special, again between the sticks. The Doncaster crowd were well and truly miffed and silenced as he walked back to the halfway line. Fair play to the Donny crowd at the end though. Although they had lost 39-0 and Bev had scored four tries, they all stood and cheered him off - unforgettable. This was new to Doncaster, but we Wires supporters watched him every week and got a thrill whenever the ball went near him. This man was truly the greatest try-scorer and winger the game has ever known.

101st and last hat-trick

The following Saturday, Warrington overpowered Barrow 33-3 at Wilderspool. Bev grabbed another hat-trick - his 101st and last. A week later, on 25 February, there was another, less pleasant, last for Bev, although no one yet knew it. Warrington lost 13-10 at home to those perennial giant-killers Featherstone Rovers in the second round of the Challenge Cup before a crowd of 15,367. Bev was never to play in another Challenge Cup-tie at Wilderspool, nor was Ally Naughton, who began the game as Bev's centre partner, but who played most of the game at stand-off after a rib injury to Bobby Greenough caused the latter to fill in as a passenger on the left wing.

With their dismissal from the Challenge Cup, Warrington concentrated on the struggle for a top-four spot and the possibility that they might just steal the Lancashire League title. Leeds had stolen a march at the top of the table and were six points clear of second-placed Wakefield Trinity. However, Trinity were only eight points ahead of ninth-placed Workington Town and it was obvious that Warrington, in third position, were going to be involved in an absolute dog-fight for a play-off berth and a shot at the Championship.

Bev scored his 27th try of the season as Warrington had all on to overcome Blackpool Borough at the seaside on 4 March, a game notable for Martin Regan's finale as a rugby league player. Five days later, Warrington announced that Ernie Ashcroft, the current Huddersfield player-coach, would take over as Warrington manager, when Cec Mountford returned home to New Zealand on the completion of his 10-year contract in June 1961. For now, however, the Wire players buckled down to giving Cec a good send-off. Eleven league fixtures remained to be played after Wire's exit from the Cup, nine of which ended in victory and one in a draw.

The team which represented Warrington in 1960-61 was nowhere near the best that ever wore the primrose and blue but it was an obdurate, determined side with that vital ingredient, spirit. March saw good home victories over Hunslet and Widnes and a draw at Salford. Easter Saturday fell on April Fools' Day in 1961, but there were no fools in the Wire camp as they inflicted Wigan's biggest defeat of the season, 17-0, before an overjoyed crowd of 17,500 at Wilderspool. Easter Monday provided an 18,000 crowd at Leigh with fewer thrills, but an equally important victory for Warrington. Leigh had led 2-0 at half-time but, five minutes into the second half, Bev had set them on the road to an 8-2 victory, when Leigh handling broke down allowing Nat Silcock to grab the ball, pass it to Ally Brindle, who in turn lobbed an awkward pass to Bev. The winger struggled through a tackle by Jim Humble and scored a try which kept Warrington on course for the play-offs. Late in the game, Bev swept into a Leigh passing move on the home '25', tipped the ball forward, juggled with it, brought it under control and shot for the posts and a little more glory. A posse of schoolboys was already rushing to greet their hero when, in shades of that Lancashire Cup final of 1950, Bev inexplicably lost the ball a couple of yards from the Leigh line. He left the field at the final whistle still shaking his head in disbelief.

On 8 April, Warrington went to Swinton and lost 22-11 before another crowd of more than 17,000, Bev's last-minute try being purely cosmetic. It was an important victory for the Lions, who were neck and neck with Warrington and St Helens in the push for a home Championship semi-final awarded to the teams who finished first and second. Warrington now had four games left, three of them tough away fixtures against teams still in the running for the top four. Their first opponents were bogey team Featherstone Rovers at Post Office Road and the bogey looked unlikely to be laid when Rovers took a 10-2 lead. However, after 32 minutes, Bev got the Wire back into the game when he cross-kicked for Terry O'Grady to score. Not long after the interval, Bev scooted over from another cross-kick from Jackie Edwards and Warrington led 19-14. A further 18 points in the last eight minutes gave Warrington a remarkable 37-14 victory.

Four days later, on Tuesday, 18 April, Warrington travelled to Oldham, a game which was to be Nat Silcock's last game in England. It was certainly a memorable occasion for the big prop. Oldham played brilliant football to lead 16-4 and looked more likely top-four contenders than Warrington. Gradually, however, Warrington crept back into the game. A try by Silcock brought Warrington within striking distance at 11-16 and then, with quarter of an hour remaining, a terrific brawl broke out resulting in the dismissals of Silcock and Oldham second-rower Geoff Robinson. Ten minutes remained when Gilfedder's superb try from Brindle's cute back-flip and Fraser's conversion levelled the scores at 16-16. Oldham could have won the game, but full-back Geoff Sims fired wide with a penalty. Two minutes from time Greenough suddenly snapped up a loose ball, shot over to the right wing and kicked towards the posts. Bev flew after the ball and was looking a likely scorer when he was obstructed by test centre Alan Davies. The referee, Tom Watkinson, awarded a penalty 15 yards out and at an easy angle. Eric Fraser kicked the winning points, while Bev "gave a fair imitation of Yuri Gagarin as he did his victory leap", according to Phil Clarke in the *Warrington Guardian*.

On 22 April, Warrington met Halifax at Wilderspool and were clinging on to a 7-4 lead early in the second half when Bev beat two defenders and slid in at the corner to effectively kill off the Thrum Hallers. He closed the scoring with a superlative 50-yard interception try as Warrington won 22-4. Featherstone Rovers did Warrington a good turn the same afternoon by beating St Helens 28-11. Victory in Wire's last game at Workington on 29 April could now secure second place in the league, although a loss, coupled with a victory for Wakefield Trinity against Leeds, would relegate them to fifth. Tantalisingly too, Swinton were dead level with Warrington in the league, but with a slight disadvantage in scoring

averages. The Lions had to visit Barrow for their last game and although they led the Lancashire League a bad result would allow Warrington or St Helens to steal the trophy from under their noses.

In the event, the games of 29 April all ended with the top four teams winning. Saints gained ample revenge on Featherstone with a 38-0 win at Knowsley Road. Leeds put paid to Wakefield Trinity with a 15-8 success at Belle Vue while Swinton won 21-8 at Barrow. The Wire came from behind at half-time in a fiery match at Derwent Park to record a 20-7 victory. Consequently they just pipped Swinton for second place, although the Lions took the Lancashire League Championship, one point ahead of St Helens and two ahead of Eric Fraser's men.

The Championship semi-finals therefore produced clashes between Leeds and St Helens at Headingley and Warrington and Swinton at Wilderspool on 6 May. Leeds despatched Saints 11-4 before a crowd of 19,393, who ignored the competition from live television of the FA Cup final between Spurs and Leicester City. Warrington, having had a short break at Cleveleys, chose to delay their kick-off until 6.45pm and were rewarded with a crowd of 24,237, the biggest at Wilderspool since the Lancashire Cup semi-final against St Helens in September 1956. Swinton had done the league double over Warrington and were the most rapidly improving side of the era, developing a host of talented players, who would reach international status and take the club to consecutive Championships in 1963 and 1964. Bev's direct opponent, left-winger John Stopford had already established himself in the Great Britain XIII.

The semi-final was a humdinger. Warrington took a five-point lead with a penalty from Fraser and a try from O'Grady, but by half-time Swinton were level at 5-5. Warrington, despite a scrum deficit of 15-24 and a penalty count of 12-16, turned on a sterling show in the second period and it was the irrepressible Bev who did the damage. He broke the deadlock on 61 minutes after Eric Fraser made a delightful incursion into the three-quarters. The full-back threw out a long pass to Bev, who went hard and fast, before triumphantly throwing himself over at the corner flag with Stopford unavailingly wrapped around him. Six minutes later Edwards made a scintillating corkscrew dash over 50 yards and kicked towards the right wing. The ball bounced invitingly for the flying Australian, who took it in his stride, slipped through Stopford's tackle and evaded full-back O'Boyle's desperate challenge to again score at the corner flag. Gilfedder's magnificent conversion closed the scoring at Warrington 13 Swinton 5.

Warrington had qualified for their first Championship final since 1955, but it was Bev who stole the headlines. The *Sunday People*, for example, blared: "It's glorious Bevan again for Wires", while the *Sunday Express* went with "Bevan sees Warrington on the way". In the event the semi-final against Swinton proved to be Bev's last hurrah and the final time that he would win a really big game for Warrington.

Although Leeds had finished five points clear at the top of the table, there was a widespread belief that they were in a false position. The next five teams were Warrington, Swinton, St Helens, Wigan and Leigh. Seven of the top 10 were clubs from the Lancashire League. Most critics believed that the Yorkshire League was an inferior competition to the Lancashire League and consequently were sparing in the credit they afforded the Loiners. Back on 20 August, 1960, in his column in the *Liverpool Echo*, Bev had aired his own view: "For a number of seasons now the type of football experienced by players travelling into Yorkshire has been one of a very tough and dour type, and as far as I can ascertain, this style of play has never varied although it has become more pronounced in the last couple of seasons... It is my firm opinion, therefore, that the standard of Rugby League in Lancashire at the present time is the best in the three counties where the code is played, and in fact has been for some time." Ironically Bev considered Hull, who finished 11th, and Wakefield Trinity (7th) to be the most formidable of the current Yorkshire teams, leaving Leeds out of consideration for honours.

Bev's last final

Cec Mountford decided to take Warrington to Ilkley before the Championship final at Odsal on 20 May, perhaps hoping that a repeat of the procedure before the Odsal replay of 1954 would have the same tonic effect on his team. He wanted to return to New Zealand on the highest possible note, and his charges would be busting their guts to oblige him. Leeds too had compelling reasons to win. Amazingly, the aristocrats of the game had never been Rugby League Champions. They had been semi-finalists 14 times and 1961 was their sixth final. Their genius of a captain, Lewis Jones, like Bev, nearing the end of his career, had won everything the game had to offer except a Championship-winners medal. This was possibly his last realistic chance.

Warrington had figured in 11 major finals, including the Odsal Challenge Cup final replay, in the post-war period and Bev was the only man to have played in all of them. The 1961 Championship final was to be his 12th and last appearance on such a stage. The teams lined up:

Leeds: Thornett; Rosenberg, Hallas, Hattee, Ratcliffe; Jones (captain), Evans; Robinson, Simms, Whitehead, Fairbank, Goodwin, Shaw

Warrington: Fraser (captain); Bevan, Challinor, Pickavance, O'Grady; Greenough, Edwards; Brindle, Harper, Arkwright, Gilfedder, Major, Naughton

Ground conditions were good at Odsal, it was a fine day but breezy - almost perfect for the great game of rugby which the crowd of 52,177 were expecting. It was a great game, but only for those of a Leeds persuasion. Warrington's pack was totally overwhelmed by the rampaging Leeds six. Hooker Barry Simms won the scrums 29-10 and created havoc in the loose, while skipper Lewis Jones played one of the games of his life. Leeds rammed the pundits' doubts about their quality down their throats and Warrington, usually so resilient under pressure during the season, had no answers.

By half-time Leeds led 10-0, and it could have been 25-0. Understandably, Bev was hardly in the game. Keith Macklin wrote:, "Only once did we see Bevan really in exciting action in a fifty-yard dash during the first half which ended when his kick ahead bounced into touch. Otherwise his contribution to the game was a try-saving tackle from behind on the runaway Hattee". Warrington trailed 18-0 before they got on the scoreboard when Challinor intercepted on half-way and outran the chasers. Jim got a second try five minutes from time which brought the score to 20-10, Gilfedder converting both efforts. Nonetheless, Leeds were always in control and it was perhaps fitting that Jones applied the *coup de grâce*, merlinesquely ripping the Wire defence to shreds for a fabulous solo try in the dying moments, to which he added his fifth goal of the match. A 25-10 defeat was not what the Warrington team, Wire fans, the corps of journalists, Bev, or Cec Mountford had been expecting. Mountford attributed the defeat to nerves. He told Jack Bentley from the *Daily Express*: "We got the flutters. They started four hours before the kick-off. You should have seen 'em. The occasion was too big for us". Bev was reported to have said: "I felt that had we had the chances in the first half we could have won. The psychological disadvantage of not getting possession caused a lot of fumbles and we could not get moving".

So the 1960-61 season ended in disappointment for Bev and his colleagues, but it had still been something of a bonus for the great man who was now nudging 37. Following on from the great triumph of the 1959 Lancashire Cup final, it had also rekindled hopes that Warrington might soon regain their status as one of the game's premier teams.

On a personal level, Bev had continued to confound the sceptics. His fitness remained phenomenal. He had played in every one of Warrington's 42 fixtures, a feat equalled only by second-rower Laurie Gilfedder. The tries kept coming too, his tally of 35 placing him fourth in the lists behind van Vollenhoven on 59, Leeds's Wilf Rosenberg on 44 and Boston on 37.

Bev's last final, Odsal 1961. Leeds crushed Warrington 25-10 in Bev's sixth
Championship final. Here Jim Challinor feels the weight of three Loiners.
Bev was confined to a watching brief.

Late in his career and showing signs of his age, Bev still gives Workington Town
defenders a lesson in deception - circa 1961.

Season 1960–61

Warrington finished 2nd in the League: P36, W27, D1, L8; For 701 Against 269
Bevan scored 35 tries for Warrington

Date	Opponent	Score	Bevan	Crowd	
13 Aug	Huddersfield	0–7		4,449	
17 Aug	**Oldham**	25–9	1T	11,010	
20 Aug	**Wakefield T**	26–5	2T	13,056	
22 Aug	Hunslet	18–8	1T	5,500	
27 Aug	Liverpool City	29–10		2,000	LC 1
3 Sep	**Workington T**	42–9	1T	6,809	
6 Sep	**Leigh**	8–9		9,951	LC 2
10 Sep	Wakefield T	9–25		14,105	
17 Sep	**Liverpool City**	38–5	2T	5,674	
19 Sep	Halifax	4–8		5,744	
28 Sep	**Swinton**	9–25		6,649	
15 Oct	Liverpool City	30–3	1T	1,060	
22 Oct	**Salford**	48–4	2T	5,891	
29 Oct	Widnes	14–10	1T	7,515	
5 Nov	**Blackpool B**	28–2	1T	4,649	
12 Nov	Whitehaven	31–2	1T	3,319	
19 Nov	**Huddersfield**	10–4		6,857	
3 Dec	**Rochdale H**	25–0	1T	3,911	
17 Dec	**Whitehaven**	45–7	1T	4,733	
24 Dec	Rochdale H	27–0	1T	2,162	
26 Dec	**Leigh**	3–4		14,081	
2 Jan	Wigan	10–5	1T	28,257	
7 Jan	**St Helens**	5–8		16,345	
21 Jan	**Featherstone R**	9–13		6,060	
28 Jan	Barrow	5–2		3,522	
4 Feb	St Helens	8–7	2T	14,833	
11 Feb	Doncaster	39–0	4T	1,448	Ch Cup 1
18 Feb	**Barrow**	33–3	3T	7,445	
25 Feb	**Featherstone R**	10–13		15,367	Ch Cup 2
4 Mar	Blackpool B	8–2	1T	1,150	
11 Mar	**Hunslet**	22–2		7,185	
18 Mar	Salford	13–13		4,891	
31 Mar	**Widnes**	23–12	1T	10,472	
1 Apr	**Wigan**	17–0		17,500	
3 Apr	Leigh	8–2	1T	18,000	
8 Apr	Swinton	11–22	1T	17,155	
14 Apr	Featherstone R	37–14	1T	8,100	
18 Apr	Oldham	18–16		10,536	
22 Apr	**Halifax**	22–4	2T	9,615	
29 Apr	Workington T	20–7		5,300	
6 May	**Swinton**	13–5	2T	24,237	CH Semi-final
20 May	Leeds	10–25		52,177	CH Final (at Odsal)

20. 1961-62 'A last indelible memory'

There was an air of anticipation and change both at Wilderspool and in the game at large as the 1961-62 season began. Warrington had, of course, lost Cec Mountford after a decade at the helm. Bev had also lost his sprinting mentor, Harry Lloyd, who had retired after so many years of putting the Wire players through their paces. Mountford had lost little time in getting into the swing of things back in New Zealand, taking charge of eight sessions with the 1961 Kiwi touring party to Europe, a team Bev would encounter twice during September. Mountford's Warrington successor, Ernie Ashcroft had been appointed on a four-year contract as team manager, but Huddersfield still held his registration as a player.

As Championship runners-up Warrington were expected to do pretty well, but there was a nagging suspicion that the team was not quite ready for top honours. Trophies would not be won on guts and spirit alone. More real class, particularly in the pack, was sorely needed. The side's continued improvement in 1960-61 had seen home crowds rise again from 8,170 to 8,775, but they were still a long way short of the halcyon early post-war days.

This season saw an added imperative to perform well. After almost annually rejecting the proposal to form two divisions, the clubs had finally agreed to the idea at the Rugby Football League's AGM on 22 June. From the start of 1962-63, for an experimental period of three years, the game would operate a two division competition, the top 16 clubs in 1961-62 forming the First Division. That meant an end to the county leagues and to the time-honoured top four play-offs. The clubs had voted 20-8 in favour. The dissenters were Barrow, Blackpool Borough, Castleford, Keighley, Salford, Swinton, Widnes and Wigan, while Dewsbury and Batley had not sent representatives to the meeting.

The season began as normal with the Wardonia Cup clash with Wigan on 12 August and, as was also becoming normal, Warrington lost 26-10, their sixth consecutive defeat in the fixture. Remarkably, the Wardonia Cup continued to attract the fans with 17,451 at Central Park. It was Bev's 14th appearance in the Wardonia Cup and his last. For only the third time in the fixture he did not score, his final tally being 19 tries, none of which counted in the official records. Almost a quarter of a million fans had attended Bev's Wardonia Cup matches.

The league season began with a good victory at Hull on 19 August. Again Bev was not among the scorers but had the satisfaction of clocking up his 600th appearance for Warrington. The following Wednesday evening a crowd of more than 10,000 saw an unseasonably early clash with Widnes at Wilderspool, won 15-10 by Warrington after conceding 10 early points.

Bev had other, exciting, things on his mind. He had been invited to Australia to take part in the Keith Holman Testimonial Carnival seven-a-side tournament. 'Yappy' Holman, widely regarded as the best Australian scrum-half of the post-war era, had played 202 games for Western Suburbs since 1949, represented New South Wales 24 times and had won a record 32 test caps. His contribution to the Australian game was rewarded with the granting of a testimonial, a much rarer honour down under than in England. In order to put more bums on seats, the organisers decided that an invitation to Bev, an enduring mystery to those Australian rugby league fans who had never seen him, would be a winner. Moreover, they were happy to pay for the whole Bevan family to travel to Sydney at a cost, reportedly, of £1,600 (Australian) - a truly extraordinary testimony to Bev's perceived celebrity and pulling power. So, on 25 August, Bev, Doreen, Jennifer and Jeanette decamped to London and thence to Mascot Airport, Sydney.

Bev had not been to Australia since 1951, so he had plenty to catch up on from the family and friends who were there to greet him. He was much in demand for radio, television and press interviews, as the Sydney rugby league and sporting fraternity clamoured to get an insight into this man, who had become such a legend on the other side of the world. He was lionised and feted wherever he went. The Lord Mayor of Sydney held a civic reception for him, there was a luncheon at the New South Wales Leagues Club and functions arranged by various sporting bodies, as well as eight or nine radio broadcasts and a similar number of television appearances.

Sevens in Sydney

The sevens tournament was set for Sunday, 3 September at the Sydney Sports Ground and was thought to be the first time rugby league sevens had ever been played in the city. There was little doubt who the major attraction was. *Rugby League News* had two full-page adverts for the event. On the back page it yelled: "Don't miss the year's greatest feast of sporting events. See Brian Bevan, the greatest try-scorer in the history of rugby league. This will be his one and only appearance during his visit to Australia". A picture showing Bev scoring a try accompanied the blurb. The inside cover declared: "See Brian Bevan, the world's greatest rugby league wing three-quarter - Coming to Australia specially to play at the Holman Carnival". It also announced that Bev would be racing against Ken Irvine in a football sprint match. There was also a centre page advert for the event repeating the exhortation to fans to come and see Bev - just in case they missed the other two pages' messages.

Bev regarded the sevens as a serious business and trained as assiduously as ever for them. He was determined to put on a good show for his homeland audience. It would have been an enormous personal disappointment if he had not performed at the optimum level, even if he was now on the way to his 38th birthday. Bev was playing in the tournament for his old club, Eastern Suburbs, and it must have been extremely strange and thrilling to turn out once again in the striking red, white and blue jersey of the Tricolours after so many years in the primrose and blue of Warrington.

A crowd of 14,200 assembled at the Sports Ground, contributing around £1,000 (Australian) to Holman's fund. Bev did not let them down, although in theory he could have been bidding them farewell after only 14 minutes had his team gone out in the first round - each game apart from the final was played seven minutes each way. Bev was in excellent form and astonished the onlookers with his speed and elusiveness - sevens was a perfect vehicle for players with his attributes. Easts qualified for the final against Parramatta, wooden spoonists that season in the NSW Premiership. In all Bev bagged five tries, including two in

THE KEITH HOLMAN TESTIMONIAL CARNIVAL

Sydney Sports Ground

Sunday, 3rd September

AT 1 P.M.

(GATES OPEN 11.30 A.M.)

DON'T MISS

The Year's Greatest Feast of Sporting Events

see

BRIAN BEVAN

The Greatest Try Scorer in the History of Rugby League.

In the picture at left he is seen scoring one of the 790 tries which he has totalled over the past 14 years.

This will be his one and only appearance during his visit to Australia.

ADMISSION BY TICKETS—
NOW AVAILABLE AT:
Western Suburbs Leagues Club;

HIGHLIGHT OF THE CARNIVAL WILL BE THE SEVEN-A-SIDE LEAGUE COMPETITION

The Rugby League News' advert for the Sevens tournament

Bevan Gives Gem Of An Exhibition

A crowd of 14,200 Sydney football supporters yesterday saw what a Rugby League "marvel" Brian Bevan is at the age of 37.

Brian Bevan in the famous tricolour jersey of Eastern Suburbs, during the Sevens tournament

215

both the semi-final and the final, and was declared player of the tournament. Easts looked well on their way to winning the competition when they led Parramatta 12-3 but the Eels stormed back to win 15-12. The *Rugby League News* on 9 September remarked that the "outstanding player on the day, apart from the mercurial Bevan, was test forward Ron Lynch who gave a remarkable display of enthusiasm, dash and stamina." It also reported that "Brian Bevan's only requirement from the masseur after last Sunday's sports ground knockout games was a rub for his right hand. Bev suffered no injuries apart from a nick over his left eye but had writer's cramp from signing autographs."

Bev did not, however, compete in the football sprint. Ken Irvine won the race ahead of Wests' reserve winger Johnny Mowbray and Fonda Metassa (Souths). Irvine's time, in full rugby kit, over 110 yards was an astounding 11.2 seconds.

The Bevan family left Sydney the following Tuesday, and arrived in London late on Wednesday night. When they arrived in Warrington on Thursday, Brian was amazed to learn that it had been reported that he was going to quit Warrington at the end of the season and take a player-coach position in Australia. He had certainly received some offers, but he was quick to inform Jack Steel and his *Guardian* readership that he had no intention of returning to Sydney, and out of courtesy would have told the club before making any announcements. A *Rugby Leaguer* report pointed out that, apart from his rugby playing, "Bevan also has a mixed business (run by his wife) and he is also engaged in the printing trade in Manchester. So he is not doing so badly over here and he writes a weekly feature, plus making occasional radio and TV appearances".

Bev was not going anywhere, but he was raring to go. Within 48 hours of his return, he was back on Warrington's right wing for the home game against Featherstone Rovers on 9 September. It was left-winger Terry O'Grady who lit up the ground, however. He ran in five tries and put Bev in for another, his first of the season, as Warrington won 33-11. Bev's centre, Jim Challinor made his first appearance of the season after a close-season cartilage operation and was unfortunate enough to damage the same leg, putting him out of the game until January.

Wire had won two league games in Bev's absence, but had been put out of the Lancashire Cup in the first round at Swinton. The match against Featherstone gave them their fifth consecutive league victory and they shared the top position in the league with Workington Town. Town and Warrington were the only unbeaten teams in the league when they met at Derwent Park on 16 September. Nothing went right for Warrington. They were without Challinor, new prop Terry Davies and Bobby Greenough for a start. Greenough had been crocked three days earlier playing centre in Lancashire's 15-13 win over the New Zealanders at Wilderspool. To cap it all, the team had to travel on the day of the match by train - no easy journey in those days - because all hotel accommodation in the area was booked. The game was played in some of the worst weather anyone could recall. The wind was so strong that passing as far as the wings was almost impossible. With the gale at their backs in the first half, all Wire had to show for their advantage was a 2-0 lead. Town made better use of it and ran out 11-2 winners.

On 20 September Bev lined up for a Rugby League XIII against the New Zealanders at Manchester's White City Stadium. The match was played under floodlights and was the first rugby league fixture to be staged at the ground. The game was to be Bev's last representative appearance and for the first time in his career in England he played on the left wing. Tom van Vollenhoven was on the right wing and both centres, Alan Skene of Wakefield Trinity and Leigh's Chris Landsberg, were also South Africans. The majority of the team were signings from rugby union.

Beating and losing to the Kiwis

It proved an entertaining affair, and Bev went out with a bang. In the first minute full-back Fred Griffiths broke through brilliantly, dummying to all and sundry before passing to Bev on half-way. Racing up to Kiwi full-back Jack Fagan, Bev nonchalantly kicked the ball over him, regathered and raced to the posts for a beautifully executed try. By half-time, the Kiwis trailed 15-5 and early in the second half Bev put the skids under their efforts to get back into the game. It was a try worthy of winning any game. Rushing back to retrieve a ball in his own half, he turned, made a monkey of one defender, found an inviting gap in the Kiwi line and accelerated through it at an amazing pace, went left and right before moving infield and thence to the posts for a try which rolled back the years. At 20-5, the game was over although, to their credit, the New Zealanders made a late rally to almost overtake the Rugby League XIII, who prevailed 22-20.

Bev's next match three days later was also against the New Zealanders, this time for Warrington. A live television broadcast of the game kept the crowd down to just short of 9,000 - a few hundred less than for the Lancashire versus the Kiwis game at Wilderspool 10 days before. The Kiwis turned on a splendid show to win 21-9 with centre Roger Bailey, one of the few really world class Kiwi players, scything through for four of their tries. Bev hardly touched the ball in what was to be his last game against a touring side.

Warrington were going through a sticky patch. Easy home wins over Whitehaven and Liverpool City, in each of which Bev scored two tries, were interspersed with disappointing defeats at Leeds and Oldham. The game at Leeds was lost by only a point, but the Wire performance was abject and Warrington were grateful that Lewis Jones missed nine shots at goal. The 35-5 defeat at Watersheddings on 21 October was costly in that debutant second-rower Mervyn Hicks suffered a serious injury, which kept him out until February. A great deal was expected of Hicks, a teenage Welsh prodigy, who had been signed from Doncaster for £5,000.

Bev had already played alongside five different centre partners - Glover, Greenough, Challinor, Thomas and Phillips - and was seeing little of the ball as Warrington sought to find the winning formula. They appeared to have found it on 28 October when 10 changes were made from the team which collapsed at Oldham for the visit of St Helens. Saints were despatched 11-7, despite a penalty count of 12-26 against the Wire, before a crowd of 14,631. A week later, Blackpool were beaten 18-6 at St Anne's Road, when team-manager Ernie Ashcroft, at last signed from Huddersfield as a player a few days earlier, made his debut at full-back, Eric Fraser being on test duty against New Zealand. Ashcroft showed some of his old flair in making the opening from which Bev scored a try at the corner.

On 18 November, Warrington went to Hunslet and won a tough encounter 11-9 with a try from Greenough four minutes from time. Charlie Winslade, the veteran forward signed from Oldham, made his debut in this match and made a big impression with his ball distribution. Bev took a heavy knock, which prevented him from playing the following week in an 18-12 home win over Swinton. He was also missing from the team which crashed 0-19 in a televised game at Featherstone on 2 December.

Bev had taken severe umbrage at the *Yorkshire Post* report of the game at Hunslet. He was so upset that he complained officially to the Warrington's chairman, Tom McLelland, although just what Bev thought that might achieve was unclear. The writer of the report was Alfred Drewry and it was headlined "Bevan only a shadow of his old self". He had written: "The under-20s among the spectators at Parkside will have written off Rugby League writers as a lot of romancers. They could not see anything in the play of Warrington's right-winger to warrant all the extravagant adjectives that have been lavished on him over the last fifteen years.

The truth is that they were not watching Brian Bevan; this man on Warrington's right wing was just a clumsy caricature of the fleet, light-as-a-feather phenomenon, who has tormented opposing defences into conceding him over 800 tries .

Rugby is a part of Bevan's livelihood, so while Warrington are prepared to keep him in employment it would be an impertinence on my part to suggest that he should retire. But there was no pleasure in watching what was once a supremely gifted player reduced by the passing years to mediocrity."

Bev came back into the team for Blackpool's visit to Wilderspool on 9 December and was played on the left wing for the first time in his career at Warrington, Terry O'Grady retaining the number two jersey. Ernie Ashcroft played alongside him at left-centre. Wire won comfortably 31-8 and the biggest cheer of the afternoon came when Bev legged it over 50 yards for a spectacular try three minutes into injury time at the close of the first half. Bev was again on the left wing on 16 December, when he bagged Wire's only try in a 12-5 loss at Whitehaven.

Terrible weather more or less wiped out rugby league for three weeks and Warrington did not play again until 6 January 1962. During that time, Ally Naughton announced his retirement. His last game had been the 1961 Championship final and injuries had finally ended his attempts to carry on. Ally had been Bev's centre partner on 80 occasions - only Albert Pimblett and Jim Challinor partnered him more often. Although Ally had preferred the left-centre spot, Bev had scored a lot of tries from his astute kicks and forceful breaks. On the other side of the coin, Jim Challinor was now fit again having missed half the season.

Oldham were the visitors to Wilderspool when the weather finally broke on 6 January but Bev was left out, purportedly because of the heavy ground. Strangely enough, mud had never been much of a hindrance to Bev up to then. Wire lost a controversial match 15-12, Eric Fraser eventually receiving a two-match ban for

Advert from the 1961-62 Warrington programme

remarks allegedly made to referee Eric Clay after the final whistle. The following week, the referee again came in for flak when Huddersfield drew 7-7 at Warrington, Bev again being left on the side-lines. Nor was he in the team which went down 11-7 at St Helens on 20 January, when van Vollenhoven scored one of his greatest tries and O'Grady was sent off after a tackle on Dick Huddart.

Inevitably matters came to a head. On Monday, 22 January the *Daily Express* headline announced "Winger Wants Lowly Club". Jack Bentley's article ran: "Brian Bevan wants to leave Warrington. The ace Australian winger... hopes to meet the Warrington board tonight and ask them for his release. Brian is hoping they'll grant him a free transfer so that he can fulfil an ambition to spend his last few playing seasons helping a lowly club. Rugby League's Stanley Matthews wants to do a 'Stanley Matthews'.

Yesterday he told me: 'I think it's time to put all the cards on the table. I'm going to see Dr. McLelland tomorrow morning and I shall ask to see the board at their meeting tomorrow night. Some time ago Dr. McLelland told me Warrington would not want me after this season. Now I haven't played for six weeks and all this fiddle-faddling is getting me nowhere. I think the sooner I can get back playing the better. Warrington have treated me exceptionally well and I think I have given them fifteen years loyal service. I don't think they'll stand in my way now.' Over the week-end Blackpool Borough were connected with Bevan... and Bevan would be interested in Blackpool... 'I've always had a soft spot for Blackpool and some time I would like to coach. I should like to attempt to build up a struggling side', said Brian. 'I reckon I've another two years of football in me. To me age doesn't count as long as you know how to keep fit'."

219

Bev got his meeting with the board but they refused to give him a free transfer or even to list him. They did, however, restore him to the right wing position for the game against Hunslet the following Saturday. Bev obliged by scoring a try from a Jackie Edwards kick, made a couple of try-saving interceptions and downed Hunslet winger Arthur Render when he looked all over a scorer, as Warrington ran out winners 22-17. At this stage in the season Warrington were eighth in the table, but the following week were beaten 16-0 at Salford.

Such form did not augur well for Warrington's Challenge Cup hopes. They had been drawn away to Wakefield Trinity in the first round on 10 February. Trinity were second favourites at 4-1 for the Cup, behind Wigan (3-1), while Wire were listed at 18-1. Trinity, the Yorkshire Cup-winners, and Wigan were running neck and neck at the top. Wakefield were a hot team, having the previous week at Halifax won their 22nd game on the trot, beating Warrington's own post-war record of 21 straight victories. Unfancied Wire were rocked when skipper Eric Fraser undiplomatically declared himself unfit to play following a contretemps with the board.

A crowd of 19,330 filled Belle Vue for what many people regarded as one of the most thrilling, but untypical, cup-ties they could remember. Trinity's star centre Neil Fox scored 22 points (4 tries, 5 goals) in a masterful display of skill and power as his side triumphed 40-18. Bobby Greenough played one of the games of his life in a losing cause, one of his lightning breaks providing Bev with his last try in his last Challenge Cup-tie for Warrington.

Transfer-listed

The directors gave the Warrington players a £4 bonus for their efforts at Wakefield and then proceeded to drop half the team for the next game on 17 February against Rochdale, among them Bev. Bev turned up for the game, expressed his disappointment at being left out and was transfer listed three days later at £3,000. Loose-forward Harry Major was listed at the same time at £8,000. Clearly things were coming apart at the seams at Wilderspool. There was a tremendous furore amongst the supporters, most of whom thought Bev was being shabbily treated. If they had to lose their hero, the least the club could do was facilitate his exit by giving him a free transfer. They had got Bev, for God's sake, for only £300, and there was no doubt they had had their money's worth. They nearly all thought that the club should do the decent thing.

Bev was still missing on 24 February, when the team went to Barrow and came away with a 17-2 victory. Then a week after being transfer-listed, he was taken off the list. Bev had requested this, clearly anxious to rebuild bridges. It had been reported that Castleford were willing to pay £1,000 for his services, but for the time being at least the great man had decided to stay where he was.

On 10 March, Bev was restored to the Warrington right wing for the home game against Hull, who were desperately battling for a place in the top 16. After 45 minutes, the Airlie Birds were leading 17-14, when their captain and inspiration, Johnny Whiteley, received a severe chest injury. Warrington took full advantage to win 26-17. Brian Batty wrote: "Not surprisingly Warrington fans saved their biggest cheer of the afternoon for Brian Bevan although he was only one of seven first half try-scorers. Bev showed all his old brilliance in attack and did more of his share of defending".

A week later at Swinton, Bevan scored Warrington's only try, when he chased a bouncing ball from a well-judged kick by Fraser, calmly and expertly gathered it and shot inside to the posts to give Wire an early 7-2 lead. Unfortunately, Swinton gained the ascendancy and won 18-9.

Warrington had 10 league games left to play. Theoretically they were still in with a chance of a top four spot, although it was obvious that they were not that good a side. Laurie Gilfedder and Eric Fraser brought good news to the club and fans when they earned selection with the 1962 Lions, but that was about as much good news as they were to get for a while. Bev was again dropped, as was Jim Challinor a little later. He seemed to take the decision philosophically this time, and announced that he would retire imminently. He requested the board to allow him to turn out at Wilderspool one last time, however, and they agreed.

In the meantime, Warrington's season fizzled out. Nine games brought just two home victories over Barrow and Workington and a lucky draw at Rochdale. There were defeats at Leigh, Huddersfield, Wigan and Widnes and both Leeds and Wigan were victors at Wilderspool. A few new men were introduced, most notably giant Welsh forward Idwal Fisher and future Great Britain tourist stand-off Billy Aspinall. The team eventually finished 14th in the league, a dramatic drop of 12 places on the previous season.

The last game of the season was a local derby with Leigh at Wilderspool on Easter Monday, 23 April. The fixture was important for Leigh, who still had an outside chance of qualifying for the new Division One. At any other time, it would have been a nondescript affair for Warrington, who had secured their place but had only pride to play for. It suddenly took on huge significance, however, when it was declared that Brian Bevan was to make his farewell appearance in rugby league - the end of an epoch, indeed.

All of a sudden, everyone who had ever seen Bev in glorious action wanted to be at Wilderspool for this momentous occasion. Warrington's biggest crowd of the season - 16,478 - turned up to watch the old maestro's swansong. The crowd was the biggest of the day in rugby league. Wakefield Trinity and Wigan both had crowds of over 15,000, Watersheddings and Knowsley Road drew attendances topping 11,000 and there were over 10,000 at Hull on an afternoon when the 13 league games played drew an aggregate 108,847 spectators. As far as most fans and the media were concerned, however, Wilderspool was the epicentre of the rugby league universe on that particular afternoon in the spring of 1962. Before the game Keith Macklin interviewed Bev for TV. The great man appeared at the side of the pitch in his playing gear, but unusually minus his usual assortment of padding and bandages. It may have been the first time his adoring public had actually seen his knees!

By the time of kick-off, Bev had donned all his customary accessories. Fittingly, he was made skipper for the afternoon and the teams were:

Warrington: Fraser; Bevan (captain), Thomas, Glover, O'Grady; Greenough, Edwards; Winslade, Dickens, Brindle, Fisher, Gilfedder, Major

Leigh: Risman (captain); Evans, Fisher, G Lewis, Hodgkiss; Smith, Brooks; Brophy, J Lewis, Owen, Higgs, Martyn, Newall

221

The game was a thrilling affair, the lead changing hands on several occasions and played in a cup-tie atmosphere. Bev Risman kicked Leigh into an early two point lead, but after eight minutes came the moment for which everyone had prayed.

Bye, Bye, Bev

According to Bev Risman's 1962 *Rugby League Football Book*: "Jackie Edwards veered out towards Bevan's wing. With his quicksilver partner Bobby Greenough flashing up from behind, Edwards dropped the ball into the stand-off's hands as he went streaking by for the line. Ten yards from the line things looked desperate for Leigh. Risman, playing at full-back, was forced to move away from Bevan's wing to cover Greenough. This left Bevan and his 'shadow' Ian Hodgkiss alone as the two wingers raced neck and neck after the Warrington stand-off. This was a situation in which the great Bev excelled. His long experience at beating a man even before he got the ball was put into effect. He slowed down noticeably as Greenough's 5-yard pass shot out. Hodgkiss hesitated, and Bev seized his chance to burst on to the pass at top speed, leaving the Leigh youngster grasping an armful of air as Bev spurted the five yards to the corner flag to touch down without having a finger laid on his famous No. 2 jersey."

Wilderspool erupted. It was Bev's 740th and last try for the Wire, nowhere near the best, nor one of the most crucial, but it was one for the memory banks of all those privileged to be present. The cold statistics of the game show that Bev touched the ball three times in the first half and only once in the second, but in touching down for that solitary try he had given the crowd what they craved, a last indelible memory of genius in action.

The rest of the game was tremendous. Leigh were striving manfully for a place in the top division and, at 17-18 to Warrington as the last quarter dawned, it was anyone's game. A final rush, however, took Warrington clear. It was 26-17 when Bobby Greenough shot over at the corner in the dying seconds to make it 29-17 to Warrington. To the crowd's obvious delight Laurie Gilfedder, who had landed four goals, declined to take the conversion and Bev was given the opportunity to kick his first goal since 1947. Heaven knows what went through Bev's mind as, for possibly the last time in his life, he walked back up the touch-line he had so often flown down. He carefully placed the ball near the right touch-line for the extremely difficult conversion kick, took five steps backwards and launched himself right-footed at the leather oval. The ball soared high and handsomely towards the posts and the crowd prepared to applaud a celestially guided goal, only for the ball to slide across the face of the uprights at the last trumpet. There was a collective groan of disappointment, referee Mr D. S. Brown from Dewsbury blew the final whistle and the curtain on Bev's incomparable career at Wilderspool finally fell.

Mike Rowan remembers that "the final whistle blew and people swarmed onto the playing surface... I can recall Idwal Fisher and Malcolm Thomas hoisting the hero of the hour on their shoulders. Fans and players of both Leigh and Warrington combined offering backslaps and hand shakes in his direction. The crowds milled around him and it took considerable time for him to make his way to the tunnel where the players of both sides formed a guard of honour. He disappeared from view but still the fans clamoured for more. 'We want Bev! We want Bev!' was the chant. Brian returned to the main stand in accordance with the crowd's wishes. It was a moment to treasure. He was joined by his wife Doreen. Although he had always felt uneasy in the glare of public limelight, this occasion visibly moved him.

We were giving it our all, singing *Waltzing Matilda*. Having released a sincere rendition of the only Australian thing we were familiar with, we added 'For he's a jolly good fellow'. Everyone seemed to join in, determined to pay tribute to the doyen of rugby league superstars. Some filed past him, some climbed the front boards of the stand to touch him, as if paying homage.

The most poignant memory of all was to see men weep unashamedly. The macho ones scoffed but that soon stopped as their words choked on involuntary sobs. Why did so many feel such pangs of emotion? They paid tribute in the most personal manner possible. One man had touched thousands and thousands of hearts. He did something that very few are capable of doing. It was unusual and today it appears to be even more so. After all, no hard sell had branded B-E-V-A-N into hearts, hides and brains of the public. No TV helped his persona. There were no agents around to give the big sales pitch that today creates the all-important image.

Bevan was, as the most non-communicative of individuals, regarded as a writer's nightmare. Yet he was loved! What was the secret? Was there a secret? I believe that it wasn't the quantity of his runs or tries that created the thrills but their quality. His unbounded magnetism was the result of him giving everything. People could see him apply body, mind and soul in those weaving runs and he returned time after time to repeat it all. Over the years he had provided heart-stopping moments everywhere so that in the end his presence illuminated the lives of thousands.

When he departed the Warrington scene on Easter Monday 1962 something of myself went with him. I was fortunate enough to see the genius of Pele and Muhammad Ali live in the flesh. I was thrilled and happy to witness their greatness but nobody got to me in the way that Brian Bevan did."

So it was over. Warrington and Brian Bevan were no longer an item. Bev was not sure what would happen next. He still hoped to be involved in the game, still hankered after that job helping out at one of the smaller clubs. He intended to keep fit, to train through the summer, in case the call came, not that he would not have done so anyway.

For now it was time to take stock. His career at Wilderspool had been truly fabulous - 16 seasons, 620 games, 740 tries, 34 goals, 2,284 points, two Challenge Cup finals, six Championship finals, three Lancashire Cup finals and six Lancashire League Championships. Forty years on no Wire player has matched his record of appearances. His 740 tries remains more than 500 more than any other Wire, the next best being Jack Fish's 215 and John Bevan's 201. It is often forgotten that Bev's points tally was a club record until beaten by Steve Hesford (a regular goal-kicker), who finished with 2,416 points in 1985. Bev's record, however, was unique in any club annals, never mind Warrington's, in being composed overwhelmingly of tries rather than goals.

A packed stand at Watersheddings sees Bev bring down Oldham prop Alf Mumberson. Warrington went down 35-5 to Oldham on 21 October 1961.

23 April, 1962. Bev touches down for his 740th and last try for Warrington, against Leigh.

Left: The teams from the Warrington programme for Bev's last match.

Below: The last farewell - Bev makes his way off the Wilderspool pitch after his finale against Leigh, whose players join in the applause.

225

Season 1961–62

Warrington finished 14th in the League: P36, W19, D2, L15; For 576, Against 335
Bevan scored 13 tries for Warrington, plus 2 for representative teams

Date	Opponent	Score	Bevan	Crowd	
19 Aug	Hull	16–14		8,697	
23 Aug	**Widnes**	15–10		10,309	
26 Aug	**Salford**	32–11	dnp	7,144	
28 Aug	Liverpool City	30–13	dnp	1,622	
2 Sep	Swinton	7–18	dnp	10,683	LC 1
9 Sep	**Featherstone R**	33-11	1T	8,037	
16 Sep	Workington T	2–11		6,400	
23 Sep	**New Zealand**	9–21		8,959	
30 Sep	**Whitehaven**	25–4	2T	5,096	
7 Oct	Leeds	9–10		13,734	
14 Oct	**Liverpool City**	27–2	2T	4,973	
21 Oct	Oldham	5–35		8,823	
28 Oct	**St Helens**	11–7		14,631	
4 Nov	Blackpool B	18–6	1T	1,000	
18 Nov	Hunslet	11–9		3,400	
25 Nov	**Swinton**	18–12	dnp	10,496	
2 Dec	Featherstone R	0–19	dnp	4,330	
9 Dec	**Blackpool B**	31–8*	1T	5,389	
16 Dec	Whitehaven	5–12*	1T	2,222	
6 Jan	**Oldham**	12–15	dnp	7,437	
13 Jan	**Huddersfield**	7–7	dnp	7,262	
20 Jan	St Helens	7–11	dnp	11,759	
27 Jan	**Hunslet**	22–17	1T	6,212	
3 Feb	Salford	0–16		3,871	
10 Feb	Wakefield T	18–40	1T	19,330	Ch Cup 1
17 Feb	**Rochdale H**	25–4	dnp	4,988	
24 Feb	Barrow	17–2	dnp	3,680	
10 Mar	**Hull**	26–17	1T	7,512	
17 Mar	Swinton	9–18	1T	8,800	
24 Mar	**Barrow**	36–9	dnp	5,075	
28 Mar	Leigh	10–13	dnp	5,682	
31 Mar	**Workington T**	37–5	dnp	5,491	
4 Apr	Huddersfield	2–9	dnp	5,045	
7 Apr	Rochdale H	8–8	dnp	1,386	
11 Apr	Wigan	15–23	dnp	18,004	
14 Apr	**Leeds**	8–13	dnp	7,338	
20 Apr	Widnes	8–11	dnp	11,257	
21 Apr	**Wigan**	10–16	dnp	11,013	
23 Apr	**Leigh**	29–17	1T	16,478	

* Bevan played on the left wing in these games. Every other club game in his English career
was played as a right winger.

Bevan's Representative Matches:

Date	For	Opponent	Score	Bevan	Venue
20 Sep	Rugby League XIII	New Zealand	22–20	2T	White City, Manchester

21. 1962-63 'If a man is still keen'

In the spring and summer months following Bev's moving finale at Wilderspool the world of sport rolled on. Wakefield Trinity and Huddersfield met each other in the Challenge Cup and Championship Finals, Trinity taking the Cup at Wembley and the Fartowners the Championship at soddened Odsal. In the world of soccer Alf Ramsey's upstart Ipswich Town were crowned champions and Spurs beat Burnley in the FA Cup Final. In Chile, England went out to the ultimate winners Brazil in the quarter-finals of the World Cup. Down under in June and July the Great Britain rugby league team, led by Eric Ashton, mesmerised and outmuscled Australia to take the Ashes, while Bev's compatriot Rod Laver won at Wimbledon on his march to tennis's Grand Slam, the first since 1938. Yorkshire won cricket's County Championship and England, under dashing Ted Dexter, flogged Pakistan 4-0.

On 26 June 1962, the *West Lancashire Evening Gazette* announced "Brian Bevan Will Be Boro' Coach". It was not much of a headline, merely the header for a single column. The big sports story in this Blackpool paper concerned flat green bowling and Blackpool Corporation's Silver Trophy competition. Peter Stephens, the local rugby league correspondent, wrote: "Brian Bevan, who holds the world record as a try-scorer, is to join Blackpool Borough Rugby League Club as a specialist coach. Mr. George Lunn, the Borough secretary, said today that Bevan, who recently retired, had accepted the club's offer of a short term contract. He accepted the offer in a letter to the club today... Bevan, who is still tied to the Warrington club for playing purposes, will take up his new duties when training begins at the St. Annes Road Stadium on July 17th. His position as a player is still undecided following talks between our club officials and Warrington over the weekend', said Mr. Lunn. When Bevan's contract expires, Borough directors will review the situation. It is his first post as a coach. The 37 year-old is famous for his wing play and has been engaged to coach Borough's stable of young wingers."

Brian had joined the game's youngest club. Blackpool Borough had entered the Northern Rugby League in 1954 and were still often referred to as the "Babes". In the eight seasons of their existence they had never finished higher than 21st in the table, a position they attained in 1960-61. They had dropped to 23rd in 1961-62.

Compared to Warrington as a rugby league centre Blackpool was a veritable backwater. If flat green bowling could generate more column inches than Bev's capture, interest in Borough's doings was swamped in the rugby league season by the goings-on at Bloomfield Road, home ground of Blackpool's first division soccer team. Just the previous season Stanley Matthews had finally left Blackpool to return to Stoke City after a beguiling career at the seaside which spanned the years 1947 to 1961, pretty much contemporaneous with Bev's Wilderspool career. The soccer side had been one of English football's giants in that period, playing in FA Cup finals in

1948, 1951 and 1953, and had, besides the incomparable Matthews, great players such as Harry Johnston, Stan Mortensen, Jackie Mudie and Ernie Taylor in the ranks. The current England captain and full-back, Jimmy Armfield was a popular columnist in the town's newspaper, a status which no local rugby league player was likely to attain.

While the soccer side was successfully slugging it out with the heavyweights of the Football League's Division One, Blackpool Borough were struggling manfully to establish the roots of rugby league. Triumphs on the field were few and far between and crowds rarely exceeded a few thousand at their St Annes Road ground, the local greyhound stadium, where the pitch was reputedly the narrowest in the game.

Certainly the millions of visitors to Blackpool were much more likely to succumb to the attractions of the Golden Mile than to become spectators at St. Annes Road. When Brian Bevan threw in his lot with Borough, the main attractions in Blackpool were Ken Dodd, the Kay Sisters and Eddie Clavert, who were appearing twice nightly at the Opera House, while Thora Hird, Michael Medwin and Freddie Frinton were starring at the Grand Theatre in *The Best Laid Schemes*, a new comedy by Henry J Meyer. The Winter Gardens featured comedian Arthur Haines with Nicholas Parsons and Joan Savage.

Despite the opposition, there were ambitious people in charge at Blackpool Borough. They had seen what might be achieved in the right circumstances and setting when the touring New Zealanders had drawn a crowd of 12,015 to Bloomfield Road in 1955, Borough sharing the honours 24-24. Bloomfield Road had also housed a massive 22,000 for Borough's third round Challenge Cup-tie against Leigh in 1957, when a 24-13 reverse was suffered. That attendance was never beaten for a rugby league match in Blackpool, but such crowds indicated an enormous potential for the game on the Fylde. The club president was Sir Frederick Emery, the team manager was Syd Abram, the first try-scorer at Wembley when Wigan won the Challenge Cup in 1929, the indefatigable George Lunn was club secretary and among the board members was Chris Brockbank, Bev's old mentor at Wilderspool.

They were men who were looking to the future and Bev arrived at a time when big changes were in store. The St Annes Road Stadium was due for demolition and Borough had undertaken to build a new ground in Rigby Road on an old gasworks site, not far from the soccer ground. The ground was to be called Borough Park and it was to be ready for the start of the 1963-64 season at a cost of £65,000, a figure which ultimately rose to more than £100,000.

Bev was part of the master-plan to raise Borough's profile. It was felt his experience and dedication would rub off on the young players and his presence might also attract other big-name players. He was no doubt impressed to hear a couple of days after joining the club that Borough had signed Joni Nabou, a Fijian second-rower, on a four year contract. Nabou had been voted one of the top five rugby union players in the southern hemisphere by an Australian magazine in 1961. At the same time it was announced that

Charles "Chuck" Wiseman, an American footballer from Michigan, was coming to Blackpool. He had played rugby union in England while in the US Air Force and had trialled at Wigan. He had reportedly clocked 9.8 seconds for the 100 yards and was earmarked for tuition in the arts of wing play by Bev, along with other promising wingmen such as Tony Wilkshire.

On 18 July Bev arrived for his first training session at Blackpool, along with 34 other registered players and trialists. It was reported that he would be working closely with the club's two coaches, Ron Fisher, a former colleague of his at Warrington, and Bill Wilkinson. Wilkinson generally sorted out the backs and Fisher organised the forwards. Bev's role as a coach was somewhat ill-defined. The club captain was Tommy Bishop, a tiny 21-year-old scrum-half, who was destined to become one of the most skilful but controversial half-backs the game has seen. It was certainly different from Wilderspool.

On 30 July Warrington finally allowed Brian to sign on for Borough as a player. Chris Brockbank was believed to have played the leading role in the negotiations between the two clubs and the fee was reported as "not a substantial amount" - a lot less than the £2,000 Warrington had originally wanted. Bev had remarked that "if a man is still keen and is capable of maintaining a high standard of fitness, then there is no reason why he should not go on". He had expressed a hope that promotion could be gained from the new second division to coincide with the opening of the new ground in 1963. Bev's fitness was not doubted by the staff at Blackpool. George Lunn declared that "he is still remarkably fast and can keep pace with any of the young men in our team now."

The 1962-63 season was different because it opened with the playing of new regional competitions, the Western and Eastern Division Championships, as a prelude to the two division format. Borough opened their campaign in the Western Division by going down to Workington Town at St Annes Road on 18 August. Bev had injured his hamstring in training and missed the fixture. He was ready to play in the fixture at Wigan, however, four days later. The teams for Bev's Blackpool debut were:

Wigan: Griffiths; Smalley, Davies, Fairclough, Bootle; McLeod, Parr; Barton, Gregory, McTigue, Cherrington, Stephens, Lyon

Blackpool Borough: Fairhurst; Bevan, Givvons, Wilkshire, Wiseman; Gee, Bishop; Hopwood, Bowden, Abram, Payne, Collingwood, Gaskell

It was like old times with a crowd of 10,661 at Central Park. Borough were given no chance despite the fact that Wigan were lacking five Australasian tourists. In the end, Wigan were lucky to take the spoils. Tony Wilkshire grabbed a try for Borough after 21 minutes and three minutes later Bev reminded the crowd that he still had what it took. The *West Lancashire Evening Gazette* reported: "He got the ball after a neat inter-passing move between Tommy Bishop, Jimmy Gee and Alex Givvons and went for the line like a ferret after a rabbit to touch down at the corner". Givvons converted and Borough led 8-0. It was also observed that "the Borough threequarter line must be one of the fastest in the game", while the Blackpool forwards were giving their opponents a torrid time. Leading 10-8, Blackpool looked set for a historic victory only for the dismissal of hooker Eddie Bowden for striking after 56 minutes to allow Wigan off the hook. Borough eventually went down 14-10. Bev's performance was highly satisfactory, his try against Wigan probably being as sweet as any of the 27 he had scored against the old enemy for Warrington, but he had paid a price. He had pulled a muscle in his leg so badly that he missed the next seven matches.

Borough had won only one fixture in that period, a Lancashire Cup-tie against Salford. They had lost all seven Western Division matches but had given remarkably good performances in most of them, against four of the game's top teams - Swinton, Wigan, St Helens and Workington Town. Bev returned to action on 29 September for the last of the regional fixtures at home to St Helens.

Borough's biggest crowd of the season - 4,750 - crammed into St. Annes Road to see an absolute thriller, the lead changing hands six times. Saints fielded their great South African wingers van Vollenhoven and Killeen but it was the old maestro who stole the show. The *Gazette* rejoiced: "This was a triumph for the 37 years old Australian winger Brian Bevan... He took over the captaincy from the rested Tommy Bishop and demonstrated the type of wing play that made him the world's record try-scorer... Bevan got his try three minutes after the restart with a 20 yards sprint when he gathered the ball from a short kick out to the wing by Alec Givvons."

Saints led 12-10 with only two minutes remaining only for Givvons to earn Borough their only point of the competition with a well struck penalty goal. The Blackpool directors were so pleased with their team's performance that they gave the players a bonus.

On 4 October Bev was awarded a further bonus when Tommy Bishop decided to give up the captaincy on a permanent basis and the directors handed the job to the willing Australian. Two days later the real business of the season started for Borough when their Second Division campaign opened with a 21-10 defeat at Rochdale. Once again the authorities had brought in a new scrummaging law, which said that the ball must pass at least three feet and emerge behind the second row. Hookers were in for a rough time from referees.

Borough played their 12th game of the season against York on 13 October. They finally broke their duck with an 11-9 victory and it was Bev who clinched the game. Blackpool led precariously 8-7 after 51 minutes, when Bev pulled one of his oldest tricks out of the bag. York were moving the ball near half-way when Bev stepped into their line, snaffled the ball, shot away and rounded full-back Willie Hargreaves before racing to the corner for a characteristic score.

The first couple of months of Bev's captaincy produced only two more victories, at Doncaster and at home against Rochdale Hornets on 10 November. The latter match was a real toughie. Hornets lost centre Norman Short after only 12 minutes but restricted Blackpool to a solitary try. That was scored by Bev after only seven minutes, the result of his gathering of a Tommy Bishop cross-kick and then foxing Hornets' giant Fijian winger Joe Levula. The only other scores were a couple of second-half goals from Bev's centre partner Alec Givvons. Three minutes from time the game boiled over and Tony Wilkshire and Hornets' loose-forward Parr were sent off.

December was more profitable for Bevan and his men, opening with a good 13-7 victory at Dewsbury. The right wing partnership of Bevan and Givvons devastated Dewsbury, claiming all their side's points in a six-minute spell before half-time.

Givvons ran in the first two tries and then Bev produced a special, careering 50 yards and beating two tacklers before touching down in the corner, Givvons adding his second conversion. A home loss to promotion-chasing Keighley followed but then a trip to Barrow brought a surprise 12-3 success. Bev had been withdrawn at the last minute because of the extremely heavy conditions. His replacement, Chuck Wiseman must have learnt something from the old man, scoring a 70-yard interception try three minutes from time to seal the victory.

The win at Barrow took place on 15 December 1962. Borough would not play again until 2 March 1963. The winter of 1962-63 brought "The Great Freeze" and winter team sports virtually shut down. For Bev it must have seemed like a re-run of his first English winter at Warrington. This time, however, rugby league fixtures were even harder hit than in 1947 with only Widnes managing to stage any games at all, courtesy of chemical treatment of their pitch. Incredibly even the supposedly more benign coastal area round Blackpool fell victim to the endless frosts. St Annes Road was covered in frozen sheets of ice for weeks on end. Players still turned up for training. At least the Borough players had somewhere to train - the sands. On Saturday, 29 December they enjoyed their first session of daylight training since the early autumn as they played soccer on the beach. Bev must have wondered why he had ever left Bondi.

Players had to travel from as far afield as Barrow, Liverpool, St Helens and Oldham for training and it said much for the spirit within the club that they continued to make the journey. Full-scale practices were held on the sands and other clubs took advantage of seaside training, Halifax, Swinton, Warrington and Wigan all taking turns on the beach. Even beach training went by the board on 26 January, however, when ice floes appeared on the sands and the sea froze for a time. Midweek evening training sessions were conducted under the lights of the promenade.

Bev's "Babes" resumed normal service along with the rest of the league on 2 March 1963 when the delayed first round of the Challenge Cup was finally staged. Blackpool, at odds of 750-1, were rank outsiders for the trophy, but their opponents Dewsbury were even longer shots at 1,000-1. Warrington were rated at 16-1, well behind 5-1 favourites Wigan. The glamour of the Cup must have seemed a distant memory for the Blackpool captain as he led his team out before a miserable crowd of 738 at St Annes Road. Givvons scored the only first half points with a penalty.

Bev only received three passes but grabbed the first try of the game after 50 minutes, finishing off a break by second-rower Alan Whitworth. A late spectacular from Wiseman enabled Borough to proceed to the second round with a 12-0 scoreline.

A fortnight later York were the visitors in the second round, by which time the crowd had risen to 1,508. It was to prove Bev's last appearance in a Challenge Cup-tie and it was a splendid game. York were one of the front runners for promotion but Blackpool gave them a fright. The *Gazette*'s headlines ran: "Thrilling Struggle At The Stadium: Late Bevan Try Failed To Save The Game". York owed much to their prop forward Vic Yorke, whose five goals were crucial in their 16-12 triumph. Bev rang down the curtain on his Challenge Cup career with a typical try from a judicious Tommy Bishop kick to the wing. It was the 64th he had claimed in Challenge Cup-ties, almost certainly another all-time record to add to his curriculum vitae.

At the time "The Great Freeze" relented, Blackpool were fourth from the bottom of the Second Division, things having clearly not gone as anticipated. However, once the weather warmed up so did Bev and his team. Of the last 14 league fixtures Borough won 10 to finish fourth from the top behind Hunslet, Keighley and York, an extremely creditable performance in the circumstances. Bev missed the last five games after taking his try tally to 10 for the season with scores against Leigh on 27 April and at Batley three days later. His try at Mount Pleasant won the game 8-7. It followed yet another pinpoint kick from Tommy Bishop which Bev gathered before dazzling the Batley full-back. Unfortunately, in touching down he sustained a bruised foot and was taken off for quarter of an hour. The injury proved more serious than it seemed and his season ended a month early.

Bev's flirtation with Second Division rugby league had ultimately given him a good deal of satisfaction. He was still active in the game that had been his life, he had finished joint leading try-scorer for the club with Tony Wilkshire, had been made club captain and had put his foot on the first rungs of the coaching ladder. Borough had equalled the club record, set in 1958-59, by winning 15 league matches during the season and hopes were high that the opening of their new Borough Park stadium would signal a golden future.

On the debit side even Bev knew that he could not go on for ever. He was coming up to 39 and his growing susceptibility to injury had seen him miss 16 of Blackpool's 38 fixtures.

Alec Givvons remembers
I played centre to Brian at Blackpool and it was a delight. We got on well together and I had the utmost respect for him.

He never altered. He remained a loner and always did his own thing. Before the games he was quiet. All his attention was on the game. He would talk to me though, if only to ask me to give him a rub and all the reserve players were happy to do little things for him. Just before we were ready to go onto the field he would ask me to rub some Fiery Jack onto his back. He loved that Fiery Jack.

He did not appreciate those players who were laughing and joking before the game and he could not understand how they could be thinking about anything but the game. His concentration was absolute.

Brian loved training - he was still keen on using spikes and relished 40 and 50 yards sprints. One of the reasons we got on was because I would join him in these activities. We would practice passing and he would talk to me about the game. I think he liked people who were prepared to work at their game. He was not a great tactician but he was an astute footballer. He knew what he could do and was exceptionally confident. We would practice moves: a lot of our combination depended on kicking. He would be running alongside me in a game, yelling: "kick, kick, kick!" Depending on where he wanted it, I would kick outside to the wing or infield and I knew he would be there going like hell. Some people thought he wanted to chase the kicks because he didn't like getting tackled, but that wasn't so. He just knew it was the best tactic.

I remember playing against Bev in the latter part of his career and he did not seem overly fast. The only problem was he could zigzag as fast as he could run straight.

There were times when I thought I had him lined up but he would just suddenly change direction and there was nothing left to tackle. I think he always knew that a lot of players were intent on knocking seven bells out of him. Second-rowers tried their hardest to get at him but hardly anybody got near him.

There was always a fear factor for opposing sides. They were frightened of playing too much on top of him, because that would allow him to exploit kicks but they dare not hang back for fear of giving him room to run.

I think Brian enjoyed his time at Borough. He was with a great bunch of lads. They were all triers and we had Tommy Bishop, of course, who was brilliant at running the three-quarters. He often played stand-off then. Everyone wanted to do well at Blackpool. We tended to split into three groups - the Oldham lads, the Wigan lads and the local lads but the spirit was good. About three times a season the directors would give us a night out in Blackpool.

It was an education and a privilege to play with Brian Bevan.

233

Season 1962–63

Blackpool finished 4th in the Second Division: P26, W15, L11; For 281, Against 247
Bevan scored 10 tries for Blackpool

Date	Opponent	Score	Bevan	Crowd	
18 Aug	**Workington T**	10–24	dnp	1,250	WD
22 Aug	Wigan	10–14	1T	10,661	WD
25 Aug	St Helens	12–21	dnp	11,214	WD
28 Aug	**Swinton**	4–14	dnp	2,000	WD
1 Sep	Workington T	4–35	dnp	3,400	WD
8 Sep	**Salford**	32–9	dnp	3,000	LC 1
15 Sep	**Wigan**	10–19	dnp	3,500	WD
18 Sep	**St Helens**	3–14	dnp	4,000	LC 2
22 Sep	Swinton	5–23	dnp	6,221	WD
29 Sep	**St Helens**	12–12	1T	4,750	WD
6 Oct	Rochdale H	10–21		3,850	
13 Oct	**York**	11–9	1T	1,500	
20 Oct	Doncaster	12–9		1,550	
27 Oct	**Dewsbury**	2–6		600	
3 Nov	Keighley	10–21	1T	3,000	
10 Nov	**Rochdale H**	7–0	1T	1,100	
17 Nov	York	7–25		2,640	
24 Nov	**Doncaster**	5–13		650	
1 Dec	Dewsbury	13–7	1T	1,000	
8 Dec	**Keighley**	0–14		700	
15 Dec	Barrow	12–3	dnp	1,783	
2 Mar	**Dewsbury**	12–0	1T	738	Ch Cup 1
9 Mar	Liverpool City	3–5	dnp	423	
16 Mar	**York**	12–16	1T	1,508	Ch Cup 2
23 Mar	**Liverpool City**	13–3		850	
30 Mar	Hunslet	2–17		2,500	
6 Apr	**Batley**	20–9		750	
12 Apr	**Salford**	11–8		1,500	
13 Apr	Bradford N	23–7		617	
15 Apr	Leigh	2–15		5,782	
20 Apr	Whitehaven	17–8	dnp	528	
27 Apr	**Leigh**	3–14	1T	850	
30 Apr	Batley	8–7	1T	1,650	
4 May	**Barrow**	12–5	dnp	800	
15 May	**Bradford N**	30–0	dnp	550	
18 May	Salford	14–3	dnp	1,298	
25 May	**Whitehaven**	24–6	dnp	800	
30 May	**Hunslet**	10–13	dnp	1,100	

22. 1963-64 'A legend's finale'

The excitement generated in the weeks leading up to the start of the 1963-64 season was almost tangible in the Blackpool Borough camp. The successful late run of the previous season and the prospect of infinitely better facilities at Borough Park promised a bright future. The Borough captain shared the general feel-good factor.

However, events did not unfold exactly as planned. To begin with, the club and Bev suffered a bad blow on 24 July, when Chris Brockbank died at the Victoria Hospital, Blackpool, aged only 62. Bev's early career in England had been shaped by Chris and, of course, he had played a significant part in his arrival at Blackpool.

Nonetheless Bev was raring to go at the start of his 18th season in English rugby league. On Bank Holiday Monday, 5 August, he took his place in the Blackpool VII which contested the Wigan Sevens. The team, consisting of Bevan, Bagshaw, Wiseman, Bishop, Nabou, Hall and Normington, put up a sterling show. To his huge delight Bev led his men to a 10-3 victory over Warrington in the first round, reviving memories of his great days with a spectacular break down the middle, which led to a try by Alf Normington. In the semi-final Borough pushed eventual winners Wigan all the way, losing 8-5 to an Eric Ashton try in extra time

The opening of Borough Park was scheduled for Wednesday, 21 August when Wigan were to be the visitors in a friendly. Unfortunately problems with the completion of the main stand meant that the opening could not go ahead and it was decided that the first home league fixture of the season against Salford 10 days later would see the historic event. A further complication arose when the players failed to agree match fees and it was not until 22 August that an accommodation was made, the Borough players reportedly obtaining the best terms ever offered at the club.

Borough began their season on 24 August when Bev led them to a good 22-16 win at Batley. It was a propitious omen for the following Saturday, when Blackpool Borough finally opened their new ground. The visitors Salford were no big attraction having finished third from bottom of the Second Division in 1962-63. Even so, a splendid crowd of 6,075 turned up, although only 4,924 actually paid at the gate. It was a grand occasion. The sun shone and the band played as the two teams filed side-by-side on to Borough's spanking new, maximum-sized pitch.

Sir Frederick Emery, who had loaned the club £50,000, gave a short speech and declared the ground open. The teams were introduced to the Mayor of Blackpool, Alderman J. H. Smythe JP, before Bev won the toss. The mayor kicked off and a new era in the club's history was launched. The game was worthy of the occasion, the *Gazette* remarking that the crowd "saw a game that will long be remembered in the town". It began badly for Borough, however, when Bev's opposing winger, Paul Murphy, shot in for a try after only three minutes. On 10 minutes Blackpool were level when Bishop developed a movement which ended with Wiseman tearing down the wing and throwing

Blackpool versus Salford, 31 August 1963 - first match at Borough Park.
Back: Bagshaw, Hopwood, Clayton, Collingwood, Whitworth, Nabou
Front: Bishop, Hall, Pimblett, Bevan, Wiseman, Gee, Hooper.

Blackpool Borough
(Tangerine, Black & White)

Salford
(Red & White)

Blackpool Borough	Salford
1. PIMBLETT	1. PEARCE
2. BEVAN	2. DORNING
3. BAGSHAW	3. HUDSON/RICHARDS
4. GEE	4. BETTINSON
5. WISEMAN	5. MURPHY
6. HOOPER	6. BRENNAN
7. BISHOP	7. DUNN
8. HOPWOOD	8. HANCOCK
9. HALL	9. PRICE
10. CLAYTON	10. HALSALL
11. COLLINGWOOD	11. WILSON
12. WHITWORTH	12. CLARE/McALONE
13. NABOU	13. CLARK

Referee : Mr. C. WHITELEY (Osset)

The teams from the Blackpool versus Salford programme

himself over the Salford full-back for a thrilling equaliser. The game ebbed and flowed gloriously and the teams left the field at half-time to a standing ovation with Borough leading 13-11. Soon after half-time, however, Borough enjoyed a purple patch to run in 18 points in the space of eight minutes. Bev's centre, Johnny Bagshaw set the ball rolling by using his captain as a foil before scything through to touch down. Bev then threw in one of his party pieces to dodge over in the corner. At the final whistle he traipsed off a happy man having led his team to a 36-16 triumph.

The festivities continued after the game. The two teams and officials were entertained at the Layton Institute and competed in a snooker match which was won by Blackpool. A new cup to mark the event was presented by Councillor R. Jacobs and was received by Bev, who paid tribute to Salford's sportsmanship.

The euphoria of 31 August evaporated the following Wednesday with a narrow defeat at Rochdale and expulsion from the Lancashire Cup at home to Workington Town on 7 September. Borough had put up stern resistance to the Cumbrians with Bev rattling them with a try just before half-time to level the scores at 8-8. It was to be the last cup-tie of any description in which the great man would play.

On Saturday, 14 September the 1963 Australians began their tour of Europe with a 28-20 victory at Warrington before a crowd of 20,090. No doubt Bev took more than a passing interest in what happened at Wilderspool but his more immediate concern was Borough's home league fixture against Whitehaven. Blackpool won an exciting encounter 20-16, Bev scoring twice, having two near-misses and revelling in the extra space provided by the new pitch. The *Gazette* reported: "The spectacular was provided by veteran winger Brian Bevan, who had the Borough Park crowd on their toes in the second half when he showed a glimpse of the form which put him among the rugby league greats. Gathering the ball from prop forward Gerry Collingwood in his own half, he raced 60 yards, outstripping all opposition for a try to give Boro' a lead which they never lost".

Two days later Borough received Oldham in their first Western Division fixture of the season, the RFL having decided to stagger the competition across the whole of the season. Borough had to kick off at 6pm in order to avoid a clash with the Blackpool versus Manchester United soccer match that evening. A crowd of 4,500 was a satisfactory reward, although a 24-10 defeat was a disappointment. Bev scored an early try just touching the ball down before Alec Givvons's long kick ran dead.

By mid-October Blackpool had won five of their seven league matches and were fourth in the table behind Oldham, Leigh and Barrow. Black clouds were looming, however, and by the turn of the New Year their season had fallen apart. The catastrophes began at Wigan on 26 October in a Western Division fixture. The *Gazette*'s headline ran: "The Slaughter At Central Park: Boro's Thin Red Line Couldn't Hold Wigan". The result was Wigan 77 Blackpool Borough 8, a record defeat for the club and the worst defeat Brian had ever experienced. There were mitigating circumstances, as Borough lost three players with concussion and loose-forward Danny Leatherbarrow injured his eye colliding with Tommy Bishop.

Bev was rested for the next game, a 7-5 loss at York, but scored a sizzling 50-yard interception try in a 25-4 home victory over Barrow on 9 November, beating three men in his race to the line. The following week Borough were leading 7-5 at Salford when the game was abandoned because of heavy fog. When the game was eventually replayed in April Borough lost heavily. There was more bad luck on 23 November when atrocious weather ruined the gate for an attractive fixture against Leigh and a 20-5 defeat was also sustained. Injuries piled up and training was only conducted once a week at Blackpool - a combination of the necessity to protect the new turf and a lack of training lights, a strange oversight in the planning of the new ground.

There was a glimmer of light when Blackpool went to Workington in a Western Division fixture, Bevan's boys returning victorious 15-9. Town were the holders of the trophy and had never suffered defeat in the competition. It was unquestionably Borough's best performance of the campaign and arguably the greatest shock result in the sport that season.

Unfathomably, it was back to square one the following Saturday, 7 December. Doncaster were the visitors to Borough Park and Blackpool managed to lose 12-11. Eric Clay, who had sent off three men in the third Ashes test at Headingley the previous week, dismissed Tommy Bishop and Doncaster's Joe Holt in the last hectic five minutes. Three minutes from time, with Blackpool trailing 12-8, Alf Normington scored a try behind the posts from an up-and-under. Full-back Tex McCarrick was mortified to see his simple conversion attempt strike the post and bounce out and two points had gone begging. Of more significance the game saw Bev score his last try in first- class rugby league. It was a good one, too, the try of the match. It arrived in the 50th minute, when he took a pass from centre Johnny Phillips 40 yards out before side-stepping past a nonplussed full-back to claim his 796th and final try.

The remainder of December brought disappointing defeats at Dewsbury and Liverpool City and a welcome 20-13 victory over Rochdale Hornets on Christmas Day. The latter game brought its own problems for Bev's team. Four selected players failed to turn up and, even though coach Ron Fisher turned out at prop, the team started the game a man short before a limping Joni Nabou eventually joined the fray. In the circumstances it was a remarkable victory, illuminated by two marvellous tries from Chuck Wiseman, who was now outshining Bev in the scoring stakes. The New Year saw Bev missing more games, either being rested or used as a travelling reserve.

He was reserve when Borough beat Doncaster 25-2 in the first round of the Challenge Cup at Borough Park on 8 February. He was, however, back in the side for the home Western Division fixture against Warrington, a game to which he had particularly looked forward. He was delighted with his team's 17-15 victory, although Peter Stephens wrote in the *Gazette*: "He got few chances on the right flank and did not have enough of the ball to score". The man wearing his old number 2 primrose and blue jersey, Jack Melling, carried on in Bev's tradition by scoring all three Wire tries.

Rugby league itself was facing dire problems. The two division system had failed to ignite crowd interest and a major shock to the system came when Bradford Northern folded in December 1963. It was no surprise when in mid-

February the league's members voted 23-4 to revert to one league for the 1964-65 season.

Against this background no one realised the significance of Blackpool's game against Oldham at Watersheddings on 22 February 1964. Borough fielded an injury-weakened team, including debutant scrum-half Brian Lennigan, on a rock-hard pitch, a third of which was covered in snow. There were 4,092 spectators on the terraces and in the stands. They did not know they were to be witnesses at a legend's finale. The *Gazette* matter-of-factly declared: "it was not a bright game".

Oldham won 18-5 to register their fourth victory over Borough during the season. They would go on to win the now meaningless Second Division title. When Bev walked off Watersheddings' freezing field that winter afternoon, it was probably not in his mind that he had played his last first class game of rugby league. For such an illustrious and spectacularly entertaining player it was the lowest of low-key finales. He had not even rated a mention in the *Gazette's* match report. The teams for Bev's final game were:

Oldham: Dyson; Sims, Donovan, Smethurst, Simms; Nestor, Gaskell; Bott, McIntyre, Wilson, Robinson, Whitehead, Major

Blackpool Borough: McCarrick; Bevan, Phillips, Berry, Bagshaw; Fairhurst, Lennigan; Hopwood, Hall, Whitworth, Nabou, Payne, Normington

Referee: Peter Geraghty (York)

... No fanfare, no eulogies, no last rites.

The following week he was selected for the second round Challenge Cup-tie against the Warrington amateur side Thames Board Mills, but he cried off with a thigh injury. Borough ran up a club record victory, 48-8, with Tex McCarrick kicking a record nine goals. A league victory at Whitehaven followed and on 14 March Borough hosted Castleford in the third round of the Challenge Cup, going down 25-4 in the rain before a crowd of 7,206 and a million or more *Grandstand* viewers.

The inevitable announcement came on Wednesday, 18 March, 1964. The *West Lancashire Evening Gazette's* sports page read: "ONE OF RUGBY LEAGUE'S GREATEST Brian Bevan has played his last game. One of the greatest careers in Rugby League is over. A series of injuries including a broken nose has persuaded him to accept medical advice and to call it a day.

There was not much more to say, certainly not in the Blackpool paper. On 26 March George Lunn, in his *Rugby Leaguer* column, "Blackpool Tit-Bits", wrote: "One of the chief topics of conversation in the Boro camp this week has been the retirement of the club captain Brian Bevan. It was perhaps not entirely unexpected, for Brian has been most unlucky in the matter of injuries since he joined the Boro... For a man who dedicated himself to physical fitness these series of injuries were disheartening, and not being as young as he was, he seemed to take longer to recover. However, as much as he would have liked to have gone on to the end of the season, his common sense prevailed. It would perhaps have been foolish to carry on and risk possibly a more serious injury.

And so a great career comes to an end for even in the twilight of it with our club he could still bring a roar from the crowd as he swerved and side-stepped down the touch-line. He will be missed, and so on behalf of all RL followers, Well Played, Brian."

239

Left: Injuries began to take their toll on Bev in his two final seasons at Blackpool. Here he receives attention in one of his last games.

Middle: the teams from the programme for his final match at Oldham

Bottom: Bevan's last first class fixture was at Oldham on 22 February, 1964 when Blackpool lost 18-5. Here Bev and a colleague fail to stop Peter Smethurst from scoring.

	THE	
OLDHAM (Red and White)	**G R E E N**	**BLACKPOOL** (Tangerine and White)
1—DYSON	**F I N A L**	1—McCARRICK
2—SIMS, G.		2—BEVAN
3—DONOVAN		3—PHILLIPS
4—SMETHURST		4—BAGSHAW
5—SIMS, T.		5—WISEMAN
6—NESTOR		6—FAIRHURST
7—GASKELL		7—BISHOP
8—BOTT		8—HOPWOOD
9—McINTYRE		9—HALL
10—WILSON		10—WHITWORTH
11—ROBINSON		11—NABOU
12—WHITEHEAD		12—PAYNE
13—MAJOR		13—NORMINGTON
	FOR	
Referee : Mr P GERAGHTY of York	**ALL** **LOCAL** **SPORT**	Touch Judges : Mr. C A. Moseley, Stretford (Yellow) Mr F Whiteley, Warr'ton (Crimson)

240

While injuries had obviously had a bearing on Bev's decision to retire, it is tempting to speculate whether he would have played on a little longer had he known just how close he was to reaching the 800 tries landmark. The try he claimed against Doncaster on 7 December had brought his grand total to 796. From a conversation he had with George Lunn, Bev seemed to believe he was still about a dozen tries short of the mark when he announced his retirement. At the rate he was scoring at that time, it would probably have been towards the end of the 1964-65 season before he registered his 800th try. Bev definitely knew what his body was capable of. His mind told him that discretion was the better part of valour.

The 1963-64 season wound down fairly aimlessly for the majority of clubs. Bev looked on helplessly as Blackpool's form dipped alarmingly, only three of the last 10 games being won. The side eventually finished sixth in the league and 10th in the Western Division. A season that had promised fireworks ended with damp squibs.

There was, however, to be a belated triumphal farewell for Bev. On 25 April, 1964 an announcement in the programme for the Halifax versus Leeds First Division match declared:

The Halifax Sevens

"Towards the end of May there will be a star-studded attraction at Thrum Hall - a Seven-a-Side Competition involving eight teams representing Scotland, Fiji, South Africa, Wales, England, Young England, Lancashire and Yorkshire. If the arrangements go according to the plans of the organising committee then such personalities as Berwyn Jones, the famous British sprinter and now a Wakefield Trinity player, Brian Bevan, making his last Rugby League appearance, and many of our own internationals will be taking part."

The event was the focal point of the testimonial year of Halifax's Yorkshire County centre, John Burnett. It was to take place on 30 May. Bev was selected to represent the Lancashire VII. Here was a chance for Bev to bow out of the game with at least some of the recognition and acclaim he merited. Moreover, the intervening three months since his last appearance at Oldham had given him time to ease his aches and pains. He would be fresh and probably in at least as good condition as the other players ending an arduous nine-month season.

Thrum Hall on 30 May 1964 was certainly a different environment from ice-bound Watersheddings on 22 February. The weather was glorious and the pitch firm. A crowd of 4,114, including the author of this book, was pretty modest but at least this time they were aware that they were privileged to be watching The Great Bev for the last time. The half-crown admission (two shillings, if the ticket had been bought in advance) was a small price to pay.

In the event Bev turned out, appropriately enough, for an Other Nationalities VII rather than Lancashire. The Other Nats took the place of South Africa when injuries made the latter an unviable proposition. So Bev once again was able to don the famous green jersey. His VII consisted of Brian Bevan (Blackpool), Barry Robinson (Halifax), Brian Saville (Doncaster), Mike Brown (Halifax), Enslin Dlambulo (Keighley), Jack Wilkinson (Wakefield Trinity) and Barney Hardcastle

(Halifax). It was a memorable occasion for all involved. The following Monday night's *Halifax Evening Courier & Guardian* headlined Roland Tinker's report: "Bevan's Tries Highlights Of Rugby League Sevens."

"There was a star-studded personality parade, headed by 39 year-old Brian Bevan, who came out of retirement to take part in the tournament. And his display for Other Nationalities, who reached the semi-finals, earned him the prize for the competition's outstanding player. He scored two memorable tries, showing that he still possesses a bewildering sidestep and a baffling swerve, and the crowd gave him a great ovation he will not forget, as he did a lap of honour after his team had been knocked out of the event."

In the first round Bevan's team beat a highly fancied Scotland 16-13. Hardcastle, who notched two, and Robinson scored tries and Saville a couple of goals but the *pièce de résistance* was a 60 yard try from Bev, arcing effortlessly round all opposition. Two minutes later he made all the running for one of Hardcastle's tries. The semi-final pitted the Others against Wales and a ding-dong struggle ensued which the Welsh finally snatched. Eric Thompson, of the *Lancashire Evening Post* had this to say: "Revealed again was a fleeting glimpse of the top class standard of Rugby League as we knew it a dozen years ago. One man who seems ageless, Brian Bevan, flitted the pages back to that great era. He scored one try, the like of which is rarely seen today. Going like a greyhound he hared for the corner in a scorching 50 yards run... Three young Welsh players, who had not even started school when Bevan was thrilling the crowds at Wilderspool, raced across to cut him off. All are reckoned pretty fast but with a superb co-ordination of brain and reflexes Bev completely bamboozled them. They were still racing toward the corner flag, unable to halt, while Bevan was sweeping majestically infield to place the ball down under the posts.

It brought the house down and Bevan was clapped all the way back to his own half. Even the trio he had beaten came racing back, shaking their heads with incredulity at the speed and swerve which had fooled them, to shake the hand of this great master of wing play. It was like an electric current passing through the crowd whenever the ball moved to Bevan."

However, even Bev's best efforts could not prevent the Welsh claiming a 14-10 victory, thanks to a late try and goal from Halifax full-back Ronnie James. Wales went on to beat Young England 15-9 in the final. At the close of the tournament Bev collected his trophy as the afternoon's outstanding performer and the crowd rose to him, demanding a lap of honour, described by Eric Thompson: "There was a touch of nostalgia and a flood of memories as the balding figure of this unique personality circled the field alone, acknowledging the cheers of the spectators and players alike - and a few eyes misted over as he made his final exit through a spontaneously formed guard of honour from leading players of today, all giving him a final pat on the back. Warrington fans would have been proud of this final curtain-call by their great idol."

And so, it really was all over now. The Great Bev bade farewell to the game he had graced at first team level for 22 years. He left the sport laden with honours, acknowledged as the greatest try-scorer anyone would ever see, the archetypal legend in his own life time - and beyond.

Thankfully, a young man from Doncaster, Bob Fox attended the Halifax Sevens and recorded images of the tournament on cine film, snatches of which appear on Micron Video's *History of the Wire* (1991). Fox, later to become secretary/commercial manager at a number of rugby league clubs and chief executive of Doncaster RLFC, certainly did posterity a favour by capturing those glimpses of the great man on the occasion of his last appearance in competitive rugby.

International Sevens Tournament, Thrum Hall, Halifax, 30 May 1964

First Round:
Young England 23 Yorkshire 5;
England 13 Fiji 10;
Wales 15 Lancashire 8;
Other Nationalities 16 Scotland 13.

Semi-finals:
Young England 14 England 0;
Wales 14 Other Nationalities 10

Final:
Wales 15 Young England 9

Season 1963–64

Blackpool finished 6th in the Second Division: P24, W12, D1, L11; For 299, Against 303. Bevan scored 7 tries for Blackpool

Date	Opponent	Score	Bevan	Crowd	
24 Aug	Batley	22–16		1,000	
31 Aug	**Salford**	36–16	1T	6,075	
4 Sep	Rochdale H	7–12		2,018	
7 Sep	**Workington T**	8–22	1T	3,500	LC 1
14 Sep	**Whitehaven**	20–16	2T	2,850	
16 Sep	**Oldham**	10–24	1T	4,500	WD
21 Sep	Doncaster	13–10		1,925	
28 Sep	**Oldham**	6–22	dnp	4,200	
12 Oct	**York**	17–10		2,450	
26 Oct	Wigan	8–77		9,686	WD
2 Nov	York	5–7	dnp	3,280	
9 Nov	**Barrow**	25–4	1T	1,400	
16 Nov	Salford	7–5*		1,500	
23 Nov	**Leigh**	5–20		1,300	
30 Nov	Workington T	15–9		1,900	WD
7 Dec	**Doncaster**	11–12	1T	1,250	
14 Dec	Dewsbury	3–7		1,600	
25 Dec	**Rochdale H**	20–13		1,350	
26 Dec	Liverpool City	7–16		438	
4 Jan	Oldham	13–18	dnp	3,908	WD
11 Jan	**Dewsbury**	8–8		1,100	
25 Jan	**Liverpool City**	8–0	dnp	950	
8 Feb	**Doncaster**	25–2	dnp	1,345	Ch Cup 1
15 Feb	**Warrington**	17–15		1,650	WD
22 Feb	Oldham	5–18		4,092	
29 Feb	**Thames Bd M**	48–8	dnp	3,214	Ch Cup 2
7 Mar	Whitehaven	15–8	dnp	877	
14 Mar	**Castleford**	4–25	dnp	7,206	Ch Cup 3
21 Mar	**Wigan**	18–25	dnp	2,350	WD
27 Mar	Barrow	8–20	dnp	3,763	
28 Mar	**Workington T**	7–21	dnp	1,750	WD
30 Mar	**Batley**	14–2	dnp	1,100	
11 Apr	Salford	8–25	dnp	1,152	
14 Apr	Leigh	14–11	dnp	3,210	
18 Apr	**Bramley**	15–14	dnp	1,200	
22 Apr	Warrington	2–33	dnp	4,211	WD
25 Apr	Bramley	7–16	dnp	1,018	

* The match against Salford on 16 November was abandoned after 32 minutes. It was replayed on 11 April.

23. Post Script

Although he was not to know it, when Brian Bevan left the Thrum Hall field after the Halifax sevens, he effectively ended his involvement in rugby league, at least in any substantial role.

Within a few months of his retirement, Jack Bentley of the *Daily Express* wrote an article under the headline "Disgusted Bevan may pack his bag". He reported, "Brian Bevan... yesterday hit out hard about his failure to get a job in the game which would enable him to pass on some of the experience he gained in running up a world record tally of nearly 800 tries. 'I am really disgusted at the way things have worked out... I wanted to stay in the game and you would have thought there was something I could do somewhere. I was looking forward to trying to put my experience to the test, but quite honestly, the way things are, I feel like packing my bag tomorrow... I have done everything. I have written to people and rung them up. I think I might even have made myself cheap - but nothing happens... I don't know whether my face doesn't fit or what. I have got the impression since I got out that no one wants to know me', the normally reticent Bevan added bitterly.

'I have spent nearly half my life in this country and I'm ready to stay here but I think the only thing left, unless something happens here, is to get out of it and get back to Australia... I think they don't think I would go back now, but if I got a definite offer, I'd be back in a flash'."

Bev never did go back to Australia apart from flying visits and he never did obtain an English coaching position, apart from his brief and nebulous flirtation with the profession at Blackpool. It is easy in hindsight to say that the game was poorer for having failed to utilise the experience of this greatest of all try-scorers but in that respect it was par for the course in rugby league. There has always been a finite number of coaching positions and even fewer in the administrative sphere. The vast majority of players, even the greatest, have consequently had their expertise under-utilised or, as in Bev's case, not utilised at all. It is no doubt a pity but it is merely the way of the world. Besides, the perception of Bev in the world of rugby league was skewed. No one would have thought of him as coaching material. How could they? Introversion has never been a prime qualification for coaching professional sportsmen. He was a complete one-off as a player. No one could coach players into being clones of Brian Bevan. Communication was simply not his game. Good coaches are usually good communicators. Failing that, they fall into the fire and brimstone category, another no-go area for Bev. A select few coaches can operate as "one of the boys" but Bev was never one of the boys.

The headline "Brian Bevan Still Active" came as something of a surprise to readers of the February 1968 edition of A. N. Gaulton's extremely accurate and reputable *Rugby League Magazine*. The small article ran: "Rugby league's most prolific try-scorer, Brian Bevan, has been appointed player-coach of the Ourimbah club for the 1968 Australian season. Ourimbah is one of the seven clubs in the Group 12 competition on the Central Coast of N.S.W., and has won the competition seven times - the last in 1960. Bevan's signing-on fee has not been disclosed, but it is said to be in the region of 1,200 dollars."

Bev did go to Australia for several months in 1968 in order to see relatives and test the water for a possible return home. While casting around for prospects, he did apparently play a few games of rugby but nothing substantial accrued and Bev returned to England, shelving the idea of a new life down under.

Even more mysteriously an Australian reference book, *The Encyclopaedia of Rugby League Players*, published in 1999, claimed that Bev returned to Australia briefly in the 1960s to captain-coach Goondawindi. This would have come as news to the great man himself. Such tales merely added even more mystique to the Bevan legend as he disappeared from public view.

In the years following his retirement as a player Bev continued to live and work in Lancashire, having moved to live at South Shore in St. Anne's in his time at Blackpool. Occasionally he would appear in a benefit or charity match - rugby, soccer and cricket - and he would always prepare and train assiduously for such events. As late as the mid-late 1970s he appeared in such games at Wilderspool in benefits for Alex Murphy and Parry Gordon and in a testimonial for the late Jim Challinor. He had passed 50, but was still able to find his way over the goal-line for tries.

However, around 1971 Bev finally decided to move south, not as far as Ourimbah or Goondawindi, but to Dorset. Doreen's respiratory condition would be alleviated there by a more benign climate. For the next decade and a half Bev lived on the island of Portland, near Weymouth, and was employed in the security section at the naval base. If he had felt isolated from the game in St Anne's, he had now descended into almost total obscurity as far as the wider world of rugby league was concerned.

Peter Atkinson remembers

I was in the Army, probably about 1968, and we had a pretty good rugby union team. We had a fixture at RAF Stafford who we had murdered the year before so we sent our second XV to play them. Brian Bevan apparently was working as a security guard in the maintenance unit there and somehow he ended up playing for the RAF team. It must have been a right scratch outfit.

When the team got back, I asked one of them how they had got on. Looking very crestfallen, he said: "We lost about 48-0. They had this bald bloke, about 50 year-old who was wearing shin-pads. We couldn't get near him. I think he once played rugby league. His name was Bevan or something like that!"

As he approached his sixties, however, belated recognition of his greatness began to emerge. On Thursday, 29 April 1982, the main stand at Wilderspool was burned to the ground within 20 minutes, as local folk ate their midday meals. Almost exactly 20 years earlier, 23 April 1962, Bev had stood alongside his wife in the front row of the seats acknowledging the homage of thousands of his admirers at the emotional conclusion his last game for the Wire against Leigh. The new stand was opened on 6 February, 1983 for a game against Hull. Eventually, it was officially and appropriately re-christened The Brian Bevan Stand, a fitting tribute to the club's most celebrated player.

In 1983 he was invited to Sydney as special guest at the presentation dinner of the Rothmans Medal at the International Hilton Hotel on 31 August. The Rothmans Medal was the highest award that an Australian rugby league player could win in the domestic game. In 1983 the medal went to Michael Eden, a goal-kicking half-back with Bev's old club Eastern Suburbs. A trip to Queensland, where he met up again with Harry Bath, a re-union with former Other Nationalities players at Balmain Leagues Club and kicking-off in the play-offs at the Sydney Cricket Ground all served to make the long journey from Dorset a wonderfully rewarding experience for Bev and Doreen. It would be Bev's last visit to his homeland.

Two years later the Rugby Football League decided to celebrate the playing of the 50th Wembley final by inviting a player from each of the preceding 49 Challenge Cup finals to be paraded before the crowd. Bev was selected to represent the 1950 final when Warrington defeated Widnes, while Stan McCormick was the Warrington selection for the 1954 drawn game against Halifax. Bev and Huddersfield's Australian winger Ray Markham, for the 1933 final, were the only overseas players in the parade. The game, played before a crowd of 97,801, between Hull and Wigan on 4 May, 1985 is now regarded as one of the all-time classic finals.

In 1988 Bev received the ultimate accolade the British game could bestow on a player. The Rugby Football League instituted a Hall of Fame beginning with an induction of nine of the sport's true immortals. There was never any doubt that Bevan would have gained entry, however stringent the qualifications might have been. On 24 October, 1988 at the Bentley Arms, Oulton, Leeds at a very moving and dignified ceremony four living members - Bev, Gus Risman, Billy Boston and Alex Murphy - received gold medals, struck by Garrards, the Queen's jewellers. Relatives of the other five inductees - Harold Wagstaff, Albert Rosenfeld, Billy Batten, Jonty Parkin and Jim Sullivan - also received Hall of Fame medals. Lord Derby, the President of the RFL, was the principal guest and met Bev for the last time, their first meeting having taken place almost 40 years ago. There is no doubt that Bev was immensely gratified at his induction to the Hall of Fame. It was conclusive proof of his legendary status in the game, an indication that he would never be forgotten, even if he did habitually shun the limelight.

The original nine Hall of Famers have subsequently been joined by Neil Fox in 1989 and Vince Karalius, Roger Millward and Tom van Vollenhoven in 2000. Bizarrely, when Bev examined his medal at home he discovered that his name had been incorrectly spelled as Beven. It was returned to the jewellers, who replaced it with a properly engraved version. The original (misspelled) medal was placed in a museum standard secure display cabinet at the Hall of Fame, alongside many of the game's historic cups and trophies. Thieves later broke in to the Hall of Fame, used concrete slabs to break into the cabinet and stole the Beven medal but nothing else.

Bev did not live to see two major memorials to himself. Had he done so, he would have been left in no doubt as to the esteem in which the rugby league fraternity held him.

Until 1993 the most notable statue in Warrington, of Oliver Cromwell, stood by the Mersey at Bridgefoot. By any standards Cromwell was a colossus in this land's history. The great seventeenth century poet John Milton famously described Cromwell as "Our Chief of Men". In many local people's eyes at least, Oliver has been superseded as the town's chief of men by Brian Bevan. On 29 August, 1993 a statue of Bev was unveiled on a traffic island, officially designated Brian Bevan Island, appropriately enough, at Wilderspool Causeway. The statue, in the shadows of St. James Church and sculpted by Philip Bews, was funded by Warrington Borough Council at a cost of around £20,000. Doreen Bevan and Colin Welland performed the opening ceremony. Very few monuments to rugby league players have ever been commissioned. Indeed the only other statues of players which spring to mind are those commemorating Wally Lewis, "the Emperor of Queensland", at Brisbane's Lang Park and the fabulous French full-back, Bev's old opponent, Puig Aubert at Carcassonne's Stade Albert Domec - august company indeed for the man from Bondi.

The proposed relocation of Warrington's home ground away from Wilderspool and a possible new road system in the next few years may, however, cause this striking monument to Brian Bevan to be moved elsewhere.

Peter Robinson, comedian, broadcaster, speaker, remembers
I recall Brian's very first game for the Wire in 1945 and his last game at Wilderspool against Leigh. I think Bev was the first goal-kicker to use a mound of sand to tee up the ball when the Wilderspool pitch was covered in sand to stem the Mersey flood. Many thousands of fans recall Bevan's long distance tries but some of his greatest were scored from 10 yards or so when he left defenders wrong-footed and grasping at his shadow.

I knew Bevan during his playing career but after those heady days I became a friend. I performed in cabaret at his daughter's wedding.

Over the years I have been involved with the Warrington Football Club as ground announcer, commentator on video, promotions, dinners and players testimonials. So, in 1991, after Brian's death I wrote to the Warrington Guardian, *proposing a permanent memorial to Brian. I actually suggested that Winwick Road should be renamed Brian Bevan Boulevard. After much discussion the Warrington Council commissioned the statue to be erected in Wilderspool Causeway. Mr Clarrie Owen, the President of Warrington RLFC, was instrumental in having the main stand at the ground named The Brian Bevan Stand. Mr Ken Foulkes was the main organiser of the service of remembrance for Bev at the ground.*

The council arranged the service for the unveiling of the statue when Colin Welland made an excellent speech. Many people were invited to the unveiling and to the buffet at the Parr Hall, which followed. Three people not invited were Clarrie Owen, Ken Foulkes and myself. Brian's widow Doreen was not happy about these omissions and I received a letter of thanks for my efforts from Brian's daughter.

At the Remembrance Service, I sat alongside Billy Boston who told me that no other wingman was fit to tie Bevan's bootlaces. Billy also said that Mick Sullivan was the hardest man to mark because he was so hard in the tackle but Bevan made you look silly. Colin Welland gave his services free for reciting the eulogy on that moving occasion.

I organised a number of charity soccer and cricket matches in the sixties and seventies and always had great support from Brian Bevan. In my team versus Crosfields Cricket Club in 1965 I had Alan Ball, Michael Parkinson, Bernard Ganley, Laurie Gilfedder, Ray Martine, Roy Hastings and Brian Bevan. A crowd of 5,000 cheered every time Bev chased the ball. The adulation for the man was enormous.

In the bar later Parky asked Bernard Ganley just how good Bevan had been in his pomp. Bernard replied, I played full-back against him at least a dozen times and the first time I ever touched him was when I shook hands with him in the dressing-room before this cricket match. Bernard assured us that Bevan often said sorry before he beat you!

I have a team photo of the XI that I arranged to play Grappenhall Cricket Club. This team included Bryn Knowelden, Ken Large, Roger Hunt, Maurice Setters, Dr. Michael Winstanley, Brian Bevan and Jim Casey, son of the great comedian Jimmy James. Brian got a couple of wickets bowling with a cap on. He was self-conscious of his baldpate on the cricket field and always insisted I found him a well-fitting cap. He called at my house to try the cap on days before the game. In addition to cricket he could also play tennis, the piano and the banjo.

I arranged to take Brian to play in a soccer match one night at Oldham Athletic. I initially arranged to pick him up at 5pm for the 7.30pm kick-off. For four consecutive days he phoned me to request the pick-up time be brought forward by 15 minutes. He couldn't stand the thought of being late.

We were among the early arrivals at Oldham. Within minutes he had the backroom staff rubbing him down, bandaging his knees, his ankles and even his toes. I felt slightly embarrassed by his demands but Ken Barnes, the Manchester City captain, who was playing in the game, said, he was the world's best so he deserves the best.

At half time the team Bev and I were playing for was leading 4-0. The opposition brought on two substitutes, Mike Summerbee and George Best. I recall Best and Bevan running for a loose ball and Bevan overtook Best. George easily repossessed the ball and eventually scored four goals. I was detailed to mark him and never touched the ball in the second half. We did, however, win the game 5-4.

In 1975 Alex Murphy was granted a second testimonial and I was on his committee. The Wire had been thrashed by Widnes at Wembley and the following Friday a testimonial game was arranged for Alex at Wilderspool. Vince Karalius agreed to come out of retirement to team up with Alex for the final time.

Would there be a poor turnout due to Wire's recent Wembley flop? I suggested we ask Bev to come from Dorset to play in the game. He accepted and trained alone for three days at Wilderspool. In the event 15,000 people packed the ground. Bevan scored twice, with a little help from his friends. I provided the commentary and for the final 10 minutes Alex took the whistle and referee Billy Thompson dropped a goal. Needless to say, the biggest cheers of the night were for Brian Bevan, the greatest of them all.

Bev eventually worked as a security guard in Dorset. He told me he played for a Rugby Union team and scored five tries in a match. Someone shopped him and he moved to another Rugby Union club some 50 miles from his work place in Portland.

It is almost impossible to explain how good the wonder winger was during his sixteen years with Warrington. I recall him receiving a standing ovation just for presenting a talent show award at the Ritz Cinema, Warrington. Another vivid memory is of seeing Brian accept the cheers from the fans, as he stood alone in the centre of the stand after that final game against Leigh.

To steal a line from Max Miller: There'll never be another.

In 1995 The Rugby Football League, under, in my view, inane leadership, made a truly horrendous botch of its centenary. Thankfully, one thing beyond its control was the Royal Mail's British Philatelic Bureau. For several years prior to the centenary the Rugby League Supporters Association (RLSA) had bombarded the Philatelic Bureau with demands that the event should be commemorated on a first day postal cover. It was a very effective campaign and helped considerably in the process of persuading the Royal Mail to issue a set of five rugby league centenary postage stamps. Their appearance was scheduled for 3 October, 1995. Commemorative stamps are prepared a long time - often years - in advance of their issue. As the RFL's archivist until April 1994, 1 was heavily involved in the creation of the stamps, providing the images, technical expertise and historical information for various presentation packs, covers, booklets and postcards. It was decided that the five stamps would feature the five dead Hall of Famers. It was an ideal solution - five stamps, five deceased Hall of Famers - a remarkably fortuitous and symmetrical coincidence. The players featured had to have passed on, as no living person, apart from royalty, can be featured on British stamps. It was agreed that Billy Batten, Jonty Parkin, Albert Rosenfeld, Jim Sullivan and Harold Wagstaff would all be further immortalised by the Royal Mail. I liaised with the commissioned artist Christian Birmingham, who duly produced five splendid paintings a couple of years before the centenary first day cover was to be released.

That, I thought, was that. All done and dusted, a relief that the job was a good one. Then on Christmas Eve 1994, 1 received a telephone call from Christian Birmingham asking for material on which to base a painting of Gus Risman, who was now going to be featured on one of the stamps. Gus had died on 17 September, 1994. So, I asked, did that mean one of the original five would be dropped? Yes, Albert Rosenfeld. I was amazed. My main source of surprise was that anyone had the power and influence to decide that Gus had to be included, especially at this late stage.

My mind suddenly leapt to Bev and I told Christian, who also had no idea whose idea all this was, that Brian Bevan had also died since the paintings had been done. If they had only been going to do one stamp instead of five, I told him, Bev or Jim Sullivan would have been the ultimate choice. So how could they leave Bev out? Christian must have passed the message on to the mandarins at the British Philatelic Bureau. Shortly afterwards I received another call from Christian telling me he had been asked to do a painting of Brian Bevan for the first-day cover. So Bev was in and Jonty Parkin was out. It was amazing that the powers that ran the operation were so flexible when they normally ran such affairs on such a long time scale.

The illustration of Gus, as had been the previous five, was submitted to me for my opinion. They were all excellent. When the illustration of Bev arrived, depicting him in action in the 1954 Odsal replay, I thought it was Captain Jean-Luc Picard, of *Star Trek - The Next Generation* fame, staring at me. When asked, I told the Royal Mail that in my opinion it just did not look like Bev, but by that stage it was probably too late to change it. At least Bev had another string to his bow of immortality. Of the five stamps which winged their way into millions of letter boxes throughout the world on and after 3 October, 1995, Bev's bore the highest tariff at 41p with Harold Wagstaff at 19p, Gus Risman 25p, Jim Sullivan 30p and Billy Batten 35p.

Stands, statues, stamps, elevation to the Hall of Fame - The Great Bev's incomparable contribution to the sport of rugby league had truly been recognised.

In 1986 Bev and Doreen had returned north to live at Blackpool's South Shore. Five years later cancer claimed Bev's life. He died, aged only 66, on Monday, 3 June, 1991 in hospital in Southport.

Joseph A. Wright of Orford remembers

On Friday, 7 June 1991 at 11.30am mourners gathered from all quarters at the Southport Crematorium to pay their respects at the funeral service of Brian Bevan. The chapel was overflowing with relatives, friends and admirers. Floral and written tributes had been received from the world of rugby, including many from Australia. Here at the service, the well-known and the not so well-known exchanged Bevan anecdotes.

We all listened intently and thoughtfully to the Reverend W. D. Thomas as he told us of Brian's family and sporting background. We gave of our best as the hymns were sung and we were silent again as Brian's favourite music was absorbed.

Then came the finale and I was spellbound. I just could not accept that the Lord's Prayer was being offered by this congregation with so much feeling, with so much sincerity, with evident emotion and with perfection of timing. The prayer was recited slowly. The phrases and the pauses were delivered and observed in absolute uniformity. I was silent. I just had to listen on this transcendental occasion. Were we at Ampleforth? Had the Benedictines assumed responsibility for the conduction of this austere and final service for Brian Bevan?

As I heard the concluding lines, "For thine is the kingdom..". I realised that I had been witness to a body of people, mostly strangers to each other, or just acquaintances, which had combined perfectly on a solemn occasion to offer their prayers to Almighty God for a deceased husband, father, friend and hero.

But how was this accomplished? How could so many people, drawn from all regions and gathered together without order or rehearsal, deliver such an unforgettable offering of the prayer Our Lord gave to us?

Had Almighty God used the occasion to make a divine expression through the medium of Brian before the rugby phenomenon was received into the Eternal Kingdom?

Brian Eyrl Bevan - the miracle man?

Within days of his death more than 20 Members of Parliament had signed a House of Commons motion extolling Bev's massive legacy to the game. The motion, tabled by Doug Hoyle, the Warrington North M.P., stated, "This House very much regrets the death of Brian Bevan, a legendary figure in rugby league. In the opinion of many he was the greatest winger to have graced the game and all of sport will be poorer for his passing".

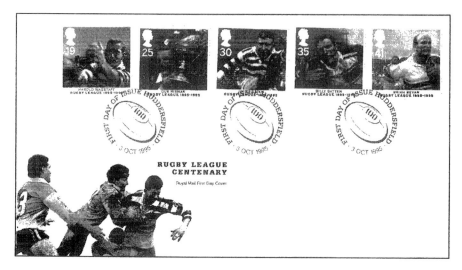

Top: The Brian Bevan Stamp
Bottom: The first day cover for the Rugby League Centenary

24. 'The try of the century'

Brian Bevan was a master of the spectacular. Many of his tries were almost indescribable although, thank heaven, the writers of the day made valiant efforts to depict them as accurately as possible. Which was the finest is obviously a moot point but generally the most recalled and celebrated was the blinder he scored against Wigan at Central Park in the Wardonia Cup on Saturday, 14 August 1948. Ironically the game was a charity match and therefore does not count in official records. Consequently Bev's try of tries is not even included in his career records. Charity match or not, no one regarded a Wigan-Warrington match as anything but a deadly serious affair in those days. The crowd of 31,960 had certainly gone to watch a real game. Excitement was palpable. Warrington's last game on 8 May had been the glorious Championship final success over Bradford Northern at Maine Road, while Wigan's, the preceding Saturday, had seen them lift the Challenge Cup with victory over Northern at Wembley. So it was Challenge Cup winners versus Champions, never mind the usual inordinately keen local derby.

It was a colourful affair, Wigan sporting unusually broad cherry and white hoops and the Wire in striking narrow primrose and blue hoops. It was a perfect August afternoon as the teams lined up:
Wigan: M Ryan; Ratcliffe, Roughley, Ashcroft, Hilton; Mountford, Alty; Gee, Egan, Barton, White, Blan, Hudson
Warrington: Jones; Bevan, Pimblett, Knowelden, Francis; Fleming, Helme; Derbyshire, Cotton, Featherstone, Atherton, R. Ryan, Palin

Of those 26 players only George Roughley, Johnny Alty, Dave Cotton, who were all Lancashire caps, and Jack Atherton never had been nor were to become Internationals. The referee was Norman Railton (Liverpool) and the touch-judges were W. Stockley (Leigh) and A. Ford (Warrington).

The first half had ended with the teams level on 5-5, Bryn Knowelden having scored Warrington's try, converted by Harold Palin. For Wigan Cec Mountford had goaled from under the posts a try from Gordon Ratcliffe. Bev's wonder try broke the deadlock early in the second half. This is how Jack Steel described it in the *Warrington Guardian*:

Brian Bevan's masterpiece had crowd and Wigan gasping

"Gentlemen, as sportsmen, you must hand out the highest possible praise to these Australians. While Ray Lindwall was making ducks and drakes of the England batsmen at the Oval in the final Test, fellow-countryman Brian Bevan was pattern-weaving a master-piece at Central Park.

Strange thing about the boys from the Dominions is their boyish enthusiasm for every sport, a must-win-at-all-costs attitude, and like the most fabulous Hollywood film producer, emphasis is generally on the spectacular.

Bevan's second-half try was so cleverly executed, so audaciously planned that journalists have practically run out of adjectives describing that 14 seconds of immense joy - a memorable try-line to try-line dash.

No doubt about it, that run bluffed everyone in the huge crowd, the Wigan team and most of Bevan's colleagues. Now I should imagine that old friend Jim Sullivan has already taken precautions against repetition.

Thrilling is hardly the word for the try, breath-taking is nearer the target and for those who missed the try of the century, well that's their fault.

Heaven-sent gift

I am not exactly a youngster - having watched R.L. since the resumption of play following World War One, but after that Bevan effort I feel I have seen practically everything the code can offer - except, of course, club achievements.

The try can never be measured in £.s.d. In fact the three points were a heaven-sent gift in the way of propaganda for the game.

How was the try scored? Here's my version. A scrum five yards from the Warrington line - the 'Wire' were defending the scoreboard end - when Dave Cotton hooked successfully. Out came Harold Palin from the pack to receive from Gerry Helme.

Risky this handling, but the ball travelled quickly and was handled crisply. Albert Pimblett took the pass, drew Hilton effectively and served Bevan at the split second.

Bev, truly the most unorthodox three-quarter in the last quarter of a century, was 'away'. No, not along the touch-line as the Wigan players had imagined, but on a diagonal run towards the centre.

Near the '25', Martin Ryan, who had hoped to link up with a possible Wigan movement, appeared likely to stop the Australian's progress, while Ashcroft and Mountford were running in to support.

Leg and body swerve took Ryan by surprise and there was a gap which the Wigan centre and stand-off could not close.

Another really wonderful swerve and swift acceleration put Bevan out of reach, and by now he was well set for the line. No wonder I had declared amid the now full-blooded Warrington supporters' roar, 'they'll not catch him now'. For Ashcroft and Hilton everything was lost, and Wigan's sole hope was the 'here, there and everywhere Mr. Mountford'. He chased, but that was all. Bevan fell flat on his tummy almost between flag and posts on the left. Not a try, gentlemen, a super try. In that run Bevan sped about 125 yards."

The report in the *Warrington Examiner* roughly concurred. *Criticus* described the try as "one of the most amazing I have seen... [Bevan] must have beaten five or six opponents and the great crowd rose to him and cheered him for several minutes."

The *Wigan Observer* reporter was also enamoured: "Warrington fully deserved to win. A wonder try from Brian Bevan, the fleet Australian wingman, alone deserved a cup. This was an end-to-end dash in which ... Bevan weaved his way through the Wigan defence and then beat everything for sheer speed. A magnificent effort."

Homer Genn, in the *Examiner*, decided to describe the try as if he were reporting on the wireless: "Helme puts the ball in, first time. It's Warrington's ball... Yes, they have it! A sharp pass to the right - Fleming, I think - to Pimblett

... Bevan has it now. He's nipped inside, fooled Hilton. He's flashed by the centres, side-stepped Mountford. He's clear! Yes, he's away! Over the '25' line, like a streak of lightning. I can see only two defenders with a hope of heading him off. He's running like the wind straight for the opposite corner. Will they get him? Yes, yes ... No, they won't! He's put on a spurt - left them standing. They're lying flat after grabbing at his shadow. He's clear away now! Another forty yards to go... not a Wigan player within a mile... He's over! Boy, oh boy! What a try! Just listen to the crowd. There must be 30,000 of us here. Bevan can't hear them. He's panned out. There goes the trainer with the cure-all sponge and bottle. He'll be OK in a minute. Listen! You should just see this demonstration - everybody on their feet! He's up now, coming back over the same course. Hands on his hips, head down. He has a sprightly walk, this lad. He's only 24. Here he is... head moving to and fro like a highly trained race-horse. Yes, sir! There's sure some speed in them thar limbs. And as his team-mates slap his back, he goes through a series of deep breathing exercises. Meanwhile the Wigan players - most of them left stranded in the Warrington '25' - trudge back. He's back in his position now and with the crowd still cheering, hardly anybody noticed Palin fail with his kick at goal."

Homer Genn then revealed he had spoken to Bev a few weeks previously and asked him which of the multitude of tries he had scored did he consider the best. Bev's response was "the one I have up my sleeve".

Of course, with the passage of time the try took on even more miraculous dimensions. Myths have grown of Bev beating all the Wigan team, some of them twice or three times, and the length of his run increased exponentially. No wonder Bev was cream-crackered as he fell on his belly in the act of scoring!

Mike Rowan recalled Cec Mountford visiting Warrington Boys Club some eleven years later, when he confirmed to the young Rowan something attributed to him in a newspaper article: "When I was a youngster in New Zealand a veteran told me a story of how it was possible to step in and out of a tackle. I just could not visualise it. I put it down to being a figment of his imagination. You see, if he did explain how it could be done, I did not grasp what he was saying. Anyway, when I cut across I manoeuvred Bev into Martin Ryan. Then before my eyes I saw Ryan grab him yet he failed to net him. Somehow his leg and upper body movement had Martin clutching thin air and away he went. He was like an India Rubberman. I gave chase but..."

Having given Warrington an 8-5 lead, Bev saw it wiped out when Ken Gee imperiously pushed Jack Fleming aside to claim an equalising try. By this time Warrington were in dire straits. Bob Ryan was hobbling about with an ankle injury which would keep him out of the game for seven months. Roy Francis was limping on the left wing and Dave Cotton then took a blow to his forehead from a Wigan knee and was led off with blood pumping from a two-inch gash. It looked as if he had retired as he had replaced his false teeth, only to remove them when he realised how hard things were becoming for his mates. He returned to the fray with his head swathed in bandages. This "friendly", played at cup-tie intensity, was no place for faint hearts. Wigan full-back Martin Ryan had also suffered a decidedly nasty head wound.

It looked as if Bev would have to break the game again. He did, with a trademark interception. Jack Steel wrote: "Wigan had not learned their lesson. They had forgotten the genius of Bevan, and when another sharp attack looked like developing an Alty pass was stolen by the Warrington right-winger. Score 11-8." Harold Palin kicked a goal to make it 13-8. The match was settled when Albert Pimblett snaffled up a fumbled pass and gave the ball to Francis, who took it one-handed and bravely half-ran, half-hobbled to score wide out. Palin goaled and Warrington had won a humdinger 18-8.

The fact that Jack Steel was prepared to use expressions like "the try of the century" and to begin his series of diagrams of Bev's classic tries is a sure sign that the Central Park touchdown was truly extraordinary. The middle of the twentieth century was not a period when sports reporters indulged at the drop of a hat in the embarrassing hyperbole that sometimes passes for sports journalism nowadays. Bev undoubtedly scored more crucial tries, the match-winners in the 1955 Championship final and the 1959 Lancashire Cup final springing immediately to mind. His tries in Bordeaux for the Other Nationalities in 1953 and a good many others, especially some of those scored in Cumberland, may actually have been more spectacular than the Wardonia Cup effort. None, however, ever appear to have more tightly gripped the imagination of those lucky enough to have witnessed his *pièce de résistance* of 14 August, 1948.

Brian Bevan's Wardonia Cup record

Date	Venue	Score	Bevan	Crowd
16 Aug, 1947	Wigan	15-28	2T	14,044
14 Aug, 1948	Wigan	18- 8	2T	31,960
13 Aug, 1949	Warrington	11-28	2T	23,300
12 Aug, 1950	Warrington	12- 7	dnp	15,608
11 Aug, 1951	Wigan	10-23		16,000
16 Aug, 1952	Warrington	9-13		19,569
8 Aug, 1953	Wigan	20-30	T	16,134
7 Aug, 1954	Warrington	27-14	4T	12,306
12 Aug, 1955	Wigan	19-10	2T	14,593
11 Aug, 1956	Warrington	15-16	T	10,000
10 Aug, 1957	Wigan	14-15	2T	15,209
9 Aug, 1958	Warrington	21-29	T	10,565
8 Aug, 1959	Wigan	22-31	T	18,701
6 Aug, 1960	Warrington	8-31	T	10,776
12 Aug, 1961	Wigan	10-26		17,451

Bevan appeared in fourteen Wardonia Cup matches, scoring nineteen tries. Those tries do not count in official records. Warrington won only three of those games. Bevan did not appear in the 1950 victory.

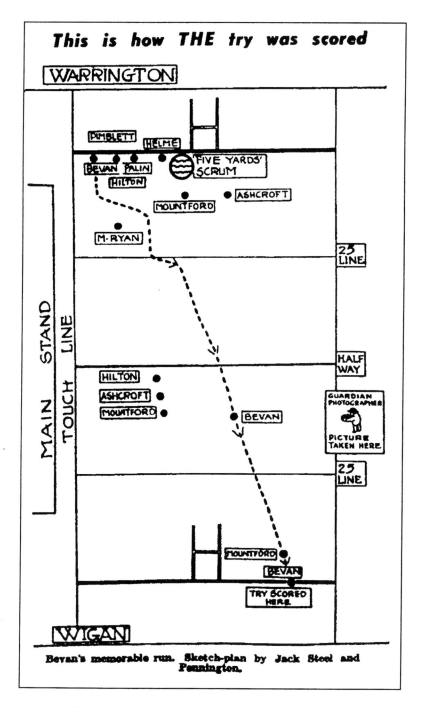

The diagram of "that try" in the *Warrington Guardian*

1948 Wardonia Cup: Bev, chased by Cec Mountford,
follows his own kick (not the try move)

A wonderful image of Bev, about to kick ahead in the
1948 Wardonia Cup game at Central Park, Wigan.

25. Memories of Bevan

Players

Harry Bath's view

"Brian Bevan has never had any counterpart in Australia in my time. Maybe Dally Messenger had the same magical effect on crowds in the early days but no player ever provided sustained thrills for so many fans over such a long period as Bevan.

He dazzled his opponents so many times and turned the result of a match so often that many deeds which would have lived forever with another player have been forgotten.

He always gave me the impression he had radar built into the toes of his football boots and that this steered him around all objects between him and the try-line."

From *Australian Rugby League's Greatest Players*, edited by Geoff Greenwood

Bob Batten

I was a winger and I played against Brian Bevan quite a few times. I remember when I was with Oldham our coach was Stan Smith, the old test winger, who was a relative of mine. Stan pointed Brian out to me before a game with Warrington. "That's Bevan, wearing the trilby," said Stan. I looked across at him and thought that he didn't look like a footballer at all.

Then when I saw him on the pitch, all covered in bandages and bald, you would not have thought there would be an ounce of football in him. But what a player. He was the best winger I have ever seen or played against - the king-pin. He could side-step you five yards before he got to you, which was amazing.

I remember once we kicked off and the ball went behind the Warrington forwards. Bevan got the ball and ran through the whole of our team and scored under the posts. Then, blow me, we kicked off after the try and exactly the same thing happened again! We changed our kick-off after that.

Jim Challinor on his wing partner

"Nobody looked less like a footballer than Brian... just skin and bone tied together with Elastoplast. Before every game he would have a couple of chaps taping him up and rubbing him down. He looked fragile. But he was out on his own. As a crowd-puller, there has never been anyone quite like him. A superb side-step he had, but what really used to make the most experienced players grasp at thin air in the tackle was his change of pace. He had a sudden fantastic acceleration that no one could anticipate. A try-scoring machine - that's what he was... Brian could tackle if he had to but he expected his centres to take his man as well if possible. In his time he had Albert Pimblett, Ally Naughton, Ron Ryder and me alongside him. He told us all that it was his job to score tries, and for my money there has never been anyone in the history of the game who could do it as well."

Jim Challinor in an interview with Bob Myers, circa 1974.

Churchill's Dream Team Winger

Clive Churchill, by popular consent the greatest full-back ever produced by Australia, chose Brian Bevan and Ian Moir (South Sydney and Australia) as the wingers he would choose for his imaginary dream team. Of Bevan he wrote:

"I played against Bevan and also saw him in English Cup matches. At the peak of his career he was a phenomenon. I've seen him gather the ball behind his own goal-line,

pierce his way through all thirteen opponents, and race the full length of the ground for a scintillating try while the crowd split the very heavens with its thrilling roars. Bevan could leave an opponent standing with his miraculous side-step at top speed. Two of England's greatest ever players, Alf Ellaby and Stan Smith concur in my rating of Bevan."
From Clive Churchill's autobiography, *They Called Me The Little Master*

Gerry Collingwood, Blackpool Borough

I played with Brian at Blackpool Borough, where I was a second-row forward. My first memory of him though was from the days when I was a schoolboy in Wigan. I was there when he scored his most famous try in the Wardonia Cup match at Central Park in 1948. I remember he ran more than the length of the field from the right corner to the left corner on the opposite side of the ground. It was a try I'll never forget. He beat man after man. They came at him singly so he beat them easily one after another. Cec Mountford, who was really quick over a short distance, had two goes at him but couldn't get near him. I have never seen anything like it and wish I had a film of it.

He was a funny character, of course. He was not a mixer, just kept himself to himself. It was a strange choice to make him captain at Blackpool because he was so quiet. I think Tommy Bishop was leaned on a bit to give up the captaincy. He did used to say "well done" to me after games though. Some people are not cut out to be coaches and I think Bev was one of them. I respected him and liked him. I would say we got on well together but I would have liked to have got closer to him. He just was not built that way.

He looked anything but a rugby player. There was nothing aggressive in his manner. There was no weight about him and he was not a robust tackler. There was no doubt how good he was though and there is no one remotely like him now.

Of course, it was different for him playing for Borough instead of Warrington. We were not a great team and Bev often grumbled about our forwards, although he did excuse me! He was always going to have a word with Gordon Emery, the chairman, about it but I don't know if he ever did.

Years later I was involved with the amateur club Blackpool Stanley. One year we invited Brian to our presentations night. We also invited Billy Boston, who I knew well. It was fantastic having the two of them there together. Everybody was getting photographed with them. It was obvious that Brian thoroughly enjoyed it. A few years later when Tommy Bishop came home from Australia we also got him to do the presentations.

Long after Brian had retired and I was still involved with Blackpool Stanley, I remember we had a young Australian player, Mark Murray. He was pretty good, could kick goals and scored a few tries. We got talking about Brian and he said he knew all about Bev. He came from the same district as Bev and everyone there knew about him. I asked if he would be interested in meeting him because I knew him and could take him to see him. He was really thrilled at the thought. When we got to Brian's house we knocked and he came to the door. He knew me, of course, but we never got across the threshold He said there was no-one else in and after a few minutes' chat Bev had run out of conversation and that was the end of our visit.

John Etty, Batley, Oldham, Wakefield Trinity and Yorkshire

When I was a teenager I was selected to play for England against Australia at Wigan, at a seven-a-side, in the company of Ernest Ward, Eric Batten and Martin Ryan. My direct opponent was Brian Bevan.

The England team was not an official one, because the knockout competition was organised by the RL Players' trade union to raise funds. A crowd of 16,000 saw England defeat Australia, when I scored a try, followed by a win over Wales, when I faced Alan Edwards.

Brian had joined Warrington in November 1945 and was an instant success. I realised his flair but, playing alongside established international players, I was confident, although I respected Brian as an elite winger.

As I was registered with the Batley club our team did not play against Warrington regularly, although I was told that the Warrington club had attempted to transfer me there at one time. In 1955 I was transferred, at 24 hours notice, to Oldham, after which I faced Brian regularly. At that time Warrington and Oldham were closely matched. Both teams had many international or county players to provide top displays. Warrington's star, among many elite players, was Brian Bevan, a true match-winner, an extraordinary try-scorer, who was prepared to use a wide variety of skills to score at any part of the line from his right wing position.

I found Brian to be single-minded - he was there to score tries - but had, in my opinion, no interest in defence. Only once did he attempt to stop me by attempting to knock the ball out of my hands, deliberately. The referee, Mr. Armitage, a schoolteacher, spoke to him, when Brian pleaded with him not to send him off. He was only cautioned, to his relief. It was only a minor incident, dealt with sensibly.

As a young player at Batley I was shown the basics of defence by coaches Bill Smith and Charlie Eaton, which I applied throughout my career. I considered that defence was important and thought deeply about it. During the Second World War British submarines sank ships carrying supplies from Italy to Rommel's Afrika Corps in North Africa, thereby creating problems for him in his struggle against the Eighth Army, notably at the turning point in the war, at El Alamein, when Montgomery and his men won a decisive victory.

I applied that strategy to defence on the rugby field. Cut off the supply of the ball to the danger men, including the best of them - Brian Bevan. It was not always possible but, with good timing, it could be effective.

Brian Bevan was a quiet man, unassuming, and a good sport, who always played to the rules. He was a prolific scorer, as all rugby fans know, who needed to be watched by opponents whenever Warrington had the ball. He graced the game of rugby league.

Bernard Ganley's nightmare

Oldham's Bernard Ganley was one of rugby league's top full-backs in the 1950s, a record-breaker in his own right. He did, however, dread the sight of Brian Bevan and, by his own admission, very rarely got near the great man. He wrote circa 1961: "Wingers always worry us. This sentiment could easily be carved indelibly on the subconscious of all full-backs. Ever since I first trod the turf with a No. 1 shirt on my back they have been the bane of my life. The first thing the full-backs always assess in the opposition is the flank man. These individuals range from weird little men with gnome countenances to hulking specimens that would petrify a battalion of Ghurkas.

As different as their physical make-up are their methods of operating. There are the crafty corkscrew runners, the duckers and weavers, side-steppers who could top the bill at any music-hall in a soft-shoe spot, sheer speed merchants, and the if-I-can't-get-round-you-I'm-going-through customers.

I've met them all. The good ones can usually combine a couple of the above qualities, while the really good ones - well, I never try to catalogue their abilities.

They use everything and invariably manage to produce one or two surprise items that you have never seen before.

Take Brian Bevan, for example. I consider Bev to be the greatest ever... Brian utilises every means of finding a way to that try-line. How he gets there is the main thing. He can perhaps jink his way through, or use a sharp burst with a swerve, while a change of pace is a variation he never fails to exploit. But the quest does not cease there. The punt ahead for him is as dangerous as any, and his uncanny sense of smell for an interception, with those telescopic arms, is unbelievable.

Bev is dangerous, not only when he is possession of the ball. He will always look for a chance to get it even if it means roving away from his beat. He never stops thinking and attempting different devices. He will dig deeper than a particularly shy mole to find new weapons for his armoury."

In an interview with Joe Humphreys the week after Bev retired as a Warrington player in April 1962, Ganley had this to say: "I have been left standing by Brian more times than by any other player. I never was able to get him in a tackle. He was most elusive. Whenever he had the ball I used to look round for help for I knew it was hopeless to try and tackle him single-handed.

His change of pace... his ability to side-step both ways kidded you. Instead of you having Bevan on the spot... he had you - and every time. You can tell the intentions of some wingers by looking into their faces as they come towards you. But not Brian. He had the same poker face all the time... and never lost his head. He was really cheeky with it. Though he looked anything but fitted for such a tough game Brian never flinched... and we used to give him some stick up at Oldham when we did cop him."

Reg Hughes

I joined Warrington, my hometown club, in 1950 on returning home from national service in Hong Kong. I played for Warrington for six years, during which time I played several games as centre to Brian Bevan and I also stood in for him on the wing. Really I was a utility back or loose-forward but mostly I played for the reserves, of which I eventually became captain.

Before I joined the club I remember watching the 1948 Lancashire Cup Final at Swinton between Warrington and Wigan. For once the Wire's form was superior to Wigan's and they were installed as favourites. Unfortunately it was reported that the Warrington players were haggling over bonuses rather than concentrating on winning the game. In the event Wigan were winning easily near the end of the game with the star Wigan winger Brian Nordgren, a New Zealander, having a blinder against Bev. Nordgren had scored two tries and Bev was just not getting the ball. Finally, Brian got one chance, beat Nordgren and cut inside to the posts, near to where I was standing. In a mixture of triumph and disgust at his lack of ball, he deliberately took the ball from under his arm and with a flamboyant gesture slammed it down to score! Unfortunately the ball hit his own knee and ricocheted over the dead-ball line. The horror dawned and the Wigan fans roared with Brian giving them looks to kill. My boyhood idol had feet of clay - until I got to know him as a rugby genius.

There was a true story about two of Warrington's old warhorse props being quizzed by a reporter about rumoured inducements and extra bonuses for Brian - long before the era of contracts. Much to the pressman's surprise they replied: "They can pay him what they bloody well like, as long as he keeps getting us winning money."

I found Brian to be a very nice man but one who could appear reticent and introverted. He tended to wait to be spoken to first. I think he was looked upon by some outsiders as a somewhat comical figure - until he scored against them. Would this controversial figure have lived in the modern era of full-time professionals with 15-stone sprinters on the wings? I sincerely hope he would, in any era.

Warrington had a team with varied temperaments. Several, including the mighty Aussie Harry Bath, would be physically sick before a game. Others needed to be slated after a poor first half - an increased win bonus was often helpful. Then they would reply with "I'll show you this half", or words to that effect. A few, like mercurial Gerry Helme, needed cajoling and to be told he was having a great game and that he could beat that mug any time. On the other hand, Brian Bevan was always prepared, single-minded and self-disciplined without any need for the stick or the softly, softly approach.

Brian once scored seven tries against Leigh and they had Great Britain full-back Jim Ledgard in their side. I think Ledgard got near enough to touch Brian every time but always failed to stop him. It was clear that Brian was over the moon, as they say.

He loved scoring. In another game against Leigh though he hardly got a chance and Albert Johnson on the other wing scored a lot of tries, much to Bev's chagrin and he clearly showed his disappointment. You have to ask was this a good point in that he merely wanted to be continually involved or was it a character flaw in a team sport?

Some people said he was timid and could not tackle - did they say that about soccer's Stanley Matthews? Yet if a try was on he would go through a brick wall to score, sometimes with two or three defenders hanging on. Also his speed at grounding the ball was amazing, whether chasing a kick through to the dead-ball line or reaching over at the corner flag. In fact the ball often spun back into the field of play with his sleight of hand.

On occasions I was reserve to travel and on such occasions you were expected to help Jackie Hamblett, the kit man/masseur and also the trainers with the customary leg massage. One trainer, Freddie Worrall, the ex-Portsmouth FC winger, used to take the complete hour before kick-off seeing to Brian. Imagine it, mid-winter and freezing outside. Inside Bev was making sure he was prepared for all eventualities. The trainer cut more than 100 strips of tape ready for action. While jerseys (sometimes two off), shorts (two off), socks and shoulder pads were on the radiators, cotton wool was applied to his shoulders, elbows, ankles and knees underneath pads. He invariably put on his boots 10 minutes before kick-off before being last on the table for a thorough massage. The rest of us had seen to the other 12! At the referee's knock he pulled up his stockings and fixed his tie-ups before going out to run the opposition ragged. Who said attention to details doesn't pay dividends?

In 1950, in my first season, I had a marvellous introduction to the game. I was a youngster in a reserve team hardened with many old pros with lots of first team experience. I played in Bev's position quite a lot and they provided me with lots of tries together with the 'A' Team Championship. Warrington were second to Wigan in the Lancashire League with two away games to play while Wigan had only to win their last game on the Saturday to clinch the title. Because both teams were in the top four play-offs and Wigan were Wembley finalists too, they fielded weakened sides. I stood in for Bevan in a team containing 10 reserves at Salford. Guess what? We won 19-0 and Wigan lost their game. This now meant that the Monday night game at Swinton was vitally important. All players reported to the club on Sunday morning with the first-teamers now volunteering for action. Manager Chris Brockbank said, No! The same team will play if everybody is fit. We had another dream game with captain Albert Naughton and myself on the right wing bagging three tries between us in a memorable 20-14 win. Needless to say, one of the first people to congratulate me was Bev although I am sure he would have preferred to play. Nevertheless he was happy with his unexpected medal. This appeared to be one occasion when he was happy to share the limelight.

On a personal note, in the 1950s I played centre to Brian against a strong Oldham team at Watersheddings. From a five-yard scrum on our own line I was given a suicide pass, receiving a reception committee of three tacklers at the same time. Fortunately, or stupidly, I managed to get a one-handed pass to the one and only Bev. From my prone position, looking through arms and legs, I saw him beat the cover down the wing before swerving past the full-back for a solo try under the posts. Imagine my delight when I bought the Saturday night football pink to read, "and Hughes sent Bevan over for a magnificent try under the posts". All my own work - some hope!

In 1951, Warrington were drawn against a very strong Workington Town in a two-legged Lancashire Cup-tie. Warrington lost the home leg against a team containing the likes of Gus Risman, Mudge, Paskins and Ivison. So with many important games coming up and several players carrying niggling injuries, Warrington sent a much weakened team north for the second leg. In a losing defensive battle I relished the chance to again stand in for Bevan. I was a bit different to Bev being 6ft 1in and 13 stone 8 lbs with a rather vigorous approach, coupled with a strong man-and-ball style of tackling, which conventional wingers did not like.

My opponent was the Scot, George Wilson, later a test winger. George was speedy but not very robust. Needless to say, I marked him very closely, often hitting him as the pass arrived. By full-time he was pleading with his centre to kick through. We managed to shake hands quite agreeably after the match, however. I had forgotten all about the encounter when Workington arrived weeks later for a league game for which I was non-playing reserve. An hour before kick-off there was a knock on our dressing-room door. A couple of cauliflower-eared forwards peered round the opened door smiling and enquired: "Wilson wants to know whether that bugger Hughes is playing or is Bevan back?" An affirmative nod towards Bev in the corner broke them up with laughter as they said, "George will be pleased!" I can honestly say I grew a couple of inches at the thought of a star winger preferring to mark the world's finest winger than risk the close attentions of an also-ran.

Colin Hutton, Widnes, Hull and Lancashire full-back

It is difficult, impossible even, to say that anyone was the best rugby league player ever. There are so many different types and so many different positions. But if anyone asks me who made the most impact on opponents, I will say Brian Bevan every time. The fact that he scored more than 200 tries more than the next highest try-scorer in history, Billy Boston, just about says it all. He was an absolute phenomenon.

The first time I played against him was for Widnes. I remember Warrington seemed to play differently from other teams. If anyone broke through the midfield they would invariably kick for Bev. As a full-back I always thought I'd get to the ball but, when Bev was playing, halfway to the ball I knew I would not. It's funny, he was more dangerous in his own '25' than the opposition's, simply because he had more room to work in. Once in motion he was truly marvellous. When he got going he didn't just beat me, he ignored me!

Once when Widnes's game was postponed I went to see Warrington play Oldham. Bev received the ball about ten yards from his own line and by the time he reached the 25 he had got clear of the cover. There was only Irving Barraclough left in front of him. Barraclough was a very competent full-back. He did everything right, pushing Bev towards the touchline, cutting down the options. Then Bev just changed tack and shot from the right wing away to the left. Poor old Irving was helpless and almost literally rooted to the spot. No one could stop Bev in that situation.

Later I remember playing for Hull at The Boulevard. Bev took 15 yards off me in 20 to get to a loose ball. They never let me forget it in Hull.

One thing a lot of people did not give him credit for was his defence. He could be very effective. Because he was so fast he could get back really quickly to pick up kicks and misdirected passes. Of course, he frightened opposition three-quarters to death because he created apprehension in them with his brilliance at interceptions.

I did not know him very well off the field but I do remember meeting him once while on holiday on the Isle of Man. Well, it was his wife who I noticed first. She was wearing a bikini, quite a daring thing to do in those days. Bev, an Australian remember, was hiding in the shade, his trouser legs rolled up to his knees and a knotted handkerchief on top of his head.

Lewis Jones

"A side-step takes you into trouble nine times out of ten, unless you are Brian Bevan". (Lewis Jones's benefit brochure, 1963) and: "Speed and pure footballing ability apart, he was an absolute past master at the art of concealing his pace. Time and again opponents, myself amongst them, could have sworn that the Warrington flier was going full bat, only to find him producing a last-second surge of pace to leave them and the spectators breathless. Unfortunately I never saw that other great Australian, Eric Harris, play for Leeds, but if he had anything on Brian Bevan in the matter of working variations on the theme of pace then he must have been a marvel indeed."
From Lewis Jones's autobiography, *King of Rugger*

Rex Mossop meets Bev

"Bevan's frail physique was deceptive. He was durable and could withstand a battering. But before they could batter the little bastard, his opponents had to catch him - and that was easier said than done. I admit I couldn't wait to get my hands on him in my first game in England for Leigh in 1951, but the old campaigner made sure my career got started on the wrong foot. Once in the game he was running with the ball, I lined him up and moved in to crunch him, then in a flash he stepped inside me. Despairingly I flung my arm out to grab his jersey and Brian ducked right into it. I'd necked him. His legs shot out in front of him and he crashed hard to the ground, landing flat on his back. There had been no malice in my tackle at all. It was purely a reflex action, but when the local hero hit the deck and stayed there crumpled in a heap, all hell broke loose. Harry Bath and his boys made a beeline to belt me, and then the crowd decided to join in the fun. About 30 of them spilled over the fence and onto the field, fists clenched and baying for Aussie blood. Trevor Allan called for our teammates to form a protective circle around me. While all this pandemonium was raging around me, images raced through my head of Custer's Last Stand."
From Rex Mossop's autobiography, *The Moose That Roared*

Brian Nordgren

It is 47 years since I last saw Brian Bevan. I first met him in late 1946. 1 was in my second season with Wigan but living in Liverpool studying law. He visited me there. I think he had a trial game with Leeds after leaving the Australian Navy and was now considering a Warrington offer. Little did 1 know that this Aussie would become a sensational winger with Warrington for the next decade or so.

I played 10 seasons for Wigan and probably had the task of marking Bevan more often than any other winger. He was fast off the mark and a skilful ball handler. I remember him most for his deceptive running, largely achieved by clever footwork and variation of pace. Year after year he was at or near the top of the try-scoring list in England. Those lists were full of wingers who were rugby league or former rugby union test players from England, Wales, Scotland, Ireland, Australia, South Africa, and New Zealand. Throughout his twenties Bevan would have been first choice in any Australian test team, if he had been eligible. At that time Kangaroo and Kiwi teams could not include players who were with English clubs. For varying periods during Bevan's prime Wigan, Warrington, St Helens, Bradford, Huddersfield, Leeds, Barrow and Workington could each field virtually a full team of past and current internationals from both codes and some other clubs could field half-a-dozen or so. The 1947 Kiwi touring team won only 14 of their 23 club games, and the 1948 Kangaroos also had a tough time against the English clubs, losing 16-11 to Wigan.

Wigan got the biggest share of honours in the 1946-53 period when it appeared in 13 finals and won all but the first and last of them. Brian Bevan's Warrington was a strong team. Only last-minute tries to Wigan stopped Warrington from going to a Wembley final in 1948 and again in 1951. Warrington won at Wembley in 1950 and drew 4-4 there in 1954 but won the replay 8-4 before 102,000 at Bradford's Odsal Stadium. Warrington won the Championship final in 1948, 1954 and 1955, and was the beaten finalist in 1949 and 1951. Warrington was beaten in two of Wigan's six successive Lancashire Cup final wins from 1946. During Bevan's first eight seasons or so, Warrington was always in or near the top four.

He was not a big bustling winger. My recollection of him at his physical peak is that he was near 5ft 10in tall and might just have tipped the scales at 12 stone. In the main, he faced stiff opposition from fast wingers weighing 12-and-a-half to 14 stone, notably Huddersfield's Aussie test winger Lionel Cooper, Wigan's Billy Boston, Leeds's Australian 100 yards record-holder Bruce Ryan, Bradford's All Black and sprinter Jack McLean and Huddersfield's All Black and NZ sprint champion Peter Henderson.

Crowds were bigger then - up to 95,000 for Cup finals at Wembley, 75,000 for a Championship final at Maine Road and up to 48,000 for Lancashire Cup finals at Swinton or for a big game at Wigan's Central Park. My impression is that none brought those crowds to their feet more often than Brian Bevan and, later, Billy Boston. Boston and I played in the same team for my last two seasons but I do not think Bevan and I ever played in the same team.

Bevan and I did not meet often off the field. Usually it was over tea and cakes in the clubrooms after matches between our two clubs. Although we probably marked each other at least 20 times, angry words never passed between us. He was not a hail-fellow-well-met type of person but he was much admired by players on both sides for his exploits on the field. I imagine most wingers of that period would rightly consider themselves handicapped by having to wear such heavy boots on so many muddy grounds. But Brian Bevan in today's light footwear on firm grounds would have been even more difficult for us to cope with!

Albert Pimblett

I got to know Brian Bevan through playing centre to him at Warrington after joining them from Halifax in 1947. I stayed at Wilderspool until I left to play for Salford in 1950 so I knew him as well as you could get to know him, which was not really well. Brian was not a good mixer. He would rather keep to himself and in those days he was in digs. We would have a few beers but I don't remember him smoking in those days although they tell me he did later. Of course, he was highly strung. I remember he used to go about in an old Australian Navy overcoat in those days. With him being in digs then you could often leave him in a pub and he would just play the piano for hours.

Although he was difficult to talk to, I think he grew fond of me. Well, I was his centre and I was the only one who would put in extra training with him after everyone else had gone home. We used to run each other to death. I enjoyed training with Brian, practising moves together, scooping up balls and perfecting our combinations. I was fast - an experienced sprinter - but carrying a ball I would say there was never anyone faster than Bevan. I used to train in spikes, he wore boots! He used to fly like a bloody greyhound.

What can you say about Bevan? I was a big, strapping bloke, but there was not a lot to him and he was white as a ghost. There's no other way to describe him. He must have been good because at Warrington, remember, we had Roy Francis and Albert Johnson as wingers as well - both internationals and both great in their own ways but nowhere near as good as Bevan. Roy was a brilliant footballer and Albert had that wonderful side-step but couldn't go 90 yards like Bevan.

There is no telling how fast Brian could have been. The famous sprint coach Matthew Clamp arranged some races for professional rugby and soccer players, which Bevan always won. Once we even had a Rugby League relay squad at one of the athletic meetings. Brian, Bill Kindon, Griff Jenkins and myself were in it. With Brian leading us off we won that too. I remember they once brought a Canadian sprint champion to Warrington for trials and coaches Chris Brockbank and Emlyn Jenkins asked me to check him out. He wasn't a patch on Brian.

One of my boyhood heroes was Alf Ellaby and I played against him a few times before he finished. He and Bevan were completely different types. Alf was tall and well built and one of the all-time greats, but no one matched Bevan really. Bev was a law unto himself - completely unorthodox. I am sure he did not know what he was going to do next, never mind his opponents. He would run towards people but never into them. He did not like being tackled so he would do anything to avoid it. He would run backwards, sideways, round in circles, right across the pitch. He could beat men, any way you can think of. The further he went, the better he went. Full-backs could not get near him. He did not need to kick past them. When I played with him he did not like people to kick for him, because the ball might take a funny bounce. He wanted the ball in his hands and he always wanted the ball. It's a fallacy that he wanted his team mates to kick the ball for him to chase - at least in my time playing with him.

In some ways it was daft, the way he played - but it certainly worked for him. People said he was lucky not to get injured but he wasn't lucky. He just made sure he kept himself out of trouble. Of course, he wasn't a tackler but that didn't matter. I used to tell him to leave it to me. I would finish anybody off who looked like getting through and there were others like Bryn Knowelden who would cover for him.

He used to score lots of tries from diagonal runs. I remember the old Wigan prop Ken Gee saying to me one game: "I'll get hold of that mate of yours one day and then he'll know about it." I said: "You'll never catch him" and Ken never did. Neither did any of the other forwards who would try to stiff-arm him as he weaved across the field. They just used to get armfuls of thin air.

Bevan loved scoring tries. Sometimes I used to pass him the ball when I could have scored just to keep him happy. He was always screaming for the ball and throwing his hands up in disgust when he did not get it. I remember my nephew, Arthur Pimblett, who played full-back for Blackpool Borough in Bevan's twilight years there, telling me he was still screaming for the ball and throwing his hands up even when he was ready for retirement. I remember a game against Leigh and Bevan had already scored seven tries. I said to him: "Next time I get the ball; I'll just boot it as far as I can out of play." Well, he played hell with me. He was still keen to run the length of the field for more tries.

By, there were some great footballers around in those days such as Gus Risman, Pat Devery. I think the best centre-wing pairings Bev and I ever played against were Devery and Lionel Cooper of Huddersfield and Ernie Ashcroft and Brian Nordgren from Wigan. Later on, there was Billy Boston who was a much better all-round footballer than Bevan but not a better winger. There will never be a winger as good as Brian Bevan.

Alan Prescott's view
"I know it is an old saying that nobody will ever be quite so good as the old favourites and that memory sometimes adds lustre, but this Bevan has caused many reassessments of opinion. I will not say there will never be a winger to compare with him, but I should say that we may never have a superior, taking into account length of service, freedom from serious injury, and consistent brilliance, season after season.

When I first met Bevan, after having heard the stories of this wonder player, and lad-like having a high regard for my tackling prowess, I looked forward to our first clash. How this slip of a player, who somehow, because of his frailty, looked out of place on a football field, could stand up to the sort of bone-shattering tackles so commonly practised in his time was something I could not understand.

Then I met him face to face. At least that was how we were for a split second and then he was gone before I had time to get to grips.

Now I never bore Bevan any animosity. In fact he was a friend of mine and I admire him greatly, but it is the duty of every player to give all he has in every tackle. Let me make a confession now. Although I played for many a long year during Bevan's peak days, I never once caught him with the sort of full-blooded tackle which I think many an opponent has had secretly stored up for him.

Bevan was ghost-like in the way he slipped away from you even when he appeared to be right in the grasp, and I always said that there was a better chance of catching one of those quick-off-the-mark trolley buses than of getting to grips with Bevan.

I have seen players with a bewildering sidestep but, apart from possibly Bevan's old club-mate Albert Johnson, none quite so accomplished. Bevan, like Johnson, could go on side-stepping man after man right across the field and then when the opening was created flash through it like an express train.

How he managed to screw up so much stamina into that sparse frame must be one of the wonders of the age. I am happy to think that having crossed his path so often and stared in wonderment at his deeds he should play his last game against my team."
Alan Prescott, one of Great Britain's finest props and captains, wrote the above in 1962 after Bev's last match for Warrington against Leigh. Prescott was Leigh's coach.

Bob Ryan, Warrington and Great Britain forward
I played with Bevan for 13 years at Warrington. Brian was a very quiet chap and never had much to say. He used to arrive in the dressing room, go straight to his changing spot and never speak a word. Freddie Worrall used to look after him. It was more or less a full-time job for Freddie, who used to have to cut up dozens of strips of plaster, all different lengths, for Bev's strapping. Bev more or less had Freddie to himself. Before Bev left the dressing room he would ask Freddie, "How many today then?" -

meaning tries - and Freddie would laugh and say "three", or whatever. It was all part of the ritual.

I remember sometimes Bev would make himself heard. He would come in at half-time and if he had not been getting the ball or things had not been going well for him, he would say, "What's up with you lot? Can you only pass one way?" Then he would go back to his usual silence.

He did not have any special mates but he did get on well with Jimmy Featherstone. Jimmy and I were both Wiganers and we used to take him back to Wigan on Saturday nights and he would return to Warrington on the Sunday. All the pubs had a piano in those days and Brian would be straight on to it. He was good and could play anything.

There certainly won't be another Brian Bevan. He could score tries out of nothing and he was more dangerous in his own half than in the opposition's. It was fatal for opponents to kick to him. He would just run back through them.

Joe Warham

Brian Bevan is the most underrated figure in our game. Underrated? Yes - because he was so good it is impossible to appreciate just how good. I have seen most of the great wingers and played against many. I have childhood memories of Johnny Ring through Alf Ellaby, Ray Markham, Eric Harris and Alan Edwards to the post-war greats Lionel Cooper, Peter Henderson, Tom van Vollenhoven, Billy Boston, Mick Sullivan and on to Ken Irvine, Eric Grothe, Len Killeen, Terry O'Grady, Berwyn Jones, John Atkinson and Martin Offiah.

What marked out Bev was this. Given their extraordinary talents - speed, strength, and skill - it was possible to accept the amazing deeds of Voll and Boston. But what Bevan did was impossible. He is the only player who has made me turn to my neighbour on the terraces and say, "That's impossible. What we have just seen happen is beyond the limits of human achievement." Searching for a comparison I can only come up with those flickering silent movies of Buster Keaton weaving and dodging his way through the entire New York police force. I think I was the first to use the hackneyed but completely truthful expression there are wingmen and wingmen - and then there is Brian Bevan.

He is a legend and as such he attracts tales - some true, some apocryphal, others purely mythical. First of all, his appearance. I was on leave from the Navy when I first saw him. Wilderspool had closed for the duration and was just re-opening. I had heard of this unknown who had played, I believe, two trials and been brought back after de-mob. There was nothing exceptional about him then. He was certainly not imposing or of particularly athletic appearance. He had a reasonable head of hair, if not the flowing locks of his brother Owen, who was to join him at Wilderspool without spectacular success. Bev had about him a whipcord tautness of sinew, a nod of the head and an almost brooding menace of impending explosion. It was the sort of pale, nervous energy reminiscent of the drawn face of another of my heroes, Alan Edwards, of whom it was said that he had a side-step which scorched the grass.

Assuredly there was nothing to cause a club to reject Brian out of hand on grounds of appearance as was alleged to have happened at Leeds. All my enquiries suggest that he was never actually interviewed at Headingley and I fear that what happened, when Bill Shankland contacted both Leeds and Hunslet to seek a game for the son of an old friend, was that harassed officials, beset by the worries of sorting out post-war playing strength, committed the unpardonable sin of not pursuing the enquiry.

Bev's cupboard full of sprinting trophies, which he proudly showed me once at his Winwick home, spoke more eloquently of freakish talent than freakish build. Later, of

269

course, the image changed. The features became more cadaverous. There came, too, the obsession with preparation - the yards of Elastoplast - and the conception that here was an athlete tied together with bandages. It was a perception he did not discourage. I remember an annual Rugby League sports day at Fallowfield. The sprint handicap race was about to start but the scratch man was missing. Heads were swivelling round looking for Brian who emerged from a friend's car in the middle of the arena. He wore a striped primrose and blue jersey, rugby shorts and stockings. In this totally unsuitable attire he joined the athletic-vested, brief-shorted sprinters on the track. Was he taking the mickey? I wish I had kept the programme. The handicaps would make interesting reading. Memory tells me that Brian was off scratch with Johnny Rock (a Powderhall man) and certainly he was giving starts to Terry O'Grady and Alan Davies, my playing colleagues.

Bev's sprinting style was all wrong. His head went up, if not back. His legs went all over the place. His arm action was across the body. Yet he covered the ground quicker than anyone else. I remembered the words of Geoff Dyson, the greatest coach I ever met, when I took the AAA's sprint-coaching award. There are only two fundamentals in sprinting - stride length and repetition rate. The latter of these is congenital and Brian Bevan - that taut bundle of nervous energy - was blessed with a particularly high rate.

Stories? Is it really true that Brian holidayed once at Butlins? That he entered the sprint handicap and the Redcoat gave this old man 20 yards start? That Brian then won by 50 yards?

Did the race against the motor-bike really happen? The story has it that an argument about acceleration arose in Harry Bath's pub, The Britannia. At first it was between the cheetah and somebody's claim that the human being was the fastest accelerating animal. Then it became man against machine. The upshot was that a match was arranged with Bev being given 30 yards start by the bike. Hundreds of people turned up at Arpley to watch the event. It was a total anti-climax. The gun goes - Bev is across the finishing line looking back at a motorbike roaring after him, but 50 yards behind.

I remember a hat-trick by Bev against Bradford Northern in their pomp - Ward, Kitching, Edwards, Davies, Foster et al. I'll swear that the first two were from his own in-goal area and the last from a five-yard scrum near the Warrington line. Harold Palin went blind and freed Bev on the touchline. Brian went as straight as a die up field, but Ernest Ward, near the centre, had spotted the danger. He turned and corner-flagged. Ernest had about 60 yards to travel, Brian about 90. As Ernest dived for Bevan, Bev dived over the line. I can see now in my mind's eye Ernest regaining his feet, turning towards Dai Rees on the bench, arms outstretched, palms uppermost and an expression that screamed, "What do you do? How do you stop him?"

Again - against Workington Town at Wilderspool. Bev tearing for the corner. Gus Risman, as sound a tackler as he was a brilliant attacker, had it all weighed up. Bev could have the outside and Gus would bury him into touch. Gus launched into the tackle but 'whoosh'. Bev had gone. There remained the sight of Gus sitting on a touch-side heap of straw clapping his hands and hailing pure genius.

When I was at Oldham, Bob Byrne was the fastest man on the books - Terry O'Grady had not then matured. However, Bob was never a regular choice so he was somewhat surprised when Stan Smith, the coach, told him he was playing at Wilderspool. "You're the fastest we've got, Bob, so you're playing. All you've got to do is stop Bevan. He's good, so watch him." Well, I think Brian scored five and Stan was moved to say, "Now, Bob, I told you to watch him." "Aye, I did", said Bob. "Isn't he a good 'un? They should handicap yon man. Make him carry a bucket of sand in each hand and catch the ball in his gob!"

In 1954, before Warrington met Halifax at Wembley and Odsal, when the Wire played away at Oldham. Oldham were a great side and were winning with minutes to go. They did not need to score but created an overlap. Roland Barrow and Terry O'Grady versus Bev - a certain try. Bev back-pedalled still facing the ball, neither committing himself to the tackle nor completely leaving the wingman. Roland was then a promising youngster. He knew there was a try on but also knew he could not go himself. In some panic he passed the ball. Instantly Bev stopped retreating. He fastened on to that ball like an osprey on a fish and was gone. Twenty thousand or so spectators felt sorry for Bernard Ganley, the Oldham full-back, as he prepared on the halfway line to stop Brian Bevan in a clear field. He hadn't a prayer and Bev had pulled another game out of the bag.

I was in the bar with Gerry Helme after this game when a spectator broached the often-asked question: "Does Bevan get paid more than the rest of you?" Gerry, an international scrum-half and a highly respected performer, replied, "I don't know what they pay him and I don't care. He's got me winning pay many a time when without him we'd have been licked."

This question of Bevan's remuneration cropped up often. In those innocent days, it was held that differential rates of pay destroyed team spirit. What if the star has an off day and some unconsidered youngster wins the match? I feel sure there was some arrangement between the club and Bevan but what is certain is that he never derived from the game the financial rewards his talents and drawing power merited. It is almost impossible to compute what his value would be in today's Sky TV-boosted economy. I remember discussing this with others in Harry Bath's pub. Harry did quite well in the traditional player's role of mine host. His advice to Brian was succinct and Antipodean. "You should take a piss-hole at Bridge Foot. They'd pay a tanner a piss to see you."

Whilst Bevan had no great reputation as a defender - indeed it was held that he couldn't tackle - not many tries were scored by the opposition on his wing. Like Martin Offiah, Brian could, without making a tackle, mess up the opposition so that a two or three-man overlap did not necessarily mean a try. Pace and a fine disregard of that shibboleth 'always take the man with the ball' saved many a tricky situation.

Seeking for cracks in the great man's armour, I once asked an old supporter, whom I knew had followed the Wire for 60 years, how did Bevan compare with Jack Fish? Fish kicked better, was the reply. When Jack Fish kicked he was under the ball when it came down. Bevan just wants the ball belted into space because he knows he'll be first to it. This I knew to be true. How often we saw him waving frantically for the ball to be kicked into an empty field. How many tries would he score today with this gambit, when modern full-backs lie up with the three-quarters? How many tries did he have disallowed for offside simply because the referee couldn't believe that any human being could get to the ball so quickly from an onside position? This certainly happened memorably during at Maine Road on the official's own admission. When Bev played at Blackpool he once told me that he could extend his career by playing at full-back. Just think of all that space to counter-attack when they kicked to him. He never did play full-back though.

I played opposite Bev once - as a right wingman myself I was usually up against that other, very different but marvellous side-stepper Albert Johnson. This time I was on the left wing. I had determined to shadow Bev wherever he went so when Dave Cotton won a scrum, as he mostly did, and Brian sidled midfield behind his three-quarter line, I did the same behind mine. "Go on, son", I thought as Bev moved to the middle. "You're only going into trouble." Just then they gave him the ball. The head went back. The neck muscles started to yammer and, 'whoosh,' he was through a gap, past me like a streak of lightning and heading for the posts before anyone could think.

I always said that he was the fastest, with ball in hand, that I have ever seen. Just one incident made me wonder if I had seen a faster man. It was Wakefield Trinity versus Hull, an overlap on Trinity's wing and a try on for Berwyn Jones. But Clive Sullivan intercepted. Jones had to stop and turn around. He pursued and caught Sullivan. Impossible! From a standing start he had given Clive Sullivan a twenty yards flying start and caught him. Had I, I wondered, seen the fastest wingman of all time?

All Bevan needed was the ball and space and he went to unprecedented lengths to secure this. More than once in his early days I saw him receive the ball in a seemingly impossible situation, even for him - ringed by opponents bent on smothering him. He had then turned and ran towards his own line like someone who had taken leave of his senses. Being so much the faster, he had opened a 20 to 30-yards gap. Then he stopped, turned again, surveyed the field and clearly said to himself: "Right. Now I have got space. Here we go!" And go he would. Bump, bump, bump. Off one foot, then the other. A trail of would-be tacklers on the ground, the ball under the sticks or by the far corner flag with seemingly 13 prone bodies littering the field behind him. Animated cartoon stuff.

Bev seldom ran down the in-goal area to place the ball behind the posts. As soon as he crossed the white line he snapped the ball down. It was as if he thought: "If you can't convert from there, let's get the game restarted and I'll score another."

The sight of him returning after scoring, shoulders hunched, chest heaving, coughing and spluttering, was so much more striking because he had generally left his team-mates so far in his wake that it took him 50 yards or so before he could receive their plaudits and backslaps.

It is not generally known that American Football was played at Wilderspool more than 50 years ago. I remember a Thanksgiving Day match between Burtonwood Bearcats and Wolverhampton Wolverines. So when the Wire restarted after the Second World War a few hundred Yanks from Burtonwood used to attend. They stood out in a khaki bunch in those neat, smooth-clothed uniforms that made their privates look like our colonels. One day, I decided to find out how Rugby League stood in their estimation vis-a vis Gridiron. I got no answer to my question. To a man the group I addressed was transfixed. Their glazed eyes looked into the middle distance and the only words they could utter were, "Bevan. That man, Bevan!"

Bevan was a pressman's dream and I still recall two of the headlines - 'All this and Bevan too' and 'Bevan, Glorious Bevan'.

I can't claim to have known Brian well as a man - few did. He was difficult to get to know but honest and reliable when you did. On Saturday nights, after our various matches around the north of England, players from the Warrington region used to meet up in Harry Bath's pub. More than once I found Brian on his own bemoaning the lack of team spirit because his own mates had left early. Whose fault it was, if anybody's, I could not say. Anyway, I would find myself driving Brian back home to Winwick. He did not have a car then. When I was coach at Rochdale I was asked to invite a celebrity to address a youth club - Cyril Smith, not then an MP, was to be present. I approached Brian and got an instant acceptance. We drove over in my first post-war car, an unheated Ford Popular, along a mist enshrouded East Lancs Road. Brian was superb. No thought of appearance money - a thoroughly uncomfortable journey, a long low-key event. Brian was just as helpful as could be in an unobtrusive manner - no publicity and no kudos.

I was once asked to appear at the Parr Hall, Warrington for some beneficiary. Bev, Alf Ellaby and other great players attended and I took the opportunity to ask Alf how Brian compared with himself and others. He replied, "Joe, if they talk about me in the same breath as this fellow, I shall be honoured." Even given the modesty which is generally part of the make-up of the stars of Rugby League, this is a generous tribute. It was well earned.

Supporters and club officials

John Blacklock

I am only in my 40s and obviously did not see too much of Bevan but I have always been fascinated by the legends about him. It's funny, but people in Wigan always talk about Boston and St Helens folk go on about van Vollenhoven and both of them constantly argue the toss about who was the better winger. None of them ever talk about Bevan though.

There is a tale about a player who worked at a Leigh colliery who was a winger with a professional club. One day some of the lads were talking about great wingers and they said to this Leigh collier, "Come on. You have played against Bevan, Boston and van Vollenhoven. Who was the best?" The collier studied it for a while and replied, "Well, Billy was the strongest, Voll was the fastest and Bevan was the most elusive." "Yeah, but who was the best?" they asked again. The collier studied it for a while again and said, "Well, Bevan was the best really. He was so good that whenever he got the ball the crowd expected so much of him that they all drew in their breath together and went 'Whoo'. It was as if all the air on the pitch suddenly disappeared and the players went light-headed and saw stars, as you do when you are starved of oxygen. Nobody could stop Bev under those circumstances."

M. Darbyshire

I remember as a young man in 1946 attending Bank Quay Station along with other Wire supporters and secretary-manager Chris Brockbank to see the arrival of a slim-built Australian sailor. Of course, I am talking about Brian Bevan. I thought at the time how shy and lost he looked. Little did I know that he would turn out to be the greatest winger I would ever see in rugby league.

He scored some fantastic tries like the famous ones against Wigan in the Wardonia Cup and in the 1954 Challenge Cup at Oldham. Another was in a second leg, first round Challenge Cup-tie at Workington in 1948 when Wire won 7-0. He took the ball 25 yards from the Warrington line and set off on a 75-yard run to score the only try of the match with Fred Worrall, our trainer, running along the touch-line with him! Fred had been a soccer winger for Portsmouth.

Although I was not a close friend of Brian, I did meet him in various locations in the town. I have always believed that Brian was a man of two personalities - one on a rugby pitch and another off it. At one time he was an insurance salesman. Once on a visit to Cec Mountford's home, when Cec was the Warrington coach, I met Brian trying to sell him some insurance! Even in business he came over as a very shy man who did not function comfortably in company. All the time he was at Cec's house he was very nervous and seemed glad to say his goodbyes.

Chris Brockbank told me that he always awaited a knock on his office door prior to home games. Brian would come in with his brown paper bags containing his

273

bandages and plasters and bring some moan or groan to Chris. My view, and Chris's too, was that it was a way of relieving his tension before a game.

Once Brian told me that although he had played against some of the best wingers ever such as Boston, van Vollenhoven, Bruce Ryan, Peter Henderson and Brian Nordgren and even raced against a racehorse, there was one player he found it hard to score against. That was Nebby Cleworth of Leigh. Nebby stuck to Brian like shoelaces. Brian did tell me jokingly that he considered asking Nebby to go to the toilet with him just so Nebby would not miss him.

Geoff Dawber

I have been a Wigan supporter for 40 years now. My grandfather started taking me to matches when I was seven. You can tell how keen on the game he was because when Wigan were somewhere we couldn't get to, we would go to watch Leigh because their fixtures were arranged not to clash with Wigan's.

Anyway, I remember as a little lad going to Central Park to see Wigan play Warrington. I vividly recall that Bevan wore white-soled boots for some reason, something I had never seen before. Well, I looked at Bevan on Warrington's wing and said to my grandfather, "look at that old man. He can't be playing."

Granddad roared laughing and then just remarked: "When you have watched Rugby League a bit longer, tell me what you think then!" I soon learnt that Bevan was like greased lightning even though he appeared all skin and bone. In fact he was just about the opposite in appearance of any super athlete.

My wife's uncle is Martin Ryan, the great Wigan full-back of the 1940s. He says that when Bevan scored that famous fantastic long-distance try against Wigan in the Wardonia Cup, he only ran so far because he was scared of being hit by him [Ryan]. He's always telling that tale.

Keith Gilbert

Brian Bevan and I have a couple of things in common. Firstly, we had the same birthday. He was born on 24 June 1924 and I was born exactly 10 years later. Then in 1991 we were both in hospital with cancer. He died and I survived.

I particularly remember two tries he scored, of all the hundreds I saw. The first came in a Lancashire Cup-tie against Barrow at Wilderspool around 1948. Bev got away on his own '25'. The Barrow fullback was Joe Jones, who was an international player. Bev flew straight down the wing, sticking to the touchline. You could see that Jones seemed to have the situation weighed up and was judging his run to hit Bev, whom he thought was going at full pelt, ball and all, into touch. He obviously thought he was timing his dive to perfection. What he certainly didn't know was that Bev was not actually going at top speed. When Jones dived, Bev revved up, and Jones went flying behind him and crashed straight into the concrete wall. They had to take him off with a dislocated shoulder.

Then there was the time Wire played St Helens not long after van Vollenhoven started playing. He was the new wonder winger and Bev was getting on a bit by then. Anyhow, Bev gets away down the touchline and the Saints full-back does all the right things in trying to hem him into a channel down the line so that he will be able to take him into touch. Van Vollenhoven is covering across from the other wing, making sure he is in position to nail Bevan if he turns infield. Bev eventually does flash in field and van Vollenhoven clamps his arms around where Bevan is supposed to be; only he ends up clutching fresh air. Somehow Bevan dematerialises and van Vollenhoven looks over his shoulder to see Brian touching down in the distance. Even seeing that try with my own eyes, I can't work out how Bevan did it. It seemed impossible. I remember van Vollenhoven walking back and shaking his head as if to say: "How the hell did he do that?" The old man had shown them all again. Saints still won 19-16 though.

He had an amazing ability to beat opponents when he didn't actually appear to do anything. So many times he got the ball and beat two, three, four or five men without any of them laying a finger on him. God knows how he did it. I certainly couldn't tell.

He always looked after himself. He would not have lasted as long as did if he had not. He wasn't one to waste energy unnecessarily. He was quick to size up any situation and he would simply walk into touch if he saw no percentage in going further, even if he had already beaten a few players. It's funny but sometimes you could see the team used to go out and play one game and Bev went out and played his own game.

He was a picture when he got going - knees up, head back. People went to games just to see him. I remember a game at the Athletic Grounds in Rochdale. Bevan scored a beauty right at the beginning and this Hornets chap turned to his mates and said: "Right, I can go home now." He knew he would not see anything better.

Bevan was not much of a tackler. Well, that's not what he was there for. He did get sent off once though at Widnes. A ball went loose and a Widnes man went down on it and I suppose that Bev had to be seen to do something about making sure that the man should be held down so that the play-the-ball was delayed for a bit. So he slid down onto the man with his knees first. There was nothing to it, of course, but he got marched.

Years after he finished playing I crossed his path in Bridge Street in Warrington. I know that he was supposed to be a very private person, but somehow our eyes met and he nodded and acknowledged me, even though I had never met him before. It surprised me, I must admit.

Jim Graves

I was fortunate enough to see Bevan at his best, if only occasionally. It was Bevan who scored the most remarkable try I have ever seen. I was 17 or 18 at the time and the try was scored about 1948 at Barrow. I was living in West Cumberland then.

Warrington were in possession on their own line. The ball was passed out to Bevan on the right wing. Bevan cross-kicked, the ball landing 15 yards or so behind the Barrow back-line just outside the Wire '25' and 10 or 12 yards infield. It was a towering kick. The ball bounced capriciously. Both sets of players seemed nonplussed.

Bevan followed his kick across the field, initially not at full pace, weaving through the Barrow players. Bevan may have hoped that his teammates would have followed up but they did not. Realising that the bouncing ball was not being collected by Barrow, he accelerated. He had a lightning brain and his speed matched it in every way. At the third or maybe the fourth bounce he zoomed in and collected the ball without even fractionally slackening pace. Seconds later he was under the posts. He dabbed the ball down for the try, tucked it under his arm and trotted back as though nothing unusual had happened.

No one had attempted to tackle or even pursue him. As he returned with the ball most of the players were still in the Warrington '25'!

The crowd's reaction was one of stupefied silence. No one cheered, I can assure you. After about a minute a Barrow supporter turned to me and muttered unbelievingly, "Bluddy 'ell. Bluddy 'ell."

Ray Hewson

I saw Bevan on several occasions, not the least of which was the 1954 Wembley final in which he produced an amazing run. I also saw him score one of his famous diagonal, corner-to-corner tries at Craven Park, Barrow. Your heart was in your mouth every time the ball went near him, both in anticipation of what you might be about to witness and also in fear that he was going to score against your team.

The best try I saw him score was at Craven Park in the 1950s. Bevan was hemmed in, 25 yards from the Barrow line, on the touchline, and would obviously be forced to run dead straight at the Barrow full-back. Thus there was no danger whatsoever of him scoring. Oh, yeah?

Well, he did run in a straight line - like a bullet from a gun. Yes, he did run, or rather was forced to run by the Barrow cover defence, right at the Barrow full-back.

You could see the glint in the full-back's eyes and the thought running through his mind: "Come to me, old man." He would clatter Bevan into touch at the corner flag. We all thought he would too.

But I tell you, when about six inches separated them and the full-back's arms were wide open, Bevan put in one of those enormous side-steps and the full-back never laid a finger on him as he went under the posts. He was left looking like a statue, fixed to the spot and bewildered, as many others were before and since, as to why he had only grasped thin air.

Homer Genn, *Rugby Leaguer*, 27 February 1954

Bevan's arrival at Warrington was unheralded, unsung. No headlines, he was just another youngster anxious to make good, with the Warrington club offering him the chance to do so. In contrast to the ballyhoo generally associated with the arrival of a new expensive signing, this young Aussie found himself among strangers in a strange land, and about as far away from home as it is possible to get. He was quartered in digs in a back street of a compact Lancashire industrial town with an English winter ahead. He had during his leisure hours much time for reflection. Lonely he must have been and homesick for the warmth and comfort of his own town of Bondi and its famous beach.

He soon became the idol of the local fans, feted and fussed on all fronts. This hospitality, often misguided, became bewildering and overpowering and in a desperate effort to avoid it all he took refuge in another town. He had a tough time that winter and, no doubt, many times may have wished that he had never taken the plunge into rugby league football...

Kindly people, including officials of the club, offered help, advice and encouragement and eventually he was found a comfortable and congenial home. It was about this time that I made his acquaintance. In the home where I lived there was Junior, a true and loyal Bevan fan. His sole desire being to have a chat with the local idol. After many disappointments he came dashing in after attending the weekly practice. I've spoken to him, he said in high glee. His mother, a dear, kindly soul answered, Bring him along to see us and the great day arrived. Junior proudly introduced Bev to the family.

Soon that austerity meal of egg and chips was served and the wizard winger seemed quite at home. It soon became noticeable that he was very shy. Not that he had any inferiority complex - he was still a stranger amongst strange folk. He was given an open invitation to come along any time and then it happened. He came to tea one day and was ushered into another room where he spotted a piano. Rubbing his hands joyously, he asked, who plays? Do you? Came the answer. Kind of, he replied shyly.

I never saw such a difference in anyone. From the moment he sat down at that piano he was a changed person. He was not a musician in a technical sense, but his manipulation of the keys was remarkable. His fingers flitted and flew across the keyboard with the same fleetness as his toes did along the touchlines. He was best as a duettist. In my limited capacity as a pianist I played on the left wing, whilst Bev would engage in all sorts of unorthodox movements with ever increasing tempo on the right, finishing in a flourishing crescendo and bringing one finger down plunk on a top note with the same emphasis as he does when grounding the ball over the try line.

Thrilled with the effort, he would sit up straight; throw back his head and laugh, usually saying Wow! Yes, the piano made all the difference. He dropped in at all hours with a blunt Hello, just a tinkle on the old Joanna! Do you mind? And away he'd go again. He called once in a serious frame of mind and enquired of my host Tom, How about running me out to Cheshire? There's a bloke got a piano for sale. OK, said Tom, and away they went. The story they told me on their return was too funny for words. Between them they tried to describe their experiences but one had to guess at the details because both were overcome with laughter.

I don't suppose Bev ever laughed so much and so continuously before or since. They saw three pianos. The first at a cafe - draped with faded satin at the front and with one of the candlesticks missing. Middle G failed to respond. The two top octaves consisted of the same cracked note only, several keys were broken and the pedals squawked but did not function and the other two pianos were in an even more dilapidated condition.

The most laughable part of the story is - Tom, a haulage contractor, undertook at each of the interviews, to accept Bev's instructions as to when the instruments should be transported, etc.

We saw much of Bevan in the summer of 1947. He was taken many times by car around the Cheshire countryside and on one occasion he seemed anxious to get back to the town. He had a date... He had found a girl, whom we had the pleasure of meeting later... the future Mrs Bevan. We attended the wedding at the quaint old Cheshire town of Grappenhall... I hope and trust that he may never be far removed from a piano. His masterpiece - *Chopsticks with Junior*.

Eric Lafferty

Although I did not start to watch the Wires until 1953, when I was 11, my memories of Brian are boundless. Although I did not know him personally he is like a member of my family whom I lost a long time ago. Even now he keeps coming up in my conversations almost daily. Funnily enough, there seem to be an awful lot of people just like me who do not tire of talking and reminiscing about him. Here are just a few memories.

We were playing Widnes at Naughton Park in the traditional Good Friday match when Bev was getting toward the end of his career. Bev was not a favourite son of the more partisan Widnesians. He had punished them too much in the past.

On this particular day three especially biased Widnes women started berating him as he took his place on the 25-yard line, referring to his physical appearance and baldness and the fact that he was past it. However, Bev had the last laugh because he scooted in for four tries. The last glorious effort saw him beat four men on the way.

Another memory from about 1958-59 was when Swinton had a great team. Warrington were playing at Station Road and losing 15-0 at half time. In the second half Bev scored three blinders. Even though we lost 22-18 it did not seem to matter. We had seen Bev score another great hat trick.

277

In 1966, four years after Bev had been finished at Wilderspool, there was a darts match to raise funds for the Jackie Edwards testimonial held at Ashton Hall, Warrington. This was played between four local leagues and there were about 250 in attendance. Brian came along to present the prizes. When he came on the stage they started to clap and I am not exaggerating when I say they applauded him for what seemed to be 10 minutes. He was truly loved in Warrington, and why not? He had given more pleasure to thousands of Warringtonians than anyone in the town's history.

I am just glad that Brian does not play for us now. I am glad he played for us when he did. It would have broken our hearts if he was playing in this era, because we would probably sell him to Wigan to balance the books. As it is, nobody can take him away from us. He was our Bev. There will never be anyone remotely like him again.

Kevin Maguire

My lasting memories of Brian Bevan stem from late 1953 to early 1954. That's when I was doing my square bashing on National Service in the RAF at Padgate. Saturday afternoons were a boon. I could visit Wilderspool. Money was short but a trip to watch Warrington play was only 1/6d (7.5 pence). It was certainly the cheapest entertainment around. I persuaded some of my pals to go to the game, people who had never been to watch rugby league. Anyway, the great man entered the field of play and my pals laughed. There was this strange-looking man with a bald head, thin as a rake and with his legs covered in bandages. They thought I could not be serious but 80 minutes later they were gob smacked - fact. Brian Bevan had scored tries that no normal rugby league player could dream about. I wouldn't mind but I contracted tonsillitis at Padgate and for several weeks was not allowed out. Meanwhile my disbelieving mates could not be kept away from Wilderspool. They went just to watch the man who was pure magic.

Bernard Mahoney

The great Jim Ledgard, the Dewsbury, Leigh and Great Britain full-back, was once interviewed on the box by Eddie Waring. When asked what was the worst thing that could ever happen to a Rugby League player during his career, Jim replied: a crippling injury to end one's career; to be suspended sine die, never to play again; and to face Bev on your own '25' line, the last line of defence, and to know that he is going to pass you whatever you do.

There was the tale told of Bev when he had a hairdressing business. An old fellow had just had his hair cut by Bev and as he was going out, he said to Bev, "You might be best bloody winger in the business but you are a bloody awful barber!"

Then there was an occasion when Albert Pimblett used Bev as a foil to score three tries. Bevan, who loved scoring, was furious, objecting that he should have had those tries. They say Bev didn't speak to Pimblett for a month. But I'll tell you what, Albert said if he had played centre to Bev for another three seasons, he [Pimblett] would have been immortalised.

They go on about Bev's lack of physique but some who know say he had a tremendously strong back. They say that from behind he looked like a professional boxer.

Tom Mitchell: One eccentric on another

"Bevan - the wonder man... and my best ever wing three-quarter... He was threat number one when we [Workington] played against the Wires. He had a phenomenal physique, quite contrary to his general appearance in civvies. With his bandaged legs,

278

his strapped shoulders, he looked more of a scarecrow or Egyptian Mummy than anything else. All skin and bone? I soon changed my opinion in the Other Nationalities' dressing room prior to a game against France. Brian was not short of muscle and his natural breast plates looked more like armour to me... That side-step, that nod, that unbelievable swiftness, that penetration through the ranks of his would-be tacklers - all put together was bewildering, pure magic."
From: *The Memoirs and Sporting Life of Tom Mitchell*, his autobiography, 1998

Clarrie Owen

I have been connected with Warrington rugby league since 1932 in a number of capacities, from being a fund-raiser to the club president. I got to know Brian Bevan quite well. In his early days Bev used to spend time in Fletcher Russell's Recreation Club in Priory Street near the ground. He was courting Doreen Allison, the daughter of a local estate agent. My wife and I, together with Harold Palin, Bob Ryan and Gerry Helme and their wives, would all be in the same room with Bev and Doreen but they would be quietly in a corner. He was always a bit of a loner, very quiet, but he was a nice chap.

There were times though when he did come out of himself. I remember a time when Dave Cotton scored about the only try he ever scored for Wire. It was against Huddersfield, in a big game. Bev took a kick deep in his own half and ran through most of the Huddersfield team. Dave Cotton had been injured way down in the other half, and when Bev got near the posts, he passed to Dave, who had been put on-side and he touched down. Everybody was thrilled to see Dave score at last. In the evening there was a do and all the team went to the concert room for a Lancashire hot-pot. Owen Bevan was there and the two of them played together at the piano and let rip singing Aussie ditties into the microphone.

I remember Bev's debut for the 'A' team in 1945. After about an hour our half-back Mel De Lloyd cross-kicked from the '25' to the corner and Brian was on to the ball in a flash to touch down. The referee couldn't believe anyone could have got there so quickly and disallowed the try for offside. That happened a lot to Bev.

When he went down to Devonport to rejoin his ship after that game he had an accident. There was a blow-back in one of the boilers he was stoking. All his arms were burnt. But it did not stop him from making his first team debut against Oldham though. He looked like a mummy in the dressing room that afternoon. His arms were bandaged from top to bottom, as well as the usual bits he used to cover.

He scored so many memorable tries. One I remember particularly was at Workington in a Challenge Cup-tie. It was always hard to win in Cumberland in those days and I think we won by the only try of the game. Workington were attacking in our '25'. Gus Risman came into the line from full-back and looked a certain scorer when Bev nipped in and intercepted. Away he went, nearly the length of the field for the winning score, but what I remember most clearly was the fact that Freddie Worrall, our trainer, who used to play soccer for Portsmouth, ran most of the way along the touch-line yelling to Bev that no one was near him and to touch down nearer the posts.

Sometimes Bev would play to the crowd. I remember when Harry Bath made his debut in an evening game against Featherstone. The ball was going out to Albert Johnson's wing all the time and I think he had scored about three tries while Bev had hardly touched the ball. Eventually the ball went Bev's way, but ended up in touch. At the same time a player was injured so Bev decided to sit on the ball over the touch-line, practically in the crowd. It looked as if he was trying to say that for all the ball he was getting he might as well not be on the pitch. It was comical.

He did depend on Jackie Hamblett a lot, but so did most of the players. They all thought the world of Jackie. To Brian, Jackie was a bit like a father-confessor. Psychologically Jackie knew just how Brian needed to be treated. He was an expert at recognising players' idiosyncrasies. He made sure everything was just how Brian wanted it.

Colin Perkin

I have watched Warrington since 1951 and must have seen Bevan play hundreds of times. I particularly remember a game at Wigan in the mid-1950s. Warrington always went to Central Park on New Year's Day at that time. On this particular occasion there was a tremendous buzz when the announcer relayed the team line-ups. Wigan had moved Billy Boston to number five, which meant that he would be in direct opposition to Bevan. Billy had only been playing for about two seasons and was the latest sensation. Quite early on Ted White, the Wire second-rower, broke through and kicked to the corner for Bevan to chase. Bev was away in a flash with a 10 yards start on Billy. Just as Bev got to the ball it bounced straight up into the air and Bev had to stop and wait for it to come down. In the meantime Billy arrived at full pelt and crashed Bev to the ground as he got the ball. I remember 30,000 Wiganers going bananas. Of course, Bev would have scored if the ball had behaved. Both Billy and Bev scored later in the game which Wire won 14-6.

One of Bevan's most important tries was the one he scored in the Cup-tie at Oldham in 1954, a fantastic interception. Earlier that same year he scored another belter from an interception. He had scored a couple at Wigan on New Year's Day when Wire just won 17-12. The following day we went to St. Helens with a really weakened team. The only try of the match came from Bev's interception when he went 60 or 70 yards to score. We won 7-2 and were the only team to win at Saints that season. We finished second in the League and Saints were third. It would have been the other way round if Bevan had missed that interception and we may never have won the treble in 1953-54.

I also remember another crucial try he scored in the Championship final at Maine Road in 1955 against Oldham. It was an awful day and the game was played on a mud heap. Bevan was trying to get over at the Kop End but was being held by Frank Stirrup. However, two Oldham forwards rushed up to help but the force of their challenge sent Bevan and Stirrup slithering over the line for Bev to touch down and Warrington won the game 7-3 and the Championship with it.

Around 1960, I remember an unusual sight. We were playing at Salford and Bevan got clear away twice with about 60 yards to the line. Both times he was comfortably caught by Wally McArthur, Salford's Aborigine winger. Mind you, Bev was about 36 by that time and McArthur could certainly shift.

Bev was different to any other winger; there is no doubt about that. My grandfather, who had been following Warrington even before they moved to Wilderspool, reckoned Jackie Fish might have been better than Bev but I doubt it. Bev would run twice round the gasworks if it meant a score. His handling was superb. I can hardly remember him dropping the ball. His technique in catching the ball was possibly unique. When someone threw a long pass to him he went to meet the ball and was actually side-stepping as he got it. He generally took it one-handed and then pulled it into his chest.

Anthony Quinn

I live in Widnes, but I have always been fascinated by Brian Bevan. In fact I am so interested that I have read all the match reports of Warrington's games between 1946 and 1962 on the microfilmed newspapers at Warrington Library and really enjoyed it.

One chap wrote into Jack Steel, the Wire reporter, saying that although he came from St Helens he watched all the games at Wilderspool just to see what Bevan would do. He reckoned watching Bevan would cure the flu. As far back as about 1959 there was a group of fans who were advocating putting up a statue to Bev, and he wasn't even retired then. They also suggested that Warrington should officially name one end of the ground The Brian Bevan End. That really shows how highly they rated him.

I remember my uncle Billy, who was a Widnes supporter, telling me that one game at Naughton Park saw Bevan having a very bad first half. He couldn't do anything right and the Widnes fans were really giving him some stick. In the second half he scored four tries, which quietened them down. Bev just shrugged his shoulders as much as to say, what do you reckon now?

Eddie Smith

I don't go to Rugby League any more. It's not the same game as it was. I did watch Warrington for all the years that Bevan played though. Rugby League and singing were my passions. Now it's just singing. Brian Bevan mesmerised us from the start. I remember a game against Bradford Northern, who were a great team then. They had Ernest Ward and, on the wing opposite Bevan, Alan Edwards. Bev got a ball about 75 yards out and began to run towards Ward and Edwards. He ended up scoring under the posts and I am sure that they never saw where he went to get there. Fabulous. Mind you, half the time I don't think Bevan knew where he was going himself.

There was another time at Leeds who used to lick us quite a lot. Their fans were catcalling and asking who the hell was that old man on the wing? You know, getting us going. Well, Bev scored two fantastic tries and to their credit they stood and applauded him all the way back both times.

Bevan was a very quiet, unassuming bloke. Once I was down at Fletcher Russells and someone said, "Come and look at this." I went into their concert room, which was empty except for Brian who was playing the piano with about four pints waiting for him on a little table at his side. He had been there playing for hours apparently.

One of my most prized possessions was an autograph of Brian Bevan. It was with some other great Wire players' signatures - Naughton, Pimblett, Knowelden and some more. I was talking to a young chap who was interested in Bevan and I gave it to him. I thought that when I've gone that young fellow will treasure it.

Peter Smith

I am 78 years old now and I have watched rugby league all my life. As a young man I remember standing behind the railings at Featherstone for a game against Warrington. As the teams came onto the field Brian Bevan passed within touching distance of me. I was with an avid rugby league man called Dick Maycock, who is now dead. As Bevan passed by Dick remarked, He has more bloody bandages on than a Ponte Hoss.

Ponte Hosses were horses that were ready for the knackers yard. They used to enter them at Pontefract Races in Sellers' Handicaps to raise a bob or two. All of these horses had had at some time ligament or tendon trouble and to cure them the vets used to fire them. In other words they welded the tendons together with hot irons to enable them to run. To cover up the torched legs they were swathed in bandages and that method is still in use today. That's why Dick likened Bevan to a Ponte Hoss.

281

Bevan looked like an alien from outer space to me with that bald, domed head. Anyway, he scored three tries that day. Dick remarked: "He must be on bloody springs." He changed from being an alien to a phenomenon and brought the house down. Dick and I shook his hand that day and I did not wash my hands for a month.

Later I remember Warrington were playing Cas at Wheldon Road. My Cas mates said, "He'll not score three at Cas." Well, he did and Cas were so busy marking him that Jim Challinor scored another three on the other wing. I feel privileged to have met this superior gentleman, Brian Bevan.

Roy Smith

I was privileged to be a spectator at Wilderspool Stadium from the start to the end of Bevan's career. He monopolised my sporting interest as a boy and teenager. Trying to remember incidents, tries, and so on, is neither difficult nor easy. I saw so many brilliant tries, many unbelievable, that they seem to have coalesced into a collective memory - they were expected to occur and they did. I have therefore chosen a few examples where it was the ambience, the atmosphere or the situation, which evokes specific memories...

Two international fullbacks and a spot on Wilderspool Stadium

On Easter Monday, 1954 Warrington were playing Leigh at Wilderspool. I was standing on the Kop with Warrington playing towards me. Warrington had possession on their left just inside their own half. The ball was passed towards Bevan's wing. He received the ball on the halfway line, swerved past his immediate marker and was into the open. Ledgard, Leigh's test full-back, moved into position. Bevan could have hared for the corner but he didn't. Instead he headed at top speed straight for Ledgard, now on the '25'. Bevan went right up to the full-back, almost running into him. Then he employed that superb side-step and left Ledgard grasping air, knees on the floor. Bevan placed the ball under the posts.

Twelve days later Warrington were at home to St Helens in the Championship semi-final. A close encounter ensued. I recall Warrington having possession again just inside their own half on the left. Stan McCormick moved play toward Bevan's wing. On receiving the ball Bevan again beat the close defence and raced into open space. Again he elected to go straight to the full-back, the Welsh international, Glyn Moses. It struck me immediately that Moses was positioned on the same spot that Ledgard had been 12 days before... and again Bevan repeated almost exactly the procedure, which had destroyed Ledgard. Warrington won the match 11-0. It was a wonderful coincidence and it will always be etched in my memory.

Mud larks, except...

This incident was related to me by my brother, Roger. He was standing on the halfway line at Wilderspool for a game against Rochdale Hornets on 4 December 1954. Warrington were champions again that season but what a scare lowly Rochdale gave the Wire that murky winter afternoon.

Hornets were in front for nearly all the game until Bevan, who hardly touched the ball, scored two sensational tries, both 70 or 80-yard specials. What added to Roger's memory of the game was his observation that due to a quagmire of a pitch, nearly every player was unrecognisable by the final whistle - but not Brian Bevan. Bev lurched off the field as clean as he lurched on to it and yet he won his team the game, which ended Warrington 8 Hornets 7.

Many a nickname

Brian Bevan had many nicknames - the 'Wizard of Oz', the 'Skeleton in Football Boots' and a lot more. One occasion I recall fitted one of his nicknames perfectly.

It was a typical December day; three days before Christmas 1956 and Warrington were at home to Oldham. Oldham were the best team in the league that season, going on to win the Championship.

A superb, close game was in progress as I watched from the clock end of Wilderspool. The weather, though, was dismal with mist, almost fog, reducing my view of the play to Warrington's half of the field. Suddenly a roar went up and I could just make out a white bobbing figure looming out of the murk on the halfway line. I saw the Oldham defence, five or six players, dashing to block the figure's progress. Now I could just make out Bevan, who suddenly switched from the touch-line and went at top speed, swerving, side-stepping in and out of the Oldham players - and in an instant he was placing the ball in front of me under the posts.

Bevan emerging from the mist - white, gaunt - was almost an apparition as he ghosted toward a magnificent match-winning try. How apt was the nickname... The Galloping Ghost!

A Springbok's introduction to Bevan

Warrington were playing St Helens in the Lancashire Cup Final at Wigan on 31 October 1959. I remember reading a preview of the game in a national daily, perhaps the *Daily Mail*, on the morning of the match. Jan Prinsloo, the Saints left winger, who was to mark Brian Bevan for the first time, was reported as saying that he had heard a lot about Bevan but was rather dismissive of him.

Later that afternoon I was standing near the halfway line in a packed crowd near the wall. St Helens kicked off towards the left touchline. The ball went to Bevan, who caught it and immediately ran towards his marker, Prinsloo. A swerve and Prinsloo was left helpless on the grass. This was Prinsloo's introduction to Bev. I felt good. Bevan scored the winning try too.

The old winner!

In the late 1960s I was employed for a short time at Deva Hospital, Chester. One late afternoon the physical training instructor came in to the ward I was assigned to and was soon giving an account of his afternoon's activities at the annual inter-sports event between Deva and Winwick Hospital, Warrington.

He said that he and others were amazed to see a bald old man win one of the main track events. He mentioned the name Bevan. I immediately realised it was the great Brian Bevan still at it. He must have been in his mid-forties. I felt good again!

Fred Worrall

My most abiding memory of Brian Bevan, besides his thrilling performances on the field, is just 25 minutes in a treatment room at Wilderspool.

Being just 14-years-old at the time, it was great to be so close to this great player. It was 1953 and I was a schoolboy boxer fighting for Lancashire. I had hurt my arm and the only place I could go for heat treatment in those days was Wilderspool. Tommy Lomax was at Warrington then. He also took the boxing at Warrington gym.

I was on the treatment couch and next to me was Brian Bevan. I couldn't believe it. He asked me what I had done and we talked about my boxing. He talked to me about rugby. We chatted for 20 minutes and it was very interesting.

The really funny thing about this was that Jimmy Challinor came in and was amazed. He told me Brian had said more to me in 20 minutes than he had to him in many games. This has always stuck in my mind and as I got older and got more acquainted with Jimmy, we often laughed about it.

Joseph A. Wright of Orford: The miracle man

When considering the justification for calling Brian Bevan 'The Wizard of Aus', we must have due regard for the high quality of the opposition that he had to face very frequently. He weighed only about 11-and-a-half stones and during his playing career there were many first-class speedy wingmen who were two, three or four stones heavier, including Billy Boston, Lionel Cooper and Brian Nordgren.

South African Tom van Vollenhoven possessed real pace but he did not surpass Bevan in weight to such extent and also played on the right wing for his club. It was, however, against van Vollenhoven that Brian scored one of his top-rated tries at Wilderspool. Although The Wizard received the ball on the Saints '25', near to touch, he cut inside to beat several defenders in sequence by a zigzag run toward the opposite corner flag.

Waiting for him there was The Van. Bevan ran straight to him at top speed but in the split second before the clash he came off his right foot in a superb side-step which left van Vollenhoven bewildered, flat-footed and clutching empty space, with Brian going on to cross the try-line in triumph - another spectacular score for the flying Aussie.

It was the strongly held opinion of many Warrington supporters that Brian Bevan rarely scored what would be considered an ordinary try. He seemed to instil every achievement with his special brand of magic. A prominent Rugby League journalist, A. N. Gaulton described this quality: "It seems impossible for a man to be in two different places at one and the same time but that is an illusion which Bevan creates with his startling side-stepping... it appears almost that he is impelled by some supernatural force." A regular Warrington player was heard to comment that Brian would burn himself out within a year. In fact he played 16 seasons with Warrington.

Bev played many times in testimonial matches. Here he lines up in the Empire XIII which beat Oldham 33-24 on 27 April 1948 in a match in aid of Edgar Brooks, Oldham's England hooker.
Back: Fred Ashworth (coach, Oldham), Paddy Reid (Huddersfield), Charlie Smith (Halifax), Chris Brereton (Leeds), Johnny McDonald (Halifax), Brian Bevan, Johnny Hunter (Huddersfield), Enoka McDonald (Halifax), Lionel Cooper (Huddersfield), Alex Givvons (Oldham).
Front: Arthur Clues (Leeds), Edgar Brooks (Oldham), Harry Bath (Warrington), Bert Cook (Leeds), Kia Rika (Halifax)

26. Poetry

The Wizard of Aus   By William Burgess

Brian Bevan the flying winger,
At scoring tries he was a humdinger.
A record breaker he proved to be.
A better one we never will see.

Aged twelve he was the sprint champion of New South Wales.
At eighteen in the Australian Navy he was on the waves,
When his ship was attacked by Japanese planes.
But Brian was unhurt and felt no pain.

To Portsmouth they sailed for ship's repair.
They gave him leave while waiting there.
To Leeds he went first of all
But they turned him down, said he was too small.

For a trial Bill Shankland sent him to Warrington.
He played so well they signed him on.
The war over, he went home to be demobbed.
When he returned he got a printers job.

For Rugby League he looked frail. Could he take it?
Very few thought that he would make it.
But with his side step, swerve and speed,
The Rugby League world soon took heed.

In his first season he scored 48 tries.
He was so elusive it was like catching flies.
A star in the making, everyone agrees,
In spite of the bandages on his knees.

Against Bramley and Leigh he scored seven.
The Warrington supporters were in heaven.
They had never seen anything like this before,
Shouting, O Come on, Brian. We want more.

He was a once in a lifetime. One can never forget
The thrill of his tries, be it dry or wet.
From right wing to left, or under the sticks,
He scored tries. He was a right bag of tricks.

His name is written in the Hall of Fame.
Another one like him, well never see again.
More than 800 tries he scored in all,
The flying Aussie with the oval ball.

We were sorry to lose him. He was bold and brave.
His bones now lie in a Southport grave.
Gone but not forgotten, springs to mind.
A real gentleman, the best you could find.

William Burgess, an 89 year-old life-long supporter of Warrington and admirer of Brian Bevan, penned the above in July 1998.

Brian Flaherty

I watched Brian Bevan play in his first match for Warrington ' A' and I watched his last match against Leigh in 1962. He was the finest try-scoring winger I have ever seen. No one will ever break his record. A lot of people say he wouldn't do it today but he would. He was a one-off. My Uncle Ted was a well-known Warrington comedian for many years and Warrington rugby team was his great love. So he wrote a song about Brian Bevan. He wrote the words to a well known tune. I have tried to find out the name of the tune but nobody seems to know it. My uncle passed away many years ago. Anyway, the words were:

Ball out, ball out. Hear supporters call.
Scrum-half, stand-off. Centre gets the ball.
It goes to Knowelden. He's a bold 'un.
Albert Pimblett hears the call.
Give the ball to Bevan! He's the man to beat 'em all.

We go to Wilderspool to watch our team play.
We do an' all. We do an' all.
We do appreciate their clever, clean play.
They pass the ball and that's not all.

We have a wingman there called Brian Bevan.
He's really good. That's understood.
When he gets the ball we are in heaven.
He scores with ease, like shelling peas.   (Back to - Ball out, ball out)

The Lament of an ageing Wirepuller By Peter Robinson

I do believe that Brian Bevan
Is up there scoring tries in Heaven.
Gerry Helme is on a darting run,
Fed by Palin from the scrum.

Les Jones is with them dropping goals,
Whilst lesser men are playing bowls.
The game's faster now, I do agree,
But the skills are missing, believe you me.

The side-step and the body swerve,
The change of pace in Bevan's curve.
We saw the skills in every game.
Now all the players do the same,

See a gap, run at it fast.
How long will these players last?
Wham, bam, slam, bash, smash, crash.
Win, win, win, we need the cash.

They only play now when it's sunny.
All that matters is the money.
Clubs have spent. Now some are broke.
Has Rupert made our game a joke?

But we'll see our heroes again some day
When we, like them , are called away
To join them in the Rugby Heaven
Where Bev will score another seven.

But before our time comes to expire
Let's change the name from Wolves to Wire.

286

Statistics

British Rugby League's leading try-scorers 1895-2002

1 Brian Bevan (Warrington, Blackpool Borough) 1945-64	796
2 Billy Boston (Wigan, Blackpool Borough) 1953-70	571
3 Martin Offiah (Widnes, Wigan, London B, Salford) 1987-2001	481
4 Alf Ellaby (St. Helens, Wigan) 1926-39	446
5 Eric Batten (Wakefield T, Hunslet, Bradford N, Featherstone R) 1933-54	443
6 Lionel Cooper (Huddersfield) 1947-55	441
7 Ellery Hanley (Bradford N, Wigan, Leeds) 1978-95	428
8 Johnny Ring (Wigan, Rochdale H) 1922-33	415
9 Clive Sullivan (Hull, Hull KR, Oldham, Doncaster) 1961-85	406
10 John Atkinson (Leeds, Carlisle) 1966-83	401

Most tries in a British season

1 Albert Rosenfeld (Huddersfield) 1913-14	80
2 Albert Rosenfeld (Huddersfield) 1911-12	78
3 Brian Bevan (Warrington) 1952-53	72
4 Lionel Cooper (Huddersfield) 1951-52	71
5 Brian Bevan (Warrington) 1950-51	68
6 Brian Bevan (Warrington) 1953-54	67
7 Lionel Cooper (Huddersfield) 1954-55	66
8 Johnny Ring (Wigan) 1925-26	63
Eric Harris (Leeds) 1935-36	63
Jack McLean (Bradford N) 1951-52	63
Brian Bevan (Warrington) 1954-55	63
Ellery Hanley (Wigan) 1986-87	63

Leading try-scorers during Brian Bevan's era

1946-47

1 Brian Bevan (Warrington)	48
2 Ernie Ashcroft (Wigan)	34
2 Emlyn Walters (Bradford N)	34
4 Roy Francis (Barrow)	29
4 Brian Nordgren (Wigan)	29

1947-48

1 Brian Bevan (Warrington)	57
2 Gordon Ratcliffe (Wigan)	49
3 Lionel Cooper (Huddersfield)	37
4 Eric Batten (Bradford N)	36
5 Alan Edwards (Bradford N)	36

1948-49

1 Lionel Cooper (Huddersfield)	60
2 Brian Bevan (Warrington)	56
3 Gordon Ratcliffe (Wigan)	36
4 Jack Hilton (Wigan)	25
4 Johnny Lawrenson (Wigan)	25
4 Stan McCormick (BVR/St Helens)	25

1949-50

1 Brian Nordgren (Wigan)	57
2 Lionel Cooper (Huddersfield)	46
3 Arthur Daniels (Halifax)	36
4 Billy Blan (Wigan)	34
5 Brian Bevan (Warrington)	33

1950-51

1 Brian Bevan (Warrington)	68
2 Lionel Cooper (Huddersfield)	59
3 Brian Nordgren (Wigan)	42
4 Eppie Gibson (Workington T)	41
5 George Wilson (Workington T)	40

1951-52

1 Lionel Cooper (Huddersfield)	71
2 Jack McLean (Bradford N)	63
3 Frank Castle (Barrow)	52
4 Brian Bevan (Warrington)	51
5 Johnny Lawrenson (Workington)	49

1952-53

1 Brian Bevan (Warrington)	72
2 Jack McLean (Bradford N)	59
3 Lionel Cooper (Huddersfield)	50
4 Brian Nordgren (Wigan)	47
5 Peter Henderson (Huddersfield)	46

1953-54

1 Brian Bevan (Warrington)	67
2 Jack McLean (Bradford N)	52
3 Drew Turnbull (Leeds)	41
4 Lionel Cooper (Huddersfield)	40
5 Steve Llewellyn (St Helens)	37

1954-55

1 Lionel Cooper (Huddersfield) 66
2 Brian Bevan (Warrington) 63
3 Peter Henderson (Huddersfield) 45
4 Drew Turnbull (Leeds) 42
5 Malcolm Davies (Leigh) 34

1955-56

1 Jack McLean (Bradford N) 61
2 Brian Bevan (Warrington) 57
3 Billy Boston (Wigan) 49
4 Frank Carlton (St. Helens) 42
5 Jim Lewthwaite (Barrow) 41

1956-57

1 Billy Boston (Wigan) 60
2 Jim Lewthwaite (Barrow) 51
3 Johnny Freeman (Halifax) 48
4 John Etty (Oldham) 43
5 Bill Kindon (Leigh) 37
- Brian Bevan (Warrington) 17

1957-58

1 Mick Sullivan (Hudds/Wigan) 50
2 Ike Southward (Workington T) 47
3 Brian Bevan (Warrington) 46
4 Malcolm Davies (Bradford N) 45
5 Billy Boston (Wigan) 43

1958-59

1 Tom van Vollenhoven (St Helens) 62
2 Brian Bevan (Warrington) 54
2 Billy Boston (Wigan) 54
4 Garry Hemingway (Leeds) 40
5 Ike Southward (Workington T/ Oldham) 38

1959-60

1 Tom van Vollenhoven (St Helens) 64
2 Billy Boston (Wigan) 47
3 Brian Bevan (Warrington) 40
4 Fred Smith (Wakefield T) 38
5 Neil Fox (Wakefield T) 37

1960-61

1 Tom van Vollenhoven (St Helens) 59
2 Wilf Rosenberg (Leeds) 44
3 Billy Boston (Wigan) 37
4 Brian Bevan (Warrington) 35
5 Bobby Greenough (Warrington) 31
5 Alex Murphy (St Helens) 31

1961-62

1 Billy Boston (Wigan) 51
2 Tom van Vollenhoven (St Helens) 46
3 Frank Carlton (Wigan) 38
4 Geoff Wriglesworth (Leeds) 34
5 Ike Southward (Workington T) 32
- Brian Bevan (Warrington) 15

1962-63

1 Ray Glastonbury (Workington) 41
2 Bill Burgess (Barrow) 37
3 Graham Paul (Hull KR) 36
3 Geoff Smith (York) 36
5 Bob Harris (Hull KR) 33
5 Tom van Vollenhoven (St Helens) 33
- Brian Bevan (Blackpool B) 10

1963-64

1 John Stopford (Swinton) 45
2 Trevor Lake (Wigan) 43
3 Keith Howe (Castleford) 36
4 Bill Burgess (Barrow) 35
5 Alan Hardisty (Castleford) 32
- Brian Bevan (Blackpool B) 7

Brian Bevan's club career records

Warrington   Debut 17 November, 1945 v Oldham (H)

	App	Tries	Goals	Points
1945-46	1	-	-	-
1946-47	42	48	34	212
1947-48	43	57	-	171
1948-49	44	56	-	168
1949-50	39	30	-	90
1950-51	40	60	-	180
1951-52	39	46	-	138
1952-53	41	66	-	198
1953-54	45	62	-	186
1954-55	37	61	-	183
1955-56	41	53	-	159
1956-57	26	14	-	42
1957-58	40	45	-	135
1958-59	40	54	-	162

1959-60	40	40	-	120
1960-61	42	35	-	105
1961-62	20	13	-	39
Totals	620	740	34	2288

Last game 23 April, 1962 v Leigh (H)

Blackpool Borough.
Debut 22 August, 1962 v Wigan (A)

	App	Tries	Goals	Points
1962-63	22	10	-	30
1963-64	20	7	-	21
Totals	42	17	-	51

Last game 22 February, 1964 v Oldham (A)

Career Record

	App	Tries	Goals	Points
Warrington	620	740	34	2288
Blackpool B.	42	17	-	51
Internationals	16	26	-	78
Representative	10	13	-	39
Grand Totals	688	796	34	2456

How Bev scored his 740 tries for Warrington

69 v Liverpool Stanley/City	21 v Leeds
50 v Rochdale Hornets	18 v Bradford Northern
40 v Oldham	18 v Huddersfield
40 v Salford	15 v Halifax
35 v St. Helens	15 v York
34 v Barrow	14 v Hull
32 v Whitehaven	12 v Dewsbury
31 v Leigh	12 v Wakefield Trinity
31 v Widnes	8 v Castleford
31 v Workington Town	8 v Orford Tannery
27 v Wigan	7 v Hunslet
26 v Belle Vue Rangers	6 v Brookland Rovers
26 v Blackpool Borough	6 v Keighley
25 v Hull Kingston Rovers	5 v Batley
25 v Swinton	4 v Doncaster
24 v Bramley	3 v Australians
21 v Featherstone Rovers	1 v New Zealanders

... And his 17 tries for Blackpool Borough

2 v Dewsbury	1 v Leigh
2 v Whitehaven	1 v Oldham
2 v York	1 v Rochdale Hornets
1 v Barrow	1 v St. Helens
1 v Batley	1 v Salford
1 v Doncaster	1 v Wigan
1 v Keighley	1 v Workington Town

How Bev scored his tries per match

	For Warrington	For Blackpool	For Rep Sides
Seven tries	2	-	-
Six tries	4	-	-
Five tries	6	-	-
Four tries	20	-	1
Three tries	66	-	2
Two tries	95	1	10
One try	204	15	9
Totals	397	16	22
No tries	223	26	4

- Bev scored tries in 435 of the 688 first class fixtures in which he played.
- His try average for Warrington was 1.194 per game.
- His career try average in first class English rugby league was 1.157 per game.

Bev scored his 740 tries for Warrington in the various competitions thus:

League matches	622	Championship play-offs	9
Challenge Cup-ties	62	ITV Floodlit Competition	4
Lancashire Cup-ties	39	Tour games	4

His 17 tries for Blackpool Borough were scored thus:

League matches	11	Challenge Cup-ties	2
Western Division	3	Lancashire Cup-ties	1

Milestones in Brian Bevan's career with Warrington

100th try	17 April, 1948	v Oldham (H)
200th try	13 Sept, 1950	v Liverpool Stanley (H) LC
300th try	30 Aug, 1952	v Salford (A) LC
400th try	23 Jan, 1954	v Rochdale Hornets (A)
500th try	15 Oct, 1955	v Huddersfield (H)
600th try	16 Aug, 1958	v Huddersfield (A)
700th try	15 Oct, 1960	v Liverpool City (A)

100th game	23 Oct, 1948	v Rochdale Hornets (H)
200th game	23 March, 1951	v Widnes (H)
300th game	26 Sept, 1953	v Whitehaven (A)
400th game	28 Jan, 1956	v Dewsbury (H)
500th game	26 Dec, 1958	v Leigh (H)
600th game	19 Aug, 1961	v Hull (A)

500th point	19 Feb, 1949	v Hull KR (A) Cup
1000th point	8 Nov, 1952	v Liverpool City (A)
1500th point	12 March, 1955	v Workington Town (H)
2000th point	27 March, 1959	v Widnes (H)

Brian Bevan's 39 Warrington centre partners

Games		Games	
181	Jim Challinor	3	Jock McAvoy
86	Albert Pimblett	3	Stan Powell
80	Ally Naughton	2	Ernie Ashcroft
65	Ron Ryder	2	Reg Hughes
39	Len Horton	2	Bill Jackson
27	Laurie Gilfedder	2	Brian Miller

27	Glyn Williams	2	Arnold Stevens
17	Ike Proctor	1	Martin Creeney
13	Fred Higginbottom	1	Terry Farrington
7	Bobby Greenough	1	Eric Fraser
7	Malcolm Thomas	1	Austin Heathwood
6	Brian Glover	1	Albert Johnson
6	Jim Honey	1	Les Jones
6	Ossie Peake	1	Billy McFarlane
6	Martin Regan	1	John Norburn
5	Alf Humphreys	1	Ivor Phillips
4	Roy Francis	1	Ray Price
4	Ronnie Herbert	1	Mike Quick
3	Owen Bevan	1	Jack Waring
3	Bryn Knowelden		

All but two of Bevan's 620 games for Warrington were played as a right-winger. On the two occasions he played on the left wing he was partnered by Ernie Ashcroft.

Brian Bevan's six Blackpool Borough centre partners

Games		Games	
21	Alec Givvons	2	Johnny Phillips
14	Johnny Bagshaw	1	Johnny Morris
3	Cliff Berry	1	Dennis Molloy

All of Bevan's 42 games for Blackpool were played as a right-winger

Representative Match centre partners

In 26 appearances in representative rugby Bevan's centre partners were:

Games		Games	
10	Tony Paskins (Workington T)	1	Jack Broome (Wigan)
7	Trevor Allan (Leigh)	1	Doug Greenall (St. Helens)
2	Lewis Jones (Leeds)	1	Percy Landsberg (Leigh)
2	Tommy Lynch (Halifax)	1	Keith McLellan (Leeds)
1	Bob Bartlett (Leeds)	1	Bill Riley (Hull KR)

All but one of Bevan's representative matches were played as a right-winger. He played on the left for a Rugby League XIII versus The New Zealanders at White City, Manchester, on 20 September, 1961, when Landsberg was his centre.

291

Bibliography

Books

Clive Churchill, *They Called Me The Little Master* (1962)
Robert Gate, *There Were A Lot More Than That* (1994)
E. M. Gibson, *The Kiwis 1947-48* (1948)
Geoff Greenwood (ed), *Australian Rugby League's Greatest Players* (1978)
Lewis Jones, *King of Rugger* (1958)
Tom Mitchell, *The Memoirs and Sporting Life of Tom Mitchell* (1998)
Rex Mossop, *The Moose That Roared* (1991)
Mike Parsons (ed), *Wilderspool Centenary* (1998)
Jack Pollard (ed), *This is Rugby League* (1962)
Keith Richardson, *Ike* (1995)
Bev Risman (ed), *The Rugby League Football Book* (1962)
Bev Risman (ed), *The Rugby League Football Book* (1963)
Jack Steel, *Warrington: Rugby League Champions 1947-48* (1948)

Newspapers and periodicals

Bradford Telegraph & Argus
/ Yorkshire Sports
Daily Dispatch
Daily Express
Daily Herald
Daily Mail
Daily Mirror
Halifax Courier & Guardian
Huddersfield Daily Examiner
Liverpool Echo
Manchester Guardian
Manchester News & Chronicle
News of the World
Oldham Evening Chronicle
Rugby League Gazette
Rugby League Magazine
Rugby League News
Rugby League Parade
Rugby Leaguer

Rugby League Record
Rugby League Review
Rugby League Week
Sporting Chronicle & Athletic News
Sunday Dispatch
Sunday Express
Sunday People
Sunday Pictorial/Mirror
Sydney Morning Herald
Warrington Examiner
Warrington Guardian
West Lancashire Evening Gazette
Wigan Observer
World Sports
Yorkshire Evening News
Yorkshire Evening Post
Yorkshire Observer
Yorkshire Post

Books available from Robert Gate

£5.00 each!!

- *Gone North: Welshmen in Rugby League* **(Volume 1)**
- *Champions: A Celebration of the Rugby League Championship 1895-1987*
- *The Struggle for the Ashes* **(1986)**
- *The Struggle for the Ashes II* **(1996)**

All the above books are profusely illustrated and are available at £5.00 each, which includes postage (United Kingdom only)

****

There Were A Lot More Than That: Odsal 1954

Also still available in limited supply £11.95 (including postage, UK only)

****

Gone North: Welshmen in Rugby League (Volume 2)

Hardback edition only, £14.99 including postage. Softback edition is sold out.

To order, send cheques (payable to R.E. Gate) to R. E. Gate, Mount Pleasant Cottage, Ripponden Bank, Ripponden, Sowerby Bridge, Yorkshire HX6 4JL (Tel: 01422-823074)

Rugby League Analysis, History & Vision

A national Rugby League magazine published twice a year

Our Game covers the history of the game, international reports, current issues, book reviews, 'changing the rules', fiction, poetry, obituaries and much more.

Regular contributors include Robert Gate, Tony Collins, Huw Richards, Michael O'Hare, Phil Melling and Craig Wilson.

Subscribe

Four issue subscription: £7.00
Special £10.00 offer:
Three issue subscription plus a copy of **one** of the following books:

• *Tries in the Valleys - A history of Rugby League in Wales*
• *From Fulham to Wembley - 20 years of Rugby League in London*
• *The Fulham Dream - Rugby League tackles London*

Back numbers available:
No. 1: Brian Bevan, Central Park, Melbourne Storm;
No. 2: 1954 World Cup, Lebanon, North America, Alex Murphy;
No. 3: 1985 Challenge Cup Final, Cumbria, Andy Gregory,
No. 4: Jim Sullivan, Ashes 1988, Hull FC.
No. 5: Bev Risman on Wembley '68, Yugoslavia, Hawaii and Salford.
£1.50 each or special offer: £6 for all five

• To subscribe, please write to London League Publications Ltd, PO Box 10441, London E14 0SB.
• Please indicate the length of subscription, book chosen if taking the £10 special offer, any back-numbers ordered and your name and address.
• Please indicate which issue you want you subscription to start with.
Cheques payable to London League Publications Ltd, no credit card orders.

Or: to order a copy post free, send a cheque for £2.00 to: London League Publications, PO Box 10441, London E14 0SB. (no credit card orders).

Our Game is also available from Sportspages (London & Manchester), Smiths of Wigan, and is on sale at all London Broncos home matches

Rugby League Bravehearts
The History of Scottish Rugby League
By Gavin Willacy
Foreword by Alan Tait

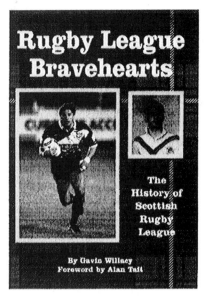

Despite never having a professional club, Scotland has a rich Rugby League history. From the sport's earliest years, there have been Scottish players in British Rugby League, including Great Britain internationals such as Dave Valentine, George Fairbairn and Alan Tait.

Since 1995, Scotland have competed on the international stage, including in the 2000 Rugby League World Cup. Since the barriers between Union and League came down in 1995, League in Scotland has developed tremendously, and the amateur, student and development parts of the game are fully covered in Rugby League Bravehearts. The book includes:

- A full record of Scotland's international matches
- Interviews with key Scottish players
- Profiles of Scottish Rugby League professionals
- Scottish players' participation in representative matches
- Scottish Students and amateur Rugby League

Lavishly illustrated, this book will be of interest to all Rugby League supporters and those interested in the development of sport in Scotland.

Published in June 2002

£9.95 net in the United Kingdom.   ISBN: 1903659-05-1

To order the book at a special offer price of £9.00 post free, please write to

London League Publications Ltd, PO Box 10441, London E14 0SB

(Cheques payable to London League Publications Ltd. No credit cards)

I, George Nepia
The autobiography of a Rugby legend
By George Nepia and Terry McLean

Foreword by Oma Nepia

George Nepia is arguably New Zealand's greatest ever Rugby Union player. This new edition of his autobiography, first published in 1963, also has new and reprinted material that gives a full picture of Nepia's life and Rugby career.

It has a new chapter by Terry McLean on New Zealand's four great Union full-backs. Other new material includes Huw Richards on the 1924-5 All Black tour, Peter Lush and Robert Gate on Nepia's time in Rugby League with Streatham & Mitcham, Halifax and Manukau, Dave Farrar on his Hawke's Bay Ranfurly Shield career and a review of the 1986 *This is Your Life* programme made 3 months before he died.

The book will be fully illustrated and of interest to followers of both Rugby codes.

To be published in September 2002 at £13.95.

Special offer to readers of this book: £13.00 post free.

Order from:
London League Publications Ltd,
PO Box 10441,
London E14 0SB

(Cheques payable to London League Publications Ltd, no credit cards)

ISBN: 1-903659-07-8

A Westminster XIII

Parliamentarians and Rugby League

Edited by David Hinchliffe M.P.

The All-Party Parliamentary Rugby League Group was set up in 1988 to promote the interests of the game in Parliament. Now members of the Group show their support for the game by writing about it in an exciting new book. Contributors include:

- Lord Jack Ashley on Memories of Widnes
- Harold Best M.P. on Leeds schoolboy Rugby League in the 1930s and 1940s
- James Clappison M.P. on Hull KR and Leeds
- Yvette Cooper M.P. on Castleford
- Tony Cunningham M.P. on Workington at Old Trafford
- Frank Dobson M.P. on York
- David Hinchliffe M.P. on Wakefield Trinity at Wembley 1968
- Peter Kilfoyle M.P. on playing against Arty Beetson
- Lord Geoffrey Lofthouse on Featherstone and BARLA
- Sir Brian Mawhinney M.P. Reflections on Rugby League
- Alice Mahon M.P. on Halifax
- Ian McCartney M.P. on Murrayfield Rugby Union to Murrayfield Rugby League
- Kevin McNamara M.P. on Hull KR
- Lord Peter Smith on Leigh's Wembley 1971 triumph
- Derek Twigg M.P. on Widnes's 2001 promotion campaign
- Derek Wyatt M.P. with a Rugby Union perspective

To be published in November 2002:

£12.95 hardback
£9.95 softback

Special offer for readers of this book: £12.00 hardback and £9.00 softback post free.

Become a Patron: Have your name in the book and receive a signed hardback copy: £20.00 - must be ordered by 20 September 2002.

All profits from this book will go to good causes within the game.

Order from:
London League Publications Ltd, PO Box 10441, London E14 0SB

(Cheques payable to London League Publications Ltd, no credit cards)

The Rugby League Grounds Guide

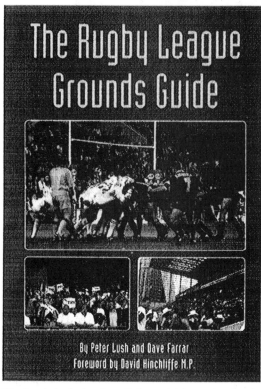

By Peter Lush and Dave Farrar

Foreword by David Hinchliffe M.P.

Travelling to watch your team play away, and visiting new grounds is one of the best experiences in rugby league. Equally enjoyable is going to watch an amateur game or a big match at a ground you have never visited before. This book will help you get to the match and use the ground's facilities when you get there.

The book includes for all the British professional clubs:
- History and description of the ground
- Telephone numbers, websites and email details
- Information on price reductions, catering and facilities for people with disabilities
- Public transport details and road directions, with a local map
- Local tourist information

It also has basic details of:
- The Australian National Rugby League clubs
- French professional clubs
- BARLA National Conference clubs
- Summer Rugby League Conference clubs

Published in April 2001. If ordered by post, includes a 2002 supplement.

Every Rugby League supporter will find this book very useful.

Special offer price for readers of this book: Order your copy for £7.00 post free (cover price £7.95) from London League Publications Ltd, PO Box 10441, London E14 0SB

(Cheques payable to London League Publications Ltd, no credit cards)

ISBN: 1-903659-02-7

Knowsley Road
Memories of St Helens
Rugby League Football Club

By Andrew Quirke

Foreword by **Mal Meninga**

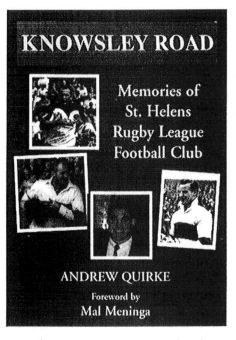

Published in September 2001, this book has memories about one of Rugby League's most successful clubs. It includes interviews with **Duggie Greenall, Tom van Vollenhoven, Alex Murphy, Kel Coslett, John Mantle, Harry Pinner, Bobbie Goulding, Keiron Cunningham, Chris Joynt** and many other Saints stars of the past 70 years along with recollections from coaches, supporters and other people involved with Saints.

Published at £9.95, the book is available to readers of this book for £9.00 post free.
Order from London League Publications Ltd,
PO Box 10441, London E14 0SB.

(Cheques payable to London League Publications Ltd, no credit cards)

ISBN: 1-903659-04-3

Sports Books available from London League Publications:

Rugby League:

From Fulham to Wembley - 20 years of Rugby League in London
Edited by Dave Farrar and Peter Lush
Published in June 2000 to celebrate the London Broncos' 20th anniversary, the book includes profiles of key players and coaches, supporters' memories, and reports of key matches.
Published at £8.75, special offer £8.00 post free

The Fulham Dream - Rugby League tackles London
By Harold Genders
The inside story of how Harold Genders set up Fulham RLFC and won promotion in the club's historic first season. Fully illustrated with full records of that great campaign.
Published in September 2000 at £6.95, special offer £6.00 post free.

London books special offer: The two books for £12.00 post free

Tries in the Valleys - A History of Rugby League in Wales
Edited by Peter Lush and Dave Farrar
Foreword by Jonathan Davies
Covers the Welsh international team, clubs in Wales and interviews with key people involved in the game in Wales.
Published in 1998 at £14.95, special offer £8.00 post free.

Cricket:

Buns, Bails and Banter - A Season watching County Cricket
By David Spiller
Foreword by Vince Wells
The author followed Leicestershire home and away in the 2000 season. Captures the unique atmosphere of county cricket today.
Published in 2001 at £8.95, special offer £5.00 post free.

Order from:
London League Publications Ltd
PO Box 10441
London E14 0SB

(Cheques payable to London League Publications Ltd, no credit cards)